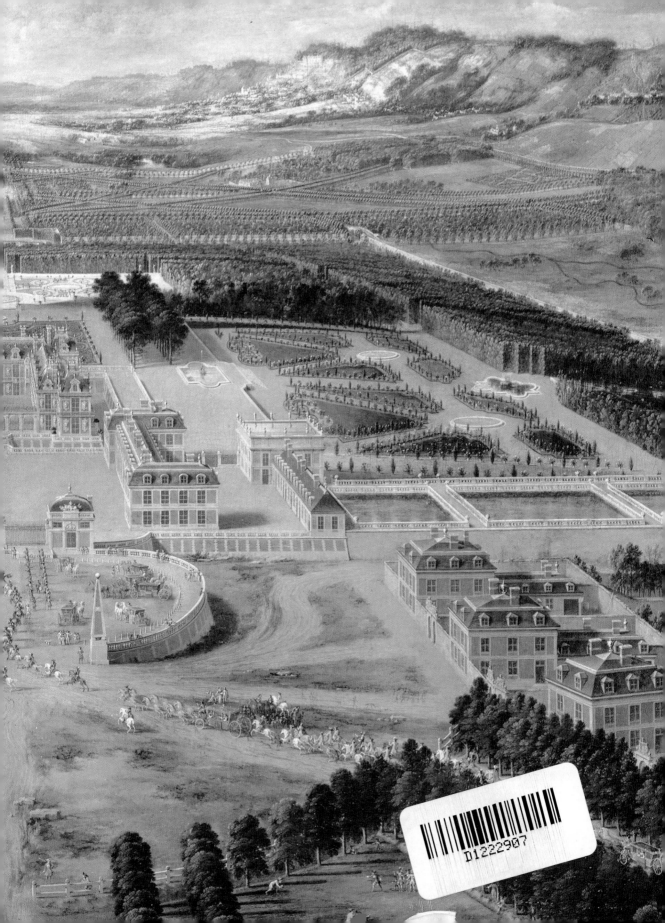

THE SUN KING'S GARDEN

Galerie des Antiques by Jean-Baptiste Martin, 1688.

THE SUN KING'S GARDEN

Louis XIV, André Le Nôtre and the Creation of the Gardens of Versailles

IAN THOMPSON

BLOOMSBURY

Published by Bloomsbury USA, New York
Distributed to the trade by Holtzbrinck Publishers

Endpapers: View of the Château of Versailles in 1668 by Pierre Patel (le Père).
Courtesy of the Réunion des Musées Nationaux.

All papers used by Bloomsbury USA are natural, recyclable products
made from wood grown in well-managed forests. The manufacturing
processes conform to the environmental regulations of the country of origin.

Library of Congress Cataloging-in-Publication Data

Thompson, Ian H., 1955–
The Sun King's garden : Louis XIV, André Le Nôtre,
and the creation of the gardens at Versailles / Ian Thompson.
p. cm.
Includes bibliographical references and index.
ISBN-13: 978-1-58234-631-1 (hardcover)
ISBN-10: 1-58234-631-3 (hardcover)
1. Le Nôtre, André, 1613–1700. 2. Gardens, French—History—17th century.
3. Gardens—France—Design—History—17th century. 4. Parc de Versailles (Versailles, France)
5. Louis XIV, King of France, 1638–1715—Influence. I. Title.

SB470.L4T46 2006
712'.609443663—dc22
2006014198

First U.S. Edition 2006

1 3 5 7 9 10 8 6 4 2

This book is printed on Gardapat.

The text of this book is set in Granjon and Centaur

Typeset by Hewer Text UK Ltd, Edinburgh
Printed in Italy by Graphicom

In Memory

Julia Darling (1956–2005)

The greater the obstacle, the more glory in overcoming it.

JEAN-BAPTISTE MOLIÈRE

CONTENTS

AUTHOR'S NOTE

By profession André Le Nôtre was a 'master-gardener'. His official titles included 'designer of the King's gardens'. In this narrative, I often refer to him simply as a 'gardener' but sometimes take the liberty of calling him a 'landscape architect' or 'landscape designer', although these terms (more or less synonymous) are anachronistic. The title 'landscape architect' was not coined until the mid-nineteenth century, when it was first used by Frederick Law Olmsted and Calvert Vaux, the designers of New York's City Central Park. My reason for associating this job title with Le Nôtre is that in terms of scale and technique he seems to have had much in common with present-day landscape architects, and 'gardener' seems somehow limiting. I have avoided referring to him as a 'landscape gardener', a term first used in the eighteenth century by England's Humphry Repton, because of its specific association with a style of landscape design that was conceived in opposition to, or in reaction against, the formal style favoured by the Sun King. To complicate matters still further, in France landscape architects are usually known as *paysagistes* ('countrysideists'), although Jean-Marie Morel used the term *architecte-paysagiste* as early as 1804.

CURRENCIES AND MEASURES

As a thoroughly mixed-up Englishman, I have used both metric and non-metric units in this book. The reader will encounter metres as well as miles, and acres as well as hectares. In Britain the metric revolution stopped halfway, so this is how most of us think. I have been similarly relaxed over the names of garden features, generally preferring the original French to an English translation (for example,

'Fer à Cheval' rather than 'Horseshoe'), but where it appeared more natural or helped the sense I have used English versions.

The pre-metric systems of measurement and currency in France and in England had much in common. British readers of a certain age will remember shopping in pounds, shillings and pence, and perhaps wondering why this was written 'l.s.d.' Before metrication, the French currency units were *livres, sols* (or *sous*) and *deniers*. Just as there were 20 shillings to a pound sterling, there were 20 *sols* to a *livre* and 12 *deniers* to a *sol*. Roughly, then, a *livre* was the equivalent of a pound; an *écu* was worth 3 *livres*, a *pistole* was worth 10 *livres* and a *louis d'or* was worth 24 *livres* (though it lost value towards the end of the reign).

The royal accounts during Louis XIV's reign were presented in l.s.d. – *livres, sols* and *deniers*. It is difficult to relate the value of the seventeenth-century *livre* to present-day currencies, but it might help to know that a vineyard worker was paid about 12 *sols* per day, while a coachman for a grand house might be paid 100 *livres* per annum. Four *sols* would have bought you a *pinte* of decent wine (0.93 of a litre) or a pair of wooden shoes. On the other hand, a courtier would have paid between 800 and 1,000 *livres* for his tunic, while in 1679 Mme de Maintenon spent 330 *livres* on a satin skirt for her sister-in-law.

The pre-metric equivalent of an inch was a *pouce*, and there were twelve of them in a *pied*, but a *toise* was six *pieds*, thus more like two yards or just short of two metres.

SUPPORTING CAST

ANNE OF AUSTRIA (1601–1666) Mother of Louis XIV. Became Regent upon her husband's death but was under the influence of Cardinal Mazarin, who was widely believed to be her lover or even her husband.

GIANLORENZO BERNINI (1598–1680): Italian sculptor, painter and architect, the dominant figure in Roman Baroque art. Louis XIV invited him to Paris to enlarge the Louvre, but his plans were rejected as too flamboyant. He met Le Nôtre at Versailles and played host to the veteran gardener in Rome in 1679.

MICHEL II LE BOUTEUX (1623–?): *Fleuriste Ordinaire du Roi*. Active at Versailles between 1668–1682, where he had particular responsibility for the flower garden at Trianon.

MICHEL III LE BOUTEUX (1648–1694): A florist, like his father. Le Nôtre passed on to him some of his duties as *Contrôleur Général des Bâtiments* in 1692. Also known as Jean-Michel Le Bouteux.

JEAN-BAPTISTE COLBERT (1619–1683): Replaced Nicolas Fouquet as Louis' finance minister. Colbert was also *Surintendant des Bâtiments* from 1664 until his death, and a powerful organising force behind the creation of the château and gardens at Versailles. He established the Gobelins manufactory in 1662. As minister for the navy, Colbert sought to strengthen French sea power, symbolised by the little flotilla on the Grand Canal at Versailles.

LOUIS II DE BOURBON, Prince de Condé (1621–1686): French general. He rebelled against the Crown during the *Frondes* but later became a staunch supporter of Louis XIV. He employed Le Nôtre to design the gardens of his estate at Chantilly.

CLAUDE DESGOTS (1658–1732): Great-nephew of Le Nôtre and one of his closest collaborators, he was sent to England in 1689 and 1698. He supervised the creation of gardens at Windsor and Greenwich. Le Nôtre passed many of his responsibilities on to him.

MARIE-ADÉLAÏDE DE SAVOY, Duchesse de Bourgogne (1685–1712). Arrived at Versailles in 1693 to marry Louis XIV's grandson, Louis, Duc de Bourgogne. She was a favourite of the Sun King. Both she and her husband fell ill in early 1712 and died within six days of one another.

ANTOINE-JOSEPH DEZALLIER D'ARGENVILLE (1680–1765): Author of *La Théorie et la practique du jardinage* (The Theory and the Practice of Gardening), first published in 1709, nine years after Le Nôtre's death, and translated into English by John James in 1712.

NICOLAS FOUQUET (1615–1680): Finance minister and patron of the arts who commissioned Le Nôtre to design his gardens at Vaux-le-Vicomte. Fell dramatically from favour in 1661 and was imprisoned for life.

FRANÇOIS FRANCINE (1617–1688): Son of the Italian fountaineer Tomasso Francini and brother of Pierre. The Francine brothers were the most significant fountaineers at Versailles. François was also prefect of police for Paris.

JULES HARDOUIN-MANSART (1646–1708): Grand-nephew of François Mansart. He effectively served as Louis – chief architect from 1673, although he received the title officially in 1681. He designed many extensions and additions to Versailles, notably the Galerie des Glaces. He also designed the Grand Trianon and the second Orangerie and was the principal architect at Marly. He was responsible for altering or erasing many of Le Nôtre's garden features, most significantly the Bosquet des Sources, which was razed to make way for his Colonnade.

HENRIETTE D'ANGLETERRE (1644–1670): Daughter of Charles I of England and first wife of Louis XIV's brother, Phillipe d'Orléans.

JEAN-BAPTISTE LA QUINTINIE (1626–1688): Lawyer turned gardener. He was put in charge of the Potager at Versailles in 1661 He was ennobled by Louis XIV in 1678.

JEAN-BAPTISTE-ALEXANDRE LE BLOND (1679–1719): Pupil of Le Nôtre who illustrated Dézallier d'Argenville's *La Théorie et la practique du jardinage*. From 1716 he worked at the Peterhof for Peter the Great.

CHARLES LE BRUN (1619–1690): Contemporary and friend of Le Nôtre. He worked for Fouquet before becoming *Premier Peintre du Roi*. He exercised a vast aesthetic influence the decoration of the royal houses, which extended into the gardens, where he often provided the sketches to which commissioned sculptors would work.

LOUIS LE VAU (1612–1670): Fouquet's architect at Vaux-le-Vicomte, he became Louis XIV's *Premier Architecte* in 1654. At Versailles he designed the Ménagerie, the Tour de Pompe, the Trianon de Porcelaine and the Enveloppe.

LOUIS XIII (1601–1643): Father of Louis XIV. Established a hunting lodge at Versailles in 1624.

FRANÇOIS-MICHEL LE TELLIER, Marquis de Louvois (1641–1691): From 1666 he functioned as Louis' war minister, officially replacing his father in 1677. Known for his ruthlessness, he became *Surintendant des Bâtiments* following the death of Colbert in 1683 and promoted the career of Jules Hardouin-Mansart.

FRANÇOISE D'AUBIGNÉ, Marquise de Maintenon (1635–1719): Widow of the poet Paul Scarron, she became the governess to Athénaïs de Montespan's children. When she supplanted Athénaïs in the King's affections, she brought piety and boredom to the court. The King gave her 200,000 *livres* with which she bought the estate of Maintenon. At the end of January 1675, the King gave her the title Mme de Maintenon. She was morganatically married to him in 1684.

FRANÇOISE-ATHÉNAÏS DE ROCHECHOUART, Marquise de Montespan (1641–1707): Became Louis' official mistress in 1677, displacing Louise de la Vallière. Beautiful and accomplished, she presided over a golden age at Versailles but was in turn rejected in favour of Mme de Maintenon.

PHILIPPE, DUC D'ORLÉANS (1640–1701): Louis XIV's brother, known at court as 'Monsieur'.

ELISABETH CHARLOTTE, Duchesse d'Orléans (1617–1680): Sometimes referred to as the Princess Palatine, she was the daughter of the Elector Palatine, Karl Ludwig. Having become the second wife of Philippe, Duc d'Orléans, she maintained a lively correspondence, which is a revealing source of information about life at court.

NICOLAS POUSSIN (1594–1665): Leading French painter renowned for his landscapes. He was summoned to Paris in 1640 by Louis XIV and is believed to have lived in a house in the grounds of the Tuileries, where Le Nôtre also had a home. Le Nôtre was an admirer and collector of Poussin's work.

DUC DE SAINT-SIMON (1675–1755): Courtier whose brilliant but waspish memoirs are a major source of information about the court of the Sun King.

MADELEINE DE SCUDÉRY (1607–1701): Often referred to as Mlle de Scudéry, she was a writer, whose novel *La Promenade de Versailles* (1669) included descriptions of Le Nôtre's gardens.

MME DE SÉVIGNÉ (1626–1696): She is famous for her copious correspondence, in which she describes life at court. She was an admirer of Le Nôtre's work.

LOUISE-FRANÇOISE DE LA VALLIÈRE (1644–1710): Maid of honour to Louis' sister-in-law, Henriette d'Angleterre, she became the King's mistress. Displaced in Louis' affections by Mme de Montespan.

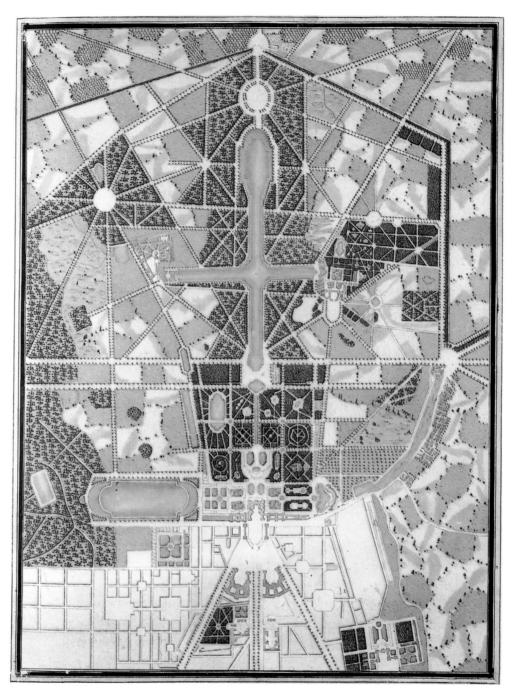

Early eighteenth-century plan of the gardens of Versailles.

Introduction

W ARMONGER, WOMANISER AND AUTOCRAT, Louis XIV, France's self-styled 'Sun King', was also history's most fanatical gardener. At Versailles, 12 miles outside Paris, he created not just Europe's most lavish palace but the most extensive gardens the Western world has ever seen.

During Louis' reign the area between the château and the western horizon, including the gigantic cruciform gesture of the Grand Canal, which threw out watery arms to north and south towards the lesser palaces of Trianon and the Ménagerie, was known as the Petit Parc, though there was never anything *petit* about it. Although reduced in its dimensions after the Revolution, it still covers 1,890 acres (756 ha), which is more than twice the size of Central Park in New York City.

Beyond the Petit Parc lay the Grand Parc, in essence a hunting forest that embraced numerous villages and hamlets and thirty-four farms. In 1689 the Grand Parc of Versailles covered in the region of 19,800 acres (8,000 ha) and was encircled by a wall almost 27 miles long, pierced by more than twenty monumental gates, for it was more important that this wall kept the King's game in than that the King's subjects were kept out. But Louis, whose territorial ambitions were reflected in the relentless expansion of his gardens, continued to add parcels of land to his estate, so that, by the end of his reign – if we include the contiguous royal lands at Marly – the hunting park covered an astonishing 37,065 acres (15,000 ha), including the whole of the forest of Marly to the north and the woods on the heights of Satory to the south.

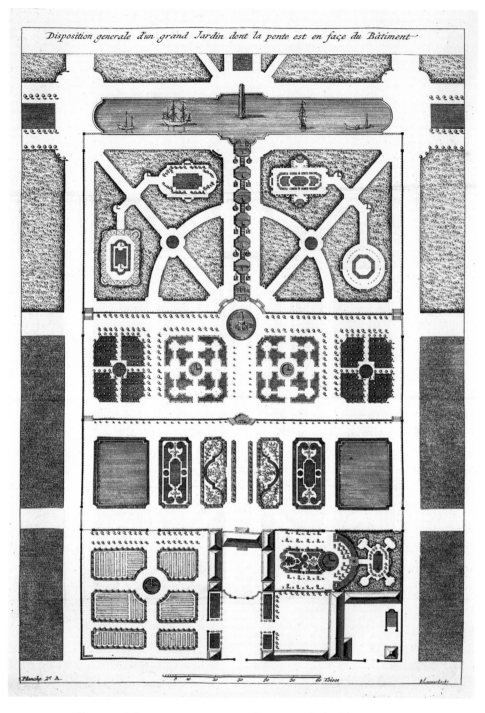

*The general disposition of a great garden facing the building, from La
Théorie et la practique du jardinage by Antoine-Joseph Dezallier d'Argenville, 1709.*

Within the Petit Parc lay the gardens proper, where vast open terraces led down to the bosky groves, or *bosquets*, which served as outdoor rooms for Louis and his court. The terraces were decorated with ornamental parterres, designs made upon the ground, usually with low box hedging and a variety of coloured earths. The woodland rooms beyond were the venues for banquets and ballets, fountains and fireworks, intrigues and courtly manoeuvring, amorous strolls and assignations. This elaborate ensemble of sandy walks, shady avenues, balustrades and basins, embroidered flower-beds, *palissade* hedges, gushing jets and gilded statues still extends over 230 acres (93 ha), which is about two-thirds of the area of London's Hyde Park. Louis had no interest in low-maintenance gardening. Here plants were to be trained and disciplined until they behaved like masonry. Although there were relatively few permanent master-gardeners on the payroll, their numbers were regularly swelled by hundreds of under-gardeners and labourers who were hired by the task or by the day. Occasionally the Sun King himself, appointed by God to lead his nation, would ask to be handed the shears so that he could add a royal flourish to the topiary.

Terracing a recalcitrant site, creating vast waterbodies and the water supply for more than twenty-four hundred fountains were engineering feats of gargantuan proportions achieved without the benefits of modern earth-moving machinery. This project occupied the King for over thirty years; at its peak thirty thousand soldiers were drafted into the enterprise, dying in prodigious numbers from fevers aggravated by the swampy conditions in which they were compelled to work.

Plants were brought from great distances. It was not just the woodlands around Paris that were plundered. Elms, poplars and limes were brought from Flanders and Indian chestnuts from Vienna. To furnish the floral displays, particularly at Trianon and Marly, hyacinths, tulips, roses and redcurrants were brought from Holland, jasmines from the royal nursery at Toulon, tuberoses and daffodils from Turkey, and oranges and carnations from Spain. Large trees were transplanted to give an immediate effect. The roads were clogged by this arboricultural traffic, a sight that prompted Mme de Sévigné to observe that the King was 'bringing all of the forests to Versailles in clumps'.

The King became so fiercely proud of the transformation he had wrought from this unpromising terrain that he often showed visiting dignitaries and royalty around himself and even wrote the first guidebook, *Manière de montrer les jardins de Versailles*. His continuing preoccupation with his gardens is shown by the number of times he revised this text. Six different manuscript versions exist, dated between 1689 and 1705, the fourth having been penned personally by Louis, while others were dictated to secretaries but corrected in the King's own hand. Louis was constantly tinkering with his gardens, adding or removing features, changing the shapes of basins or altering *bosquets*, so he felt that this regular updating of the guidebook was necessary. The garden guide was not an established genre, so his directions can seem a little imperious – 'One will pass over the road where there are jets on two sides, and one will make a tour of the large pond: when one is at the bottom, one will pause to consider the wreaths, the shells, the basins, the statues and the porticos ...' The *Manière* is more like a training manual for courtiers than a readable companion, but it reveals both the King's pride in his gardens and the extent to which he liked to be in control. Those who have tried to tie it into some governing iconographic programme have been disappointed. There is no obvious route or sequence in which to view Versailles, but Louis was keen that his visitors should be directed systematically, so that nothing might be missed. The route took in the Orangerie, the Labyrinthe and the Salle de Bal before arriving at the Fountain of Apollo. Here Louis gave his visitors a choice. If they wished to see the Ménagerie and the Trianon on the same day, they were to go there before viewing the fountains. Since these two features were at opposite ends of the cross-arms of the Grand Canal, this was good advice. Favoured guests might be taken there by boat, but even without this excursion a trip around the rest of the park could take several hours.

In these times of instant makeovers it is difficult to conceive of a garden project quite so daunting. The gardens of Versailles were not made easily. In particular there was the persistent problem of finding enough water to fill the basins and run the multitude of fountains. Here Louis' preoccupation escalated to the level of a costly and damaging obsession. The network of reservoirs and canals he created to feed his fluid fantasies stretched for 18½ miles beyond the château, but even this was insufficient. A monstrous pumping machine was built to bring water from the Seine. Although it was regarded as the Eighth Wonder of the World, it still did not produce enough water. Ultimately Louis was driven towards an extravagant plan to bring water from the River Eure, over 60 miles away, an engineering project for which a large part of the army was requisitioned. Responding to reports of deprivation and deaths along the works, a contemporary commentator, the Duc de Saint-Simon, remarked that the project would be the 'ruin of the infantry'.

Helping Louis to realise his dream was a gardener from a family of modest rank called André Le Nôtre. Le Nôtre's character and temperament were as different from those of his sovereign as it is possible to imagine. Louis was ruthless and driven. Le Nôtre was down-to-earth, witty and amiable, though also phenomenally talented. Though the King could strike fear into the highest in the land

4

with just a look, with Le Nôtre he enjoyed a warm friendship that transcended the vast gulf between their respective positions.

Under Le Nôtre the French formal garden reached its apogee. The Grand Style he brought to perfection, not just at Versailles but in such gardens as Vaux-le-Vicomte, Saint-Germain, Chantilly, Saint-Cloud, Meudon and Sceaux, dominated Western garden tastes around the end of the seventieth century. This style would be imitated throughout Europe. Yet about Le Nôtre, the man, we seem to know very little. One commentator has likened him to Shakespeare, similarly known through his works but hardly at all as an individual. Le Nôtre wrote no books and left no great correspondence, nor have many of his drawings survived. But he did leave traces of the private man. We find him in literary locales, such as the letters of Mme de Sévigné and the memoirs of Saint-Simon. He had his portrait painted by Carlo Maratta wearing a medal given to him by the King; his name appears regularly in the building accounts for Versailles; his favourite nephew wrote a warm eulogy; the *Mercure de France*, which carried all of the news that would interest the court, printed a glowing obituary; an inventory of his possessions when he died shows him to have been an enthusiastic collector of paintings, engravings and medals but not much of a reader. He features in numerous anecdotes, some backed up by primary sources, others handed down across the generations. Perhaps most revealing of all, at least in terms of his contribution to garden design, is a book by Antoine-Joseph Dezallier d'Argenville called *The Theory and the Practice of Gardening*. This treatise, first published in 1709, nine years after Le Nôtre's death, and translated into English by John James in 1712, hardly mentions the master-gardener at all, even though one of his pupils drew the pictures in it. Yet it is beyond doubt that the design philosophy presented was Le Nôtre's and that the methods so meticulously described and illustrated are identical to those which would have been used in the creation of the Sun King's garden.

The fashion used to be to heap all the praise for Versailles – or, for those critics who disliked formality, all the blame – upon Le Nôtre alone, as if the French style had been created unaided and from scratch on his drawing table. Recent scholarship has shown this to be wrong. Le Nôtre was working within a tradition, and his efforts were shored up by gardeners who shared his cultural background and assumptions. Though the gardens were the brainchild of the shared vision of a gardener and a king, they were also the result of an immense team effort.

If gardens came with rolls of credits as films do, we might wonder which names would appear first and in the biggest letters. Louis would be the producer, naturally, though it would be more accurate to call him the producer-director, and we might find his name appearing elsewhere in the credits as a set designer and even as one of the dancers. Jean-Baptiste Colbert, Louis' minister of finance, was also *Surintendant des Bâtiments*; historians have likened him to a book-keeper, but we might think of him as the principal production assistant. He was directly answerable to the King, and he was also Le Nôtre's immediate superior, yet he seems to have acted almost like a clerk-of-works, personally assuming much of the responsibility for progress on site. He had a meticulous eye for detail, exactly the quality one looks for in a supervisor, and his nickname was 'North Wind', such could be the iciness of his displeasure. Le Nôtre, meanwhile, was not just the King's 'designer of gardens' but also, for much of his career, a *Contrôleur Général des Bâtiments*, which is to say a high-ranking member of the royal administration. We can regard him as the gardens' creative director. But we must also recognise that he had co-directors who, while not directly responsible for the gardens, influenced them in significant ways.

Louis Le Vau was one of these. His title was *Premier Architecte*, and as such the château was his main concern. But he also designed structures within the gardens, including the octagonal pavilion of the Ménagerie and the Water Tower, which he devised with the help of Denis Jolly, Louis' less than trustworthy fountaineer. Fortunately Le Vau and Le Nôtre had collaborated previously on the design of Vaux-le-Vicomte, and they got on well. Another key figure was Charles Le Brun, who bore the title *Premier Peintre du Roi*. He is usually thought of as Louis' interior designer and as the head of the Gobelins, the manufactory where the carpets, furniture, tapestries and silverware that dress the château were produced, but he also devised the allegories for the statuary in the gardens, including the Apollonian theme which predominated in the early years. In fact he often provided the sketches to which sculptors were required to respond, and also designed many of the permanent decorative features, from urns to gates, as well as the temporary structures erected for the many fêtes that punctuated Louis' reign.

The Italian sculptor Bernini, whose relations with the French court were strained, observed that 'Colbert behaves to Lebrun as to a mistress and defers to him entirely.' Le Brun could be tyrannical, and his control over the artists who worked at Versailles was a good match for Louis' absolutism. It was difficult for any painter or sculptor to receive commissions unless they had Le Brun's approval, but he and Le Nôtre were friends, having trained together in their youth in the studios of the painter Simon Vouet. Le Brun was influential in securing Le Nôtre the biggest opportunity of his career: his commission by Nicolas Fouquet, the King's first finance minister, to design the gardens at Vaux.

For special effects Le Nôtre and Le Brun turned to their fountaineers and firework-makers. François and Pierre Francine were the sons of a Florentine fountain

A great wood of forest trees pierced with a double star, from La Théorie et la practique du jardinage by Antoine-Joseph Dezallier d'Argenville, 1709.

designer called Tomasso Francini. François was the more creative of the brothers, specialising in the designing of the fountains, while Pierre, who worked under him, dealt with the less glamorous but essential pipework.

Versailles was also a musical spectacular, its soundtrack provided by the Italian-born Jean-Baptiste Lulli, who, like the fountain-making Francini brothers, decided to Frenchify his name to Lully for greater acceptability at court, for this was the century when things French were going to surpass things Italian. Louis adored music. Twenty-four violins would play as he dined, and when he took to the waters of the Grand Canal in the royal barque, Lully and his musicians would be floating alongside.

If life at Versailles resembled a theatrical production, there were many occasions for plays within this play. Not only was the young King an accomplished ballet dancer who liked to take centre stage; he also liked to celebrate his success at war by mounting dazzling fêtes which incorporated comedy-ballets written by Molière and staged by his troupe to music by Lully. Since the guest list was often enormous and there were no rooms in the château large enough to contain such spectacles, these performances took place within structures specially constructed in the gardens. Le Nôtre was called upon to respond to this need for outdoor spaces suitable for nocturnal shows and alfresco supper parties. Versailles' *bosquets* in effect served the court as a palace outside the palace. Some of the names of these features make their relationship with architecture very clear, for there is a Salle de Bal, or Ballroom, and a Salle des Marroniers, or Chestnut Hall, and one progresses towards the Grand Canal along the Tapis Vert, or Green Carpet.

There is a sense in which the whole of life at Versailles was minutely choreographed, with Louis playing the leading role while some of the once-powerful nobility were lucky to get walk-on parts. The King quite deliberately excluded them from power, nullifying them through elaborate entertainments and costly pleasures while subjecting them to elaborate rituals of etiquette. All advancement became a matter of catching the King's eye, so it was necessary for the ambitious to remain at court. While under Louis' watchful gaze, trailing behind him on his tours of the garden or impoverishing themselves at the gaming tables, they could not be getting together to fester and plot.

Although it would be wrong to give the impression that there was much social mobility in seventeenth-century France, some were lucky enough to be able to impress by their ability and get on. Sébastien le Prestre de Vauban, the great military engineer, was one of these. His father was a member of the petty nobility – in English terms a squire – and he started his military service as an infantry cadet. But he rose through merit to become a Marshal of France. It may seem odd to

The general disposition of a magnificent garden all upon a level, from La Théorie et la practique du jardinage by Antoine-Joseph Dezallier d'Argenville, 1709

draw a parallel between the vocations of gardening and military engineering, but Vauban and Le Nôtre had more in common than their modest origins. Garden design on the scale practised by Le Nôtre owed much to earthwork techniques developed by the military. The canals, terraces and retaining walls of his gardens had their equivalents in the moats and revetments of Vauban's fortresses. Both men rose in society because they knew how to manipulate the land. Considering Louis' consuming passion for his gardens, it is not surprising to find Vauban summoned away from his defensive responsibilities on several occasions to give advice regarding the water supply for Versailles' fountains. Indeed Vauban was put in charge of the disastrous scheme to divert waters from the Eure, though the blame for its failure does not rest with him.

Though Louis' reign is often taken to be the epitome of an absolute monarchy, it was not a police state and, whatever his failings, the Sun King was no Stalin. Repugnant though absolutism might seem to twenty-first-century democrats, it is arguable that for a country which by the seventeenth century had developed no democratic traditions, it was the only alternative to the civil warfare that had dominated Louis' youth. A fractious nobility had played the greatest part in these disturbances, and it became a central policy of his reign to keep his nobles in line. His way of doing this was subtle. Having declared that he would take personal responsibility for government, he moved his entire court to Versailles. Anyone with any ambition had to follow him and it was there, by the simple expedient of making all advancement dependent upon himself, that he kept the court under his nose and within his power. It suited Louis well that Versailles became a cockpit of ambitious manoeuvring.

We might wonder how an affable man like Le Nôtre was able to hold his own in a court riven with petty intrigue and jockeying for position. Maintaining the King's goodwill was no easy matter, and many fell from grace. The playwright Racine reacted against the back-biting literary world by becoming a royal historiographer, but his religious views put him out of favour; Le Vau was never entirely trusted by Colbert and died penniless; mighty Le Brun lost his power upon the death of Colbert; the sculptor François Girardon received few commissions in his later years; even Vauban ended his career in disgrace for speaking out against the iniquities of the tax-collection system. The competitiveness and roller-coaster quality of life at Versailles are captured in a remark by Marèchal de Villeroy: 'When a minister is in power, you hold his chamber pot for him, but as soon as you see that his feet are beginning to slide, you empty it over his head.' Unusually, although Le Nôtre lost influence in old age, he never lost the affection of the King.

Nineteenth-century writers described Le Nôtre as a *bonhomme*, essentially a good-natured but rather naïve fellow, a bit of a rustic. If that were really so, it is difficult to see how he could have survived, let alone prospered, at court. He was promoted to the aristocracy and died the owner of five houses and a considerable art collection. If he was such a bumpkin, would he have kept the respect of men like Le Vau, Le Brun or François Francine, all of them recognised as outstanding practitioners in their fields? How would he have avoided the envy of less-favoured gardeners? How could he have coped with the King's incessant demands for design changes, or with the court's other dominant personalities, including Louis' rivalrous mistresses, Mme de Montespan and Mme de Maintenon? Surely it is more plausible that Le Nôtre was not only a cultured individual but also a consummate courtier. He emerges from contemporary accounts as a man of disarming simplicity and a natural diplomat. When Louis decided to ennoble Le Nôtre, he asked the gardener what he might take for his coat of arms. Le Nôtre replied that he would like 'Three snails and a head of cabbage – but I must not forget my spade for it is due to my spade that I am the recipient of all the kindnesses with which Your Majesty honours me.' It must have been difficult to feel any resentment towards a man of such self-effacing wit.

The chapters that follow tell the story of the triangular relationship between Louis, Le Nôtre and the gardens they fashioned together out of an unregarded swamp. The King's passion for his gardens can be linked into both the patterns of his complicated love life and his military adventures, for it seems that he celebrated every conquest, whether of a new territory or of a new courtesan, with an extension to his garden. Visionary yet practical, Le Nôtre was exactly the person the King needed in order to fulfil his gardening ambitions. They were very different personalities separated by a vast social distance, yet, as the snobbish and waspish Saint-Simon had to admit, when it came to Le Nôtre, 'the King liked to see him and talk to him.' If it is possible to talk about a God-given demiurge having friends, then Le Nôtre was the Sun King's friend, and their friendship had its foundation in a mutual love of gardening.

NICOLAS FOUCQUET.
Procureur General au Parlement,
Sur-Intendant des Finances et Ministre d'Etat
Né en 1615. Mort le 23. Mars 1680.

Nicholas Fouquet. Portrait by René Gaillard, seventeenth century.

I

The Fateful Party

ON 17 AUGUST 1661 Nicolas Fouquet, Louis' finance minister, had little inkling of the calamity he was about to bring upon himself. Fouquet was finalising the arrangements for a glorious party at which he would celebrate the completion of his new château at Vaux-le-Vicomte, 32 miles outside Paris. He was expecting six thousand guests, representing the highest echelons of French society, and had made provision for a sumptuous feast that would run to six courses. Later, if everything ran to plan, they would retire for entertainments in the gardens, newly laid out by the designer André Le Nôtre, a man as yet little known though already in middle age, whose talent Fouquet prided himself on having spotted. There would be a play by Molière and a ballet by Lully on a specially constructed set, followed by a fireworks display. Fouquet was particularly looking forward to the moment when an enormous whale, illuminated by *petards* within its belly, would start to swim up Le Nôtre's Grand Canal. The most important guest at this celebration was to be the young King, Louis XIV.

The fête of 17 August was not the first of that summer. On 12 July Fouquet had received the widow of Charles I, Henriette of France, accompanied by her daughter, Henriette d'Angleterre, and her son-in-law, the Duc d'Orléans, Louis' brother. Although the King had not been in the party, he had heard glowing reports of the occasion. These must have piqued his curiosity, for although he was already secretly turning against his *Surintendant*, he expressed a desire to visit Vaux and be honoured by a fête. This must have seemed like a godsend to Fouquet, who

Jean-Baptiste Colbert by Jaques Lubin

had aspirations to become first minister. Preparations began almost straight away. The sculptors Girardon and Nicolas Legendre were employed to assist Charles Le Brun with the decorations. It was decided that the fête should be a nocturnal event illuminated by lanterns hung from the cornices of the château and ranged along the terraces and walks; it would be brought to a climax by a display of spectacularly noisy fireworks. Everything was calculated to astonish. But Fouquet misjudged the King's mood completely.

Well before his arrival at Vaux that August evening, Louis had grown deeply suspicious of his finance chief. During the King's minority, France had been ruled by the Italian-born Cardinal Mazarin, and Fouquet, thinking that the young Louis was a malleable ninny, planned to follow the Cardinal's example and become the de facto head of state. He was unaware that his rival, Jean-Baptiste Colbert, a minister no less able but a good deal more honest, had been briefing young Louis against him. In the dialect of western France, the name Fouquet means 'squirrel', and the family incorporated this canny animal into their coat of arms, an appropriate emblem, perhaps, for someone who would be accused of hoarding treasure that did not belong to him. In contrast, the Colbert arms feature a snake, and while this appears to be a grass-snake rather than a viper, those who think that Fouquet was deceived by his enemy are quick to point out the appropriateness of the imagery.

As was customary under the complicated financial system that operated in seventeenth-century France, Fouquet had raised loans for the Crown, putting his own property up as security. The loans would be repaid from taxation, but there was plenty of scope for embezzlement. Fouquet's defenders, and even today there are still many, argued that he behaved no worse than previous finance ministers, and that he had to keep up a lavish front to give his investors confidence. But this was where the real trouble lay: the front was too lavish. Fouquet might have believed he was about to impress the King. In fact he was going to confirm all of his worst fears.

Vaux-le-Vicomte was not Fouquet's first or only garden. He also had an estate at Saint-Mandé, which was renowned for its library and its two hundred orange trees, though there was nothing distinguished about the design of its garden. Saint-Mandé was as lavish as Vaux, however, and it was there that Fouquet began to gather around him the most talented writers and artists in France. However, Saint-Madé was a private house, whereas Vaux was something more: a showcase and stage for Fouquet's taste, wealth, influence and patronage. In creating Vaux, Fouquet was behaving in a kingly fashion. It was this that would get under Louis' skin.

The château and gardens at Vaux impress with their outstanding unity. House and garden belong together, and the whole composition seems to fit its site perfectly and to know its limits. Although in landscape architecture it is never right to compare a site to a blank canvas, since the pre-existing character and topography must always be reckoned with, at Vaux the constraints were few and the opportunities many. Fouquet provided the funds, the labour and the support. For Le Nôtre, who was already in his mid-forties, it must have seemed like the commission for which he had been waiting all his professional life. Le Brun and Le Vau were, similarly, middle-aged men at the peak of their powers. To create the ensemble of château and gardens, three villages – Vaux itself and the two hamlets of Jumeaux and Maison-Rouge – had to be completely flattened. Vaux had been a significant settlement with a church, a cemetery, cottages, various mills and a farm. One can only imagine the consternation of the local peasants as Fouquet's surveyors strode among their crops with their ranging poles.

When works began at Vaux in 1657, an army of labourers was assembled, including masons, carpenters and gardeners. In all eighteen thousand men are reported to have been employed. The château's great dome was up within a year, though finishing touches were still being applied five years later. So many employees were injured during construction that a hospital had to be set up in a neighbouring village. All of this activity was highly visible, and even the insouciant Fouquet began to worry about the ammunition he might be providing to his detractors. According to Anatole France, Colbert himself visited the construction site in secret but was spotted by Fouquet's major-domo François Vatel, the same man who would later serve the Prince de Condé and – so the story goes – commit suicide following a banquet in the King's honour for three thousand guests because he had failed to ensure the arrival of the fish course. The Marquise d'Huxelles wrote to Fouquet on 10 August, only days before the proposed fête, to warn him that the Queen Mother had been speaking against him. 'The King would like to be rich,' she is reported to have said, 'and he does not love those who are more so than he, because they undertake things which he cannot do and he has no doubt that the great wealth of these others has been stolen from him.' Fouquet told his supervisors to hurry the works along and to tighten site security, pressing ahead despite the smear campaign.

Had Fouquet's downfall not been so resounding, he would probably be remembered more for his role as an outstanding patron of the arts than as hubris personified. Under Mazarin's predecessor Cardinal Richelieu, the Marquise de Rambouillet had set herself up in Paris as the arbiter of good taste and culture (for which she would be satirised in Molière's *Les précieuses ridicules* – The Pretentious

Ladies). The marquise had held fêtes in the gardens of her country château and dreamt of pulling down this relic to replace it with a beautiful modern house. Fouquet and the figures he assembled around him – the playwrights Molière and Pierre Corneille, the novelist Madeleine de Scudéry, the letter-writer Mme de Sévigné and the poet Jean de La Fontaine – kept this literary circle going; in building Vaux, Fouquet not only achieved Rambouillet's vision but successfully transplanted the artistic salon, usually an urban phenomenon, into a countryside setting. This too was a problem for the King: there could not be two suns in the same sky.

Fouquet had demonstrated an early interest in gardening by supporting Claude Mollet, a royal gardener from the generation to which Le Nôtre's father had belonged, with the publication of *Théâtre des plants et jardinage*. This book, which contained many delicate drawings of complicated parterre designs reminiscent of the floral ornamentation found in fine needlework, introduced the idea of the *parterre de broderie*, or embroidered parterre, into gardening theory. The book was ready for publication in 1610, but it did not reach a wide audience until Fouquet took an interest. The second edition of 1652 included a four-page dedication to Fouquet from the publisher: 'With your protection and under the authority of your name, I expose this work to the eyes of the public and by this means give it a second birth.'

Le Nôtre was already known as a designer of parterres when he was recruited by Fouquet, although in later years he tended to look down on them as mere pattern-making. Gardening was, for him, a three-dimensional art, a matter of space, enclosure and form, more like architecture than embroidery. At Vaux – his first opportunity to garden at such an extensive scale – he demonstrated his ingenuity at manipulating levels and space. He was determined to exploit the advantages of the site, which straddled the shallow valley of the Anqueuil, thus providing an opportunity to employ terraces, skilfully arranged to create optical effects. The orientation of the house and garden had been decided before Le Nôtre was brought in; fortunately the main axis, which runs from north to south, was roughly perpendicular to the valley. So the broad basis for the garden could be established in the form of an orthogonal grid.

The garden at Vaux is in essence a rectangle, and the whole design attaches to an axis that runs like a spine from a circle of trees to the north through the courtyard and château, across the terraces, down towards the Canal, then up the slope beyond to the upper park. The design gets much of its strength and originality from an interplay of levels that creates shifting perceptions and suddenly reveals unseen parts of the garden. It is held together by enclosing walls of clipped

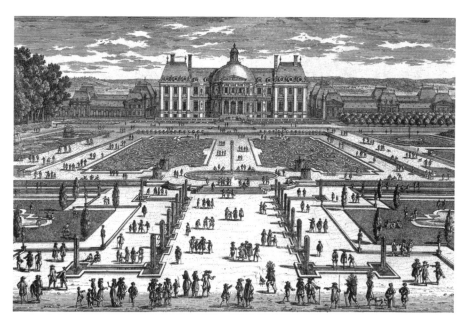

View of the château of Vaux-le-Vicomte. Engraving by the Perelle Family

*View of the Grotto and part of the Canal at the château
of Vaux-le-Vicomte. Engraving by the Perelle family.*

horn-beam hedges, for, despite its extent, this is essentially an enclosed garden, like a vast outdoor room. Le Nôtre used the underlying grid to develop permutations of pattern and enclosure. What at first sight appears to be a perfectly symmetrical garden reveals itself to be something altogether more subtle and interesting, since the apparent symmetry turns out to be composed of carefully juxtaposed dissimilar elements. At Vaux, as at Versailles, it is the variety within the apparently rigid framework that makes the garden lively and engaging and saves it from being stiff and boring.

The poet La Fontaine, who would suffer later for his support of the disgraced Fouquet, wrote that on the evening of 17 August 1661 the weather was perfect: 'Vaux will never be more beautiful.' Setting off from Fontainebleau in mid-afternoon, the royal party, which included the Queen Mother; Philippe, Duc d'Orléans, known to all as 'Monsieur'; and his wife, Henriette, the daughter of Charles II of England, arrived at about six o'clock, clattering through the great stone gateposts of Vaux with their distinctive two-headed herms.

No doubt they were impressed. Arriving at Vaux is still one of the finest architectural experiences that France has to offer. The reason why Vaux works so well lies in the complex relationships between the château, an edifice of glowing yellow limestone; the handsome outbuildings of brick and stone that flank it at a respectful distance; the elegant gate and railings interspersed with a rhythmic row of stone columns; the sequence of courtyards through which one must pass en route to the château, and the hidden moat, which comes as the first of many surprises. As at Versailles, the gardens are almost completely hidden behind the château's façade, though the moat and glimpses of formal gardens to left and right suggest that there are many delights to come. Anyone who has ever played a video-game will be familiar with the way that perspectives change as one moves through space. Needless to say, Le Nôtre and Le Vau achieved their symphony of forms without access to three-dimensional computer simulations, although they may have made models, a common practice at the time. The fact that they achieved the results they did by 'walking through' in their shared imagination makes the results even more astonishing.

It was, by all accounts, gloriously sunny as the King, accompanied by his brother, Fouquet, the Prince de Condé and the customary retinue of brightly attired courtiers, beribboned and plumed for the party, began their promenade around the grounds. Thoughtfully Fouquet had provided light, open-topped carriages called *calèches* for his royal visitors; the Queen Mother kept to hers throughout. According to Helen Fox, one of Le Nôtre's biographers, the garden designer accompanied this party; this seems probable since the King would have expected an account of the design and no one would have been better placed to give it. A small room had been made available to Le Nôtre under the roof of the château so that he could be available to supervise the works and, no doubt, act as a guide on occasion. Le Vau and Le Brun had similar lodgings. The fountaineer Robillard had fine-tuned his water displays, and there was a lively debate among the courtiers as to which feature was the finest, the Cascade, the Couronne or the Gerbe d'Eau. In terms of sheer height, the Gerbe, or Water-stack, would have been the winner, with its jet as thick as a man's waist and its height of 5 metres. The anonymous author of the *Relation*, a contemporary account of the festivities, thought it was one of the best things of its kind in Europe.

Today visitors can retrace the path the royal party would have taken on that portentous day, descending from the terrace to the central path, which extends from the house towards an apparently rectangular pool fed by grottoes. The *Relation* describes this central walk, noting that 'instead of the usual espaliers it is bordered by a channel where the water runs between grass banks, and more than two hundred jets of water, each of the same height, make a pleasant murmur, and one sees fifty fountains playing in the diverse compartments of the parterres, each making a different figure.' This *allée d'eau* was the forerunner of similar features at Versailles such as the Allée des Marmousets. (Today the jets have sadly gone, replaced by plant-filled pedestal basins.)

Walking down this axial path at Vaux, the first of Le Nôtre's optical illusions becomes apparent. The pool, which seemed to be rectangular, is actually square. The grotto, which seemed to lie just beyond it, is seen to be some distance away and separated from it by the declivity which contains the Grand Canal, the dramatic waterbody Le Nôtre created by damming the modest Anqueuil. To reach the grottoes today, one has to walk around one end of this 1-kilometre-long transverse canal, but in Fouquet's time small boats were provided to take visitors across, and on the day of the fête the host had provided a wooden bridge. It also becomes apparent that the row of jets that had been visible as one approached the square pool is only the top of the Grandes Cascades. Though there is scarcely a trickle in them today, in Le Nôtre's time there would have been a tumultuous roar as water gushed down tiers of shell-like bowls into a rectangular pool below.

As one approaches the canal, the distant ends of the water are not in view – it seems as though it might stretch to infinity. Only upon reaching its banks does the visitor learn the true nature and extent of this waterbody. It gets its nickname of 'La Poèle', or 'Frying Pan', from a circular basin at the eastern end that was used for turning boats. From a distance, the grottoes beyond the Canal seem to have niches containing statues, but drawing closer one discovers that they are nothing more than concatenations of stone and concrete, another of Le Nôtre's optical tricks. At either end there is a statue of a river god. One represents the Nile, the other the Anqueuil, elevated into distinguished company by means of the landscape architect's art.

When the King reached the Cascades he was arrested, says the *Relation*, 'by their beauty and by the great quantity of water that he saw there'. Nothing in the whole of Italy, a country celebrated for its spectacular gardens, could be compared to the magnificence of Vaux. Then the party climbed beyond the last cascade to the height from which the Gerbe d'Eau shot its astonishing jet skywards.

Most designs for formal gardens work best when viewed from the terrace in front of the house. One of the great virtues of the design at Vaux is that the composition works equally well when viewed in the opposite direction. Looking out from the house, it is the statue of Hercules at the top of the slope which operates as the focal point. Looking back from the upper park, the château and its outbuildings seem to float serenely and resplendently on the horizon. On still days – and there must not even be the slightest puff of wind – the château's façade and dome are perfectly mirrored in the Carré d'Eau, an effect that must have required the careful calculation of distances, levels and angles of reflection.

Perhaps Fouquet should have anticipated trouble. When the King reached the far end of the garden, where the statue of Hercules now stands, he looked back over the three-quarters of a mile that separated the party from the great domed château, then turned to Fouquet and said, 'I'm surprised.' 'I'm surprised you're surprised,' retorted Fouquet, thinking that the King had paid him a compliment that deserved a witty reply. His astonishment would be much greater three weeks later when, while on a visit to Nantes, the musketeer D'Artagnan, familiar to readers of Alexander Dumas' novel *The Three Musketeers*, would place him in custody for the crimes of peculation and lese-majesty.

After the walk came dinner, marshalled by Vatel. Serenaded by Lully's violins, the guests were treated to a banquet that included pheasants, ortolans, quails, partridges, bisques, ragouts and abundant quantities of wine. The food was served on plates of gold. Some accounts say that there was also a lottery in which jewellery and choice weaponry were given away. As evening turned into night, events unfolded smoothly. The guests had gathered in front of the terraces forming the base of the water feature known as the Grille d'Eau, which had been made into a stage for the evening. When the show was about to start, Molière appeared wearing his everyday clothes. He began to apologise. It seemed that some of his performers had been taken ill and would not be able to entertain the King. While the crowd was still considering this announcement, strange things began to happen. An artificial rock broke open, becoming a shell out of which stepped a nymph who, with much grace, began to recite the prologue for the show. In the King's name the nymph commanded sculptures to walk and trees to speak. Molière's troupe emerged from their various hiding places, the violins and hautboys struck up, and the first ballet began.

After the dancing came the comedy, a performance of *Les Fâcheux*, Molière's play about a man tormented by irritating people – a lightly disguised satire of various personalities at court, many of whom were present to see themselves lampooned. Between the acts there was more light-hearted ballet around a curious assortment of themes; according to the *Relation* there were dances based on the games of *paulme, mail* and *boules*, but performers also appeared as cobblers, as Basque shepherds and in Swiss costume.

After the comedy came the fireworks, which Louis watched from the centre of the garden, just above the Grandes Cascades. The show began one hour after midnight, the blackness of the night adding to the splendour of the display. A thousand rockets shot out of sight, carrying gunpowder into the heavens, then fell in a thousand blazing figures – fleurs-de-lis, stars and names written in fire. On cue the enormous whale made its way up the Canal, launching rockets which snaked across the water. There were so many fireworks and so many reflections that it was hard to judge what was water and what was fire. The rocket salvos lit up the night sky, making it as clear as day. The spectacle was accompanied by the trumpets and drums of the King's musketeers, making it seem as though some epic battle was under way. When it seemed as though the extravaganza was coming to an end, the King mounted his carriage to return to the château. At that instant a million rockets soared skywards from the dome and the whole of the garden became a vault of fire. Thankfully the indefatigable Vatel had assembled a late-night collation.

By the time the court guests boarded their coaches bound for Fontainebleau, their weary heads must have been filled with a kaleidoscope of images. They had walked and talked, laughed and applauded, gasped and guffawed, been wined and dined. But what of Fouquet? There is a story that towards the end of the evening he offered the King his château and gardens as a gift. If there is any truth in this anecdote, we might wonder why he should have been inclined to make such a generous offer. Perhaps he had begun to have doubts about his position and thought that this offer, though bound to be refused, would put him in better odour with the King. Maybe he even thought that the gift would be accepted, but that the loss of Vaux would be a price worth paying if he could realise his ambition of becoming the effective ruler of France. But Louis was a great dissembler, and keeping people guessing was to become one of his most effective tools of government.

Even on the morning of his arrest, timed to coincide with the King's twenty-third birthday, Fouquet believed that it was Colbert whom the King was likely to dismiss. In fact it was his rival who had drawn up the plans for his arrest.

Fouquet's trial was a drawn-out business. Mme de Sévigné, in a letter dated 20 November 1664, recorded a particularly poignant incident that occurred when the former minister, under escort by D'Artagnan, was passing the Arsenal in Paris. He noticed some workmen, and – when he asked what they were doing – was told that they were laying the base for a fountain. 'Don't you wonder what I'm up to?' he quipped to his custodian, going over to speak to the workmen. 'It's just that long ago I used to be quite good at this sort of thing.'

Fouquet was imprisoned for the remainder of his life in the fortress of Pignerol in the Alps. If this seems like a ruthless punishment, we should remember that Louis was a young king determined to stamp his authority on all who served him. There was no better way to do this than to make an example of one of the highest in the land. One cannot help thinking that Fouquet should have seen it coming.

With Fouquet gaoled, Louis proceeded to pillage Vaux. He took tapestries, brocade hangings and silver ornaments from the house, and statues and young trees from the garden. All the orange trees were transferred to the orangery he built at Versailles, along with thousands of shrubs to *pepinières* (nurseries). It seems that Mme Fouquet was paid some compensation for these confiscations. Louis also commandeered Fouquet's entire design team, the architect Le Vau, the interior decorator Le Brun and the landscape architect Le Nôtre. Thus, as Fouquet fell, Le Nôtre stepped up to the position that would make him France's most celebrated garden designer. Other significant figures also went to Versailles, including the fountaineer Claude Robillard; the stonemason Villedo, who had constructed the grotto and lined the Canal; the sculptors Anguier and Girardon; and Antoine Trumel, the flower gardener who had been responsible for the planting-out of the parterres. Another gardener who joined Louis' line-up was Jean-Baptiste La Quintinie, who as a young man had given up his legal career after an educational trip to Italy and a visit to the botanical gardens of Montpellier, which were the oldest in France. La Quintinie had become fascinated by the techniques required to produce fresh fruit for the table and had been persuaded to set up the *potager*, or vegetable garden, at Vaux.

The gardens of Vaux were exemplary in showing how the traditional formal components – terraces, pools, *allées*, hedges, parterres and fountains – could be put together in new ways to reinvigorate old ideas. They were a showcase for Le

Nôtre's talents and expansive vision. We might wonder what he made of Fouquet's cataclysmic fall. It cannot have been pleasant to watch the work of five years systematically dismantled. On the other hand, he had been singled out by the King, which was more than just an honour; it was more like a calling from God. Érik Orsenna suggests that Le Nôtre was dazzled and went willingly. Helen Fox imagines a scene in which he felt sympathy for the young, uncertain King when the latter was confronted by his minister's brilliant achievements. In the face of Vaux's glory Le Nôtre feels it necessary to reassure the King, saying, 'Your Majesty has grandeur of the spirit.'[19] The suggestion is that Le Nôtre was on the King's side all along and that he dropped all associations with Fouquet once the latter had been exposed as a crook.

What is clear is that Le Nôtre does not seem to have spent much time at Vaux after Fouquet's arrest. But this is understandable. The place had the whiff of treason about it, Le Nôtre had plenty of other work to get on with, and no designer could take pleasure in watching his masterpiece fall into ruinous neglect. Unlike Mme de Sévigné or La Fontaine, Le Nôtre wrote nothing in support of his former benefactor, but the garden designer was not a writer, so this is also not surprising.

Some facts point towards there having been residual contact between Fouquet and Le Nôtre. In her description of Vaux-le-Vicomte in her novel *Clélie* (published in ten volumes between 1654 and 1660), Madeleine de Scudéry describes two miniature pyramids, modelled on originals near Memphis in Egypt. They are described as standing on an irregular spot of land facing the Carré d'Eau. The novel was written while the gardens at Vaux were in progress, and there is no evidence that these features were ever built, though the intention to do so was clear. It seems that they would have housed two Egyptian sarcophagi which Fouquet had bought at Marseilles and was storing at Saint-Mandé. They never got as far as Vaux, however. When some of his possessions were sold off at auction, these artefacts were bought by a sculptor who then sold them to Le Nôtre, who sited them close to his house at the Tuileries in Paris. Perhaps it was simply opportunism that prompted him to buy the sarcophagi. On the other hand, it is not hard to believe that sentiment played a part and that he liked the idea of having something which linked him, however tenuously, to Fouquet and to Vaux.

Perhaps more telling is the detour that Le Nôtre made on his journey to Italy in 1679. While crossing the Alps he stopped at Pignerol to visit Fouquet and spend some time with him. It is poignant to consider the trajectories of these two men, Le Nôtre, received by the Pope and by the famed sculptor Bernini, Fouquet languishing in his mountain prison, where little had been done over the years to ameliorate the conditions of his captivity. In stopping at Pignerol, Le Nôtre was risking the King's anger, but he was already sixty-six years old and protected by his reputation and their long friendship. The episode nevertheless shows that he had not forgotten Nicolas Fouquet nor the crucial part this broken man had played in promoting his illustrious career.

André Le Nôtre. Portrait by Carlo Maratta, 1687.

II

Born to Garden

I T WAS ALMOST INEVITABLE that André Le Nôtre should have become a gardener. French society was rigorously stratified, and public offices were passed on according to the hereditary principle. For example, the royal mole-catchers always belonged to the Liard family. As the son of a *jardinier ordinaire* and growing up watching his father at work in the gardens of the Tuileries, André's destiny must have seemed settled.

Just as the term 'engineer' has always been stretched to cover everyone from Isambard Kingdom Brunel to the humble train driver, the term 'gardener' is very elastic, ranging from upper-class garden-makers to municipal parks managers and jobbing lawn-mower men. Jean Le Nôtre was a few rungs up this hierarchy, for the position of *jardinier ordinaire* was not ordinary at all. It is probably easiest to think of him as a privileged contractor who worked for the Crown. One contractor might be responsible for clipping *palissades*, another for tending parterres and yet another for tending to the orangery. Each would employ under-gardeners to carry out much of the labour. If they were prudent, these *jardiniers* could live handsomely, but if an individual neglected his duties, he might be required to reinstate his section of a garden from his own purse. André's father was careful, and the family prospered, living in a house adjoining the Tuileries.

Throughout history the members of trades and professions have banded together for mutual support. On the positive side this has facilitated the development and transmission of expertise and guaranteed levels of competence, but such

27

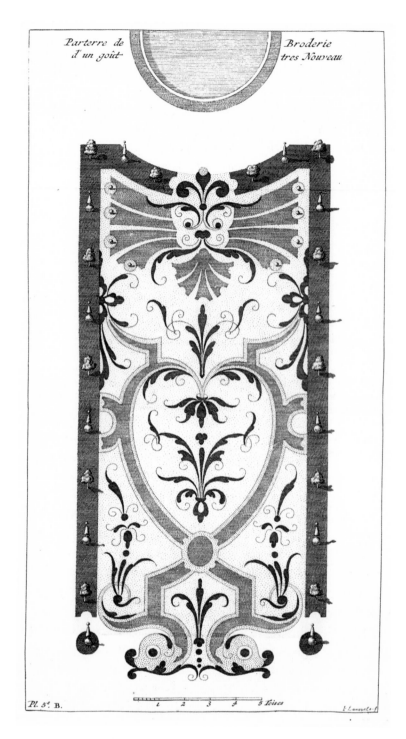

Parterre de
d'un goût

Broderie
tres Nouveau

Pl. 5⁵. B.

1 2 3 4 5 Toises

I. Lanvelo. f

Parterre of embroidery of a very new design, from La Théorie et la practique du jardinage by Antoine-Joseph Dezallier d'Argenville, 1709.

associations also lean towards self-interest and the exclusion of competitors. So it was with this élite group of master-gardeners drawn from the vineyards, orchards and market gardens that abounded in the fertile plains around Paris. To become a master-gardener, a four-year apprenticeship under an established master was deemed necessary, followed by either the production of a 'masterwork' or a two-year period of practical experience. Growing up in the grounds of a royal palace, and having a father who was already a master-gardener for the Crown, these requirements were little obstacle to André. His father wished to pass on not just his skills but also his position to his heir. Nepotism was the norm in seventeenth-century France.

The Le Nôtres were one of a half-dozen families who filled most of the important positions in the King's gardens. It is not too fanciful to suggest that they were as much a dynasty as the Bourbons themselves. The Dupuis, Trumel, Collinot, Masson, Bouteux and Desgots families all play a significant role in this history, but it is the Mollets who deserve particular mention. The first Jacques Mollet, whom garden historians dignify with the regal-sounding title of Jacques I, was the head gardener to the Duc d'Aumale. His son, Claude I Mollet, was the senior gardener at the Tuileries when Jean Le Nôtre was a *jardinier ordinaire*. As well as designing the gardens of several châteaux for Henri IV, Claude I wrote a book on gardening entitled *Théâtre des plans et jardinages*, which was published posthumously in 1652. Jean Le Nôtre and Claude I Mollet were both appointed as 'Dessinateurs des Jardins du Roi', a status that André would also come to enjoy.

One of Claude's sons was also christened André. He travelled widely, designing gardens for royalty in England, Holland and Sweden. He laid out the gardens of St James's Palace in London, then crossed to Holland, where he worked for Prince Hendrick of Orange. In 1644 he returned to France and lived briefly in a house not far from that of the Le Nôtre family, before his inclination to travel took him away again. At this time it was André Mollet, not André Le Nôtre, who was the *Premier Jardinier du Roi*. The latter would have to wait another ten years for his great opportunity.

Claude I Mollet had four further gardening sons: Pierre and Claude II, who joined their father at the Tuileries; Jacques II, who was placed in charge of the gardens at Fontainebleau; and Noël, a lesser-known *Jardinier du Roi*. Though they would in time be eclipsed by André Le Nôtre's rising star, the Mollets were an influential clan, and some of the praise that has been heaped upon Le Nôtre should rightly be shared with them.

The royal gardeners of seventeenth-century France were entwined by marriage as much as by professional calling. Consider the marriage choices of André's three sisters. Françoise wed Simon Bouchard, who was in charge of the orangery at the Tuileries. They were the parents of two girls, Anne and Françoise. When Simon died, his wife and daughters continued to tend the oranges. Élisabeth meanwhile married Pierre Desgots, who was responsible for the *palissades*, and their grandson, another Claude, became André's assistant and ultimately carried on his work, for he had no son of his own. Only Marie struck away from gardening circles, and she had to find herself a sleek Parisian bourgeois in order to do so.

It was quite normal for children to embark upon their professional careers when they were as young as thirteen, for to be a child was not a favoured condition. Children were expected to grow up quickly and take their places in society. It was fairly common for young boys to be given swords, authentically sharp ones, as tokens of their impending manhood, and duels between ten-year-olds were not uncommon. We can only imagine the discussions that went on in the Le Nôtre household when young André expressed the desire, and showed the talent, to become a painter rather than to tread in his father's muddy footsteps. Although fate and family seemed to have marked him out as a gardener, there were numerous specialisms from which he might have chosen. He could have become a nurseryman, or *pépinièriste*; a *fleuriste*, an expert in the cultivation of flowering plants; or a *treillageur*, a specialist in the design and construction of the trellis-work which often assumed architectural levels of complexity; or, like La Quintinie, he might have devoted his life to the perfection of horticultural techniques in the *potager*. Knowing what we now know of Le Nôtre, all of these routes seem too narrow. For a man who understood how to embrace the horizon, the walls of a vegetable garden would have seemed like a prison, and the perfection of horticultural technique would have provided insufficient outlet for his creative vision. Perhaps designing trellises could have interested him for a while, but eventually he would have become bored.

It is more than likely that the Le Nôtres were familiar with the opinions of Jacques Boyceau de la Barauderie, a royal steward and the highest-ranking employee at the Tuileries or, indeed, at any of the royal gardens. Boyceau's strong views on the proper training for a gardener were published posthumously in 1638 in his influential *Treatise on Gardening According to the Reasons of Nature and of Art*. Here he remarks that the ideal apprentice should be chosen in the same way that one would choose a young tree; one should look for a specimen 'of straight trunk, well-grown, well-supported by roots on all sides and of good descent'. The scion of a gardening family would, by analogy, be likely to be of good breeding. Physically he should be 'good spirited, the son of a good worker, not delicate and thus likely to grow physically strong with age'. Dubious though this genetic prescription might seem today, it is clear that André Le Nôtre filled it perfectly.

Boyceau's prescription for the apprentice gardener did not completely conflict with the young Le Nôtre's artistic leanings. Though he thought that practical experience was important and believed that a young gardener should 'work with the spade with other labourers, learning well to cultivate the earth, to bend, set right and bind the wood for works of relief, to trace upon the ground his design … to plant and clip the parterres, and trim the *palissades* with a long-handled sickle, and several other particulars regarding the embellishment of gardens of pleasure,' unusually he did not suggest a programme of lessons in horticulture or agronomy for the protégé gardener. Instead he recommended first that the apprentice must be taught to read and write, and then to draw. His idea was not that the student gardener should be turned into a painter or a sculptor, but that he should be sufficiently capable with pen and pencil to design the patterns used to make parterres. The aspect of his father's work that pleased the young André the most was observing him at the draughting table, planning and plotting the elaborate designs he would later see transferred to the ground.

If the trainee showed promise in drawing, Boyceau suggested that he should be encouraged to study geometry, so that he might plan the partitions and compartments of gardens. Next, that he be taught architecture, so that he could undertake construction, and also arithmetic, so that he might work out the costs of his various proposals. This programme bears a striking similarity to the syllabus of a present-day landscape-architecture course. It seems that seventeenth-century master-gardeners were landscape architects in all but name.

Perhaps Boyceau's way of thinking softened Jean Le Nôtre's attitude towards his son's aspirations. Maybe he foresaw that artistic training would lead André back to gardening in time. Whatever his reasoning, this wise parent did not stand in his son's way.

If fortune had favoured André with a father well placed in gardening circles, it had also given him the huge advantage of growing up within walking distance of the most significant concentration of artisans in France. The former King Henri IV had installed a colony of craftspeople in the Grande Galerie of the Louvre, a short distance from where the Le Nôtre family lived. While André was still in his mid-teens he was apprenticed to one of their number, the painter Simon Vouet. As a young man, Vouet had travelled with the French ambassador to the Ottoman lands, studied the decorative arts of Islam and painted a lifelike portrait of the Sultan at just one sitting. Joining Vouet gave André an entrée to a creative treasure house. It was as if he had graduated to the most liberal university in the world. If he wished to, he could discuss the construction of mathematical instruments with Étienne Flantin, or matters of engineering with Jacques Alleaume, who was an

31

Habit de Jardinier

Habit de jardinier. Anonymous, seventeenth century.

expert on military fortifications, or the crafting of geographical globes with Marin Bourgeois. All of these men worked in the Grand Galerie. André's education was clearly not confined to the potting shed, but flourished in the stimulating light of the atelier.

One of the explanations advanced for André Le Nôtre's interest in architecture is Thierry Mariage's observation that the royal architect Louis Lemercier, the designer of the Palais-Royal, collaborated with both Vouet and Jean Le Nôtre. André would also have had access to Vouet's library, which contained over forty books on architecture and perspective and other works related to painting. It is not hard to imagine the young Le Nôtre being given the task of filling in the background landscape for one of Vouet's compositions, this being common practice at the time, and discovering, little by little, that it was the landscapes rather than the biblical or mythological groups in the foreground that most interested him.

Alternatively, André's return to gardening may have had a parallel with the career path of William Kent, the eighteenth-century English landscape gardener whose first ambition was to become another Raphael. Despite his long apprenticeship in Rome, Kent's first commissions failed to impress the critics, who thought he had a shaky eye for human proportions. He fared better as an architect – the Royal Mews, the Treasury and Horse Guards in London are all his work – but it is as a designer of landscapes that he is mostly remembered. Horace Walpole went so far as to say that Kent had been 'born with the genius to strike out a great system from the twilight of imperfect essays'. It seems likely that the young Le Nôtre mistook his métier in just the same way but realised his error before it cost him too much in time and disappointment.

Whatever the reasons, there came a moment when André had to choose between a career as a painter or a return to the family business, and the pull of the soil and of tradition proved the stronger. He put away his brushes and returned to work with his father in the Tuileries. In 1635, still only twenty-two, he obtained his first serious position, working as first gardener for Gaston, Duc d'Orléans, no less a person than the brother of Louis XIII. At this time the Duke lived in Paris, at the Luxembourg Palace, whose gardens had been conceived by the aforementioned Boyceau. Le Nôtre soon took over in the Luxembourg Gardens. Though his apprenticeship at the Louvre and his close observation of gardening practice in the Tuileries would have given him the best possible grounding in the arts of gardening, it must still have proved difficult for a young man to step into the boots of one as renowned as Boyceau, but at least the old gardener had provided him with the best possible set of instructions.

*　　　*　　　*

Le Nôtre's love of art and his affinity with artists remained throughout his life. His friendship with Le Brun, a fellow student under Vouet, became the basis of a lifetime collaboration. Before working for Fouquet at Vaux, Le Brun had been to Rome in the company of Nicolas Poussin, a painter whose reputation would eventually surpass that of Vouet. Though Poussin remained in Rome for most of his life, he was summoned back to Paris in 1640 to decorate the Long Gallery of the Louvre and was given a house in the grounds of the Tuileries, which would have made him a close neighbour of the Le Nôtres. Poussin's stay in Paris lasted for a little over eighteen months and was not a happy period. Vouet, whose Baroque style was at odds with Poussin's Classicism, regarded him as a rival, but Le Nôtre became an admirer. Later, when he had sufficient wealth to collect paintings, the gardener acquired seven of Poussin's canvasses, among which was one, *The Woman Taken in Adultery*, which he commissioned himself in 1653. He also admired the work of Claude Lorrain, another Frenchman who was happiest when working in Italy.

We might wonder why these artists appealed so strongly to Le Nôtre. The most straightforward answer is that both liked to paint landscapes, yet the kinds of scene they depicted were not at all like the formal gardens of Italy or France. Both set their subjects in landscapes that were intended to evoke a Classical Arcadia, drawing upon the Roman Campagna for their inspiration. These scenes were quite shaggy, without the clipped hedges and straight lines of the geometrical garden. In the eighteenth century these same painters would be greatly admired by the English land-owning classes, who, with the help of gardeners like Kent, Lancelot 'Capability' Brown and Humphry Repton, would seek to adjust their portions of the rolling English countryside to match these painterly visions. It is no accident that the figures in Poussin's paintings often seem like actors posed against a backcloth. The artist's method was to build a sort of peepshow with a miniature stage and small wax figures dressed in scraps of drapery. From about 1640 his interest in the backdrop began to overtake his interest in the little figures in the foreground. Lorrain's paintings, on the other hand, are softer and more bucolic, and were inspired by Virgil's evocations of the ancient Roman countryside. Gods, hunters, shepherds and flocks of sheep animate scenes in a barely tamed Nature to which rocky arches and promontories, ruined towers and temples add an atmosphere of nostalgia and melancholy. It is not difficult, when viewing such paintings, to see how they influenced English landscape gardens like Stourhead or Stowe, but the landscapes of Poussin and Lorrain do not demonstrate the absolute dominion of Nature that was generally exercised in the gardens of Le Nôtre. Perhaps the answer can be found in the Bosquet des Sources at Versailles, where he utilised a marshy spot to create a garden of winding paths and meandering streams, sporadically embellished with statues. Here the geometry was subtle, just the sort of veiled control that one might find in a painting by Poussin or Lorrain. This suggests that Le Nôtre was ahead of his times and that he had an eye for what would later become known as the Picturesque. The court was not enthusiastic, however, and the Bosquet des Sources was erased in 1684 to make way for the Colonnade. Le Nôtre, understandably disgruntled, managed to recapture the informal atmosphere in his little Jardin des Sources at the Grand Trianon, which proved to be a popular success.

In 1637, when André's father decided that it was time to retire, Louis XIII was happy to appoint André to succeed him as *jardinier ordinaire* at the Tuileries. André must have performed his duties for the Duc d'Orléans well, because the document that confirmed his appointment opened as follows: 'In response to the good and laudable report on the person of our dear and beloved André Le Nôtre and in full recognition of his sufficient loyalty, wisdom and experience in the matter of gardening, expedience and fidelity, for these reasons and others besides, we confer and grant to him the Status and charge of Gardener of our Tuileries gardens.'

Three years later, at the age of twenty-seven, André married Françoise Langlois, the daughter of an artillery officer, further confirmation of his improving status at court. It was also, as we shall see, a useful professional connection. The witnesses to the marriage included two prominent gardeners, Michel I Le Bouteux, who served the Duc de Vendôme, and André's brother-in-law, Pierre Desgots. Also present at the ceremony, which took place in the church of Saint-Roch, were François de Montigny, captain and governor of the Tuileries château, and M. de Belville, equerry to the Royal Stables. The Langlois family could be considered lesser nobility, so this was a propitious match for the young gardener. The in-laws also provided a dowry of 6,000 *livres* for the newly-weds, to which Le Nôtre's parents added a gift of 3,000 *livres*, another indication that the groom's family was flourishing and well established.

The Le Nôtres' marriage was stable and prosperous, though tinged with sadness. Nancy Mitford, no cheerleader for the medical profession, suggested that in seventeenth-century France doctors were among the greatest threats to human life. The staple treatment for most ailments, whether fevers, inflammations or infections, was blood-letting; it was even used for haemorrhages. After bleeding, the patient generally felt much worse, which was considered such a hopeful sign that the veins would be opened again. The benefits of this universal remedy were extended to infants, who very often died as a result. Only the affluent could afford

Grand Portique de Treillage

1   2   3   4 *Toises*

A large portico of trelliswork or treillage, from La Théorie et la practique du jardinage by Antonie-Joseph Dezallier d'Argenville, 1709.

such dubious medical attention, which may be why ten of the seventeen children Louis had with his wife or principal mistresses did not survive beyond infancy. André and Françoise had their own portion of grief. They had three children: Jean-François, who was born two-and-a-half years into the marriage, and two girls, Marie-Anne and Jeanne-Françoise, who were born much later, when Le Nôtre's career as a royal officer was settled but before his involvement with Versailles had begun. Little is known about these children, not even the dates of their deaths, but we do know that they all died very young.

Whatever the sadness at home, professionally Le Nôtre continued to prosper. In general there was little scope for social mobility in seventeenth-century France, but a connection with royal building works did offer opportunities to some. There were no clear demarcation lines between masons, architects and building contractors, so someone like Jules Hardouin-Mansart could train as a mason and become a royal architect and, ultimately, *Surintendant des Bâtiments*. Boundaries on the gardening side were equally fuzzy. There were many lowly journeymen gardeners and pieceworkers but far fewer master-gardeners, and at Versailles less than ten *jardiniers en chef*. Under Colbert these included men like Marin Trumel, who was in charge of the Orangerie; Henry Dupuis, who took that responsibility over after Trumel's death; and Michel II Le Bouteux, the specialist in flower-gardening who also acted as the concierge for the Trianon. With the single exception of Jean-Baptiste La Quintinie, who was ennobled for his services in the kitchen-garden, none of Le Nôtre's gardening contemporaries got anywhere near the top of the social ladder.

The accession of Louis XIV in 1643 made little immediate difference to Le Nôtre's status, but in 1657 he was appointed *Contrôleur Général des Bâtiments du Roi*, answering directly to the *Surintendant*, who at that time was Antoine de Ratabon. (Colbert would take over in 1664 and keep the post until his death in 1683.) The *contrôleurs* were senior administrators, but they worked in rotation, taking up their duties for one year in every three. As was customary, Le Nôtre had to purchase this position, at the cost of 40,000 *livres*, a significant sum considering that it carried an annual gratification of just 3,000 *livres*. It also gave him the title of *Conseilleur du Roi*, and – more importantly – it established his position firmly within the court hierarchy.

The administration Le Nôtre joined grew to be a significant branch of government, employing more than a hundred officers including architects and artists. His duties involved supervising all sorts of works related to the royal buildings, not just the gardens, though these were, naturally, his special province. He had to verify the accounts submitted by contractors before they went to the treasurers for payment. Here is another respect in which the myth of the genial rustic is at odds with reality. Le Nôtre was clearly very much at his ease in matters of money, whether he was looking after it on behalf of the Crown or accumulating it in his own right. In seventeenth-century France there were none of the strictures that now prevent public servants from seeking their own profit. As a royal gardener and court official, Le Nôtre remained free to undertake lucrative commissions for private clients. In this context, his investment in acquiring high position seems shrewd as it was certain to enhance his reputation and attract more custom. It has been estimated that he was earning about 40,000 *livres* per annum by the end of his life, and his fortune has been estimated at 540,000 *livres*. Martin Lister, an English doctor who travelled to France in 1698, visited the elderly Le Nôtre and was proudly shown his collection of medals. 'The French King has a particular Kindness for him,' the guest observed, 'and has greatly enricht him.'

At one and the same time Le Nôtre was a contractor who provided services and also a senior figure in the administration. This confusion of roles may seem odd to our eyes, but it was normal in seventeenth-century France. Le Nôtre was also the *Dessinateur des Jardins du Roi*, and it was in this capacity that he provided the overall designs and plans for the setting out of the grounds. Good contractors and efficient administrators are not so hard to come by, but men with creative vision are harder to find. It was Le Nôtre's ability to visualise that won him favour with the King.

Yet, despite his status and success, as the master-gardener entered middle age there was little to indicate that his destiny would be much different from that of dozens of other gardeners who gave satisfactory service to the Crown. At the Luxembourg Gardens, laid out by Boyceau, there had been no scope for design innovation. In Le Nôtre's youth the Tuileries had been sacrosanct, and any radical dreams he might have cherished had been hidden away like tulip bulbs in a closet. His opportunity to remodel the Tuileries would not come until 1664, by which time he would already have begun his work at Versailles.

It would not be true to say that Le Nôtre was unregarded before his ability was recognised by Fouquet. His involvement in some of the gardens attributed to him is by no means certain, but it has been suggested that while working at the Luxembourg Palace he collaborated with the architect François Mansart at the châteaux of Blois, Petit Bourg and Maisons. The mitre-shaped garden for Archbishop Bousset at Meaux was certainly a Le Nôtre design, undertaken when he had just turned thirty. A year later he worked at Fontainebleau, where he modified the Jardin de la Reine. This was an important commission but not the stuff of a great reputation, although Louis XIV would ask him to work at Fontainebleau again in 1662, by which time the major works at Versailles had begun. Charles II chose this unfortunate moment to invite Le Nôtre to England. The tone of Louis XIV's reply was positive: 'I shall willingly allow him to make a tour of England since the King desires it.' But it appears that Louis must have changed his mind, because there is nothing to suggest that Le Nôtre ever went.

Throughout the period during which he worked for the Sun King, Le Nôtre also took other clients, and their names read like a *Who's Who* of late seventeenth-century France. The King was not the only one to have been impressed by the gardens at Vaux. Louis II de Bourbon, Prince de Condé, descended from an uncle of Louis' grandfather Henri IV, had been in line for the French throne before Louis' birth. A great military leader with a string of victories in Flanders, in 1652 he had led an unsuccessful insurrection against the Crown, but his rebellious fire burnt out in his later years, and he recognised that if he wished to live as a great prince, he would have to be content to reflect the light that emanated from the Sun King. His ancestral domain was at Chantilly; the château dated from the middle of the previous century, when most of it had been built by Condé's famous forebear Anne de Montmorency, the *Connétable*, or supreme commander, of the French armies.

The fate of Fouquet was a salutary lesson to anyone who had delusions of glory, but Condé was an exception, a Prince of the Blood and a reformed rebel who had pledged his devotion to the King. He was now perceived as a loyal member of the family, so the King did not view the château and gardens of Chantilly as threats to his own authority and prestige.

Condé, like Louis, wasted little time in commissioning Le Nôtre, but the task that faced the landscape architect in 1662 at Chantilly was very different from the proposition at Versailles. Condé did not follow the vogue for knocking down old buildings, and this presented Le Nôtre with an impediment. The château was irregular in plan, not quite a triangle and certainly not a rectangle, and it sat at the centre of an even more irregular moat. The usual ploy of developing an axis to bisect the main building and extend into the park at a right angle to the main elevation was simply unavailable. Le Nôtre's solution, every bit as daring as the transverse canal at Vaux, was to set the axis parallel to the front of the château. He placed an impressive equestrian statue of the *Connétable* in a key position on the Grande Terrace and cut the axis south for several miles through the forest. It was so conceived that for anyone arriving from this direction, horse and rider would be constantly in view. As one approaches today, it stands out against a light background of sandy paths; as one gets closer, it is silhouetted against the sky. The château only comes into view as one reaches the moat, for this is a design in which the gardens dominate the architecture. Nor do the gardens to the north come into view until the Grande Terrace is reached. This shifting of goals is another manifestation of the designer's skill.

A massive flight of stairs descends from the Grande Terrasse to the level of the water parterres. Although the stairs were designed by the architect Daniel Gittard, it was Le Nôtre, drawing on his recent experience designing the grotto at Vaux, who decided that there would be nymphs and river gods in the niches of the towering retaining wall. Versailles was to be far richer in jets and fancy waterworks; at Chantilly Le Nôtre used expanses of still water, hardly troubled by fountains. Here the reflective qualities of large, peaceful sheets of water fascinated him. The enlarged moat, the Grand Canal and the ten simple pools arranged in the Grand Parterre were like mirrors reflecting the immensity of the sky.

Le Nôtre was involved at Chantilly for twenty years, a time-span that bears comparison with his engagement at Versailles. His experience working for Condé must have offered a contrast to, and perhaps a relief from, his work for the King. Although Condé was a domineering person with a quick temper, he seems to have treated his garden designer well. While the Prince did not have the almost unlimited funds that the Sun King had at his disposal, at Chantilly there were no accountants like Colbert to look over Le Nôtre's shoulder. The garden designer also had the assistance of a favourite nephew, Claude Desgots, and difficulties over the water supply did not loom over every design proposal, since the River Nonette provided for all the garden's needs. Certainly Le Nôtre thought very fondly of Chantilly, where he is remembered by a statue in the grounds. Two years before his death, he was corresponding with the Earl of Portland concerning a possible commission from the English King. 'Remember the gardens you have seen in France,' he wrote. 'Versailles, Fontainebleau, Vaux-le-Vicomte, the Tuileries and above all Chantilly.'[17]

Those not of Condé's rank were more careful. No one wanted to follow Fouquet into oblivion. Garden parties became rare, though this did not concern anyone too much since there were always so many diverting parties at Versailles. Colbert waited for nine years before he purchased a country estate. In 1670 he began to build himself a château at Sceaux where he employed Le Nôtre for the gardens, but although the place is grand, it does not have the opulence or the ostentation of Vaux. At Sceaux Le Nôtre created a cascade of eighteen basins linked by a watery staircase which flowed down to a pool called the Octagone, where the most powerful fountain in France rose to a height of 25 metres. Nothing at Versailles could rival it until François Mansart's son Jules Hardouin-Mansart created the Hundred Pipes at the beginning of the eighteenth century. At Sceaux Colbert was restrained by his natural fiscal prudence as much as by his wariness of the King.

He even resisted the suggestion that there should be a canal because he thought it would be too expensive. One was built eventually but not until Sceaux passed to Colbert's son, the Marquis de Seignelay.

Le Nôtre also laid out the garden at Saint-Cloud, a difficult site halfway up a slope overlooking the Seine, for Philippe d'Orléans, the King's only brother. At Saint-Germain-en-Laye, where there were two royal palaces on the same site, Le Nôtre undertook one of his greatest works of engineering, the Grande Terrasse, an airy walkway 30 metres wide, stretching uninterrupted for 2,400 metres, high above the Seine, which required the construction of massive retaining walls to keep its path straight along the crest of the slope.

There is a phrase in the Duc de Saint-Simon's eulogy to Le Nôtre which provides us with a key to understanding the gardener's success. 'He was of charming simplicity and truthfulness,' wrote the diarist. It appears that gardeners often enjoy the privilege of closer communication with their royal patrons than do senior courtiers. In Britain one can think of 'Capability' Brown, who had the ear of George III and even urged him to abandon his American war, and of the chemistry between Queen Victoria and John Brown, who, though not a gardener, occupied a similar position as a highly trusted outdoor servant. Le Nôtre had this sort of relationship with Louis XIV, even though contemporary accounts mention the terror that proximity to the King could induce in members of his retinue.

One might have thought that Le Nôtre's position as a royal favourite would have attracted poisonous darts, for courtiers were jealous in their pursuit of royal favour, but one cannot detect the slightest whiff of malice, though Saint-Simon, in a more liverish frame of mind, could write disparagingly about the design of the château and gardens of Versailles in his memoirs. Unlike many around him, Le Nôtre never appeared to be on the make. He would defer to others, was always happy to share the credit for his work and did not like to criticise.

Only at the very end of his life was there any perceptible cooling of Le Nôtre's relationship with Louis, and even then it had more to do with the King's wish to take more personal responsibility for the design of his gardens than any ill feeling towards his favourite gardener. To understand Le Nôtre it is necessary to appreciate that he always thought himself the luckiest of men. At an age when most would have abandoned any thoughts of greatness, he was handed the opportunity to create the most lavish and extensive garden the Western world had ever seen. This opportunity came to him not from a wealthy financier, merchant or noble but from a monarch regarded as a god-king. Le Nôtre continued to be dazzled by the Sun King for the whole of his life but never to the extent that he missed his footing or was blinded to the requirements of good design.

The young Louis XIV goes hunting. Portrait by Jean de Saint-Igny.

III

The Sun Rises

Everything we know about André Le Nôtre – his amiable disposition, his easy relationships with co-workers, his long and devoted marriage – suggests that he must have had a secure and contented childhood, sheltered behind the walls of the Tuileries. The same cannot be said for the Sun King. Not only did Louis come from a family which, by contemporary standards, could be labelled dysfunctional, but his formative years coincided with a period of political unrest that put his very life at risk.

Louis became King in 1643 on the death of his father, Louis XIII, a brusque and sometimes boorish man whom the young Prince can hardly have known. His father and his mother, Anne of Austria, had little in common; indeed they spent so little time together that the birth of an heir after twenty years of loveless marriage was considered a miracle, and the first of many epithets that would be attached to Louis was *le dieu-donné*, or 'Gift of God'. He was only five when he acceded to the throne. Louis XIII had foreseen that his wife would lack the political nous to rule as Regent, so he had made provision for a Regency Council to support her, but Anne persuaded the Parlement de Paris (a group of lawyers rather than a democratically elected chamber) to set this aside. She fell under the sway of Cardinal Mazarin, her brilliant but unscrupulous and manipulative first minister; there have even been suggestions that the two were secretly married. Mazarin was the de facto ruler of France for eighteen years, not counting two brief periods when he became so unpopular that he thought it better to remove himself. He managed to upset everyone, the Parlement, the Princes of the Blood and the population in general. It cannot have helped that the government was now perceived to be in the hands of two foreigners. Despite her title, Anne was the daughter of Philip III of Spain, while Mazarin was a naturalised Frenchman thought of as the 'Italian Thief'.

In French history the mood of the Parisian mob has often proved decisive. While Le Nôtre, now in his mid-thirties, continued to lead a settled existence in the grounds of the Tuileries, barely a stone's throw away at the Palais-Royal the young King was in mortal peril. The civil wars that troubled France from 1648 until 1653 are known as the *Frondes*, a name derived from the word for a slingshot, the sort of weapon easily improvised by the members of a mob. This was a period of confusion and shifting alliances as various sectors of French society sought their own ends with little regard for one another. The Princes of the Blood would have been happy to have deposed Mazarin; the Parlement was eager to increase its control over government; the poor just wanted some relief from crippling taxation and the poverty that came with it.

In August 1648, when Anne tried to arrest three prominent members of the Parlement, there was trouble in the streets, with barricades thrown up and the air thick with stones. The *Frondes* had begun. Within two days Anne had to back down and an uncertain peace was restored, but she decided that Paris must be subdued by force. Before she could do this, the ten-year-old King would have to be smuggled to a place of safety. At this point, the Prince de Condé was prepared to offer the monarch sanctuary at Saint-Germain. On 5 January 1649, the ladies of the Palais-Royal having gone to bed, the doors were all locked. At three o'clock in the morning the Maréchal de Villeroy went to the King's bedchamber and woke him gently; then the royal party crept to the garden gate of the palace, where a coach was waiting. Their flight through the dark and frosty streets and their clandestine and ignominious arrival at Saint-Germain, where no fires had been lit, the wind howled through glassless windows, and there were no decent beds to sleep in, left a mental scar on the young monarch. He grew up with a need for stability that was almost pathological. It would find its most creative outlet in the geometrical order which, with Le Nôtre's assistance, he would impose upon the ground at Versailles, but towards the end of his reign, as youthful manifestations of glory ossified into sterile conservatism, it was expressed through overblown etiquette and the inflexible clockwork of courtly life.

Later on in 1649, Condé made a speech to the Parlement, hoping to win over the people by suggesting that the way to put an end to the country's troubles was for Mazarin to leave. But the Cardinal refused to go. In January 1650 Anne took the momentous step of ordering the arrest not just of Condé but of his brother and brother-in-law. By this time the court had returned to the Palais-Royal, but once again the Queen Mother thought it wisest for Louis, now twelve years old, to leave the capital. So there was another secretive and wintry departure, this time for Rouen in Normandy.

While Condé remained imprisoned, there could be no peace, and the following winter found the court once more under siege at the Palais-Royal. The wily Mazarin thought it prudent to slip away to Cologne until the situation improved. Now the King's uncle, Gaston d'Orléans, that same Duke who had written such a glowing recommendation for the youthful Le Nôtre after his work in the Luxembourg Gardens, sent the captain of the Swiss Guards to make sure that Louis had not been spirited away once more. He wanted to keep the King in Paris, where pressure from the Parlement and fear of the mob might have forced Anne to dismiss her first minister and release the royal captives. Whoever had possession of the boy might be the ruler of France. The angry crowd that seethed around the Palais-Royal would not accept the captain's assurances that Louis lay sleeping and demanded to see the King for themselves. The Queen Mother decided to take an enormous gamble and opened the doors to the rioters. Whether the King genuinely slept through the events that followed or whether he had been instructed to feign sleep we do not know, but the mob, which had seemed so threatening moments earlier, now melted into tender admiration. Once their leaders had seen the boy resting peacefully in his bed, they became loyal subjects once more, and another crisis was defused. On the following day the princes were released.

Anne's high-risk tactic had paid off. In September 1650 Louis reached his thirteenth birthday, the date on which his minority was supposed to end. Preceded by liveried footmen and pages sporting white feathers, the King, dressed in a golden suit and mounted on a bay charger, led a glorious cavalcade through the streets of Paris to cries of 'Vive le Roi!' The Parlement that had so recently plotted to usurp his power was now forced to listen in solemn silence while he declared his wish to take the government upon himself. But it was a sham; Louis also had to tell the lawyers the news they hoped to hear, which was that Mazarin would remain in permanent exile. In truth Mazarin, who had been like a father to Louis, was the only person he could trust, aside from his mother. In seeking their own interests, the greatest names in France, her finest generals and even the King's own uncle had sided with France's old enemy Spain. While the capital was seized by unrest, there was a war raging at France's frontiers and it was not going well. The release of Condé and the return of Mazarin brought on the last spasm of the insurgencies. A royal army under Turenne was sent to engage Condé, who was now in full revolt. With Spanish support and the aid of Mlle de Montpensier, the daughter of Gaston d'Orléans, who had raised a regiment, the Prince succeeded in occupying Paris on 2 July 1652, one of the hottest days of that year. The rebels were outnumbered, having only five thousand men against a force of twelve thousand loyal to the King. Like all internecine struggles it was a grim business. The Queen Mother waited and prayed in a convent at Saint-Denis while the nuns brought her intermittent news of the deaths of her relatives; meanwhile the Prince de Condé, in a battered cuirass and caked in blood and dust, found Mlle de Montpensier near the Porte Saint-Antoine and declared that their victory had come at a great cost: 'I have lost all my friends.'

Although the battle of the Rue Saint-Antoine left Condé in possession of Paris, he had failed to seize the King. The *Frondeurs* soon began to chafe under his leadership, and the rapacity of his ragged army antagonised the citizenry. Within three months he was obliged to leave the city in the hope of meeting up with his Spanish allies. The way was open for Louis to reclaim his capital.

With the abject collapse of the *Fronde*, Louis' life, which had thus far been characterised by periods of flight and virtual imprisonment, was suddenly transformed. The pitiable, harried boy now met with flattery and subservience on every side. He began to sense his destiny, though he kept his ambitions hidden behind a mask of indolence, courtesy and laddish playfulness. With the aristocratic leaders of the *Fronde* in exile and disgrace, the Parlement was soon put in its place, and all the resolutions it had passed since 1651 were annulled.

Louis' coronation, delayed by the *Frondes*, took place with sufficient pomp at Rheims in 1654, but he was not yet the ruler of France; Mazarin would continue to occupy that position until his death. Louis owed too much to his mother and to the scheming Cardinal to wrestle them for power, so he bided his time, content to be thought of as a mediocrity and a fool by many at the court.

Mazarin had a shrewd plan to marry Louis to the Spanish Infanta, Marie-Thérèse, a union that could secure peace between France and Spain. This would be the culmination, the keystone, of the Cardinal's diplomacy, but he almost wrecked his initiative when he brought his own three nieces to court. The teenage Louis fell for the youngest of them, Maria Mancini, a tall, dark-eyed, intelligent girl who shared the King's fondness for dancing and for outdoor pursuits like hunting and rowing. Although this love match would have united his family with the Bourbons, Mazarin knew he had to oppose the relationship. When the lovestruck Louis came to see him to express his intention to marry Maria, Mazarin told him that it was impossible. For there to be any hope of peace between France and Spain, Louis had to marry the Infanta; for him to marry the niece of the

Louis XIV wearing the costume of Apollo to dance in the ballet La Nuit. Anonymous.

detested Mazarin was to risk another *Fronde*. Louis wept and raged, but he knew the Cardinal was right. At the age of twenty he was forced to say goodbye to his first love and sign a contract of marriage with Marie-Thérèse. In light of this love-less union, it would not be long before Louis lost his heart to a mistress.

In Louis' early years there were few signs of the gardener-king to come. His life had not been sufficiently settled for him to have developed strong attachments to places, though his ambivalence towards Paris can surely be traced to his fear-ful peregrinations. As he was shy and withdrawn, many thought him dim-wit-ted, but he showed physical prowess. His favourite pastimes included fencing and jousting, just the sort of activities one would hope a future military leader might enjoy, and from an early age he distinguished himself through his horsemanship. Before he was much older, he would be leading his troops into battle, demon-strating tireless energy and coolness under fire. Another of his favourite activities was ballet dancing; there was certainly nothing namby-pamby about the rigorous training he embarked upon while still in his minority. Dancing and the martial arts have much in common – set moves, good posture, balance and control. Louis, the tongue-tied future King, discovered that he could express himself through dance; indeed he could astonish. It would not be going too far to say that he dis-covered his potency in his dancing classes. Before he could become a king, he had to learn to carry himself like one, and it was through ballet that he acquired the necessary control and poise. He made his stage debut at the age of thirteen in the ballet *Casandre* and would appear in more than forty major ballets before bowing out in February 1669 in the *Ballet de Flore*. It was a career worthy of any full-time professional.

In the darkest depths of the *Frondes*, Louis discovered that when he danced those around him would forget their enmities for a while and watch him. His grace and prowess would strike them dumb. For the duration of the dance, their private worlds would converge and centre upon the compellingly graceful figure of the King. In 1653, with the *Fronde* shattered, Louis made his first dazzling ap-pearance before the court in the costume of Apollo, wearing a golden wig, an em-broidered tunic and a pink-and-white plumed head-dress, laden with diamonds and rubies and bursting with solar rays, while little suns blazed forth from his garters and the buckles of his high-heeled dancing shoes. With some astute tutor-ing from Mazarin, Louis had begun to fashion his own image. Here was France's rising sun, the victor over the *Frondes*.

In another *ballet de cour* Louis as Apollo boasted of having vanquished 'that Py-thon who devastated the world, that terrible serpent whom Hell and the Fronde had seasoned with dangerous venom'. The destruction of the Python would provide the theme for the fountain that Gaspard and Balthasar Marsy would create for the Bassin du Dragon at Versailles. Soon this Apollonian symbolism would be inescapable. It would be reiterated in ever more lavish theatrical extravaganzas but also in miniatures, murals, medallions, statues and fountains. It would not be possible to stroll in a royal garden without encountering some reminder of the power of the King and the folly of insurrection.

On 1 November 1661, after a labour that almost killed Marie-Thérèse, the Dauphin was born. In June of the following year, Louis put on a show in Paris both to celebrate the birth of an heir and to set the seal on his ascendancy over the one-time *Frondeurs*. At the time this event was called the *Course de Bagues*, a name that links it to a mediaeval joust, but history remembers it as the *Grand Carrousel*. The equestrian ballet that opened the tournament was propaganda on horseback.

The *Carrousel* was a foretaste of the great fêtes that would be staged at Versailles, but this was just one year after Fouquet's arrest, and work on the château and its gardens had scarcely begun. If there was to be a great spectacle, it would have to be in Paris. An arena was formed between the Louvre and the Tuileries, with viewing stands sufficient to take five thousand guests. Less favoured spectators lined the route of the parade.

The *Carrousel* consisted of three days of contests between five brigades of horsemen. Louis' masterstroke was to flatter the vanity of his great nobles by inviting them to lead the brigades but then to choreograph an opening extravaganza in which they would willingly demonstrate their subservience and loyalty to the Crown. Each quadrille was turned out in costumes which represented a great civilisation. The King, suitably enough, was dressed as the Emperor of Rome, with a golden cloak, a silver helmet with fiery plumes and a shield carrying a solar device and the inscription *Ut vidi vici* – 'I no sooner saw than conquered'. Next came the Persians, led by Monsieur, the King's brother, whose escutcheon bore the symbol of the moon and the words *Uno soli minor* – 'Only the sun is greater'. The Duc d'Enghien led a band of Indians dressed in yellow and black, while the Duc de Guise, shining in a silvery fish suit and crowned with coral, headed a posse of Native Americans. But it was the presence of the Prince de Condé, the one-time rebel, dressed as the Sultan of the Turks and displaying the crescent moon as his device, that brought the political message home. Whatever light the moon possesses comes ultimately from the sun. There could hardly be a more fitting symbol for Condé's relationship with Louis.

Just as the sun takes time to burn away the morning mists, so Louis' ascension from mere mortal to demigod was a gradual progress. He kept his developing astuteness hidden and his anger cloaked, and there were many ready to dismiss him as a country-loving playboy. They did not do so without reason. Louis certainly loved dancing, parties and balls, he adored hunting, and increasingly he pursued beautiful women with as much eagerness as he followed his hounds. At 5 feet 4 inches he was not tall, and writers have made much of his lofty wigs and high-heeled shoes, but since most men at court dressed in similar fashion these devices cannot have done much to compensate for his lack of stature. Louis had the bearing of a king, and in battle he liked to lead from the front. He was immensely dignified and courteous and hardly ever lost his temper – he once beat a footman for stealing a biscuit from the table, but he had just learnt of the cowardice in battle of his son, the Duc du Maine, and he needed to displace some of his fury. This exception is so rare that it is always mentioned. As he grew into his role, Louis learnt that he could be far more intimidating by maintaining a stately politeness and an impenetrable reserve than he could ever be if he were to rant and rave. Most of the court was terrified of him.

In the speech Louis gave to the princes, dukes and ministers of state on 10 March 1661, one day after the death of Mazarin, he made it clear that the Italian would have no successor. Henceforth the King would be his own first minister and would have to approve all governmental decisions, even the signing of a passport. No one quite believed him, but Louis was as good as his word. The hatred of disorder that had grown within him during the *Frondes* now manifested itself in a desire to put himself at the head of an utterly ordered state. Many kings would have fled from the minutiae of government, but Louis saw them as a necessary duty and from the outset devoted two or three hours each morning to the business of ruling.

Louis did, of course, come to rely on certain people – not least Colbert, who as minister of finance and *Surintendant des Bâtiments* had two of the most important posts in the administration – but he was a hands-on sovereign who kept an eye on everyone. He listened to the advice of his ministers, whom he generally appointed from the ranks of the lesser nobility, but he took the decisions himself. The princes and great nobles were excluded from the business of government almost entirely.

Everyone who has studied French history knows that Louis XIV declared, '*L'état c'est moi*,' identifying his personal destiny with that of France, but there is doubt amongst the experts that he ever used this specific phrase. It is one of those probable misquotations that has stuck because it seems to contain an aspect of the truth. In seeking to glorify himself, Louis was also seeking glory for his country, but it was a quest that could overlook the little man, the peasant farmer struggling to pay his taxes and to keep food on the table, the villagers whose fields became battlefields or the labourers killed in the building of a palace or the excavation of an ornamental lake.

Louis claimed that his right to rule was divinely given. He was as far above the ranks of ordinary men as the heavens are above the earth, yet his status beneath God was difficult for this 'Most Christian King', especially in the early years of his reign when his morals earned him the disapproval of churchmen. He did not like to be told what to do nor, more significantly, what not to do, by priests. In side-stepping the symbolism of Christianity and identifying himself with Apollo, he made a positive choice, since this deity represented order, harmony and civilisation. Apollo was a cultured, rational and hard-working god, at least by comparison with other Olympians. Every morning it was his task to harness his chariot and draw the sun across the heavens. This was a fitting image for the young Louis, a conscientious ruler who would, through his own brilliance, animate his countrymen and bring happiness, harmony and prosperity to France. Although Louis did not invent the badge of the radiant sun to use as his emblem – he copied it from his ancestors – he made more extensive use of it. It would be inlaid into furniture and marble floors, woven into carpets and ballet costumes, wrought into gates and grilles, carved into marble vases for the garden and into the door panels of staterooms at the palace. In styling himself *Le Roi Soleil*, Louis XIV chose what he thought was the perfect image for a great king. The sun was incomparably the most glorious object in the heavens, yet in itself it was serene and imperturbable. This was how Louis intended to present himself to the world.

The identification with Apollo would became the leitmotif of the first half of Louis' reign. It was a theme that was consciously pushed by the members of the *Petite Académie*, Colbert's back-room advisors on aesthetic matters. Classical imagery would soon be everywhere, not least in the gardens of Versailles, where two of the most significant focal points on the main axis would be devoted to the god himself, at the reigns of his solar chariot, and to Latona, his mother. It would be many years before Louis decided to move the whole court to Versailles, of course. To begin with, some relatively minor building works were ordered: repairs to the roofs, some new outbuildings to house kitchens, stables, and some living rooms. Pavilions were built at the entrance to house the King's musketeers. In 1661 Le Vau was instructed to turn what was then a little lodge into an elegant pleasure-house where Louis could entertain guests. The King proved himself to be a good host for, as Colbert wrote, 'Every day there were balls, ballets, comedies, music, both vocal and instrumental, violins, promenades and hunting.' There was not

Parterre a l'Angloise

fig. 1ere

1   2   3   4 Toises

*A parterre in the English manner, from La Théorie et la
practique du jardinage by Antoine-Joseph Dezallier d'Argenville, 1709.*

Parterre de pieces coupées pour des fleurs

fig. 2.

A parterre of cutwork for flowers, from La Théorie et la
practique du jardinage by Antoine-Joseph Dezallier d'Argenville, 1709.

Parterre de Compartiment

A parterre of compartments, from La Théorie et la practique
du jardinage by Antoine-Joseph Dezallier d'Argenville, 1709.

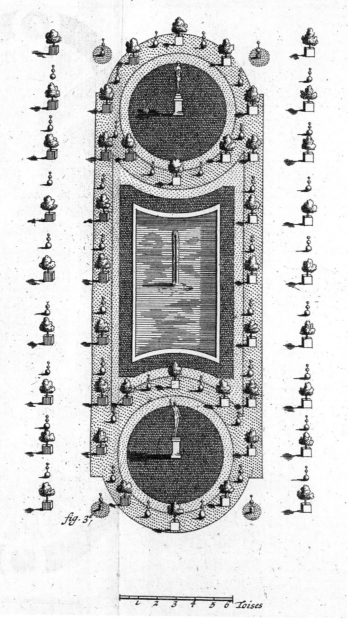

fig. 3.

1 2 3 4 5 6 Toises

*A parterre of orange trees, from La Théorie et la practique
du jardinage by Antoine-Joseph Dezallier d'Argenville, 1709.*

much accommodation, but those fortunate enough to be allocated an apartment would find it furnished and supplied with firewood and candles, which had not previously been the practice in royal houses. Perhaps Louis had in mind his own frosty reception as a child at Saint-Germain.

Olivier de Serres, a sixteenth-century rural gentleman who got caught up in the Wars of Religion on the Protestant side, found sufficient tranquillity to write the most influential French book on horticulture and agronomy of the 1500s, the *Théâtre d'agriculture et mesnage des champs*. In it he wrote:

> all sorts of people have honoured gardening. Emperors, kings and other great lords have been seen at work, supervising their gardens with their own hands, opting for such work as relief from their grand affairs. Their names, written into the names of many herbs and fruits to perpetuate the memory of their labours, show how agreeable such exercises were to them. We read in the herb loosestrife (*lysimachie*) of King Lysimachus; in the gentian, of Gentius, King of Ilyria; in the artemesia, of Artemis, King of Caria; in the achillea, of Achilles; in agrimony (*eupatoire*), of King Eupator; in water germander (*scordium*, also called *mithridates*), of Mithridates, King of the Pontus and of Bithynia; and there are many others.

We cannot know for sure whether Louis read De Serres's book. The King was not renowned for his scholarship, but it is conceivable that he read what interested him. He never became the agricultural reformer his country badly needed, but as a gardener he can easily be imagined sharing the sentiments expressed in this passage. The warrior-king was as happy in his gardens as he was on horseback supervising a siege. Nicodemus Tessin, a Swedish architect who visited Versailles in 1687, was taken aback to find the King in the Bosquet du Théâtre d'Eau with pruning shears in his hands. Other accounts confirm that the King's involvement with his gardens sometimes went beyond supervision. Like beard-trimming or table-polishing, hedge-pruning is one of those inherently satisfying activities which consist in the restoration of a degree of order. It is not hard to imagine its appeal to one as fastidious as Louis, and it may also have had some symbolic purpose. For here, in miniature, was what Louis sought to do, not just in the gardens but in the countryside beyond, indeed for the whole territory of France.

For a king or for a gardener, keeping order is not enough in itself. Just as in a well-kept garden plants will flourish, in a well-administered state people will prosper. Louis was aware of this parallel. In his memoirs he remarked that when strangers visited a country and found it flourishing, it created a perception of magnificence and power that reflected well upon the ruling prince. This explains not only his own dedication to his gardens but also the pains he took over writing and rewriting the guidebook to them and his wish to conduct important visitors around personally. The gardens were the embodiment of his rule, representations of good government. Louis was motivated not so much by a taste for power (he had been given that as his birthright) but by an appetite for *gloire* – the French word carries more connotations than its English equivalent, 'glory'. Though it is a difficult concept to pin down, *gloire* included anything and everything that would broadcast Louis' magnificence, not just throughout his own lands but all through the civilised world. *Gloire* was intangible and mysterious, but it could be accumulated, and, like gold in a vault, it outlasted the person who had gathered it. Louis cared deeply about posterity. Successful wars and successes in building – these above all else – were the things for which princes were remembered. For Louis, gardening was not just a hobby, nor merely a respite from military campaigning; it was showmanship, propaganda, a continuation of policy and a contribution towards the immortality of his reputation. Could he have known that his gardens would survive into the twenty-first century, that thousands would visit them, and that books would be written about their creation, it would have delighted him.

Plan of the park at Versailles, c. 1662, known as the
'Du Bus plan' because it was discoverd by Charles Du Bus.

IV

The Unpromising Site

SAINT-SIMON, admittedly not the most reliable of witnesses, did not share Louis' enthusiasm for Versailles. In his opinion it was '… the saddest and most barren of places, with no view, no wood, no water and no earth, for it is all shifting sand and marsh and the air, consequently, is bad …' Giovanni Battista Primi Visconti, an Italian adventurer who became one of Louis' courtiers, thought similarly. 'The very landscape is unpleasant,' he wrote. 'There is nothing but sand and smelly swamps, and you could say that the king has introduced novel elements by bringing in woods, trees and water.' The surprising thing is that this last assessment was written in 1680, eighteen years after Louis had begun his improvements, but for much of this period the place had been a construction site. Those who make gardens, particularly on this scale, have to take the long view. By the end of the century, Versailles, château plus gardens, had become the paradigm for courts throughout Europe.

At the beginning of Louis' reign, however, most of his courtiers would have shared Saint-Simon's opinion. Compared with the pleasures of Paris, there was little at Versailles to detain them. Apart from the deeply unfashionable château, there was a peasant village clustered around a twelfth-century church. It had a pond, which Le Nôtre would in time enlarge to form the immense mirror pool known as the Pièce d'Eau des Suisses. There were a few other hamlets in the vicinity; their names are familiar because in time they would become the sites of other great houses such as Trianon and Clagny. But in 1661 they were utterly unmemorable.

59

The château of Versailles stood on a hill of sand – fortunately of a type that compacted readily – and the site was, at least, well above the water-table. The area where the gardens would be laid out was not so blessed, for here the geology consisted of impermeable layers of clays and marls. Unable to soak away, water sat on the surface in numerous pools and marshes. The water-table today is still little more than a metre deep during summer and only 60 centimetres in winter. The dampness of the ground would present Le Nôtre and his colleagues with serious difficulties when they came to build in the lower regions of the site. Soils like these were also a headache for gardeners and silviculturists since they would get churned to mud in the winter, yet turn to hard-pan under a hot sun. Keeping trees alive in such conditions was no easy matter, particularly as the King was impatient for immediate effects and often asked for mature trees to be brought from elsewhere. The mechanics of this would have been difficult enough on mud tracks, but the survival rates were also dismal.

Despite everything, there is no doubt that Saint-Simon exaggerated the defects of the site. The village of Versailles was on a drove road between Paris and the pastures of the Orne. With a population of five hundred and four inns, it was prosperous enough. Areas in the surrounding woods had been cleared for the cultivation of cereals and vines, and the ponds in the vicinity of the château, which writers have often referred to in derogatory terms, had been used for cultivating fish. The countryside was remarkable neither for its affluence nor for its beauty, but it was not barren, and the large swathes of wetlands and forests were rich in game.

Louis XIII, the Sun King's father, had first got to know the place in 1607 at the age of six. The Dauphin had been taken along on a falconry expedition and had immediately been taken with the area. When he became a young man he asked a Parisian mason called Nicolas Huau to build him a hunting lodge there. This was in 1623. In comparison to the edifice that occupies the site today, it was tiny, with a central block that measured a mere 35 by 6 metres. The Maréchal de Bassompierre wrote in his memoirs that Louis XIII was not one to build at the expense of the country 'unless one wishes to reproach him for the lowly Château de Versailles, in whose construction even a simple gentleman could not take pride'. However, the King had not wanted this house for show but as a place where he could get away from the women in his life and spend time with his male cronies. Significantly there was no accommodation for the Queen. A windmill was knocked down to make way for the modest building, and courtiers would later quip that though the mill had gone, the wind remained. Louis XIV would also come to view Versailles as a retreat, but – unlike his father – he liked to surround himself with female company.

Louis XIV Giving Orders to His Master of Hounds
by Adam Frans Van der Meulen, c. 1664. This view from
Satory shows Le Vau's orangery and the village of Versailles.

This first building was enlarged by Le Roy in 1631, a year before Louis XIII purchased the seignory of Versailles, thus establishing a royal domain. Saint-Simon referred to it scathingly as 'the little cardboard château which Louis XIII had built so that he would no longer have to lie on straw'. The young Louis XIV would in turn become deeply attached to this cheerful brick-and-stone mansion, which was ranged around three sides of a quadrangle and surrounded by a moat. He first visited Versailles at the age of twelve, in the company of his governor, the Maréchal de Villeroy, whose job it was to introduce the boy to the kingly pastime of hunting. The chase appealed to Louis immediately. It was thrilling to gallop through the woods in pursuit of a fox, a hare, a stag or even a wolf, for there was always the risk of a fall and a wound. Louis preferred shooting and hunting with hounds to falconry. Pursuit on horseback developed strength and fortitude and was regarded as the most excellent peacetime preparation for warfare. Giving trackers and huntsmen their dispositions was not unlike directing troops on a battlefield, and the horns and the liveried costumes of the hunters added to the martial atmosphere. Throughout his life Louis would hunt two or three times a week. There was even an occasion in February 1685, recorded by the Marquis de Dangeau, when the King, who was usually such a workaholic, abandoned a meeting of the royal council in favour of the hunt. He was so fond of his shooting dogs, Bonne, Ponne and Nonne, that he commissioned Alexandre-François Desportes, who specialised in portraits of animals and hunting scenes, to paint them.

Although Louis XIV's lifelong love affair with hunting goes some way towards explaining the attraction that Versailles held for him, it is surely insufficient to explain the depth of his infatuation. The King was, by nature, more fond of the countryside than of the city, and this is why, as a young man, he became so attached to the modest hunting lodge that had belonged to his father. His need for a rural retreat became more urgent when he became enamoured of Louise de la Vallière, a beautiful teenager recently arrived from the Loire valley and introduced to the court by his playful sister-in-law, Henriette d'Angleterre. To pursue this affair Louis needed to be out of the way of a disapproving older generation of royals, including his mother, who had become close to Marie-Thérèse, bonding with her as another foreigner stranded at the French court. To give himself maximum freedom from censure, Louis ordered that no one should follow him to Versailles on these occasions without his express permission. A select few, the so-called *Gardes de la Porte*, were permitted to ignore this rule. They were distinguished by the *justaucorps à brevet*, a special uniform of blue coats lined in scarlet,

Louise-Françoise de la Baume-Le-Blanc, Mademoiselle La Vallière, represented as a companion of Diana, goddess of the hunt. Portrait after Claude Lefebvre.

each embroidered in gold and silver with a distinctive design. Only members of the royal family, Princes of the Blood and fifty chosen men were allowed to wear this coat, which was similar to that worn by the King himself.

The cult of romantic love was strong when Louis took the throne, and since marriage was usually a matter of business or diplomatic convenience, no one was surprised when he took lovers; in a sense it was expected of him, for virility was a kingly virtue. One of his predecessors, the fifteenth-century monarch Charles VII, had set the pattern when he had granted the semi-official position of *mistress declarée* to his lover Agnès Sorel, so Louis was following a well-established tradition. He even began a flirtation with Henriette, his brother's wife, but when gossip began to circulate, she suggested that he should pretend to court one of her ladies-in-waiting and pointed him towards Louise.

Henriette was surrounded by the most beautiful high-born girls in France, collectively known as the 'flower garden'. Louise was not the only blossom the King plucked from this source. We naturally associate gardens with fertility and fruitfulness, and since Eden they have been connected with love and passion. Gardens have also provided lovers with opportunities for concealment not so easily come by within the confines of castles or country houses. The mediaeval courtly garden was not just a pleasure site for the senses but also the perfect place for a tryst. We know that Louis and Louise used gardens for their liaisons from an account by the hapless Abbé Locatelli, an Italian visitor to the court, who stumbled upon one of their secret promenades one morning while exploring the grounds at Saint-Germain. He fell to his knees and begged forgiveness for disturbing the amorous couple. Louis verbally boxed his ears and sent him away.

Though formal gardens had sweeping expanses of terrace and monumental vistas where all could be seen, they were well provided with hidden places, *bosquets* tucked away amidst groves, and secluded arbours where infidelities might flourish. Fumbling amongst the foliage was perhaps not Louis' style, for he liked his comforts, and in time he would build party-houses within his gardens for purposes of pleasure, of which the Trianon would be the most important.

It is not difficult to see why Louis preferred Louise, the sporty outdoor girl, to frumpy, stay-at-home Marie-Thérèse. Locatelli was unimpressed by La Vallière's looks but admired her abilities as a horsewoman. 'I saw her once at the Tuileries,' he wrote, 'which are the King's pleasure gardens in Paris, mount and ride a Barbary horse bareback, stand upright on its back while it was in full gallop and reseat herself again, repeating this manoeuvre several times, aided only by a silk cord passed through the horse's mouth in place of a bridle.' For the King, with his passion for hunting, Louise, despite her demure femininity, could be a tomboyish

Plan of an early parterre at Versailles, from
Jacques Boyceau's Traité du Jardinage, 1638.

Plan of an early grass parterre at Versailles,
from Jacques Boyceau's Traité du jardinage, 1638.

companion. According to Locatelli, even professional hunters could not excel her in swordsmanship, pistol shooting or horse-riding. Louis was also a crack shot – he once brought down thirty-two pheasants with only thirty-four rounds – and he loved his hounds so much that he kept several of them in his own rooms and fed them by hand. For such a country-loving couple, Louis XIII's old hunting lodge at Versailles must have seemed the ideal rustic hideaway.

In his *Mémoires* Charles Perrault recollected that in his youth the King was afraid of the power wielded by women. He told his ministers that if they noticed any woman getting dominion over him they were to bring it to his attention and he would disencumber himself within twenty-four hours. Despite these precautions there is no doubt that Louis' mistresses did hold sway over him. This was evident throughout his reign, particularly when it came to plans for building or the development of the gardens. The initial development of Versailles was undertaken out of love for Louise de la Vallière, and before she lost the King's affections around 1668 she had a significant influence over the gardens and the programmes for the first of the great fêtes.

Because the lodge was initially so small, the first parties Louis threw to please Louise took place in the modest formal garden that had been laid out for his father by Jacques Menours. The latter had determined the main east–west thrust of the axis and created an array of *compartiments de broderie*, picked out with box hedging and infilled, for the sake of colour, with gravel, crushed brick or slate. The present Parterre du Nord maintains the essential design, though Le Nôtre doubled the original in size. The term *parterre* (literally 'on the ground') usually refers to a flat terrace close to a house, laid out in decorative patterns but not necessarily including any flowers. The simplest form was the *parterre à l'anglaise*, a turf lawn with a design cut into it, very different from the intricate arabesques of the *parterres de broderie* made popular by Claude Mollet.

Louis understood, even at this early stage when little had been done to the house, that it would take time to establish a garden. So in 1661, André Le Nôtre was put to work on what would become history's greatest makeover. Unlike the quick-fix domestic transformations to which we have become accustomed, this project would keep the master-gardener occupied for the next thirty years.

As the son of a royal gardener, it was natural that André should be a royalist, but his devotion to Louis was without reservation. There was an age difference of twenty-five years, and their relationship had something of a father–son quality. Le Nôtre was open, honest and amusing, so it is not difficult to see why the King, who had to be so much on his mettle with many of his courtiers, would have

Charles Le Brun. Portrait by Nicolas de Largillière.

appreciated the relaxing company of this older man who bore him nothing but goodwill and enjoyed nothing so much as talking about gardens.

With the loot from Vaux and a ready-made design team, Louis was in the mood to start straight away, and the first renovations began at Versailles in 1662, despite careful Colbert's protests about the likely expense. Colbert would have much preferred the King to lavish his money and energy on the Louvre, which he thought would make an appropriate residence for a great monarch. But once Louis had made his mind up about something, there was little that could be done to deflect him.

Whatever errors of taste he might later commit, Louis had a better visual imagination than most of those around him. This is not a quality that everyone possesses. Le Nôtre certainly had the gift of foresight – indeed it was the basis of his profession – but Louis had it too, and this might account for the strength of the bond between the two men. When it came to design, they understood one another's language.

Pierre-André Lablaude observed that when it came to the design of his gardens, Louis XIV, in his role as patron, client and producer all rolled into one, was only prepared to place his trust in two people. At the start of his reign, this was certainly true. One was Le Nôtre's old friend Le Brun; the other was Le Nôtre himself. Le Brun determined most of the themes and allegories for the fountains and sculptural groups, while Le Nôtre was responsible for the overall layout of the gardens, its levels, water features, vistas and intersections, as well as all matters relating to planting and horticulture.

Louis liked to talk directly to his architects and gardeners, and this made Colbert uneasy. He saw the way in which Le Vau and Le Nôtre, in particular, were encouraging the King in his grand visions for Versailles, instead of the Louvre, his own preference. In a letter to Louis he wrote, 'Your Majesty will observe, moreover, if it pleases him, that he is in the hands of two men who know him almost exclusively at Versailles, that is to say, in pleasure and entertainment, and who don't know the love he has for glory at all …' Colbert thought that Louis' designers were leading him on: '… they will pull you along from plan to plan in order to make their work immortal, if Your Majesty isn't wary of them.'

When it became evident that Louis was not going to change his mind about Versailles, Colbert became reconciled to the project, though his opinion of Le Vau did not improve much. A natural risk-taker, the latter obtained a licence to produce tin plate in 1665 and began a parallel career as an entrepreneurial industrialist. Soon the architect would also be producing cannons for the navy, an enterprise that literally backfired when some of the guns blew up during testing. This

*The château constructed by Le Vau, 1674. Illustration from
Pierre De Nolhac's La Création de Versailles.*

cannot have helped Le Vau's standing with the minister, for whom the navy's development was a personal project. Le Vau's architecture was a chancy mixture of Baroque and Classical styles and received a mixed reception from critics, some praising its nonconformist innovation, others seeing only faults and damning it for its lack of unity. Torn between too many activities, Le Vau – it has been suggested – skimped on the details and his buildings suffered as a result. His standing with Colbert was sliding badly by 1670 and might have fallen further had the architect not died in that year at the age of only fifty-seven. Le Nôtre, conversely, rose steadily in Colbert's regard. The finance minister might not have liked to contemplate the vast sums that were being spent on the gardens of Versailles, but we hear no more of the suggestion that Le Nôtre was manipulating the King. The gardener's probity was beyond reproach, and he became a trusted figure in Colbert's administration. Le Nôtre had big ideas, but they could hardly have been grander than those of Louis himself, and Colbert knew the limits when it came to restraining the King. As we have seen, when Colbert went looking for a landscape designer for his own estate at Sceaux, it was to Le Nôtre that he turned.

It is extraordinary to think of mighty Colbert, who almost wielded the authority of a Richelieu or a Mazarin, acting as a landscape clerk-of-works, but he paid close attention to the day-to-day activities on site. 'Make a count of Colinet's boys,' he told one of his overseers, referring to one of the royal gardeners, to 'ensure that he has as many as he said he would'. This workaholic bureaucrat put in fifteen-hour days and supplied Louis with a constant stream of facts and statistics, not just about the state's finances but about the numbers of soldiers digging a lake and the rate at which they were shifting earth. The King enjoyed his pleasures too much to work as hard as Colbert, but he liked to know exactly what was going on and must have appreciated his finance minister's meticulous mind – just as long as Colbert did not try to preach prudence. Under such a regime there was no place for slackers. Le Nôtre, we can be sure, worked extremely hard, and the puzzle is how he managed to find the time to dream and to draw. This mystery starts to dissolve, however, when we realise that Colbert was the sort of line manager who was willing to shoulder a lot of the responsibility for detail. The royal building accounts of 1671 contain much detail about the mundane services that Le Nôtre had to provide. At the Tuileries these included 'cleaning, packing down and raking the great terrace in front of the said palace' and the maintenance of 'eight squares of *parterres en broderie* which are to be clipped and tidied throughout, along with the flower-beds and transverse *allées* and the area around the basins'.

In the early years of his reign, Louis shuttled between the courts at the Louvre and at his birthplace, Saint-Germain-en-Laye, which remained the principal

Parterre of compartments, from La Théorie et la practique
du jardinge *by Antoine-Joseph Dezallier d'Argenville, 1709.*

royal residence until 1682. His youthful zeal for military campaigning often took him away to the borders of France, but wherever he was he asked for daily reports about the progress of his building and garden improvements at Versailles. When it became clear that he intended to spend most of his time there, his courtiers began to refer to the place as his 'undeserving favourite'.

Although he was too sentimental to have his father's hunting lodge demolished, Louis' vision of Versailles grew into so grand a conception that no one could think that he was just tinkering with a place made by someone else. Unlike the older palaces, Versailles would be an entirely Bourbon creation, the embodiment, in clipped hedges and serried formations of trees just as much as in masonry blocks, of the Sun King's glory.

It was typical of Louis' obstinacy that he should have fastened upon such a recalcitrant site for the location of his great ensemble. In his *Mémoires* he wrote that 'It is in difficult things that we show our virtue.' It was as if he delighted in the challenge of bringing the land under control, just as he intended to bring his subjects into line. True to the Cartesian spirit of the times, Versailles would be the site for a demonstration of what the human intellect could do.

Shrewd Colbert could see what was coming. His assessment of the existing garden at Versailles was gloomy; it 'will not be possible to occupy more ground', he predicted, 'without reversing everything and incurring a prodigious expenditure'. He was right. According to the building accounts, the total expenditure for earthworks, which included excavations, levelling and the lining of basins with clay, eventually was 6,038,035 *livres*, in other words 7 per cent of the total cost of all the building works at Versailles and the later sites of Trianon and Clagny. Only the items for masonry and for the ill-fated aqueduct across the Eure amounted to more. Those who criticised Louis for his devotion to this swampy place had a point. Thousands would be killed or maimed before the gardens were completed.

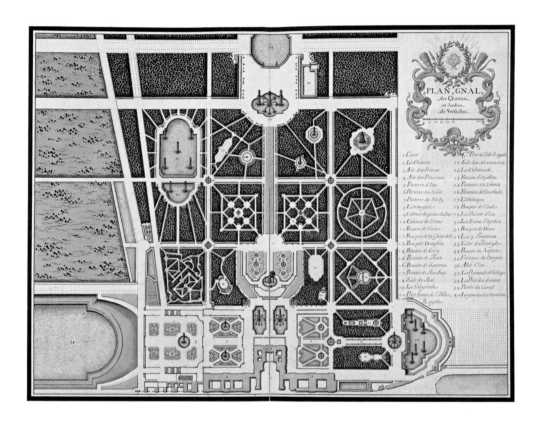

Plan of the gardens of Versailles. Drawn by Jean Chaufourrier, 1720.

V

Geometry and Earthworks

B Y THE TIME Le Nôtre was summoned to Versailles, things had got out of
hand amongst the gardeners on the site. One of them, Guillaume Masson, had fallen out badly with Henri de Bessay, Sieur de Noiron, the
King's concierge. This seems to have been a clash of personalities which escalated
into something more litigious and damaging. Masson accused Sieur de Noiron
of having cut down some of the best espaliered fruit trees in the park and said
that the concierge had threatened him with his sword. De Noiron laid counter-
accusations that Masson had been cutting wood in the royal estate and selling it
for his own profit.

It seems likely that Guillaume's brother, Hilaire II Masson, was also caught up
in this quarrel, because in September 1660 he was peremptorily sacked, an event
almost unheard of in royal gardening circles. He was condemned, without appeal,
for his poor conduct and for the degradation he had caused to the gardens. Quite
what Hilaire did to bring such stern retribution upon himself remains vague. His
brothers Mathieu, Claude and even the troublesome Guillaume continued in royal service, seemingly unaffected by this family disgrace.

Hilaire's dismissal followed swiftly upon the arrival of a trouble-shooter. Louis had perhaps already decided to spend more time at the château when he dispatched his *valet de chambre*, Jérôme Blouin, to investigate the mismanagement of
the estate. It was not only Hilaire II Masson who was found wanting. There was
some suggestion that Sieur de Noiron had been disposing of furnishings for profit,

and Blouin was asked to take an inventory. Soon afterwards Sieur de Noiron and his wife were ordered to leave Versailles and to take up residence in rooms on the kitchen-court at Saint-Germain. This was clearly a punishment rather than a promotion. The following year Blouin, who had served both Richelieu and Mazarin, was given authority over everything that went on at the château and in the park of Versailles. By the time that Le Nôtre and his colleagues arrived in 1662, order was well on the way to being restored.

Le Nôtre was able to draw upon his family's connections to surround himself with close gardening allies. By 1664 Marin Trumel, whose mother had been a cousin of Jean Le Nôtre, was in charge of the Orangery. His daughter Geneviève married Henry I Dupuis, who was also a gardener at Versailles from about 1664, and was given special responsibilities for the upkeep of the Petit Parc. The close ties that had bound the gardening families together at the Tuileries remained strong once Versailles became the principal centre of activity.

Le Nôtre had two strategic weapons with which to subdue the recalcitrant landscape – geometry and earth-moving. Both had been fundamental to the design of the major Italian gardens of the previous century, but these were attached to hillside villas where strict geometry often had to bow to the constraints of contours. On the French plains there were no such hindrances. Houses could be symmetrical about an axis that could extend towards the horizon. Fortuitously for Le Nôtre, there was already such an axis at Versailles, albeit not a very extensive or developed one, and it ran towards the west, which meant that, give or take a few degrees, the sun sank every evening at its visual limit. So it would be easy to plan the Sun King's garden around a solar theme.

Extraordinary gardens had been created in Italy throughout the sixteenth century. There was the Villa Lante, built for Cardinal Gambia, where the house was split into two separate *casinos* so that the garden axis could pass through the middle on its way down the hillside. A stream tumbles down a long central channel constrained by crayfish claws carved of stone, then spills over a cascade flanked by loafing river gods. The channel forms a watery rectangle in the middle of a stone dining-table, then appears in a many-tiered fountain ingeniously set into a massive masonry retaining wall. Finally, tamed and humanised, it fills the quadrants of a water parterre. Or consider the Villa D'Este at Tivoli, built for Cardinal Ippolito II on the steep western slopes of the town, where Pirro Ligorio assembled a funfair of water effects ranging from the magnificence of the Pathway of One Hundred Fountains, to the ingenuity of the water organ, to the awesome roar of the Dragon Fountain, to the delightful novelty of the automata, for example the bronze birds which sang tunefully until startled by a mournfully hooting owl.

For the use of geometry, Le Nôtre did not have to look as far as Italy for his precedents, since Italian ideas had been seeping steadily into France ever since Charles VIII had led his armies across the Alps and briefly seized the throne of Naples in 1495. The ensuing Italian Wars rumbled on inconclusively for fifty years, and in the process many French soldiers, travellers and statesmen got their first taste of Italian Renaissance architecture and garden design. Soon it would be Italian artists, designers and craftsmen who would be invading France. Charles VIII himself coaxed the Franciscan friar Fra Giocondo to come to France by offering him the position of royal architect. Giocondo was knowledgeable about hydraulics and helped Charles to plumb the fountains and water-jokes that were introduced into the royal garden at Amboise. Another Italian recruit, Pasciello de Mercoliano, came with a reputation for laying out gardens. When Charles died suddenly in 1498, his successor, Louis XII, retained the services of both men. At Blois, Mercoliano surrounded the garden with an elaborate arboured gallery reminiscent of a mediaeval cloister or ancient Roman peristyle.

The Italian experts who went to France were constrained by their clients' conservatism. Garden design thrives best in settled and prosperous times, and conditions in sixteenth-century France were seldom favourable. It might be objected that a century later, under Louis XIV, the country was more often at war than at peace, but Louis carried his fight to the boundaries, which he was always trying to expand, and used the expertise of Vauban to strengthen the borders by building and reinforcing fortresses. Those who owned estates in the body of France could sleep secure in the confidence that their territories were unlikely to be overrun. In the later sixteenth century, conversely, France had been wracked by the bloody Wars of Religion, when the country's internal tensions, social and religious, had become fatally entangled with dynastic rivalries. The Italians had demonstrated how it was possible to create gardens which were extensive and outward-looking yet in perfect unity with their houses. Radical rebuilding was often required, however, and few in France had the appetite for it.

There were of course exceptions, with which Le Nôtre would have been acquainted. Forty-eight miles to the south-west of Paris was the château of Anet, designed by Philibert de l'Orme for Henri II's mistress, Diane de Poitiers. When she was only sixteen, Diane had married Louis de Brézé, Steward of Normandy, who was forty years her senior and known as the 'great huntsman of France'. Through this marriage Diane gained access to the highest court circles, becoming lady-in-waiting to Queen Claude, the wife of François I. Widowed at thirty-five,

Sébastien Le Prestre, Seigneur de Vauban.
Portrait by François de Troy (atelier), seventeenth century.

Diane sincerely mourned the loss of her elderly husband, whose passion for hunting she had shared. Beautiful, intelligent and dressed in widow's silks of black and white, Diane made a powerful impression upon the timid and taciturn Prince Henri, who was still a teenager. Despite the twenty years that separated them, she would become his official mistress. De l'Orme's redevelopment of Anet was in part a tribute to Diane's husband – there was an inscription to that effect – and partly a love retreat for Diane and Henri.

One can trace many parallels between Anet and the future Versailles. Both were built for the sake of a royal mistress. Both involved difficult sites – De l'Orme had to drain marshes to make the gardens at Anet, just as Le Nôtre would later have to do at Versailles. In both cases a skilful architect succeeded in preserving an old manor house while adding radically new buildings. Both places possessed a powerful iconographic programme: inevitably, given the name of the mistress of the house and her deceased husband's enthusiasm for the chase, Anet was dedicated to Diana, goddess of the hunt, who was associated with the crescent moon, which Diane assumed as her insignia. The mythical Diana used to bathe in a grove with her nymphs; Diane would also bathe every day in cold water, something unusual for the times. A bathhouse was situated in a moon-shaped pool formed in the moat that ran along the northern garden wall.

The château and gardens at Anet were organised in a symmetrical fashion around a central axis, a sequence of spaces that gave a foretaste of the plan for Versailles. The visitor entered through a gatehouse flanked by ornamental trees – another reminder of Diana's grove. Then came an inner courtyard similar to the Cour de Marbre at Versailles. The gardens, as at Versailles, lay beyond the château. They were laid out as parterres held in place by a regular grid of intersecting paths. The garden was entirely flat and was enclosed by an arcaded wall. This arrangement was essentially conservative and owed much to the inward-looking mediaeval traditions of the cloister. In the seventeenth century, Anet passed into the hands of the Maréchal Louis-Joseph de Vendôme, one of the Sun King's military commanders. He employed Le Nôtre to draw up plans for the garden. As one might have expected, André's most significant alteration was to demolish the surrounding walls, which he must have regarded as stifling and antiquated, and to replace them with a canal. Sadly the château suffered badly during and after the Revolution. In the early years of the nineteenth century, the main building was blown up and all of the trees in the park were felled.

The gardens laid out by Étienne du Perac for Henri IV at Saint-Germain-en-Laye at the very end of the sixteenth century mark another development of the Renaissance style in France. Du Perac had travelled in Italy and in 1573 published a collection of views of the Villa D'Este which he dedicated to Catherine de' Medici, Henri II's Italian wife. There are aspects of the design for Saint-Germain which were clearly influenced by Cardinal Ippolito's garden and also by the grounds of the Villa Lante. Although the sites of French gardens tended to be much flatter than their Italian counterparts, at Saint-Germain the Château Neuf, begun by Henri II about 1556, lay at the top of a slope overlooking the Seine, opening up the possibility that a series of terraces could be created below. Like the Italian gardens that had provided the inspiration, this ensemble, a sort of French Hanging Gardens, was made possible by the use of massive amounts of masonry and fortification skills developed during the Wars of Religion. Linked by stairs and landings, the terraces were laid out in geometrical and symmetrical fashion, embroidered with parterres and embellished with fountains, while the walls were honeycombed with grottoes.

Henri IV, whose second wife, Marie de' Medici, was also Italian, drew upon this connection when he persuaded his father-in-law, Francesco de' Medici, Grand Duke of Tuscany, to send him the fountaineer Tommaso Francini to work at Saint-Germain. The vaulted galleries beneath the terraces were interconnected so that visitors could pass from one to another. Francini devised an elaborate system of plumbing which utilised the water stored in subterranean reservoirs to power a variety of automata. On the third landing there were three grottoes, one in which a nymph played an organ, another devoted to Neptune and encrusted with *rocaille*-work, and the third in which a dragon beat its wings and vomited gobbets of water. Sadly nothing remains of this complex showpiece. It proved difficult and costly to maintain and had a short life.

Le Nôtre – who was to work with Tommaso's descendants at Versailles, as we have seen, would also have learnt from the Luxembourg Gardens, where he had worked as a young man. They had been laid out for Marie de' Medici, and evidence points to Jacques Boyceau as the designer, not only of three of the parterres but also of the overall plan. Boyceau's client had not relinquished her Italian roots and yearned for a *palazzo* in Paris. She employed a French architect, Salomon de Brosse, and instructed him to create something like the Pitti Palace in her native Florence. She did not get quite what she was looking for, since the Luxembourg Palace, with its corner pavilions and steeply pitched roofs, is decidedly French. If the Luxembourg was supposed to look like the Pitti, then it seems likely that the Luxembourg Gardens were expected to resemble the Boboli Gardens, also in Florence. Those who have studied and measured these two gardens have found strong similarities in their dimensions and arrangement, but when one transfers a plan designed for a slope on to a site that is essentially flat, the copy looks very different from the original. There were no automata in the Luxembourg Gardens, no water-jokes nor heraldic topiary; Boyceau turned his back on all that fussiness and frivolity to produce a design with dignity and a simple strength. The Luxembourg Gardens were the first in France to be laid out on such a cohesive, monumental and decorous plan. They represented a major step towards the mature style of André Le Nôtre.

The Luxembourg Gardens also represented a physical demonstration of Boyceau's theory that even a symmetrical garden should contain diversity. This is something akin to the Oriental notion of 'occult balance' whereby dissimilar objects can be placed in equilibrium. The impression that greets the visitor to the Luxembourg Gardens is one of monumental harmony, and it seems at first that the symmetry is absolute. But this turns out to be an illusion; within the *bosquets* and *cabinets* there is subtlety and variety. Le Nôtre would employ exactly this principle at Versailles.

The English diarist John Evelyn was impressed by the Luxembourg Gardens, particularly by the walks, which he described as 'exactly fair, long and variously descending, and so justly planted with limes, elms, and other trees, that nothing can be more delicious, especially that of the hornbeam hedge, which being so high and stately, butts full on the fountain'. Any present-day designer of parks would be delighted if one of their projects were as successful in attracting the variety of people that frequented the Luxembourg Gardens; according to Evelyn's account there were gallants and ladies, jovial citizens, serious scholars and melancholy friars. Some groups sat in quiet contemplation while others danced and sang and still others played at bowls. Evelyn says that this was possible without disturbance because the place was large enough; he himself took 'extraordinary delight … in the sweete retirements'.

As both theorist and practitioner, Boyceau recognised the importance of water in a garden. In his *Traité du jardinage* he wrote that 'its vivacity and movement are the most living spirit in gardens,' but he also noted that it was most uncommon to find naturally bubbling water in the place where one wished to make a garden, so it was usually necessary to find a source at a higher level and bring it to the site via pipes of wood or lead. In this respect, too, the Luxembourg Gardens prefigured Versailles, because the Aqueduct of Arcueil had to be constructed to bring water from sources at Rungis and Wissous. Still functioning today, the Arcueil aqueduct must be judged a success – a second storey was added in the nineteenth century by Baron Haussmann and the engineer Belgrand. But when Louis XIV tried to follow this precedent and feed his fountains from the Eure, the results were calamitous.

The extent of Boyceau's involvement in the creation of the small garden that served Louis XIII's 'cardboard château' is uncertain. In his *Traité* there are two parterre designs which he specifically refers to as having been made for Versailles, one of which resembles the embroidered parterre he designed for the Luxembourg Gardens. He also refers to the well-ordered diversity of the designs made for Versailles. The original garden was modest; beyond the parterre a central avenue ran a little way through woodland towards a quatrefoil basin on the site of what is now the Bassin d'Apollon. There were just three fountains along this central axis. There is documentary evidence that Boyceau's nephew, Jacques de Menours, participated in the layout of the gardens. It seems that the two men were very close. Even if Menours was the principal author of this design, he would have followed his uncle's precepts closely. Le Nôtre, in his turn, would follow the principles first set down by Boyceau, but he would have the clients, the resources and the imagination to realise them on a scale of which his predecessor could only have dreamt.

Was Le Nôtre daunted by the sheer size of the task he was given at Versailles? There is no evidence that he was anything but sanguine. He knew what the King wanted and had promises that the necessary resources would follow. The site had been surveyed in 1660, but like any present-day landscape architect Le Nôtre must have walked over the ground until he felt he knew it intimately. He would have looked for the difficulties – the cold slopes and the marshy hollows – but also for the opportunities – the falling ground that would lend itself to terracing, the low spot that might take a lake. It is no accident that the Pièce d'Eau des Suisses was eventually constructed on the site of a former duck-pond.

In England a century later, 'Capability' Brown would earn his nickname from his quirky way of referring to such possibilities. He would reassure his clients by telling them that their site had 'capabilities' – in modern terms, potential. However, he and Le Nôtre – history's most celebrated garden designers – seem superficially to have employed contrasting methods. Le Nôtre, heir to Descartes' rationalism, made nature subject to geometry, while Brown, the English empiricist, studiously avoided straight lines and sought to enhance the natural beauties of each site. But this contrast has been overstated, and at a more subtle level Le Nôtre and Brown had much in common. Though the sorts of designs they produced look very different, both took account of the 'capabilities' of their sites. Both had a sort of formula which they sought to marry with the topography of their sites. In Brown's case the formula consisted of a serpentine lake, usually made by damming a river, an enclosing belt of trees and carefully deployed clumps of

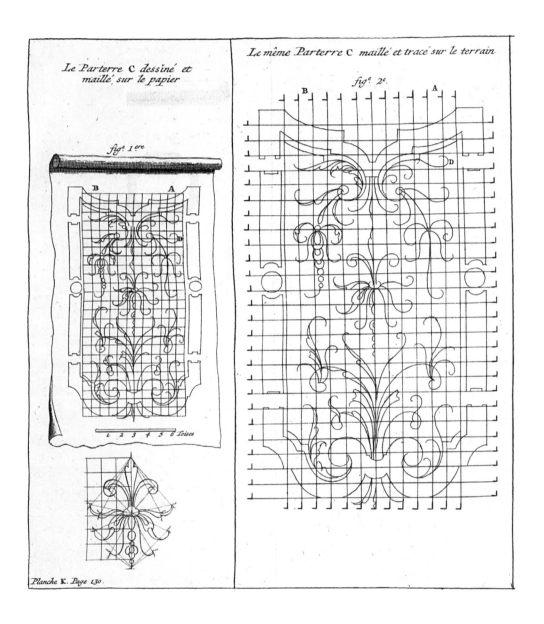

The parterre drawn and squared over upon paper, from La Théorie et la practique du jardinage by Antoine-Joseph Dezallier d'Argenville, 1709.

*The Semi-circle, from La Théorie et la practique du
jardinage by Antoine-Joseph Dezallier d'Argenville, 1709.*

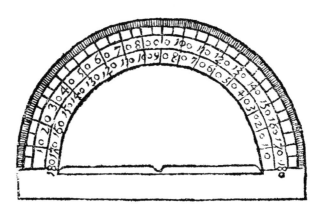

*The Protractor, from La Théorie et la practique du
jardinage by Antoine-Joseph Dezallier d'Argenville, 1709.*

trees within a park. For Le Nôtre it involved an axis with various cross-axes and the geometrical subdivision of a garden into areas which would in turn become parterres, *bosquets* or reflecting pools.

Their methods of construction, too, were not so different, because both lived before the age of the mechanical excavator. To create their landforms, they had to move vast quantities of muck from place to place and had at their disposal picks, shovels, carts, horses and large numbers of men. In Le Nôtre's case the latter were often soldiers and subject to military discipline, which might not have improved the quality of their lives but which made the master-gardener's job much easier.

It has been suggested, perhaps because so few drawings in Le Nôtre's hand have survived, that he designed on the land itself, only making drawings after the work was completed, but this seems improbable. It is a technique that might work for the broad outline of a garden but not for the sort of complex features introduced by Le Nôtre, and certainly not for an elaborate parterre. Some of the drawings that have come down to us, like his sketch for the alignment of the Avenue de Picardie at Versailles or his doodles suggesting the shape of the Bassin du Dragon and the configuration of a grand stairway at Saint-Cloud, suggest a designer working out his ideas on paper. Then there is his more elaborate sketch design for a cascade at Versailles, which was never built, and the drawings he made for sites which he never visited, such as the gardens of the Queen's House at Greenwich. It is the very sketchiness of these scraps, along with their numerous annotations, that show that he thought with his pen. Indeed, although Le Nôtre had a reputation as a fine draughtsman, it is finished drawings that we lack. Perhaps he had little interest in producing 'as built' plans and left that to others.

Le Nôtre left no written explanation of his working practices. But as we have seen, Dezallier d'Argenville's instruction manual *La Théorie et la practique du jardinage* closely reflected his philosophy of garden design.

It is in the second part of Dezallier's book that we find a chapter devoted to 'some practices in geometry, described on paper, with the manner of marking them out truthfully upon the ground'. First the author introduces his readers to the essential tools of the trade. There is the Semi-circle, a brass protractor with a swivelling arm, mounted upon a centre-pin, which carries two upright sights that 'direct and guide the visual ray'. In the middle there is a 'sea-compass', and the whole instrument, used in the setting-out of angles upon the ground, is usually supported on a tripod. For setting out right-angles a simpler apparatus can be used. Called the Square or Whole Circle, it is no more than an iron ring with two sets of diametrically opposed sights. For marking out lines upon the ground

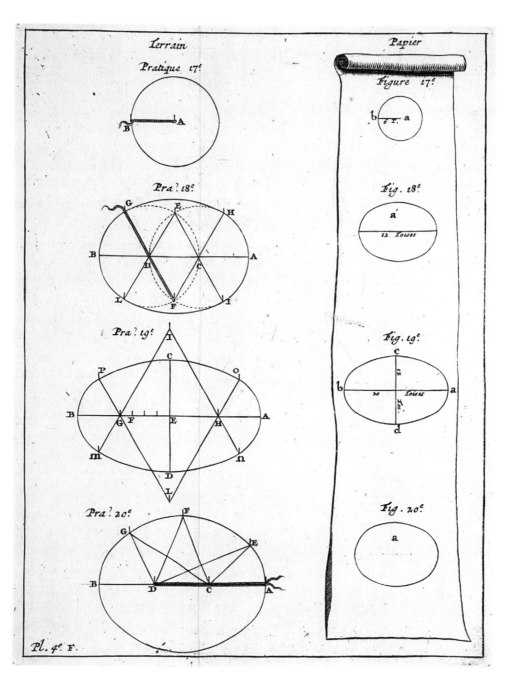

Practices, numbers 17–20, from La Théorie et la practique
du jardinage *by Antoine-Joseph Dezallier d'Argenville, 1709.*

there are stakes and ranging rods; the gardener also needs a line wound around a stick, measuring rods and, for longer distances, a measuring chain. 'The terms of staking out, aligning, ranging and bourning, all signify the same thing,' says John James in his English translation; they refer to the operation whereby the gardener, 'shutting one eye, and opening the other, applies it to the head of the ranging-stick, to direct all the others in the same line, which we call the Line of Aim, or Visual Ray.' For drawing out their designs on the ground, Le Nôtre and his contemporaries would have used a tracing-staff, a long stick tipped with a triangular piece of iron, 'flattened like a cat's tongue'.

Dezallier d'Argenville wished to spare those who used his book the need to read any 'treatise of practical geometry'. Instead they could work their way through his intensive course, which was designed to teach them all they needed to know. In all, he described twenty Practices, starting with the simplest, 'To draw a straight line on the Ground, with the cord', then mounting in difficulty until, by the time the tyro had reached number fourteen, he was ready to tackle the *pentagone, exagone, eptagone, octagone, ennéagone, décagone, endécagone* and *dodécagone*. The trickiest challenge of all was kept until last; this was the Gardener's Oval, which used a length of line tied into a loop around two stakes driven into the ground. Using the tracing-staff to keep to keep the line strained around these fixed points, the gardener could score a sweetly proportioned oval into the earth.

Le Nôtre would have learnt these techniques from his father and from the other gardeners at the Tuileries. Reading Dezallier d'Argenville or John James, it is easy to picture a bewigged and frock-coated Le Nôtre bending to squint through the eyepiece of his tripod-mounted Semi-circle, then straightening up to wave directions to his pole-carrying assistants. The work must have been slow and the equipment heavy and cumbersome, but setting out the garden was relatively easy work. Only hard physical effort could transform a site.

When landscape-architectural contracts are let today, the first items in the Bill of Quantities are usually concerned with site clearance. On the sorts of sites that landscape architects are called upon to deal with now this can include the demolition of buildings and the treatment of contamination. The task that faced Le Nôtre's men was simpler since the site was essentially undeveloped, but there would have been huge quantities of scrubby vegetation to clear before anyone could think seriously about levelling and setting out, and this work would have been done with hand tools such as axes, spades and mattocks. Dezallier d'Argenville noted that 'when the ground is too uneven or rough, one must begin, first of all, to break it up with the plough, to destroy the weeds, and then harrow it to level the hillocks and fill up the cavities. This serves, likewise, to render the earth more workable, both for removal and for transporting, as for driving in the poles and stakes, as necessary.'

For a formal garden there were two general conditions of slope that were desirable. The first was the absence of any discernible gradient at all, which was called reducing the ground to its perfect level. The essentials of this operation remain the same today. To create a level area on a slope requires material to be cut from the upper parts and deposited lower down. By careful balancing of 'cut' and 'fill' it is often possible to create a level area without importing or exporting any earth to or from the site. If this operation cannot be done without creating banks that would be precipitously steep, then a retaining wall is required. The other advantageous condition was that of a regular slope. Sometimes all that was needed to make a naturally sloping site seem uniform was to fill any holes and flatten any humps. Apart from requiring much less labour to achieve, regularly sloping sites shed surface water easily. In his various garden designs, Le Nôtre was able to combine these conditions in a masterful way. The sequence of gently sloping terraces, steeper banks and retaining walls provided sequences of views but also hidden areas awaiting discovery. The most striking example is at Vaux-le-Vicomte, where the Grandes Cascades and the whole of the Canal formed from the Angueil are invisible from the central axis until one is right above them. In 1665 Le Nôtre created a similar effect at Versailles, where he concealed the Jardin Bas below the massive curving ramps and staircases of the Fer à Cheval. Here he laid out parterres and basins which were hidden from view from the château terrace. In 1668 the space embraced by this curving masonry wall would become home to the first version of the Fountain of Latona, executed by Gaspard and Balthazar Marsy.

Creating features like the Fer à Cheval required extensive earthworks, and it is easy to overlook the difficulty that these must have presented before the advent of power tools. 'When the earth is to be dug or cut to make a terrace, a bank, a bowling-green or a canal,' wrote Dezallier, 'they make use of mattocks, pickaxes, spades and shovels, with workers who remain behind those who dig and fill baskets, scuttles and wheel-barrows.' There were four ways of carrying the earth away. It could go in carts pulled by horses, wheelbarrows pushed by men, panniers carried by asses, or baskets on men's backs. In John James's translation, with cost-conscious English landowners in mind rather than an autocratic French king to whom money was no object, the horse and cart are regarded as too expensive. Using men ought to be cheaper, James argues, but because people are 'generally intolerably lazy, and have no concern but to spin out the day', his own preference is for donkeys. In France, he notes, they have *piqueurs*, or overseers, to stop workmen from loitering and 'holding discourse'.

The face of a deep excavation could become unstable. Dezallier observed that the common method was to 'undermine the foot of it with a pick-axe, and hollow it a little before them towards the bottom; with this precaution, that no one walk upon the ground above, for fear that it should collapse and injure those who are working below'. When all went well, the labourers could bring down 'vast quantities of earth at once', but if they met with rocks, it might be necessary to detonate small barrels of gunpowder placed at the bottom of the excavations.

Landslips were not the only dangers associated with such works, as it was not uncommon for carters to be crushed by their vehicles. Cinchona bark, imported from South America, was used as an analgesic for the injured. Quinine is a product of cinchona bark, so this substance would also have been useful in fighting the malarial fevers that beset the works. Frédérick Tiberghien has studied the compensation payments made to injured workers at Versailles. Using the building accounts, he estimates that 700 payments were made for injuries sustained on the works between 1660 and 1700. This figure includes those who were hurt while working on the château but not the large numbers who died or were maimed during the construction of the aqueduct at Maintenon. The stratification of society was reflected in the payments; an injured labourer would be paid between 10 and 20 *livres*, whereas a stonemason in similar circumstances might get 40 *livres*. This inequality persisted in death. A dead labourer was worth 20 to 30 *livres* to his family, whereas the settlement for a deceased foreman was 50 *livres* and that for a master-craftsman was 60 *livres*. There was not much difference between the value of a human being and that of a horse – Tiberghien noted a payment of 30 *livres* for a lost horse in 1684. Those injured during earth-moving operations would have been at the lower end of this social hierarchy; but even the top payments look niggardly when we consider that 60 *livres* was only enough to feed a family for a couple of months.

La Théorie et la practique du jardinage has much to say about levelling; indeed several Practices are described in detail, each with a helpful diagram. In every case the essence is the same. The gardener uses stakes and an instrument called a mason's rule to establish a level line against which the amounts of necessary cut and fill can be determined. The First Practice, 'to set out a level line upon the ground', is followed by the Second Practice, 'to lay a piece of ground straight and even, according to a level line', and a Third, 'to dress an entire piece of ground, however large, and to lay it level'. The author adds an observation to this last exercise. It would prove too expensive, he suggests, to make the whole ground according to this method, so 'one might just dress and lay even those places that will be exposed to sight, such as those that serve for parterres, halls, galleries etc.' In the areas that

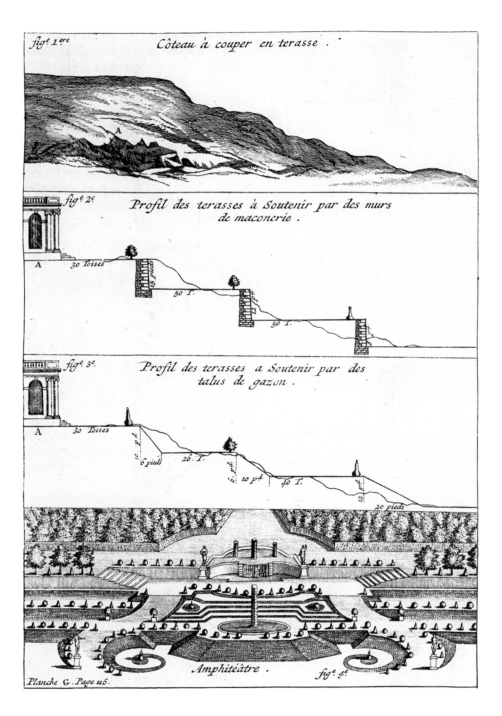

The hill to be cut into terraces, from La Théorie et la practique
du jardinage *by Antoine-Joseph Dezallier d'Argenville, 1709.*

are to be mostly wooded, it is only necessary to dress the *allées* and the rides. The squares and middle parts of the woods can stay uneven and natural.

Practices One, Two and Three are all concerned with the production of perfectly level ground, but the Fourth Practice concerns that other desirable condition, the regular slope. In this case the gardener must fix two 4-foot stakes, one at the top of the slope and one at the bottom. He then drives in intermediate stakes at regular intervals, making sure that their heads are in line with the 'visual ray' that connects the tops of the stakes at the extremities. Next, he takes a 4-foot-long gauge-stick and lays it against each stake in turn to determine whether earth needs to be added or taken away. Dezallier d'Argenville closes this chapter with a wry observation on some other practices he has noticed. 'This is the best way that I know,' he writes, 'to level and to dress ground, and the easiest and least burdensome in the execution. Here are none of the bad customs that are followed by ordinary levellers, amongst others, that of lying along the slope on their bellies, digging holes in the ground to sit in, and kneeling down to the height of the ruler.'

Another chapter of Dezallier's indispensable book is devoted to the treatment of steeper slopes, where 'terraces sustained by walls of masonry' or 'supported by banks and slopes of turf' are required. For this more serious undertaking additional equipment is needed, not just stakes but also poles of 15 to 20 feet in length, a plumb rule for setting them straight, lengths of cord to strain between them and a 'mason's long ruler'. The author cautions his readers to 'avoid the defect of heaping terrace upon terrace, it being very disagreeable in a garden to be constantly going up-hill or downhill, without finding any resting place'. Again there are four Practices, with diagrams and step-by-step instructions, but it is the incidental remarks that throw the most light on the difficulties that Le Nôtre and his men would have faced at Versailles. 'It is much better to cut banks out of solid ground,' writes Dezallier, 'which is to say firm ground, than to build them up with made ground and hurdles; they keep better when they are natural and cost less.' Sometimes the construction of such artificial slopes will be unavoidable, suggests the author, in which case layers of earth can be laid, sandwich-like, between beds of willow-wattle hurdles, which will reinforce the slope. Many important areas at Versailles, including the forecourt and the site of the stables, consist of entirely made-up ground.

A little further on, when discussing the foundations for retaining walls, Dezallier d'Argenville remarks that those who build walls to hold up terraces must 'consult the natural bottom of the soil; for the masonry must be set upon firm ground and a good earth. In ground that is sandy, loose and boggy, one makes use of gratings of timber-work, platforms and piles, upon which to secure the foundations of the walls.' At Versailles, many of the structures in the lower parts of the site had to rest on timber piling.

Most of the difficulties that Le Nôtre and his army of labourers faced on site were concerned with water, water of the wrong sort and in the wrong place. In the ecologically attuned twenty-first century we may be starting to value our wetlands and to cultivate a new aesthetic around them, but for most of history such places have been thought of as unproductive, unhealthy and ugly. The solution at Versailles was to drain them, but into what? There was no river on the site, just a stinking little stream called the Galie. The marshy pools were turned into decorative water features by lining them with stone and controlling the inflow and discharge. Le Nôtre proposed a large octagonal pond, for example, in the swampy area to the south of the château, though this plan lapsed until 1678, when excavations for the Pièce d'Eau des Suisses began in the same area. A network of *pierrées*, or drystone drains, was excavated, which, if all the various branches were measured, amounted to a total length of over 30 kilometres. *Pierrées* were trenches about half a metre deep, backfilled with rubble, which served to dry out the surrounding soil. In the English-speaking world they are still known as 'French drains', and because they are cheap, low-tech and efficient, they are still much favoured by landscape architects.

The boldest step in Le Nôtre's approach to the drainage problem was the construction of the Grand Canal, a vast cruciform waterbody that is 1,800 metres in its longest dimension and covers an area equivalent to about fifty-seven football pitches. This was not begun until 1667, but it cleared the way for the extension of the park and made a virtue out of a necessity. It was not just a matter of digging – the earth removed from the excavation had to be carefully placed elsewhere. The Canal was to be surrounded by a shelf of level ground, so much effort went into the filling of hollows and the correction of irregularities. As with maps of pirate treasure, the simplest, boldest mark that one can make on a plan is a cross – X marks the spot – and the Canal at Versailles, as well as being a potent religious symbol, is like an inscription that draws attention to the supreme importance of the place.

The arms of the Canal, stretching off like the points of a compass, form the axes of a great co-ordinate system. René Descartes, the inventor of co-ordinate geometry, died in 1650, so it is tempting to apply the label 'Cartesian' to Le Nôtre's designs. Descartes, however, had left his native France to work in the less stultifying intellectual atmosphere of Holland. Although he taught that Creation was orderly because God made it that way, the Catholic Church disapproved of his books, and

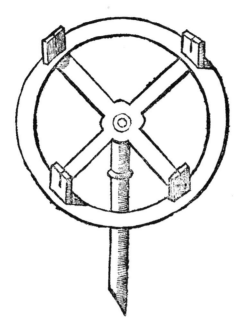

The Whole Circle or Square, from La Théorie et la practique du jardinage by Antoine-Joseph Dezallier d'Argenville, 1709.

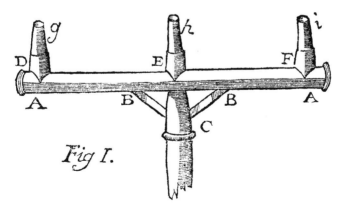

A level with vials, from La Théorie et la practique du jardinage by Antoine-Joseph Dezallier d'Argenville, 1709.

so, in his turn, did Louis XIV. There is no evidence that Le Nôtre ever read any of them; it is more likely that he got his ideas on geometry from gardening circles, from the books of Serres and Boyceau, or from his friendly contacts with military engineers. Nevertheless his designs will continue to be associated with Descartes' rational and systematic approach, whereby the surest road to truth was through mathematics.

Before construction of the Grand Canal could begin, it was necessary to obtain some measure of the slope. According to Charles Perrault, this task was first given to the masons and fountaineers who were working in the area. Denis Jolly, the King's fountaineer, reported that there was a difference in level of 10 feet between one end of the proposed Canal and the other. Colbert was sceptical and brought in Abbé Jean Picard from the Academy of Sciences, a renowned astronomer, geodesist and surveyor, to check the results.

Jolly and his team had two sorts of apparatus available to them. There was the ordinary level, essentially the A-shaped mason's level with a plumb-line added. This was a standard piece of equipment for gardeners, and it is illustrated in Dezallier d'Argenville's book, but it was inaccurate over long distances – it could be out by 10 metres over a kilometre. There was also the water-level, illustrated in *La Théorie et la practique du jardinage* in the section devoted to hydraulics. In his translation, James calls this the 'Level with Vials'. It consisted of a tin pipe, about an inch in diameter and 3 or 4 feet long, which could be mounted on a stake. 'Upon the upper part of this pipe,' says James, 'at the two ends and in the middle, are soldered three other ends of pipe, which communicate one with the other ...' Tubes or vials of glass were then fixed into these openings with wax or mastic and the apparatus filled with water. By keeping the same amount of water visible in each of the vials, the device could be set level. This was an improvement on the ordinary level with its plumb-line that could be blown about by the wind, but it still was not accurate enough for sighting over any great distance.

Abbé Picard and his associates at the Academy, however, had devised an instrument that was, and measuring the levels for the Grand Canal was an early test for his invention. It used a plumb-line, but for the sake of precision a long human hair was used rather than the usual length of cord, and this was encased within a sealed tube with a viewing window, so a calm day was not required for its use. A more radical design improvement was the addition of a telescope, similar to the one developed for astronomical purposes by Galileo around 1609, thus increasing the effective range of the level to as much as 400 metres. Abbé Picard reported that the difference in level between the ends of the Canal was only 2 feet, a result significantly at variance with the previous measurements. Colbert and Le Nôtre readily accepted the

Academician's levels over those of the hapless fountaineer, and they were right to do so, for when the Canal was excavated Picard's levels were found to be out by only a *pouce* or a *pouce-et-demi*, which is to say a thumb or a thumb-and-a-half.

As Le Nôtre and his men grappled with the site, Colbert grumbled, but more about the cost than anything else. In 1665 he wrote a very carefully worded letter to the King, making a well-judged appeal to Louis' vanity and thirst for glory:

> Your Majesty knows that, apart from the glorious actions of war, nothing celebrates so advantageously the greatness and genius of princes than buildings, and all posterity measures them by the yardstick of those superb edifices which they have erected during their life. O what a pity were the greatest and most virtuous of kings, of that real virtue which makes the greatest princes, to be measured by the scale of Versailles!

At this stage Colbert was not party to Louis' grander vision, or perhaps the King himself only dimly perceived it. In any case, Colbert was wrong.

View of the Château of Versailles in 1668 by Pierre Patel (le Père).

VI

First Plans

L E NÔTRE WAS CERTAINLY kept busy during his early years at Versailles. As early as 1660 Louis started to acquire parcels of land in order to consolidate and extend the boundaries of his estate. This included some plots in the village of Versailles which were needed to regularise the boundaries of what was then his orchard but would one day become the Parterre de l'Orangerie. The villagers must have had mixed feelings about the attention the King was showing towards their modest settlement. Louis Gourlier the Eldest, uncle of one of the royal farmers, lost a barn, three stables and a pigsty, together with a considerable area of cultivated land, and he was not the only one to forfeit fields or gardens in this way. In a similar fashion, with the aim of consolidating the boundaries of the Grand Parc, Louis began to buy up all the remaining land between the villages of Choisy-aux-Boeufs to the west, Satory to the south and Trianon to the north, and had this terrain surveyed even before the accounts had been settled.

Le Vau's minor improvements to the château included new staircases, a balcony and two new buildings housing the stables and the kitchens. Painters were brought in to renovate rooms which had not been redecorated for twenty years. The Petite Château, as it came to be known, is illustrated in a famous painting by Patel, which shows the carriages of the King and Queen clattering along the rutted avenue towards the embrace of the curving, harbour-like walls of the Place d'Armes. Their procession winds towards the grille leading into the forecourt, which is flanked by the new stables and kitchens. The château lies across a dry moat, through an arcade,

*The ancient Cour de Marbre. Illustration from
Pierre De Nolhac's La Création de Versailles.*

and is arranged around three sides of the Cour de Château, later known as the Cour de Marbre. In the painting, the château and the vast gardens beyond, revealed by Patel's bird's-eye perspective, are devoid of people and wait to be animated. The picture is dated 1668, and its great sweep shows the scale of achievement in the gardens by that year. The central axis stretches to the horizon, punctuated by shining basins of water. Large vessels float on the Canal, which has not yet been expanded to its full cruciform extent, but the rectilinear framework of the gardens is already well established. Though the plantations to either side of the Canal look immature, the trees closer to the château have grown up sufficiently to form solid blocks of woodland, and clipped *palissades* of architectural rigidity are already in evidence. Since work started in earnest in 1663, Patel's painting is testament to five years of prodigious effort by Le Nôtre and his fellow gardeners.

Having acquired hundreds of orange trees as booty from Vaux, the King, who loved their scent, was eager to provide them with a new home, so the construction of an orangery was one of the first significant tasks given to Le Vau. The best place for such a structure was to the south of the château, where it could take most advantage from the warmth of the sun. Le Vau utilised the sloping ground in this direction, embedding his building into the hillside, so that its level roof could form the Parterre des Fleurs, also known as the Parterre de l'Amour. The width of this first Orangerie was fixed by the dimensions of the southern elevation of the château, with which it was exactly aligned. It would stand for twenty years, by which time massive extensions to the château and gardens would make it seem inadequate and out of scale. It would be replaced by a new structure, twice the size, by Le Vau's successor as *Premier Architecte*, Jules Hardouin-Mansart. In the meantime, this parterre, with its gilded balustrade and bordering cypresses, was filled with flowering plants, for which Louis had much more of a passion than Le Nôtre. It became one of the King's favourite places, and its necessary destruction was one of the motives for the later development of the flower gardens at Trianon.

Building the Orangerie and levelling the terrace on the garden front of the château were major works of construction. Louis Petit, a member of Colbert's administrative staff, wrote to his master that 'Our *terrassiers*, eighty in number, are working as I told you in my last report. They have assured me that another brigade will arrive on Monday. Three hundred and thirty *terrassiers* are moving earth from the Orangerie and from the Demi-Lune at the end of the large parterre, and also cultivating the garden of the Château Vieil.'

*   *   *

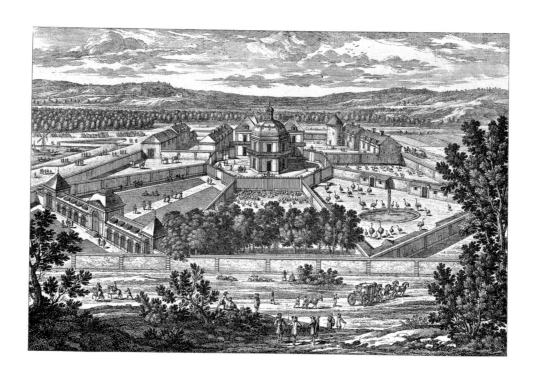

Perspective view of the Ménagerie and its enclosures. Engraving by the Perelle family.

The clearest indication of Louis' vision of Versailles as a place of pleasure and diversion was his decision to build the Ménagerie on the old road to Trappes. The site was about twenty minutes' walk from the château, a location chosen perhaps out of considerations of hygiene – the King did not want livestock odours too close to his main residence – but also to provide a suitable terminus for promenades through the gardens. There was nothing new about the taste for keeping rare birds and animals; indeed the practice had ancient Roman precedents which would have appealed to Louis. The emperors of Antiquity had paraded the elephants and big cats they had captured while on military campaigns, prior to slaughtering them as a demonstration of imperial power. Harnessing big cats to chariots for processional purposes was also known, and wealthy Romans liked to embellish their villas with aviaries, fish-ponds and animal pens. These tastes persisted throughout Europe during the Middle Ages; Lorenzo the Magnificent held parades of lions and elephants at the end of the fifteenth century. Francis I of France is said to have kept a lion or a snow leopard at the foot of his bed, and Louis XIII, while only a child, witnessed dogs being set on a bear in the oval room at the château of Saint-Germain. The cruel pitting of wild animals against domestic animals – not just strong ones like bulls or mastiffs but also docile creatures such as cows or donkeys – was a particularly unsavoury aspect of this bloodthirsty appetite, but it was consonant with seventeenth-century notions of hospitality according to which a host was willing to sacrifice valuable animals in certain carnage for the delectation of his guests.

The Ménagerie at Versailles marked a significant shift, however. It was not that Louis was any more tender-hearted than his contemporaries; indeed he kept a seraglio of fighting beasts at Vincennes until 1700. The collection at Versailles was more for show than for sport, however, and can be regarded as the first modern zoo in the West.

The Ménagerie commission was given to Le Vau, who produced a unique and jaunty miniature château centred on an octagonal pavilion with an eye-catching cupola. On the first floor there was an eight-sided salon from which windows in seven of the walls looked down upon seven animal enclosures. The word *ménagerie* is derived from *ménages*, which refers to housekeeping or farm management, and this domestic aspect was represented by the inclusion of domesticated animals like deer and fowl. There were even stables, a dovecote and a dairy, so as well as being a zoo, the Ménagerie had many of the characteristics of a model farm long before Marie-Antoinette notoriously developed her taste for rustic make-believe at the Hameau.

In 1665 the Italian traveller Sebastiano Locatelli was impressed to find at

Tree-planting. Illustration from La Quintinie's
Instruction pour les jardins fruitiers et potagers, 1690.

Versailles 'more than 40 species that I had never seen before, nor even heard spoken of'. These included pelicans, flamingos, pigeons, chickens, turkeys, swans, herons and ducks. Gentle herbivores like cows, horses, deer and gazelles were kept in proximity to foxes, bears and wolves, and fierce imports including crocodiles and lions. Most of the exotic species came from North Africa or the Levant. Tropical birds, including humming-birds, birds of paradise, parrots, lorikeets, toucans and cockatoos, were splendidly housed in an aviary that had the form of a small château with a central, domed volary flanked by low wings attached to end-pavilions with pointed roofs.

The design of the Ménagerie, with its central salon offering elevated views over a fan-like array of animal pens, was echoed in 1791 by Jeremy Bentham's design for an ideal prison, the Panopticon, where a centrally placed warder could keep a large number of cells under surveillance and this is more than a coincidence. For both buildings were about control. Only a mighty king could have brought together so many rare, exotic and wild beasts in one place, where they were kept penned for his scrutiny and pleasure. Like Le Nôtre's gardens, which were focussed on the King's chambers, the Ménagerie was an example of the 'visual politics' of Louis' reign. The prisoners in the Panopticon would never know when the guard was looking at them. One wonders if the courtiers at Versailles sometimes felt the same way.

It is possible to hazard some guesses about Le Nôtre's approach to the planning of the gardens in its early stages. It seems that his procedure was to set up a linear framework based around the central axis and its cross-axes. Having established this general composition, he would divide it up into sections and design each part in turn. Close to the house there would be parterres, since no tall hedges or woodland should interfere with views to or from the building. Elsewhere it was a matter of creating variety and balancing the solid elements, such as the *bosquets*, against the open features, such as the canals and basins or the lawns known as *boulingrins* (a corruption of 'bowling greens' although they were not used for bowling).

Planting was used as a form of green masonry. In the Grand Parc and also within the square woodland blocks of the Petit Parc, the dominant species was oak, with a sprinkling of chestnut, beech, ash and wild cherry. However, oaks made poor trees for formal training, so other species were used for the surrounding *bosquets*. Sometimes areas were planted with a single species such as lime, elm or chestnut, while yew was prized because it was evergreen and malleable; it could be clipped to any height and brought to just about any form, making it eminently suitable for Le Nôtre's type of horticultural architecture. Straight walks, known as *allées*, were lined either with trees or *palissades*. Hornbeam was the most popular choice for *palissades*, though beech, yew and maple were also used. Elms, limes and chestnuts were favoured for planting in lines. The *bosquets* were cut through with walks or, in the case of the larger ones, might enclose an outdoor room, or *salle*. Often the *allées* created vistas, and there would be an object of interest – a building, statue or fountain – at the far end to punctuate the view. In his journal of his French travels, John Locke described the hedges he saw at the Tuileries: '… most of them are of maple whereof some only are cut up the sides and so let shoot up. Others are shorne also on top & kept soe & grow & looke very well, being green quite to the bottom.'

Recent restoration works are bringing back the flavour of Le Nôtre's plantings, but there is a romantic softness to the gardens today that is misleading. In engravings by Adam Pérelle, Israel Silvestre or Jacques Rigaud, one can gauge the strictness of the contemporary maintenance regime; the hedges are so immaculately clipped that they look like walls, sometimes towering to 30 feet in height.

A plan known as the Du Bus plan after Charles du Bus, who discovered it, shows the gardens as they were in 1662, before Le Nôtre's arrival. It is not reliably accurate for it shows the garden site as almost square, whereas it is trapezoidal, but it establishes that Louis XIII's garden broadly corresponded to the extent of the Petit Parc today. The rudimentary grid that Le Nôtre was to adjust and develop was already in place, as was the main western axis, running from the embroidered parterre close to the château to a quatrefoil pool at the furthest boundary, punctuated midway by a circular pool at the intersection of two diagonal paths. The basic division of the lower garden into twelve squarish blocks is also apparent. It was within this chequerboard layout that the complex game of *bosquet* design was played out over many years. Outdoor rooms were fashioned and refashioned, while sculptures were moved from place to place like so many chess pieces.

Le Nôtre's geometry was a suitable antidote to Louis' unpredictable temperament and boundless ambition. The grid can be the basis of very flexible planning, particularly in places where, as in the cities of the American Midwest or the plains of seventeenth-century France, there seems to be plenty of available land. At Versailles there were few limits, as the subsequent development of outlying pleasure palaces at Trianon and Marly demonstrates, yet the *bosquets*, which played such an important role in the schedule of entertainments at Versailles, had to be a reasonable distance from the palace. The quatrefoil pool, that marked the boundary of Louis XIII's plot remained the limit of the lower gardens. When the Sun King stocked it with swans, it became known as the Bassin des Cygnes, but it was destined to be the Bassin d'Apollon and change its character, becoming an important 'hinge' between the gardens and the Grand Canal. In pre-Canal plans, from about 1664, there is a circular space known as the Grand Rondeau from which five *allées* extended into the countryside beyond, including the diagonal walks that led to the Ménagerie and in the direction of Trianon. This was an example of the *patte-d'oie*, or 'goosefoot', because it resembled the webbed footprint of an enormous bird.

Close to the château, Le Nôtre replaced the original parterre by Jacques de Menours with one that was slightly elongated so that it would appear square in a perspectival view. Le Nôtre made use of earth from the excavations for Le Vau's orangery, but this part of the site was destined to be worked over again, for it was where various versions of the water parterre would be tried out. From the new parterre one could descend a flight of steps to the central *allée*, which Le Nôtre broadened as far as the little circular pool. In 1667 he would widen this as far as the Bassin de Cygnes, and it would become known as the Allée Royale. In 1680 the centre of this walk was grassed and became known as the Tapis Vert.

Le Nôtre's first essays in the creation of outdoor rooms were the relatively modest twin *bosquets* which would later bear the names Girandole and Dauphin, criss-cross configurations of paths forming symmetrical, diamond-like patterns to either side of the principal axis. Though they appear to have played little part in the Sun King's lavish programme of entertainments, the form of these decorative *bosquets* did not change during his reign, though they were replanted in quincunx fashion in 1775–6.

Throughout this period Le Nôtre worked closely with the members of Colbert's *Petit Académie*, although their main concern was with the iconographic programme of the gardens rather than its geometry. As far as the layout was concerned, it was Le Nôtre's opinion that carried the most weight, though at Versailles nothing could be attempted without the sanction of the King. Nevertheless we can attribute the decision, around 1664 or 1665, to create a major new cross-axis, running from north to south, to the royal gardener. The idea was to move the existing cross-axis – which ran through the centre of château itself, bisecting the north- and south-facing façades – by taking it further west so that it would run across the terrace, parallel to the garden front of the building. This was a major undertaking because it involved doubling the width of the northern parterre. It was part of a larger plan that involved the construction of the sweeping walls of the Fer à Cheval to separate the Jardin Haut from the Jardin Bas. The new layout had considerable advantages. Now when the King stepped out on to the terrace of his château, he was in a truly commanding position, the point at which all the major axes of the garden converged. Doubling the width of the Parterre du Nord made possible the creation of some of Versailles' most impressive features: the

Dragon Fountain, the Neptune Basin, the Allée des Marmousets and the *bosquets* of the Trois Fontaines and the Arc de Triomphe.

If this sort of vision does not come readily to every garden designer, it also takes a particular kind of confidence to instruct works which will occupy a large labour force for weeks on end before one can judge the results. Many painters are able to work quickly on canvas with relatively inexpensive materials, and, if the outcome does not please them, it is not so difficult for them to start again. Architects have a more difficult life, because they must work though plans and the labour of others, while their buildings, sometimes consuming vast resources, have not only to satisfy the aesthetic yearnings of their clients but also meet their functional needs. Arguably landscape designers have it harder still, since they share many of the problems faced by architects, but they also have to work with growing materials that, by their very nature, change over time. It can take years for a scheme to resemble the mature vision that was in its designer's mind. Perhaps a landscape design is never completed, since it continues to alter beyond maturity as trees become old and ultimately die. Because results often come at great expense and effort, and come slowly, the landscape architect must be a seer who can conjure images of places that do not yet exist.

Le Nôtre often toured the works in the company of the King, trailing behind them a wake of ministers, contractors, architects and hangers-on. One of the stories told about the master-gardener is that on a particular occasion during the construction of the first parterre, he improvised a table from planks and trestles and proceeded to unroll one of his plans for the Petit Parc. The King was pleased with what he saw and said, 'Le Nôtre, I will give you twenty thousand *livres* for this.' Murmuring his gratitude, Le Nôtre unfurled a second plan and the King was similarly impressed: 'I will give you twenty thousand *livres* for this one too.' Flushed with success, Le Nôtre produced a third drawing with the same result: 'Le Nôtre, this is magnificent, I must give you another twenty thousand *livres*.' The King looked expectantly at the remaining drawings lying upon the trestle, but Le Nôtre, smiling, covered them with his hand. 'Sire,' he said, 'you will see no more, for otherwise I should ruin you.'

Gilles Loistron, Sieur de Ballon, who was director of the King's nursery in the Faubourg Saint-Honoré, close to the Louvre, played an important role in selecting and delivering plants to the various royal gardens and is often mentioned in the building accounts for Versailles. He was sent on missions to Flanders to select plant material for transportation there. The accounts show, for example, that on 6 January 1669 he was reimbursed for an expedition he had made the previous year in the company of Pierre Desgots and two other gardeners to source limes and elms. He appears to have made another trip at about the same time to find a variety of poplars known as *ypreaux* because they grew in the region of Ypres.

As numerous entries in the building accounts testify, the quantities of trees brought to Versailles were prodigious. On 21 February 1668 a gardener called Thuileau was paid 87 *livres* for fifty-eight hundred young elms for the nursery at Versailles, while on the same day Jacques Julienne was paid a total of 678 *livres* for a further forty-two thousand elms and a quantity of young hornbeams. In December of the same year a *terrassier* called Nicolas Binet received 117 *livres* 11 *sols* for 14,300 young chestnuts and 6,350 young hornbeams, oaks and other trees for the Grand Parc. Where the accounts mention young trees, it is likely that they refer to what today would be called 'seedlings' or 'transplants' – plants less than two years old – particularly where the quantities are large and the species are those which were favoured for hedging or the creation of *palissades*. But there is evidence that much larger trees were also acquired. In February 1669, for example, René de Lalun was paid 360 *livres* for six hundred walnut trees, supplied for an avenue in the park.

In order to transplant mature trees in enormous numbers, Le Nôtre used machines with pulleys and levers. Such machines were so vigorously effective that the workmen nicknamed them 'the Devil'.[15] The gardening writer Dezallier d'Argenville recommended two types of these machines:

> … if your tree should be very big, the clod of earth of great compass, and the head large and well furnished, as are the great trees planted in the royal gardens; you must have a machine on purpose to remove them, which is a kind of skid or sledge, upon which the tree is set a little leaning, and supported at the head, for fear the branches should break. There is also a very useful machine which is a sort of cart, with two great screws and chains for lifting and suspending the rootball, to support it without tiring it during transportation and then to lower it into the hole.

Mme de Sévigné wrote in a letter that while out riding she had seen 'entire leafy forests being carried to Versailles' and noted how the trees swayed unsteadily in ox-drawn wagons.[17] Dezallier d'Argenville thought that it was a mistake to try to transplant trees that were too large, noting that 'more of these great trees die, notwithstanding all the precautions that can be taken.' To safeguard trees that had been moved, he recommended that they be planted in ground similar to that from which they had been taken; that they be planted in November or December, so that their roots could settle over the winter; and that planting be done in dry weather; and that watering be frequent and plentiful, since 'a drop of water thrown into a great fire only irritates the flame more.' The best times for watering, he suggested were morning and evening; he also understood the principles of mulching, observing that the best practice was to spread a layer of manure or litter around the foot of the plant before applying the water. Despite this knowledge of good horticultural practice, trees died in their thousands and had to be replaced.

The preferred species for lining out parterres was box. Dezallier distinguished between *Buis d'Artois*, a dwarf form with hard green leaves resembling myrtle, which was essential for the embroidery of parterres and the making of edgings for borders, and the box-tree of the woods, which grows much higher and is therefore suitable for *palissades*.

Le Nôtre's apparent coolness towards parterres has become part of his legend. In 1663, while working at Versailles, the gardener was also employed at Saint-Germain. A letter dated 11 October 1663 from Le Vau to Colbert reports that 'Monsieur Le Nôtre is here with a number of workmen to make the parterre opposite the end of the Grande Galerie of the King's Apartment ... the earth is levelled and they will begin planting the box hedging tomorrow.' According to Saint-Simon, Le Nôtre thought that parterres were best viewed from an upper-storey window and that consequently it was nursery maids, tied to the upper rooms by their childminding duties, who got the most pleasure out of them.[23] Whether this is a true reflection of the gardener's sentiments or just a prejudice of the waspish Duke is impossible to tell. It is not difficult to believe that Le Nôtre was more concerned with the overall structure of his gardens and with the stunning effects that could be produced through the expansive deployment of water than with the elaboration of parterres, but Saint-Simon concedes that Le Nôtre's designs for the latter were every bit as good as his work in other parts of the garden. The Swedish architect Nicodemus Tessin wrote of the terrace at Trianon: '... the parterre is perfectly beautiful; and represents the genius of M. Le Nôter [sic]'.

As we have seen, Colbert began to think well of Le Nôtre, who became an accepted member of the *clan Colbert*. It must have helped the gardener's cause that he was an ally of Le Brun, for the latter was the dominant personality in the Académie Royale de Peinture as well as the director of the Gobelins manufactory. The precise nature of the relationship between these two artists remains hazy, although the fact that they trained together, then worked together for three years at Vaux and for a further thirty at Versailles, with hardly any recorded friction between them, suggests that they remained friends as well as artistic collaborators. Their talents were complementary, since Le Brun was concerned with interiors and Le Nôtre with outdoor design. When it came to the sculptural embellishments of the park, both had their say, with Le Brun largely responsible for setting the programmatic brief for the artworks and commissioning the artists, and Le Nôtre advising on the overall siting of the works, as well as the design of their immediate settings.

Charles Perrault, a man of letters who is now mostly remembered for his re-writing of folk-tales such as 'Red Riding Hood', was also a commissioner for buildings and a member of Colbert's kitchen cabinet, the *Petite Académie*, a group of cerebral taste-formers which met every Tuesday and Friday in Colbert's house to discuss the progress of the King's image. There was nothing naïve about the company that Le Nôtre kept; on the contrary these men were opinion makers and arbiters of taste. Searching among classical sources such as the second book of Ovid's *Metamorphoses,* this tight clique of artistic spin-doctors began to develop a vision of Versailles as 'the Sun's bright palace'.

*View of the Bassin d'Apollon and the Grand Canal with its fleet by
an unknown French artist in the reign of Louis XIV.*

VII
The New Rome

I F A TIME-TRAVELLING JOURNALIST were to profile the Sun King's enthusiasms in bullet-point fashion, high on the list, higher even than dancing, playing cards, bedding courtesans or following his beloved hunt, would be gardening and making war. In many ways these activities were complementary; both were driven by a quest for glory. In Louis' view there were two ways in which a great king could earn the respect of posterity. The first was through military success, so he set himself the objective of extending France's borders until they stretched from the Rhine to the Alps and the Pyrenees. The second was through building, whether roads, canals, aqueducts or great houses. His writ would run along new highways and waterways and extend throughout his realm. Versailles would become the centre of this great rational network of communications, and Le Nôtre's gardens, similarly incised with canals and *allées*, would become the perfect expression of Louis' territorial ambition.

The garden scenes depicted in contemporary engravings look so tranquil that it is easy to forget that seventeenth-century France was a martial state. To be at war was the normal condition during Louis' reign, which was punctuated by only short intervals of peace. Nancy Mitford estimated that the country had 150,000 men in arms even in peacetime. In such prints lovers stroll arm in arm through *bosquets*, while family groups attended by prancing little dogs pause to admire the fountains. If anything, there are more men than women, which is perplexing because for much of the time all the young men, and many of the not so young, would have been away at the front. Soldiering was one way to win Louis' favour, and many seized the chance to display battlefield valour. Unfortunately the nobility were better known for reckless acts of bravery than for their discipline or grasp of tactics, and widows were commonplace at the court of Versailles. One wonders if the young men depicted in the engravings by Pérelle and others actually got to see much of the gardens in their summer prime, since the more clement months were favoured for military manoeuvres. Nor do there seem to be any amputees in these peaceful scenes, yet the increasing use of artillery meant that many soldiers who escaped death were horribly mutilated. There must have been many veteran officers hobbling around Versailles on crutches and peg-legs, but theirs were not the images that Louis' propagandists cared to show. And this despite the fact that Versailles was not just the headquarters of the French military; at times it became more like a military hospital.

Louis considered military leadership to be the greatest of professions. It seems that his presence on the battlefield genuinely raised the morale of his troops, although some historians have suggested that he was not the strategist he thought himself to be, and that his generals were happier when he stayed at home. He certainly enjoyed warfare and shared many of the risks and privations of his troops; he also cared enough about their welfare to establish the Hôtel des Invalides in 1674 for wounded and homeless veterans, and ex-servicemen were also given a monopoly of the sedan-chair business in the royal palaces. But it is difficult to separate Louis' true military accomplishments from the myth-making that surrounded him. In 1672, during the Dutch War, the *Gazette de France*, an official court journal, trumpeted the news that 'everyone is on fire with a noble ardour to seize the opportunity of distinguishing himself, inspired by the presence of this great King whose continual activity one cannot cease to admire – His Majesty himself giving those orders, by day and by night, which he judges necessary and taking less repose than any officer in the army.'

Louis was particularly fond of sieges and was present at eighteen of the forty successful operations undertaken by Vauban. Seventeenth-century warfare was no less gruesome than conflict in any other century; the wounds were as gory and the mutilations just as distressing. There was, however, something theatrical, indeed entertaining, about siegecraft, as long as one was not on the receiving end. Vauban's scientific approach to siege warfare brought with it a degree of predictability; the commanders of a siege army could estimate the time and resources it would take to reduce a fortress. If they got it right, the King and his guests could be on hand to witness the surrender. Sometimes an orchestra would strike up an overture to the detonation of the mines. There were strong

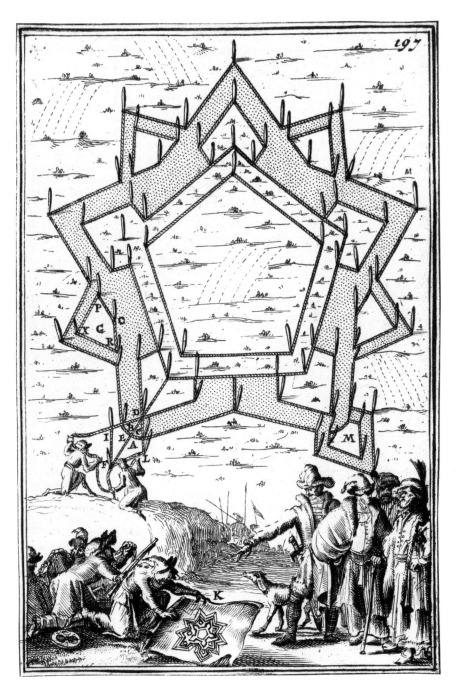

*Layout for a new fortress. Illustration from Les Travaux de Mars
by Alain Manesson Mallet, 1684.*

similarities between these battlefield performances and the peacetime firework spectaculars Louis liked to stage at Versailles. Siege warfare also appealed to the King's taste for earthworks and engineering. The system of parallel trenches employed during the First World War was essentially devised by Vauban for the siege of the fortress of Maastrict in 1673.

The fact that Le Nôtre and Le Brun were to be found at the siege of Valenciennes in 1677 is perhaps less unlikely than it might seem. Louis himself wrote to Colbert to say that 'Le Brun and Le Nôtre arrived this morning with Van der Meulen. I am very glad that Le Brun will see the disposition of this siege because it is very fine.' Le Brun and the Fleming Adam Frans van der Meulen could be classed as war artists. Shortly after his arrival in France, Van der Meulen was commissioned to paint a series of views depicting Louis' military successes. One of his paintings, *Louis XIV au siège de Tournai, le 21 juin 1667*, shows the King scrutinising trenches which zigzag towards the smoking city walls; it has been compared to a painting by Jean-Baptiste Martin that depicts Louis inspecting the reservoirs built on the heights of Montbauron to feed the fountains in his gardens. Engineering for warfare and engineering for the pleasures of peacetime were both considered worthy artistic subjects, and in both paintings the King, dismounted from his white charger, surveys the scene with a satisfied, proprietary gaze.

What was Le Nôtre doing at the siege of Valenciennes? Though he had also trained as an artist, he certainly was not there to gather material for paintings. Perhaps it is enough that he was a friend of Le Brun and by now one of the King's favoured circle. Le Nôtre was a courtier as much as a gardener, and it would have been normal for him to have shown an interest in warfare, since the nobles around him still saw themselves as part of a warrior caste and must have talked frequently about martial matters. It is not hard to imagine him discussing military tactics and engineering with his father-in-law, François Langlois, Sieur du Hamel, who was a *Conseiller Ordinaire de l'Artillerie de France*. It has also been suggested that Le Nôtre could have been introduced to the principles of fortification during his time with Vouet. Jacques Alleaume, who helped to design some of the strongholds in eastern France, also had a study in the Grande Galerie of the Louvre.

From the moment that Le Nôtre started to design on an extensive scale, he turned instinctively to garden features analogous to military earthworks. As Chandra Mukerji has observed, if one draws a section along the main axis at Vaux-le-Vicomte and compares it with a cross-section through the system of battlements illustrated in Allain Manesson Mallet's *The Art of War*, a seventeenth-century military manual, there is a surprising correspondence. Not only are some common elements used, such as stone-faced retaining walls, earth banks and moats (or canals), but the general sequence in which these are combined is also similar. The heights, angles and proportions may not be identical, but the resemblance is indisputable. It seems understandable that the master-gardener, having learnt about fortifications from his teachers and relatives, and having already used comparable features in his garden designs, should have grasped the opportunity to see a live contest between artillery and earthworks at Valenciennes. It also seems that he enjoyed the spectacle enough to want to repeat the experience; Dominique Garrigues tells us that Le Nôtre joined the King at the siege of Cambrai in 1687.

Louis' military campaigns were more than adventurism or vainglorious posturing. Two years before Le Nôtre began his work at Versailles, the Peace of the Pyrenees (1659) had brought to a close almost half a century of dynastic warfare between Bourbon France and the Hapsburg powers of Spain and the Holy Roman Empire. It was as part of this settlement that Mazarin had compelled Louis to marry Marie-Thérèse, a union which, before many years had passed, would provide Louis with a pretext for attacking the Spanish Netherlands. In 1661, however, France was almost as exhausted as the rest of Europe, and although little of the fighting had taken place on French soil, the King was aware that her borders were pitifully weak. On the eastern front, under the terms of the Peace of Westphalia, which ended the Thirty Years' War, the French had gained Alsace and the strongholds of Metz, Toul and Verdun, but Strasbourg remained a free city, and they had no title to the territory of Lorraine. To the north-east things were even worse. In 1636 a Spanish army had penetrated almost to the suburbs of Paris, and there had been other dangerous incursions during the *Frondes*. While invasion routes were severely constrained in the south and south-east by the Pyrenees and the Alps, there were no such natural barriers to the north-east. The Spanish Netherlands, an unwelcome reminder of Hapsburg encirclement, remained a likely springboard, but with the exception of Alsace, Louis' dream that the Rhine might one day become France's border had to be adjusted to political reality. It was not something that the rest of Europe was likely to allow.

Weak though France might have seemed at the close of the *Frondes*, it did not take Louis long to galvanise his countrymen and restore France to a fighting condition sufficient to exploit the power vacuum left at the close of the Thirty Years' War. Louis had a capable war minister in Michel Le Tellier, who began the process of reforming the army that was carried through by his talented but abrasive son, François Michel Le Tellier, Marquis de Louvois, who took over from him in 1666. At the start of Louis' reign, armies were still assembled in the feudal manner, but the King's experience during the *Frondes* had taught him that he could not always count on the loyalty of his noblemen. The latter saw leadership in combat as their calling but had no more appetite for peacetime square-bashing than their soldiers. All this would change. The most important reform was that by which the King took control of all appointments of officers of rank. Although he was unable to abolish the practice of purchasing commissions, he did establish a parallel ladder of promotion with the unpurchasable ranks of major and lieutenant colonel. In this, as in so many areas, Louis, the absolute monarch, was a surprising meritocrat, and the quality of leadership in his forces improved as a result.

Implementing Louis' policy, which was yet another means to curb his fractious nobles, did not make Louvois a popular man, nor did the subordination of army commanders to royal authority happen quickly or easily. Mme de Sévigné recounts an incident that took place in the gardens of Versailles, when Louvois sought to rebuke M. de Nogaret, an aristocratic courtier, for his derelictions. 'Sir, your company is in a very poor state,' barked the war minister. 'I did not know that,' replied Nogaret. 'Then, Sir, you should have known it,' snapped Louvois, getting crosser. 'Have you seen your company?' 'No, Sir'. 'Then you should have done so, Sir.' And then the closing put-down, which must have left Nogaret smarting: 'You must choose, Sir, either to be a mere courtier, or to perform your duties if you are going to be an officer.'

With control of the officer class established, the way to further reform was open. Conditions for the soldiery began to improve as rations were regulated and barracks constructed. The issue of respectable uniforms did much to raise morale; by 1680 all the royal regiments were kitted out in blue, with red for the Swiss Guards. Louvois established a network of *magazins*, or supply centres, which ensured that troops were kept supplied with food and equipment. But along with this concern for their welfare, the men were subject to tighter discipline; one of Louvois' inspectors of infantry, Jean Martinet, was so keen on drilling that his name entered the English language as a term for an over-strict disciplinarian.

Putting France on a war footing involved more than recruiting and training a large army. Civil and military engineers were put to work to provide the necessary infrastructure. This went beyond the more obvious military requirements like arsenals, garrisons and fortifications; it included new roads, canals, bridges and aqueducts, all of which served not only the needs of the generals but also those of a king determined to centralise his power and demarcate an enlarged France bounded by fortifications, whether natural or engineered.

Colbert approved of the orderliness Louis was imposing upon the land, for the new highways, inland waterways and harbours also improved the prospects for French commerce. Much attention was given to surveying and cartography during the Sun King's reign, these being the prerequisites for works of civil and military engineering. Although Britain would not get its first Ordnance Survey maps until 1790, Colbert saw the strategic importance of good topographical information as early as 1668, when, on the recommendation of the Abbé Picard, he invited the Italian astronomer and cartographer Gian Domenico Cassini to join the Académie des Sciences.

Part of Colbert's enthusiasm for surveying, beyond his natural taste for inventories and order, was connected to his ambition to build up the French fleet, for as well as being responsible for finance and for buildings, he was also minister for the navy. While Louis dreamt of expanding and consolidating France's land boundaries, Colbert, like Richelieu before him, saw a great future across the seas, setting up trading companies and persuading his King to spend money on building a navy. France had virtually no fighting fleet in 1660, and things might have remained that way since Louis showed little interest – he had not even stepped on to the deck of a ship until a visit to Dunkirk in 1680.

The little fleet that gradually appeared on the waters of the Grand Canal at Versailles was Colbert's way of getting his master to share his enthusiasms. In time there would be two gilded galliots, a brigantine, a felucca, nine shallops, two English yachts and a light frigate called the *Modèle* with fluttering pennants and bristling cannons, for when the Grand Canal was finished it had sufficient area to be used by Louis' naval architects for testing scaled-down prototypes of ships of the line. Some of the most beautiful vessels were built on site at Versailles: these included the *Grand Vaisseau*, designed by the Marquis de Langeron and launched by the King in August 1685. It carried thirteen bronze cannons and lanterns for giving orders to the rest of the fleet. The *Grande Galère*, launched in November of the same year, was hung with crimson brocade, while the *Dunkerquoise* was constructed by Flemish boat-builders. Other vessels were brought in and had to make part of the journey overland, such as the two gondolas that came as a gift from the Senate of Venice, complete with genuine gondoliers who lived in a waterside village called Little Venice, which was built around 1674 and functioned as a dockyard.

This pocket-sized fleet had a political significance that went beyond its dimensions. It was there to demonstrate to visitors that France was an up-and-coming maritime power. It was even considered important enough to have its own admiral, the Marquis de Langeron, under whom served 262 officers and men. When tourists take out boats and scull about as if on a municipal lake, or when the rowers from the local club slice the waters at Versailles in their swifter, more elegant craft, one has a faint sense of how Louis' colourful fleet must have animated the view and captivated spectators. In fact France was to have two fighting fleets, one comprised of sailing ships operating in the Atlantic and the other consisting of galleys ready for action in the Mediterranean. The sailing fleet would be crewed by professional seamen, while criminals and slaves would man the oars in the galleys alongside troublesome Protestants and other political undesirables.

In 1660 the French navy had just nine ships, but thanks to Colbert's efforts there were 112 by 1683. Figures supplied by British naval sources give some idea of the quantities of timber that must have been involved. It has been estimated that about thirty-five hundred full-grown oaks were needed to provide enough timber for a large ship of the line and that HMS *Victory*, Admiral Lord Nelson's flagship at the Battle of Trafalgar, launched in 1765, could have required five thousand oak trees from over 60 acres of forest. Louis' flagship, *Le Soleil Royal*, launched from Brest in 1669, was of comparable size, with 108 cannons bristling from three decks, and it was as beautiful as it was ferocious. Le Brun exerted his usual authority over the sculptural embellishments, bringing on board the same motifs that adorned the château and gardens of Versailles. The taffrail was embellished with a rendering of Apollo drawn across the sky by his familiar team of horses, while the figure-head took the form of a seahorse flanked by winged maidens.

To ensure that France would have sufficient supplies of timber for the construction of such vessels, Colbert sent his surveyors into the woods. His *Ordonnance des Eaux et Forêts* issued in 1669 brought forest management firmly under his control. Before Colbert intervened, French forestry had been regulated, after a fashion, but it had not been well organised. Habits of clear-felling with no thought to re-planting had failed to conserve the pines and slow-growing oaks most needed by shipbuilders. Colbert wanted to know not only the extent of the royal forests but also the magnitude of the available timber reserves, so maps were made and data collected concerning the age of trees, their species and their condition. In place of haphazard exploitation he wanted to see planned cycles of felling with provision made for regeneration. The system was administered by a corps of royal forest-ers – splendidly uniformed in blue velvet overcoats, gold vests and cocked hats – backed up by armed forest guards. Each of Colbert's *Grands Maîtres* had to send their chief an annual report stating the amount of wood sold in his jurisdiction and 'the sums … set aside for sowing and replanting empty areas, and clearing dead and stunted woods.'

When Colbert first turned his attention to France's forests, he found that the incumbent officers were far more crooked than the trees they were supposed to protect. The 'North' Wind' blew mercilessly through their ranks. The master of the Champagne forests was executed; others were heavily fined, dismissed or, in

Profile of a System of Earthworks. Illustration from
Les Travaux de Mars by Alain Manesson Mallet, 1684

some cases, exiled, while lesser officials were flogged or sent to the galleys. While the minister lived, his rigorous forest code was enforced, though it hurt the peasants who had been accustomed to gather acorns, chestnuts and firewood in the royal woods. In the bleak winters towards the end of Louis' reign, the officials turned a blind eye: whatever could be scraped together from the forest might mean the difference between life and death.

Accurate maps also helped Colbert with the collection of taxes and efficient recruitment for the army, but Louvois, as minister of war, had a more immediate need for surveyors. He ordered the construction of massive relief plans (mainly 1/600 scale) depicting all the major fortified sites in France. These huge, meticulously detailed models were regarded as top secret until as recently as 1952. It is puzzling that the first contour map was not drawn until 1782 – it was produced in France by Marcellin du Carla-Boniface – since the surveying expertise needed to produce these accurate but unwieldy models had been available a century earlier. That they were still judged to have military importance long after the development of the folding contour map says much for the power of three-dimensional representation. Le Nôtre knew nothing of contour plans, but a remark in a report addressed to Colbert from his son, the Marquis d'Ormoy, suggests that that there was an intermediate step between the production of a drawing and the work being executed on site. Discussing Le Nôtre's design for the feature known as Les Sources at Trianon, D'Ormoy remarked that 'the King approved Le Nôtre's drawing; from it one will make a model.'

Though apologists for Louis' militarism might point to the pressing need to establish precise borders and make France secure, it is clear that this was overtaken by an altogether more grandiose ambition. Rulers have often sought to boost their prestige through flattering associations with heroes of old. For Louis and his image-makers, it was not enough that the King should be identified with Apollo. In the court ballets that were performed during the 1660s, Louis also appeared as Alexander, as Cyrus, King of Persia, and as a chivalric hero called Roger. Writers of the day compared him with Charlemagne and Clovis, but he was also a new Solomon, a new Constantine and a new Justinian. The fourth-century Arch of Constantine in Rome provided the model for several triumphal arches in Paris, though their designers saw fit to bump up the dimensions, while many equestrian statues of Louis were based upon the representation of Marcus Aurelius that stands on the Capitoline Hill. In particular the King was likened to the Emperor Augustus, who restored peace to Rome after a hundred years of civil war and maintained a sound government under which the arts flourished. The writers

Virgil, Horace, Ovid and Livy all lived under Augustus' patronage, while his enthusiasm for building is shown by his well-known boast 'I found Rome a city of brick and left it a city of marble.' The inscription on a bust of the Sun King at the convent of Mathurins reads 'more august than Augustus'. There was nothing modest about these comparisons. Louis saw himself in the guise of a Roman emperor, and France, with whom he was so personally and inextricably identified, was to be the new Rome.

Louis wished to outstrip the glory of papal Rome as well. It was necessary that France should surpass Italy, not just in military might but in every area of cultural endeavour. Louis' self-confidence was demonstrated as early as 1662 by his reaction to a scrap between the Pope's Corsican Guards and the French ambassador's guards in Rome. The Most Christian King did not hesitate to demand an apology from the Holy Father; indeed he even forced the Pope to erect a pyramidal monument in Rome to mark the incident.

Another sign of France's ascendancy was the French court's less than hospitable treatment of the Italian architect and sculptor Bernini. Colbert prevailed upon the King to invite Bernini, who, after his reconstruction of Rome, was considered the world's greatest living architect, to prepare plans for the rebuilding of the Louvre, which at the time was an untidy assortment of buildings rather than an impressive palace. The Pope took a little persuading, but Bernini arrived in France in 1665 and swiftly fell out with most of the artists, architects and government ministers he encountered. In particular Charles Perrault started a whispering campaign against him. Louis, on the other hand, was initially delighted to have this great Roman architect at his court, such was the cultural power of the Italian Baroque which he represented. The architect, in turn, was impressed by the Sun King's ability to read his plans.

Bernini would become a casualty of France's growing self-confidence. He drew up plans for the Louvre after his return to Italy, but they were rejected by the *Petite Académie*. He prepared a second scheme, which the King is said to have liked, but Colbert, with others murmuring in his ear, brought up all manner of objections. It was the archetypal clash between the visionary architect and the practical man with an eye for detail. Bernini had suggested a large arcade, but surely this feature, ideal for Italy, would not be suitable for a cold northern climate? Where exactly were the servants to sleep, and how would food be delivered from the kitchens? Whether or not these were just criticisms, Bernini did not get the commission, which went instead to Claude Perrault, assisted by Le Vau and Le Brun. The long, stately colonnade that was actually built marked a complete break with the voluptuous curves of the Italian Baroque. It was a decisive moment, for in producing this simple, sober alternative, Perrault returned to ancient precedents. France had not only found a new style; in doing so she had wrestled custodianship of the Classical tradition away from Italy.

Bernini's trip to France had not been a complete waste of time, however. The marble bust of the Sun King that he carved during his visit is the best contemporary effigy of Louis. Louis must have been pleased with this work, because he also commissioned an equestrian sculpture, which Bernini was to complete at his leisure once he had returned to Rome. The convoluted and controversial story of this piece is further proof of French artistic autonomy and also reveals much about the way aesthetic decisions were made at court.

Bernini did not rush to complete this commission. It was carved between 1671 and 1677 by students working at the French Academy in Rome. The master supervised their work and personally carved the head. When Le Nôtre went to Rome in 1679, Colbert asked him to inspect the sculpture and give his opinion, at the same time writing to Charles Errard, the Director of the French Academy, asking him to make arrangement for its transportation. We can only assume that Le Nôtre's report was favourable, though when Bernini died in 1680 the piece had not left Rome. Colbert must have had some misgivings, because in 1682 he wrote to the Duc d'Estrées in Rome, mentioning diverse reports he had received concerning Bernini's work and asking the Duke to gather together some experts to see if it was suitable to bring before the King.

Colbert died in 1683, but his successor, Louvois, also dawdled over the issue. The statue was eventually shipped late in 1684, arriving at Le Havre in February of the following year, where its appearance was marked by the discharge of cannon and muskets and the detonation of bombs and shells. It was then placed on a small Dutch vessel to make its way by river via Rouen to Paris. It had been intended for a public site opposite the Tuileries, but a week later it was hastily repackaged and sent on to Versailles.

Louvois was responsible for the initial judgement, since Louis was not in Paris at that time. The minister concluded that 'The equestrian figure of the King by the Cavalier Bernini is so ugly that there is no likelihood when the king shall have seen it that he will let it be as it is.' When the work reached Versailles it was set up in the Orangerie for Louis to inspect. The Marquis de Dangeau describes this encounter in his journal entry for 14 November, 1685. The King 'walked in the Orangerie, which he found to be of an admirable magnificence; he saw the equestrian statue by the Cavalier Bernini . . . and found that the man and the horse were made so badly that he resolved not only to have it removed from there, but also to have it broken into pieces.' The King, who prided himself on his horsemanship, disliked the rearing pose, and the awkward way in which he was shown in the saddle, while cascades of hair and tumultuous folds of drapery added to a generally wild appearance inconsonant with royal dignity. Yet once he had got over his initial shock, he recognised that the sculpture had some aesthetic merits and granted it a reprieve. It was placed within the parterre of the Orangerie, though later relocated on the northern side of the Neptune Basin.

The principal problem with the sculpture was that it was unacceptable as a royal portrait. The waggish suggestion that it would be satisfactory if it had a different head provided an aesthetic solution. Someone at Versailles, perhaps François Girardon, saw how the sculpture could be converted into an image of Marcus Curtius, a mythological Roman hero. This was duly done. In 1702 the modified statue was moved again, this time to the far end of Le Nôtre's Pièce des Suisses. This has often been presented as a banishment, as if Louis thought so badly of the statue that he wanted it put out of sight, but the head of Le Nôtre's lake is not such an ignoble place, though most visitors, only seeing it from a distance, will not know whether they are looking at a high-born Roman or the King of France.

One respect in which the age of Augustus can be safely compared with seventeenth-century France is that both were periods in which the arts flourished. The seventeenth century will always be regarded as *Le Grand Siècle*, a golden age, even if it presaged the decline of the monarchy and the turmoil of the Revolution. Against Virgil, Horace, Ovid and Livy can be set Racine, La Fontaine, Corneille and Molière. Conventional wisdom suggests that great art is unlikely to be produced under state control, and it is true that the *Petite Académie* achieved a certain bureaucratisation of taste. While control of the performing arts was less strict than that exercised over the visual arts, most of what was created reflected the outlook of the uppermost levels of French society, which took the existence of the monarchy, the dominance of the Church and the social order for granted. Le Nôtre's well-ordered gardens are the perfect metaphor for a Classically disciplined literature, which may today seem mannered and artificial. In drama, for example, playwrights adhered to the Classical unities of time, place and action, which meant that plots were often laboriously contrived and characters were given to long speeches describing events which had taken place before the time-frame of the action.

There were certainly no revolutionaries in literary circles. Jean-Baptiste Poquelin, better known as Molière, may have been a satirist who poked fun at the aristocracy, but he was an entertainer rather than a radical, and specialised in social, rather than political, lampoons. Like Le Nôtre, he had grown up in close proximity to the court – his father had been one of eight *valets de chambre tapissiers* who looked after the King's furniture and upholstery – and this had given him a sharp eye for the blemishes of upper-class society. Molière set his plays in or around Paris and ridiculed the types he found there: social climbers, posers, libertines, misers and hypochondriacs.

Though Molière could be the scourge of society, mercilessly exposing its hypocrisies and petty foibles, he did not advocate any great changes in the existing order, though on occasion he could fall foul of the religious authorities. After his admonitory tale about false holy fervour, *Tartuffe*, was premièred during the fêtes held at Versailles in 1664, some thought it an attack, not just on hypocrisy but on the Church. Louis, who had read the script prior to production, greatly enjoyed the show but had to ban its performance in Paris to allow the storm to subside.

Under Louis, Versailles rivalled Bernini's Rome as a magnet for cultural tourism. It was fashionable to be French, to the extent that many of the Italians who were attracted to the French court changed their names. These included, as we have seen, Louis' court composer, Lully; the heirs of Tommaso Francini, fountaineer to Henri IV, who were known as Francine; and Tuby, sculptor of the Apollo Fountain.

In rather the same way that British culture would spread around the world in the heyday of the Empire, or the manner in which American culture has swept the world in our own times, French tastes under Louis were hugely influential abroad. When he took the throne, the stylish élite would have been purchasing their fabrics from England or Holland. By time he moved his court permanently to Versailles, aristocrats from the rest of Europe felt obliged to make pilgrimages to the seat of the Sun King and mingle with the modish set there, for this was where trends were being set.

In contrast to the austere fashions of the sixteenth century – the dark, tailored tunics of the Hapsburg court, the Puritan simplicity of Dutch costumes and the stiff 'whisk' collars of Elizabethan England – men at the French court draped themselves in floral patterns, in ravishing coats of wool, silk or pastel satin trimmed with exquisite ribbons and intricate lace collars. Women had abandoned the cumbersome farthingales and bum rolls in favour of a softer, more flowing look, with layers of floating silk. Having forsaken doublet and hose in favour of coat, vest and breeches, seventeenth-century men followed Louis himself in the showy elaboration of their costumes with fancy ruffles and ribbons and preposterous 'petticoat breeches'. When Louis' towering coiffure began to be undermined by baldness, he set a new fashion for lofty powdered wigs. It is difficult to look at pictures of the Sun King and his nobles and to imagine them as tough fighting men, but in the symbolic language of the era, garlands of flowers were associated with military victory.

The ascendancy of French fabrics and fashions owed much to the activities of Colbert, whose family had made their money in textiles. Always keen to improve France's trading position, he knew the significance of cloth as an item of international commerce. Colbert established factories throughout France, extending his influence and control over the regions as he did so. The two most famous workshops were the Gobelins and the Savonnerie, both in Paris. The Gobelins took its name from the brothers, Jean and Philibert, who had invented a special scarlet dye in the fifteenth century. In 1662 Colbert took over their premises, and they became the Manufacture Royale des Meubles de la Couronne. Although the Gobelins made items as diverse as fireplaces, silverware and doors, its reputation rests on the output of the 250 or so Flemish weavers installed there by Colbert, under the direction of Le Brun, to produce tapestries for the royal châteaux. In theory the Gobelins would fabricate items for anyone who could pay, but in practice nearly all of its work was for the King or his court. The Savonnerie, so named because it was located in a former soapworks, was famous for its elaborately patterned carpets.

The patterns of the parterres which Le Nôtre laid out in his gardens, developing the traditions of earlier generations of French gardeners, have much in common with the designs found in the borders of Gobelins tapestries and the figures that swirl across carpets from the Savonnerie, as well as the motifs with which courtly costumes were decorated. A visual language of arabesques, tendrils, scrolls, vines and foliage swags is held in common. The garden writer Dezallier d'Argenville tells us that parterres can be made in various ways. They can be made up in compartments containing grass-work scrolls combined with knots of shrubs and borders of flowers, with narrow paths surfaced with tile-shards or brick-dust between them; they can be cut into beds for flowers, edged with box; they can be laid out in the English manner – the plainest and meanest of all – with a large grass plot 'cut but little' with a simple border of flowers; they can even be made out of water. He saves his greatest praise for the *parterre de broderie*, far more intricate – and more French – than all of the others.

It is arguable that the parterre evolved from the knot gardens found in mediaeval cloisters and Italian Renaissance gardens. Both the Italian and French traditions were influenced by the designs found on the Oriental carpets that were imported into Europe in significant quantities during the sixteenth century.

Plan of the Bosquet de l'Étoile showing its pentagon shape, c. 1685-86.

Although the term *parterre de broderie* suggests that such features were developed in conscious imitation of designs on fabric, some recent writers have questioned this, suggesting that those ladies at Versailles who liked to pass their time in embroidery only had to look out their windows to find suitable patterns. It is likely that the influence passed in both directions, that the inventions of the gardeners were taken up by those who worked with needle and thread, just as the gardeners might view the clothes of their noble clientele as animated pattern-books or find woven inspiration hanging on a wall or spread along the floor of a gallery.

The development of Louis' gardens slowed down at times of war and accelerated during the short periods of peace. But there were direct and specific references to warfare at Versailles. Le Nôtre's Salle des Festins, one of the *bosquets* featured in a series of paintings by Jean Cotelle, clearly resembles the footprint of an old castle, the sort that had round corner towers and a moat crossed by drawbridges. It was not just children who used the Salle de Festins as a giant play-fort. Nobles who walked their dogs there and ladies who strolled arm in arm might also imagine themselves defending the realm, just as the spectators at Louis' firework displays might see themselves at the siege of some great border fortress but without the fear of taking a musket shot. A smug optimism prevailed at Versailles for most of Louis' reign. France's dominant position in Europe meant that Versailles was protected, so there were no real defences around the château, only symbolic ones, a condition the Revolutionaries were able to exploit in 1789. Indeed the extent to which Louis lived his life in public view and the lack of security around him seem astonishing in our age of international terrorism. Rather than laying down arms when entering the palace, courtiers were expected to carry swords as marks of their rank.

Military geometry was also evident in the layout of the Étoile, one of the *bosquets* Le Nôtre created to the north of the central axis. Though it was called the Star, in plan it was a pentagon, one of the most common shapes employed in the construction of fortresses. In 1941, when it was decided to rehouse the scattered offices of America's War Department in a single building, it took Brigadier-General Brehon B. Somervell and his principal architect, George Bergstrom, less than five days to come up with the site plan for the Pentagon in Arlington, Virginia, the largest office building in the world. Whatever conscious or subconscious influences were at work, these military planners hit upon an efficient shape, for although there are 17½ miles of corridors, staff can reach any point within the building by a walk of not more than six minutes.

Seventeenth-century military engineers like Vauban would probably have suggested the same solution. Le Nôtre understood the efficiency and symbolism of the pentagon, but to make the Étoile more interesting, he playfully placed the figure within a circular path, itself connected to the broader grid of *allées* by diagonal passages at the corners. As the whole figure was surrounded by trees and the paths were bordered with lattice-work covered in honeysuckle, the Étoile had some of the characteristics of a maze. Before one could find the satisfyingly direct path that led to the centre, it was necessary to negotiate some twists, turns and changes of direction. In 1671 the fountain known as the Montagne d'Eau was added to the centre, as a suitable reward for those who made their way there.

The artworks with which the gardens were liberally decorated were replete with military connotation. Though children play, cherubs make music in marble and bronze, and nymphs ply goddesses with bunches of grapes, there are far grislier scenes, like the groups depicting combat between animals that decorate two *cabinets* off the main water parterre. One lion has killed a wild boar, and another is mauling a wolf, while a tiger has prevailed over a bear, and a drooling bloodhound has brought down a stag. Elsewhere the statues are an assorted lot. Mixed with contemplative philosophers, dreamy semi-naked goddesses, and personifications of the seasons, the elements and the hours of the day are dying gladiators, warlike gods and busts of military commanders: Alexander, Hannibal, Octavius, Marcus Aurelius and Septimus Severus. The statues line the *allées* and principal spaces like soldiers on guard, and topiary bushes are often pressed into similar service.

Physical strength, courage and raw power are admired at Versailles, and war is seen as the vehicle that can carry a great leader to glory, but the militaristic aspects of the gardens are softened by artworks which depict the pleasures of peacetime. The two great vases that stand on the terrace reveal these two facets of Louis' reign. They correspond to two rooms within the château at the extremities of the Hall of Mirrors; the War Room, painted by Le Brun to depict the great military exploits of Louis' reign up to the Peace of Nymegen, and the Peace Room, also decorated by the *Premier Peintre*, but this time to illustrate the benefits that flow from the successful completion of hostilities. Similarly the *Vase de la Guerre* by Antoine Coysevox carries bas-reliefs which show France, on one face clad for battle, accompanied by Hercules and carrying an Austrian eagle upon her shield, laying into an army of turbaned Turks (a reference to the [limited] role that French troops played in the defence of Vienna in 1664), and, on the other face, receiving a submissive Castilian lion, an allusion to Spain's apology after a quarrel over ambassadorial precedence in London in 1662. The *Vase de la Paix* by Tuby shows Louis dressed as a Roman emperor, sitting on a dais, attended by Hercules and

Louis XIV Visiting the Reservoirs of Montbauron by Jean-Baptiste Martin, 1688.

View of the Bosquet de l'Arc de Triomphe by Jean Cotelle, 1693.

receiving the benefits of tranquillity – a cornucopia, an olive branch and a redundant lance – from a procession of womanly incarnations of Peace.

Just as the decoration of whole rooms in the château would be dedicated to Louis' victories, so too would some of the outdoor *salles* and *bosquets*, the most striking of which would be the glade containing the Arc de Triomphe, created in 1677 at the summit of the Sun King's reign. Although designed to be in scale with its garden setting and thus much smaller than its Parisian namesake commissioned by Napoleon, it was similarly inspired by Roman precedents.

Glorious though Louis' gardens might have become under Le Nôtre's guidance, the Sun King would not be content until there were also fountains, and hundreds of them. Louis enjoyed the sight and sound of splashing water for their own sake, but he also saw fountains as symbols of France's superiority in engineering. In this regard they were as essential to his visions of glory as his military campaigns, his building projects and the artistic embellishments of his houses and gardens. When offered the choice between an ingenious underground siphon and a massive aqueduct on the Roman model, it was inevitable that Louis should choose the latter. How could an invisible conduit compare with a towering feat of engineering? This was a choice that would bring privation, sickness and death in its train.

Louis XIV and the Dauphin in Front of the Grotte de Thétis. French school, c. 1673.

VIII

Divertissements

I N 1664, ONLY THREE YEARS after the momentous fête at Vaux and with Fouquet's lengthy trial finally drawing to a close, Louis decided that it was time for a demonstration of his authority. He too would throw a party, inviting six hundred members of the French élite, but his fête would outshine the spectacle delivered by his erstwhile finance minister. It would drive home the message that only the King, the personification of the state, was in a position to mount such a sumptuous extravaganza.

Louis himself chose the theme for *The Pleasures of the Enchanted Isle*. The general narrative was based on Ariosto's *Orlando Furioso*, or *Roland Furieux*, which tells the story of the mythical hero Roger and his band of knights, held captive on an island by the sorceress Alcina (Handel would one day write an opera on the same theme). The prisoners were enslaved by the hedonistic lifestyle which the enchantress was able to give them through her magical powers, until Roger, realising where his duties lay and summoning up his military virtues, broke free of the spell, but not before he and his knights – and therefore the guests at Louis' fête – had enjoyed themselves thoroughly. Louis must have smiled inwardly when he selected this theme, for did he not intend to do to his nobles exactly what Alcina had done to Roger and his companions? This was the first great social occasion at Versailles, setting the pattern for the reign, and although Louis' courtiers grumbled initially about having to leave Paris and sleep on straw in stables because there was so little accommodation in the château or at the local inns, they were nevertheless flattered to receive invitations and came willingly, though unwittingly; they had no idea that the King intended to ensnare them in a labyrinth of pleasure.

Although the festivities were officially dedicated to the Queen and the Queen Mother, it was undoubtedly the King's mistress, Louise de la Vallière, who provided the ulterior motivation. Happily for Louis, his chosen theme allowed him to dress up as a hero, displaying his equestrian skills, his manly virtues and his virility. Mounted on a charger and dressed in the costume of a warrior from Antiquity, his silver breastplate encrusted with jewels, he led a procession of knights into the ring that had been laid out in the place where the Fountain of Latona now stands. Louis had inveigled a host of dukes and counts into playing the other members of his troop, for, just as he had at the earlier *Carrousel*, he would get the mightiest in the land to follow his script. A mediaeval tournament followed, and it was perhaps no surprise to anyone (since the King was judging) that it was won by the Marquis de la Vallière, Louise's brother, who was awarded a golden sword studded with diamonds as his prize.

A collation followed, preceded by another extraordinary procession through the gardens. It was headed by Mlle du Parc, one of Molière's company, representing Spring and mounted on a lively Spanish horse, surrounded by gardeners carrying preserves. She was followed by Sieur du Parc, symbolising Summer, riding on an elephant supplied by the Ménagerie and leading a group of harvesters. Then came Sieur de la Thorillière as Autumn, mounted on a dromedary and accompanied by grape-pickers. Finally Winter, personified by Sieur Béjard astride a bear, made its contribution to the feast in the form of ice, carried in bowls by a company of old men. The meal itself resembled a ballet, since it was set to music by Lully, while the costumed servants performed their tasks rhythmically, as they had been schooled by the Comte de Saint-Aignan, *Premier Gentilhomme de la Chambre*, who had choreographed the entire proceedings. Two hundred masked servants carried white wax torches to illuminate the tables where the court feasted.

The fête began at six o'clock on the evening of 7 May and lasted for a whole week, with the Roger story played out by the end of the third day. The rooms within the château being generally too small for such a large gathering, the main events took place in the gardens, where temporary structures had been erected at various points along the principal axis. For the second evening's entertainment a proscenium arch was constructed a little further away from the château, framing a vista of the garden. This temporary theatre was hung around with tapestries to prevent the wind from blowing out the hundreds of candles that lit the scene. Here Molière's troupe staged a play-within-the-play, a new comedy-ballet called

La Princesse d'Elide, which included a number of pastoral interludes that mirrored the setting surrounding the audience. Just as Le Nôtre's gardens mixed heroic grandeur with the simple charms of nature, so Molière's prancing satyrs and bucolic dancers played sophisticated games that mixed simplicity and artifice. The plot revolved around a princess who was apparently immune to love but who was eventually won over by a young man who feigned indifference in order to entice her. At the outset Princess Elide was presented as a spirited beauty who loved hunting more than she sought love, and it cannot have been an accident that Louise de la Vallière was dedicated to the chase. Indeed the whole play might be seen to justify Louis' passion for her. Louise's hold on him was at its greatest; two years later, upon the death of Anne of Austria, he would be prepared to recognise her as his 'declared mistress', although for Louise this would not be a triumph that would last for long.

The third evening saw the action transferred to a stage erected on the rim of the pool at the farthest extremity of the garden, where Carlo Vigarani had created the enchantress's castle to which a barge disguised as a marine monster bore Alcina. When Roger (no longer played by the King, who had rejoined the audience) routed the sorcerer's army of dwarfs, demons and giants, the whole edifice was blown up by spectacular fireworks. One of the more unusual entries in the royal building accounts is a payment to a clothes-seller for 'fourteen demon costumes for the artificers who lit the fireworks at the Fête at Versailles'.

As on Alcina's island, so at Versailles, the entertainments flowed on as if by magic, though in reality a small army of performers and servants was required to create this effortless effect. In the darker days that lay ahead, courtiers would look back on the fêtes as times of abundance, though they were in reality a closed world that shut out the realities of life for the majority of the French people.

On the fourth day there was a jousting competition in the dry moat of the Petit Château, another opportunity for Louis to show off his equestrian prowess. The fifth day saw an excursion to view the exotic birds housed at the Ménagerie, followed by a performance of Molière's *Les Fâcheurs*, which had been the highlight of Fouquet's party. On the sixth day, after a frivolous lottery for the ladies, there came the première of Molière's *Tartuffe*, a darker play that castigated aristocratic hypocrisy. On the seventh day, yet another of Molière's works, *Le Mariage forcé*, was performed in the vestibule of the château. On the eighth day the court left for Fontainebleau.

The crowd that departed from Versailles at the end of this extraordinary week, their heads reeling from the bombardment of music, pomp, luxury, spectacle and

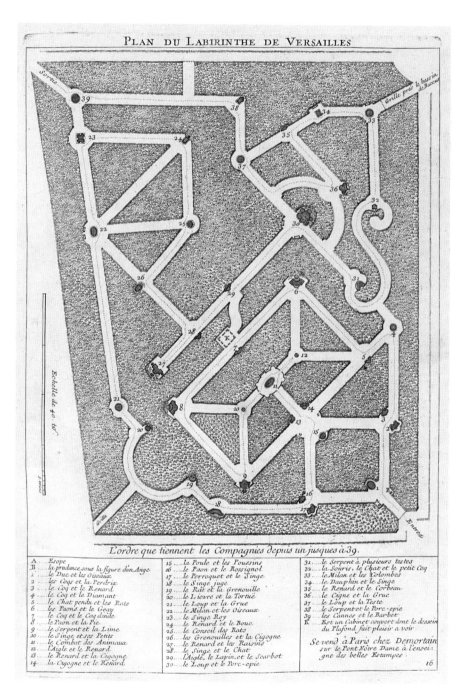

Plan of the Bosquet du Labyrinth, c. 1714.

entertainment, must have wondered if they would ever see anything like it again. As events turned out, they would not have to wait long, because the next great fête would be staged in the gardens in 1668. In the meantime, *Les Plaisirs* was only a punctuation mark in the development of the park, and work resumed immediately. On the central axis, the Fer à Cheval, with its impressive staircase, was fashioned, below which the Nouveau Parterre, or Jardin Bas, was laid out. Construction of two of the most famous features of the seventeenth-century gardens also started about this time. One was the Labyrinthe, cut into woodland to the south of the main axis according to a design by Le Nôtre; the other was the fabulous Grotte de Thétis, conceived by Charles Perrault and erected on the northern side of the château by his architect brother, Claude. Sadly neither of these features has survived. The Grotto had to be demolished to make way for the North Wing of the château, while the Labyrinthe, pride of the Sun King and his gardeners, was replaced in the early years of Louis XVI's reign by the far less interesting Bosquet de la Reine, which still exists today.

Labyrinths were extremely popular features in gardens of the Middle Ages and the early Renaissance. Though they often symbolised a religious or romantic quest, they were just plain fun, and it is entirely consistent with Louis' attitude towards his pleasure-park that he should seek to build one so soon. The Labyrinthe can be found on plans dating from around 1665 though work may not have begun until the following year. Like so many of the important features at Versailles, it was a team effort; in fact Louis had Fouquet to thank for first bringing the members of this *équipe* together. Le Nôtre, of course, was responsible for the ground plan and the horticultural aspects, but the two literary figures associated with its content, Charles Perrault and La Fontaine, regularly attended the salon at Vaux, as did Le Brun, who oversaw the twenty sculptors who worked on the decoration of the maze.

In 1668 La Fontaine published his first volume of verses based upon Aesop's fables. They were a popular success, and further volumes followed in 1678, 1685 and 1693. Although La Fontaine was in disgrace, having spoken up in defence of Fouquet, his poems seem to have provided the theme around which the sculptures and fountains of the Labyrinthe were designed. The idea of siting fountains representing stories from Aesop in this way probably came from Perrault, whose *Contes de ma mère l'oye*, or *Tales of Mother Goose*, of 1697 retells half-forgotten folk stories like 'Puss in Boots' and 'The Sleeping Beauty'. The King was so proud of his Labyrinthe that he commissioned Perrault to write a guidebook, which was published by the Imprimerie Royal in 1677 and 1679. Bound in red morocco and embossed with the royal monogram, copies were kept in the royal library and

The Entrance to the Labyrinthe, showing the statues of Aesop and Cupid, by Jean Cotelle, commissioned in 1688.

given away to important guests. Perrault also wrote the following description of the Labyrinthe in 1675:

> It is a square, young wood, very thick and luxuriant, cut into a great number of paths, intermingled with such artifice that nothing is so easy nor so pleasant than to lose one's way. At the end of a part, and wherever they cross, there are fountains, so arranged that wherever one finds oneself, one always sees three or four and often six or seven of them at once.

In total there were thirty-nine fountains in the area covered by the Labyrinthe, incorporating over three hundred animal sculptures, at least a hundred of which spouted water. The animals were sculpted in lead, painted in realistic colours and grouped around rockwork basins beneath lattice-work canopies. Working out the sculptural programme, producing the sculptures, creating their settings and plumbing them in was a lengthy undertaking, and the Labyrinthe did not reach its completed form until 1673/4. The water was not just incidental; it was used in an expressive way to animate the animal characters. In Perrault's words:

> These animals are so well made and lifelike that they seem yet to be in the action that they depict, one could even say that in some way they speak the words that the fables attribute to them, since the water they spout forth at one another seems not only to give them life and action, but serves them also as a voice to express their passions and their thoughts.

At the entrance to the Labyrinthe there were two sculptures, one of an aged and ugly Aesop, the other of a beautiful and youthful Cupid. Perrault imagined a chance meeting between Apollo and Cupid in the grounds of Versailles, with the youthful god addressing his senior as follows:

> I'll leave you all the glory and permit you to direct everything, so long as you grant me the arrangement of the Labyrinthe, which I love passionately, and which entirely suits me. For you know that I myself am a labyrinth, where one easily gets lost. My idea would be to create a number of fountains there and to adorn them with the most ingenious fables of Aesop, in which I would conceal lessons and maxims for the guidance of lovers.

While order and geometry might rule the Parc, this passage suggests that the Labyrinthe was constructed according to the very different logic of love. It was a place

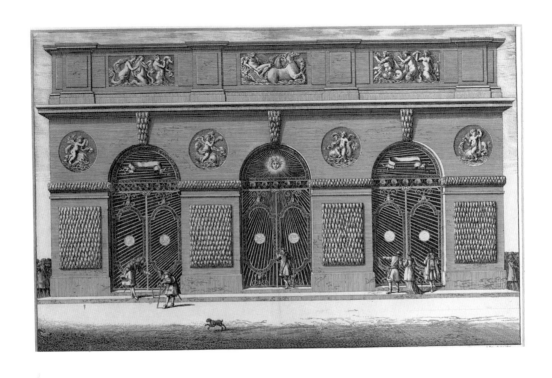

Exterior of the Grotte de Thétis by Jean Le Pautre, 1672.

where mortals might get lost, though the statue of Cupid at the entrance helpfully proffered a ball of string. The layout of the Labyrinthe was unusual since it had no central goal and allowed glimpses ahead, but it was clearly intended as a place for moral education, where men and women could wander in search of hidden truths. In particular, the lessons to be learnt between Le Nôtre's 15-foot hedges were intended for the young Dauphin.

One of the sculptural groups illustrated the fable of the horned owl and the birds. The poor owl is set upon by the other birds because of his dismal plumage and harsh song and henceforth dares only show himself at night. The moral, according to Perrault, was that any prudent man who wished to pass unscathed through love's labyrinth had to be gentle in his language and pleasing in his manners and dress. In the fable of the peacocks and the jay, a misguided jay dresses himself one day with discarded feathers gathered from several peacocks. Thus disguised, he thinks he will be accepted by them, but they turn on him mockingly, pecking him horribly. The moral is one that would have appealed to the courtiers at Versailles – that it is no use trying to feign a gallant manner if one is not born to it.

Innocuous as the Labyrinthe's sculptures might seem at first, this grove of love was not free from the sort of political messages that were starting to be stamped all over the rest of the Parc. Many of the fables featured life-and-death struggles similar to the scenes of animal combats featured in the *cabinets* off the water parterre. Some carried messages about the ordering of society and the role of the King. In 'The Frogs and Jupiter' the frog nation asks Jupiter to send them a king, and he sends them King Log, who lands with a splash but then does nothing. The frogs complain that they would like a more active monarch, so Jupiter, annoyed, sends them King Crane, who eats them for breakfast, lunch and dinner. The moral is that subjects should accept the king they have got, for another might be much worse.

Grottoes, no less than labyrinths, were features of Renaissance gardens that harked back to Antiquity. Like the labyrinth, the grotto, as an amalgam of the natural cave and the Roman bath, occupied that tantalising zone where nature mingled with the artificial. First in Italy, then in France, grottoes were created as fabulous and exotic retreats, encrusted with precious stones, mirrors and mosaics, where life-affirming fountains would play in an atmosphere that mixed sacred memory with pure whimsy. Construction of the Grotte de Thétis, which depicted the descent of Apollo into the sea at the end of his daily ride across the heavens, began in 1665, while Louis was still firmly under the spell of Louise de la Vallière, but

*The Marquise de Montespan Surrounded by Her
Legitimate Children, attributed to Charles de La Fosse, c. 1677.*

Charles Perrault claimed credit for the concept and the detailed design was certainly done by his brother, Claude. Deliberately sited close to the King's bedroom so that no one could miss the association, the Grotte presented a simple one-storey façade to the Parterre du Nord. Although Le Brun exercised his usual control over the sculptural components, Claude Perrault's responsibility for much of the ornamentation was made clear by Charles: 'My brother also made designs for all the other ornaments of this grotto, figures, rock-work, paving, etcetera.' Claude also 'designed the gate, which was very beautiful: it was a golden Sun that spread its rays, also of gold, over the extent of the three gates, which were of iron bars painted green. It appeared as though the Sun was in the Grotto and that one saw it through the bars of the gate'.

Inside there were three niches embedded with pebbles and seashells, a form of encrustation known as *rocaillage*. The *rocailleur* in this instance was Jean de Launay, who took two years to finish the work. A sculpture by Girardon and Regnaudin occupied the central niche; it showed Apollo resting after his day's work attended by the sea goddess Thetis and her nymphs, while to either side his horses, their fires almost exhausted, were groomed by Tritons. There was also a novelty called the water organ, which reproduced the twittering of birds, though their presence in a realm more suited to fish is difficult to explain. Mlle de Scudéry reported that 'one might well fancy oneself in the middle of a grove, where a thousand birds answer one another, and this natural music, joined with the murmur of water, produces an almost indescribable effect'.

Like many of the other significant features at Versailles, the Grotto was years in the making. By the time it was completed in 1666, Louise de la Vallière had lost her place in the King's affections. It took Denis Jolly three years to move and install the water organ, which was bought from Sieur Desnots at Montmorency, 8 miles north of Paris.

When the Grotto was demolished, the evicted Sun God, Sun Horses and their attendants began their nomadic wanderings around the park. They were lodged in the former Bosquet de la Renommée for twenty years, its name changing to the Bains d'Apollon for the duration. In 1704 some of them were moved to a site at the end of the Bosquet du Marais, but all were happily reunited during the reign of Louis XV in a romantically rocky grove designed by the artist Hubert Robert.

In 1686 Louis' mother, Anne of Austria, died after a long struggle with cancer. Even a Sun King, granted the divine right to rule by God, has to pay some attention to his mother. But with her passing, he felt a new expansiveness, an awareness of the possibilities that were now open to him. His love life had also taken an interesting turn.

Françoise Athénaïs de Mortemart had first come to court in 1660, the year of Louis' marriage, and though she married the Marquis de Montespan three years later, it seems that she had always had her sights set on the King. It must have galled her that he had taken up with Louise de la Vallière instead, but Athénaïs was not a woman to be easily deflected. She made friends with Louise, using her to get closer to the King. (There was a pattern to Louis' most important affairs – each mistress was a friend of the last.) Mme de Montespan also enlisted the help of a fortune-teller called Mme Voisin who dabbled in the black arts, and even of a priest who was willing to risk his soul by assisting the two women in arcane rituals. Something must have worked. On 2 December 1666 both La Vallière and Montespan danced with the King in a production of Lully's *Ballet des Muses* at Saint-Germain, but when the King went off to besiege Lille in 1667, he took Athénaïs de Montespan with him as lady-in-waiting to the Queen. La Vallière followed the royal party, desperately hoping to be taken along, but the King was in no mood to have his hand forced and sent her away. Soon, heartbroken, she would be begging to join a nunnery, a wish that would eventually be granted in 1674.

Louis once told the Princess Palatine that he liked clever, amusing people. Athénaïs was known as much for her conversation and her wit, which could be malicious, as for her sensuous beauty. High-born, highly spirited and thoroughly cultivated, she was also voluptuous, though her full figure would eventually run to fat. At this point in her life, even without the services of Mme Voisin, she was considered a bewitching woman. Louise de la Vallière was no match for her. When she became the royal mistress, Athénaïs would exercise a significant degree of patronage, and her tastes would be less constricted than those of the King, for whom Classical precedents always tended to stiffen into severity. Some of the most playful features in the gardens at Versailles were created during the decade in which Athénaïs held sway.

Louis' marriage to Marie-Thérèse, empty shell though it might have been, gave him the pretext for an attack on the Spanish Low Countries following the death of Philip IV of Spain in 1665. Louis advanced an imaginative but spurious argument that evoked an old Flemish law to establish his wife's claim to Spanish territory. When this claim was rejected by the Spanish Queen Regent, he dispatched an invasion force of twenty thousand troops under the command of Turenne, which, with the help of Vauban, successfully laid siege to the towns of Douai, Charleroi, Oudenarde and Lille. Louis, in the flush of his new love affair, was a fiery leader, personally leading the attack on Tournai and joining the assault at Douai on a white charger, with a showy white plume in his hat. Meanwhile another force, under Condé, captured Franche-Comté, a campaign fought in the middle of winter. By the spring of 1668, Louis was in a commanding position and willing to negotiate a favourable peace. By the terms of the Peace of Aix-la-Chapelle, signed in May of that year, France magnanimously restored Franche-Comté to Spain but kept most of her conquests in the Spanish Netherlands. It had been a relatively quick and easy war which had given Louis his first taste of blood and of territorial aggrandisement. Naturally he planned a celebration at Versailles.

Louis must have been dreaming of the show he would put on while the treaty negotiations were still under way, because from the first week in June his staff began to transform the park for *Le Grand Divertissement Royal de Versailles*. They had only six weeks to get the place ready. The Duc de Créqui, *Premier Gentilhomme de la Chambre*, was placed in charge of the comedy and the Maréchal de Bellfond was given responsibility for the catering, while Colbert, Le Vau and the designer Henri de Gissey put their minds to the buildings and the decorations, and Vigarini, the king of theatrical wizardry, devised his machines.

The fêtes that punctuate Louis' reign can be thought of in many ways; they were celebrations of success, massive propaganda exercises, events which marked shifts in his self-perception and one of the means by which the nobility could be kept dazzled and subdued. From an entirely practical point of view, they were also very useful for imposing deadlines. If the King intended to hold a party, everyone was obliged to work exceptionally hard to get the château and park ready. The fêtes were also laboratories in which new aesthetic ideas could be tried out. At Versailles, their architecture and decoration did not slavishly follow those of the château; it was often just the opposite way round, with the design vocabulary explored in canvas and cardboard later made permanent in bronze or marble. These extravaganzas were staged not just for the court but for the whole nation and for those beyond France's borders who needed to be impressed. It was no accident that the writer Félibien was usually at hand to create a detailed account, preserving a transient event for posterity but also ensuring that the reputation of Versailles would spread throughout Europe. Naturally these essays in propaganda seldom mentioned the labours of Le Nôtre or the sweat of the under-gardeners, nurserymen, labourers, masons, fountaineers, carpenters and artists who made such displays possible. The spectacles were described as if they flowed directly from the King's command, conjured by his majesty.

For the *Divertissement*, the mediaeval trappings of *Les Plaisirs* were abandoned and even the mythological theme was toned down, since Louis had now won a

145

The fête given by Louis XIV at Versailles in 1668. Engraving by Jean Le Pautre.

war and was starting to think of himself as the equal of the ancients. Whereas the festivities of 1664 had lasted for a week but had been confined to the Nobles of the Sword, the *Divertissement* concentrated its delights into a single evening but was open to wider participation. Félibien tells us that the King instructed the Marquis de Gesvres, captain of the Swiss Guards, to open the gates so that no one would be excluded. This was to be a celebration that the whole of France would remember.

The *Divertissement* began at six o'clock on Wednesday, 18 July 1668, with a tour of the gardens. The King and his entourage descended via the parterre to the north of the château to inspect the newly installed Dragon Fountain. This work, created by the Marsy brothers after an idea by Le Brun, represents the legendary Python, a huge snake that terrorised humanity until slain by Apollo. The allegory embodied here, as in the Fountain of Latona, referred to Louis' triumph over the monstrous rebellion of the *Frondes*. As described by Félibien, the fountain featured a 'bronze dragon, which, pierced by an arrow, seems to vomit blood from the mouth heaving a cloud of water into the air which falls as rain covering all the basin'.

So that the King could show off the latest garden embellishments, the royal party made several detours before arriving at the Bosquet de l'Étoile, where a collation had been laid out for them. Aligned with each of five converging *allées*, five tables were arranged, making a star-like configuration at the centre of which was a rockwork fountain, which produced an agreeably noisy spout of water. One of the tables resembled a mountain, with caverns on its slopes holding many kinds of cold meats. Another supported a sugar-and-marzipan palace that was merrily besieged, broken up and eaten once the royal party had passed by. Félibien paid a rare tribute to the gardener who had industriously bent and tied the branches of the encircling trees into architectural shapes. Some of the trees within the *bosquet* had been hung with candied fruits, while in the surrounding *allées* fruit trees had been placed in large vases. One walk was lined with Portugal oranges, another with cherry trees, a third with apricots and peaches, a fourth with currant bushes from Holland, and the last with various sorts of pears.

Upon leaving the *bosquet*, the court took to a variety of carriages to make their way to the theatre, taking a turn around the Bassin des Cygnes en route. The Salle de Comédie was over 30 feet high and had seats for an audience of more than twelve hundred. It had been erected on one of the side *allées* parallel to the Allée Royale, at an intersection with one of the cross-walks, where the Bassin de Saturne stands today. Vigarani had constructed a proscenium arch framed by twisted columns of bronze and lapis lazuli, wrapped with golden vines. The theatre was hung with tapestries and lit by thirty-two crystal chandeliers, each bearing ten white wax candles. When the curtain rose, the audience got a surprise, because the scene on stage took them straight back outside to the gardens. The canvas back-cloth had been painted, in trompe-l'oeil fashion, to resemble a beautiful garden of the sort that Le Nôtre might have created. In this dazzling theatrical box, erected just for the occasion, Louis' guests enjoyed a kind of Royal Command Perform-ance, consisting of the comedy *George Dandin* by Molière and Lully's first opera, a pastoral pastiche entitled *Fêtes de l'Amour et de Bacchus*.

When this lengthy entertainment ended, there was a substantial supper in the Salle de Souper, an octagonal structure with a dome that reached 50 feet and was decorated inside in gold and silver on a green background. This building was lo-cated at another intersection of walks, the present site of the Bassin de Flore. The temporary decorations for this midnight supper included a marble fountain and a model of Mount Parnassus complete with figures of Pegasus and of Apollo play-ing a lyre. The meal consisted of five courses, each brought in on fifty-six large dishes. For a hundred of Louis' élite Swiss Guards, the evening's duties included carrying in the meat course. Louise de la Vallière sat at the King's table. Although she was carrying his child, she was unhappy because his attention was elsewhere. There was much more laughter on the table shared by Mme de Montespan and a certain Mme Scarron, soon to become the governess of Athénaïs' children. Past, present and future were thus represented, for though Mme de Montespan was al-ready replacing the unfortunate Louise in the King's affections, she in turn would be unseated by Mme Scarron. But for the moment she harboured no suspicions, and the two women enjoyed one another's company.

There were some carping voices who objected to the 500,000 *livres* it cost Louis to stage the *Divertissement*, voices which said that the money would have been better spent helping demobilised soldiers, but there was no doubt about the spectacle it-self. Much of it seems to have gone up in smoke. After the ball that followed supper, the château was lit up like the palace of the sun with forty-five fiery figures, rep-resenting trophies of war and musical instruments associated with Apollo, while the balustrades were bordered with flaming urns. At the intersections of avenues throughout the vast Parc, antique sculptures were suddenly lit up in many col-ours. The display continued below the Fer à Cheval, where

> a thousand fireworks emerged from the middle of the water which, as if furious and escaping from a place where they had been held by force, scattered to every side of the parterre. An endless number of further fireworks left the mouths of the lizards, the crocodiles, the frogs and the other bronze animals around the fountains, seeming to go to the aid of the first ones, flinging themselves into the

water in the form of many serpents, sometimes separately, sometimes joined together like great balls of string, having an angry quarrel.

Just when the display seemed about to end, there would be another surprise. A great number of rockets were fired from the top of the Tour de la Pompe, built by Le Vau in 1665 to raise water for the fountains. Exploding stars filled the night sky with light, and the inverted 'L's of the royal cipher, traced in figures of fire, floated above the astonished crowds. Thus the great celebration finally came to a close as the first rays of daylight stole upon Versailles.

The *Divertissement* was an ephemeral event, gone in an evening, but it ushered in a new era at Versailles. At the end of Anne of Austria's drawn-out illness, Louis confessed that he could not stand the sight of the Louvre, the place where his mother had died. His grief is evident from his memoirs, in which he observes that he had formed the habit of sleeping under the same roof as his mother, eating at the same table and seeing her every day, no matter what the pressures of work. When she died, Louis went immediately to Versailles, where he could be alone. In the past the château had been a place for youthful escape, but Louis was now approaching thirty, and he was wearying of the traditional peripatetic life of the court, always on the move between his various châteaux. Colbert still hoped that Louis would settle upon the Louvre as his principal residence, but that possibility was already receding. Although there would be only one more fête that could rival the festivities of 1664 and 1668, Versailles was growing in significance, and Athénaïs would soon be its mistress.

View of the Bosquet du Théâtre d'Eau by Jean Cotelle, commissioned in 1688.

IX
Pleasure Works

ANDRÉ LE NÔTRE may have liked to present himself as a simple man of the
soil, but in reality he was an accomplished psychologist. He knew how to
survive and prosper in a court riven with competition and jealousies, and
above all he knew the mind of his King. He instinctively understood that the sort
of garden he had created for Fouquet at Vaux-le-Vicomte would not satisfy Louis
for long. Purely in terms of design, connoisseurs are agreed that Vaux is the finer
creation. It has the quality of unity for which designers strive, and which, when
achieved, means that a garden is sufficient and could only be damaged by additions or subtractions. Versailles, on the other hand, seems to go on for ever.

From the outset Le Nôtre gauged the King's personality perfectly and knew
there was no possibility that he could quell his ruler's restless disposition. The
gardens were there to be used, adapted, altered and extended as royal enthusiasm
dictated. They had to keep pace with every extension of the King's power, his
need to celebrate every conquest, whether at war or in the bed-chamber, as well as
his developing conception of what it meant to be an absolute monarch.

How was Le Nôtre to deal with this? In some ways Louis was the worst sort
of client. Most designers prefer to work for someone who can give a clear brief,
someone who understands enough about design to appreciate it but does not wish
to interfere, who does not have changes of heart in mid-construction, who does not
meddle with the implementation of works, who recognises when the job is done,
and who pays up promptly, making provision for the design to be maintained

unaltered in perpetuity. This perfect client may not exist, but Louis clearly fell far short of the model. He had firm ideas and could convey them, but he was wont to change his views, even while work was in progress. He did not mind the expense involved in tearing down a building shortly after it was finished, simply because he had come up with a better idea. After the château took its final shape under Jules Hardouin-Mansart, the west terrace and its parterres were completely rebuilt. Their present form includes the two giant mirrors of the Parterre d'Eau, which effectively serve to unite the house with garden. Design critics agree that this is the perfect solution, though there is no such unanimity about the attribution. It has been suggested that the King proposed it himself and that it was designed in detail by Le Nôtre, but there are some who would give the credit to Mansart. Whoever was responsible, it took ten years of trial and error to find the answer.

Louis' greatest frustration at Versailles at this time was that he could not get all of the fountains to run. It hurt his pride to have fountain-lads darting about behind hedges switching them on and off as he approached and departed. In the light of what was to follow, his ambitions in 1672 seemed modest: he would have been satisfied if he could have placed some fountains close to the château – in the spot once occupied by Menours' square parterre, where they could easily be seen from the windows on the garden front – and ensure that these, at least, were always playing. But even this presented difficulties. The only reservoir high enough to feed them was on the roof of the Grotte de Thétis, and it did not have sufficient capacity. The Francine brothers had an answer: it would be possible to construct three cisterns *underneath* the parterre. These would act as a sump, collecting the water used in the fountains and recycling it to the tank on the grotto roof by means of two horse-driven bucket-chain systems (known as 'Jacob's Ladders'). By the time this solution was suggested, Louis had launched his Dutch War and was away on campaign in eastern France, but he was impatient to know whether the system would work. Colbert sent him a message reassuring him that 'Sieur Francine is doubling the capacity of the pump which raises water from the parterre to the upper reservoir,' but Louis sent a stern instruction back: '… you will make a test of the eight fountains which you have already tested together with the last two of the parterre, because they must always work, so that I can regulate the times that they will play and the size of the jets'. This attention to technical detail on the part of a monarch who one might have thought would have had weightier matters on his mind is further proof of Louis' passionate involvement in his garden, but those who served him must have felt that they were forever under his eye.

With the technical problem solved, aesthetic questions remained. Where there had formerly been a *parterre de broderie* and, later, four compartments of lawn, there could now be a water parterre, but what shape should it be and how should it be decorated? Le Nôtre produced a design that was both delicate and complicated. It consisted of a circular central pool surrounded by four pools whose unusual shape is difficult to name – 'clover-leaf' is an approximate description. This fancy configuration included all sorts of sculptural embellishments and employed water in a variety of ways; there were fountains and superimposed basins and jets which formed arcs that people might walk beneath. The sculptural programme was equally elaborate. Colbert issued a *Grande Commande* in 1674 that commissioned twenty-four sculptors to illustrate six themes, each represented by four statues. There were to be Four Elements, Four Seasons, Four Continents, Four Humours, Four Poetic Genres and four groups representing Classical abductions.

This first Baroque scheme for the water parterre shows some of the dangers inherent in the formal style. It is a mistake that new students of landscape design often make, as do those who buy their nymphs and urns from the garden centre. One can easily get carried away and produce something which is fussy and over-elaborate. Most of this scheme was built, although the sculptural programme lagged behind and was eventually overtaken by alterations to the château. This parterre looked its best when seen from the balconies on the first floor, but when the building was enlarged in 1678 it had to be modified.

As if Louis' changeability was not difficult enough to handle, the King also liked to tour the works on a daily basis. Most designers would find this level of attention at least disconcerting, if not stressful or downright terrifying, but Le Nôtre did not mind. He enjoyed his walks with the King. In addition, he had now grasped that, as far as the gardens were concerned, the King's purse was virtually bottomless, which must have relieved much of the psychological pressure. It is one thing to have a client who wants changes but will not pay for them, quite another to have a patron who will bankroll every suggested improvement to a plan.

In the face of Louis' unpredictability, the basic ordering device of Versailles, the grid, really came into its own. Le Nôtre needed a design strategy that could cope with incessant demands for innovation. He found it in a spreading geometry that was anchored by the central axis and its regularly spaced cross-axes. Elements of this grid are also found in the Parc, but there the diagonal *allées* become more important. In a flat landscape this geometry could, in principle, be extended infinitely, while the strong framework it provided could accommodate changes within the parterres and *bosquets* it held in place. The geometry also extended into the town of Versailles, where, in 1664, Le Nôtre turned town-planner and laid out the three avenues, each 8 miles long, that converge upon the Place d'Armes.

The years of relative tranquillity that followed the Peace of Aix-la-Chapelle saw new projects launched at Versailles. In this interlude, while Vauban was dispatched to build a string of border fortresses, Louis commissioned Le Vau to enlarge the château and had Le Nôtre dig the Canal and add to the *bosquets*. Le Vau's Enveloppe, as its name suggests, was the ingenious means by which Louis could make his château more palatial without having to knock down his father's original building, to which he was sentimentally attached. The little hunting lodge was encased on three sides by new additions in stone. The pleasing proportions of the inner courtyard were retained, but the Parterre des Fleurs, on the south side of the building, had to be destroyed.

It has been said that the new additions were more like bookends than an envelope, since the old château was sandwiched between two blocks of new accommodation, the Grand Appartement to the north, and the Appartement de la Reine to the south. On the western front, these bookends protruded beyond the line of the original building, so a new façade was conceived that included an open arcade at ground level, supporting a generous terrace accessed from the first floor. This unusual feature gave the western elevation much of its character, and also provided the King and his guests with a raised platform from which to enjoy the patterns of the water parterre. But this was not to be the last enlargement of the property: Louis would one day ask Mansart to make it much bigger still, and in the process this delightful viewing area would be demolished.

Wilful though the King might have been, he could also be gripped by indecision, and Le Vau did not have an easy run-in to his commission. Colbert was characteristically sceptical about the whole project, doubting that it was possible to build a great house in the space available. Construction had already begun – indeed some of the new walls had reached first-floor level – when Louis suddenly announced that there was to be an architectural competition, something of a novelty for the time. The brief for the competition was a mess, for it required the competitors to keep the portions of the Enveloppe that had already been built, but now, in a complete volte-face, the old château was to be razed. Work on site stopped while six of the best architects in France – Le Vau, Le Pautre, Jacques IV Gabriel, Claude Perrault and Vigarani – burnt candles through the night to complete their drawings.

It soon became clear that the competition had been a failure, and the King and Colbert decided to return to a version of the original scheme built around the old château. Perhaps the King also realised that if he went ahead and pulled down his father's old lodge, he would have nowhere to stay at Versailles for about three years, an unattractive proposition as his relationship with Athénaïs de Montespan gathered pace.

It came down to a decision between the designs of Le Vau and Perrault. Ultimately Le Vau's was favoured because, in Colbert's words 'it preserves all that is made'. However, Le Nôtre and François d'Orbay, who would take over the role of *Premier Architecte* in 1670, after Le Vau's death at the age of fifty-seven, were asked by the King and his minister to scrutinise the plans, and they suggested some changes. The whole episode must have been very frustrating for Le Vau, although he might have brought it upon himself though his entrepreneurial dabbling in cannon-forging and other industrial activities which distracted him from his architecture and irritated Colbert. It is surprising that such a patchwork of a building, the product of much dithering and the work of so many hands, was nevertheless an architectural success.

The charming French word for a building site is *chantier*; this is what the château became in 1668, although excavations for the Grand Canal had already begun by 1667. When one looks at a plan of Versailles, it is the great cross formed by the Canal that makes the most immediate impression. This is by far the largest feature on the site – the main reach is over a mile long – but, considering its distance from the château, it needed to be big if it was going to register in views from the terraces. In keeping with the quadruple themes of the first water parterre, the Canal has four arms stretching towards the four cardinal points of the compass, emphasising Louis' authority over the whole of France and the outward thrust of his power. A cruciform layout also seemed appropriate for a monarch who styled himself the Most Christian King, and it had the practical benefit of linking the Ménagerie (and the little palace of the Trianon de Porcelaine, built a few years later) to the central axis and thus to the château via the Allée Royale. It was more than just a conceptual linkage, since expeditions to these outlying pleasure-houses could now go by boat.

The Grand Canal is the outdoor equivalent of the Galerie des Glaces. The two are linked by the seventeenth-century fascination with reflecting surfaces and a more general interest in optical phenomena. Members of the educated élite were fascinated by lenses, mirrors and prisms and kept them in their curiosity cabinets for the amusement of their friends, while hydraulics as a popular science was represented not just by fountains but by water-driven automata such as singing birds and organs powered by air displaced by water. For example, Solomon de Caus published a treatise entitled *The Relations of Motive Forces, with Various Machines as Useful as they are Pleasing*. In general, however, Louis' taste was for fountains rather than gimmicks. In the case of the Grand Canal, optics triumphed over hydraulics, because it was decided that there should be no fountains to trouble its glass-like surface. This liquid mirror would be inlaid into the French countryside, where it would slice through the woods in the strongest and simplest of ways, pulling down the sky – perhaps even God – to anchor them within the King's territory.

The main reach of the Grand Canal is 62 metres wide, but when it was time to excavate the cross-arms, Le Nôtre increased their width to 75 metres, thus compensating for the foreshortening that would otherwise have made them seem narrower than the waters that lay along the central axis. Having trained as a painter, he understood the principles of perspective and how to compensate for distortions. If he wanted a pool to appear square when viewed from a distance, he would make it a rectangle; if a basin had to look circular, he would make it an oval. Perspective can be a help, not a hindrance, for the designer who understands these matters. One of the cues to distance is the way in which parallel lines appear to converge. If apparently parallel lines, such as the rows of trees in an avenue, actually come together slightly, the effect is to make the farthest ones seem even further away. This effect, known as 'accelerated perspective', can be used to make small areas seem bigger. Features which seem generous on plan can seem niggardly in three dimensions, which is the reason Le Nôtre chose to elongate the main axis of the Grand Canal following the construction of Le Vau's Enveloppe. From the upper-storey terrace the Canal simply did not look big enough. Colbert summed up the expansive spirit of the era when he wrote: '... we do not live in a reign which is content with little things. With due regard to proportion, it is impossible to imagine anything which can be too great.'

The Apollo Fountain, a major component in the iconographic programme for Versailles, was created at this time on the site of the Bassin des Cygnes, the hinge-point situated at the far end of the Allée Royal. The sculptural group commissioned from Tuby in 1668 to sketches by Le Brun was put in place in 1671. It provides a sense of arrival for anyone who has followed the Tapis Vert from the terrace of the château, but this is also the point where the axis is relaunched across the waters of the Canal. Here the Sun God, refreshed after a night with the nymphs of Thetis, emerges from a cloud of foam at the reins of his mighty chariot to begin another day's work. Thoughtful visitors might think that the Olympian air-traffic controllers have got something wrong, since his trajectory is eastwards towards the palace rather than towards the end of the Grand Canal where the sun

View of the Bosquet du Marais by Jean Cotelle, commissioned in 1688.

sets, but aesthetically he is urging his steeds in the right direction. He also seems
to be flying to the assistance of his mother, Latona, who is being tormented by
Lycian peasants at the other end of the Tapis Vert. As conceived by Le Brun and
realised by Tuby, Apollo and his gilded horses form the most dynamic group in
the whole of the gardens. Dolphins surge aside while Tritons blow on their conch
shells to clear the way. On a bright day when the fountains are playing, the sight of
Apollo bursting from the waves is glorious. The sculpture looks moodily marvel-
lous on misty mornings when the chariot seems to struggle to escape the vapours.
Perhaps it is its appearance on such occasions that has earned it a nickname among
the *Versaillais*; according to Pierre-André Lablaude, the sculpture is known as the
Char Embourbé, the chariot stuck in the mud. In Marsy's sculpture of Latona for
the lower garden of the Fer à Cheval, the goddess has successfully petitioned her
lover, Jupiter, to turn some disrespectful Lycian peasants into frogs. These un-
fortunates are still there, in four concentric rings, croaking spouts of water from
their wide-open mouths. The inspiration came from Ovid's *Metamorphoses*, and
the sculpture is another reference to the *Frondes*, in particular to the indignities
suffered by Anne of Austria.

Le Nôtre's situation was complicated and precarious, because – in addition to
the King – other powerful personalities at court sometimes took an interest in
his endeavours. The whimsical feature known as the Marais, or Marsh, is a case
in point. It was conceived by Mme de Montespan while she was at the height of
her influence with the King. In the centre was a bronze tree with tin leaves that
sent forth water from the tips of its branches. In the corners of the pool there were
metal reeds and bulrushes which also spouted jets, while four gilded swans nested
amongst them squirted additional streams towards the tree from their beaks. To
each side of the *bosquet* were the equally remarkable Buffets d'Eau, which consisted of tiers of red and white marble upon which was laid a mock collation in
richly gilded urns and vases, around which the water tumbled in cascades.

Nothing like this had previously been seen in France, and, according to Helen
Fox, the whole thing was too frivolous for Le Nôtre, who distanced himself from
it. The grounds for this interpretation are provided by an account Colbert gave to
the King on 17 July 1672 in which the minister seems to have assumed responsibility for the construction. 'The stem of the tree in the Marsh, which is cast iron,' he
wrote, 'is in place, and several of the branches have already been welded. All of the
foliage has been put right and is in a state to be joined with the branches.'

It is probably going too far to say that Le Nôtre washed his hands of this project.
It was too fussy for his tastes, no doubt, and he would have been happy to have left

the concept to Athénaïs, the water ornaments to François Francine and the site management to Colbert, but it is likely that he played some part in the setting out of the *bosquet*. When Mme de Montespan fell from favour, all traces of her influence in the garden were removed, and the Marais became the site of the Baths of Apollo, where the various displaced gods, horses and nymphs from the Grotte de Thétis would find accommodation.

Another feature which has not survived is the Théâtre d'Eau, represented in two paintings by Cotelle. If the Marais was Mme de Montespan's own initiative, created with only reluctant help from Le Nôtre, the Théâtre d'Eau is reputed to have been the King's – but this time Le Nôtre was an enthusiastic collaborator. The Théâtre *was* a theatre, but not one in which human actors strutted their parts. Here the performers were the fountains. The *bosquet* makes excellent use of the principle of accelerated perspective; taking advantage of the natural slope, Le Nôtre created three tiered avenues of water which converged upon circular space divided into amphitheatre and stage. Each of these avenues tapered significantly, making them appear much longer than they really were. Water coursed down these *allées*, but, as Cotelle shows clearly, there was also a rhythmic pattern whereby it was launched overhead in delicate arcs or lanced upwards like fenceposts. This *bosquet* was a genuine team effort, with the theatre director Vigarani, the Francine brothers and the fontaineer Claude Denis all assisting. Félibien describes it thus:

> Each canal seemed like a long allée in the shape of a bower, decorated with many large jets at intervals throughout the space. Sometimes they are like fences made of crystal spears which separate the canals and the allées. Sometimes, indeed, their crests brush the trees. Finally the water spouts out of these places with such abundance and in so many different ways that it is impossible to comprehend the diverse effects that one sees.

The Marais and the Théâtre d'Eau are just two of the *bosquets* created in the period between 1666 and 1683, the most prolific era of *bosquet*-making at Versailles. The expansion of the gardens reflected the optimism that accompanied Louis' successful foreign policy. Among many others were the Salle de Conseille, otherwise called the Salle de Festins, which looked in plan like the outline of some great fortress that Vauban might have built; the Renommée, which featured a hexagonal basin at the centre of which was a fountain built to celebrate the Sun King's fame; the Berceau d'Eau, a water-arbour with arching jets under which one could walk and only get a little wet; the Île Royale, at the centre of a large ornamental pond; and the Bosquet de l'Encelade with its great gilded-lead giant.

Even though Versailles was vast, there was a limit to the number of *bosquets* that could be created within easy reach of the château. This practical limit, combined with the King's unsettled tastes, accounts for the number of changes within the gardens. Particular features would lose favour and be erased to make way for new conceptions. Another of Le Nôtre's creations, the Bosquet de l'Etoile, created in 1668 on the northern side of the gardens, became the Montagne d'Eau in 1671. Its pentagonal star of converging walks was retained, but a miniature mountain of rockwork was added at the centre. This *bosquet* was one of the garden features, already sadly neglected, that was devastated by the storm of December 1999, but at the time of writing it is being restored by the landscape architect Pierre-André Lablaude and his team. Two of Le Nôtre's very earliest designs, the Bosquet de la Girandole and the Bosquet Dauphin, remained intact until they were replaced by simple quincunxes during the replanting ordered by Louis XVI in 1774. They were recreated as part of the 1998–2000 replanting programme, which sought to restore the gardens to their condition at the close of the Sun King's reign. Considering the buffets and collations that Louis used to provide for his guests, it does not seem inappropriate that the Bosquet de la Girandole is now the site of a brasserie.

Louis now needed a secluded retreat where he could make love to Athénaïs de Montespan. Le Vau and Le Nôtre were dispatched to produce designs for a house to be built at the northern end of the cross-axis of the Grand Canal. The site was the village of Trianon, which Louis had bought in 1688. He had promptly razed the whole place, including its church. Sufficiently distant from the palace for secret sexual encounters, it was also well located to serve as a place of refreshment for hunting parties in the Grand Parc.

Louis had acquired the fashionable taste for chinoiserie, and, though Le Vau would have been more comfortable producing something in the Classical idiom, he was persuaded to cover the roof with glazed faience tiles from Saint-Cloud and Normandy in an attempt to make it look a little like the Imperial Palace of Nanking. China urns along the roof ridge gave the building an appropriately jagged silhouette. This new edifice, known as the Trianon de Porcelaine, stood where visitors today will find the Grand Trianon, which replaced it in 1687.

A high-priority project, the Trianon de Porcelaine was built very quickly. 'This palace was seen by everyone as an enchantment,' wrote Félibien, 'for it was not started until the end of winter and was finished by Spring, as if it had sprung out of the ground along with the flowers in its gardens.' It seems likely that it was

Perspective view of the Trianon de Porcelaine from the garden side.
Engraving by the Perelle family.

built in the winter and spring of 1669–70 but not occupied until September 1670. According to the diarists of the day, Trianon was a light-hearted place, where there were frequent collations, suppers, concerts, dances and recitals throughout the spring and summer, including a brilliant fête held on 27 July 1685 to celebrate the marriage of the Duc de Bourbon and Mlle de Nantes.

The most significant room of all, given the pavilion's primary purpose, was the Chambre des Amours, decorated in white, silver and blue, which was equipped with an extraordinary bed. With a large mirror at the head, an elaborate canopy, flounced curtains, and trimmings of silver and gold, this exuberant piece of furniture gave excellent service, since Athénaïs remained Louis' official mistress for twelve years and bore him six children. When the King was ensconced here with her, behind the drapes and beneath the gilded canopy, thoughts of Louise de la Vallière must have been far from his mind. Although she readily agreed to return from her convent once she thought she had regained the King's affections, it would prove to be a temporary triumph. In the larger battle for the King's heart, Athénaïs was in the ascendancy, though even she would not be able to hold on to him for ever.

This first Trianon was essentially a garden-house that gave Louis the opportunity to indulge his love of floral displays. To please Athénaïs and to compensate for the destruction of the Parterre des Fleurs during construction of Le Vau's Enveloppe, the parterres at Trianon were filled, not with coloured gravel but with jasmines, jonquils and wallflowers, the King's particular favourite. Louis can be included amongst the ranks of the 'curious florists', those wealthy and erudite nobles who liked to collect rare varieties, though, being the monarch, he naturally had to have far more of them than anyone else. There were so many scented species at Trianon that on one occasion the King and his courtiers were forced to leave because their perfume had become overpowering. Félibien called this place the 'Abode of Spring' since 'whatever season one goes there, it is enriched with flowers of every kind, and the air that one breathes is perfumed by the jasmines and the orange trees beneath which one walks'.

The plant list at Trianon was certainly extensive. There were tulips, narcissi, hyacinths, veronicas, valerians, carnations, pasque flowers, feverfews, tuberoses, violets and white lilies. When it came to flowers, Colbert's usual stipulation that everything should be sourced from within the borders of France simply did not apply; oranges, jasmines and carnations came from Spain, narcissi from Constantinople and valerians from Greece. Louis was not immune to the tulipomania that had swept through Europe. Elizabeth Hyde describes one of the flower-beds in which tulips alternated with hyacinths (which were the latest fashion) and white narcissi. Perennials were planted between the rows, including veronicas, orange hyacinths, sweet williams, cornflowers, pasque flowers, violets and Spanish carnations. In the centre of the bed was a row of taller plants including feverfew, valerian, bellflowers, wallflowers and white lilies.

The gardens at Trianon were a smaller version of those at Versailles, with parterres close to the house and woodland blocks at a distance, containing outdoor rooms. Between the flower-beds and the groves, however, was an area occupied by the trellis-work arbours of an open-air orangery. At the foot of the garden was a *boulingrin* with a large circular pool in the middle. The garden included two cascades designed by Le Nôtre which were warmly praised by Nicodemus Tessin when he visited in 1687.

When Louis had demolished the village at Trianon, it had been like handing Le Nôtre a clean sheet of paper. This was quite a rare situation for the mastergardener, who usually found himself amending and enlarging existing gardens rather than creating entirely new ones. The problem he faced was that the King did not give him an entirely free hand. In his diplomatic way André confided to his friend, the sculptor Pierre Puget, that the true author of the Trianon gardens was Louis himself, who had become the King of Gardeners. Here, even more so than at Versailles, he chose to be involved personally, even to the point of direct interference.

The man in day-to-day charge of the Trianon gardens was Michel II Le Bouteux, who was related through his marriage to Marguerite Bouchard to Le Nôtre; Le Nôtre's sister, Françoise, had married Marguerite's brother, Simon Bouchard, the gardener in charge of the orangery at the Tuileries. Like the Le Nôtres, the Le Bouteux family had been in the business of gardening for generations, and Michel's father had been one of the witnesses to André's marriage.

Le Bouteux's name is mentioned in the building accounts for 6 August 1668 for providing the festoons, bouquets and floral ornaments for the temporary rooms erected in the gardens for dining and dancing during the *Divertissement* of that year, for which he was paid 900 *livres*. As a specialist *jardinier-fleuriste*, he was held in as much esteem for his production of flowers as La Quintinie was for his fruits, though being held in high regard did not spare him from the King's impatience, and Colbert was often breathing down his neck. In the minister's 'Orders and Regulations for the Buildings of Versailles' of 1674, Colbert instructed his officers to 'visit Trianon often; see that Le Bouteux has flowers for the King for the whole of winter'.

The principal floral area at Trianon was the orangery, and it was here that Le Bouteux showed himself to be an innovator. The orange trees were not trundled out in clumsy tubs from indoor storage but were planted directly in the ground, or rather they were placed into iron buckets that were then sunk into the soil. They remained in place throughout the winter, protected by an ingenious collapsible greenhouse, their roots protected by layers of straw.

The Sun King liked to defy winter and was prepared to go to great expense to keep his gardens in a summery condition, whatever the season. The only way to do this was through the expedient of bedding out, also much loved by the Victorians and still practised by municipal parks departments today, but thankfully not quite with Louis' fervour. At certain times of the year, Le Bouteux and his men were required to change the plants every day, and sometimes twice in one day. Louis liked to take his guests on a winter stroll to the Trianon. Having admired the beds on the way into the building for luncheon, how astonished they must have been when they emerged after the meal to discover fresh flowers of different colours in the borders they had seen not long before. To appreciate the scale of this achievement, it is worth noting that the planting plan just for the main border required 96,000 plants.

Tessin described Trianon as a garden 'always full of flowers, which are changed every season in their pots and one can never see a dead leaf or a shrub that is not in flower'. To facilitate the industrial levels of horticultural production involved, there were permanent greenhouses not far from the demountable ones, and the gardeners employed two million clay pots, which were in continual circulation. The building accounts seem to bear out these extraordinary numbers, showing purchases of close to 170,000 pots in 1687 and a further 100,000 in the following year. The pots were expensive, costing about 15 *livres* for a hundred.

The land at Trianon, like much of the park at Versailles, was boggy and not well suited to horticulture. There are frequent references in the building accounts to the delivery of good-quality soil. Large quantities of manure were also used, along with other ameliorants, such as the 6,346 litres of pigeon droppings and the 10,459 litres of *mar de vigne* supplied by Gentien Duval in December 1690.

To stock the flower-beds many plants were purchased in Holland. Colbert's network of royal nurseries also played a crucial role, particularly the Pépinière du Roule and the significant garden established at Toulon in 1681. The head gardener at the Pépinière told Martin Lister that furnishing the Trianon 'with Flower Pots in season, every 14 days in the Summer, took up no less than 92,000 Pots from hence'. He also boasted that 'he could Plant and furnish in 14 days time, any new Garden the king should Cause to be made'.

Le Bouteux was handsomely rewarded for his expertise. His annual wages for maintaining the Trianon gardens were 17,500 *livres*. This compares very favourably with the salary of 20,800 *livres* paid to Le Brun, who is the top earner mentioned in the accounts. Even Colbert only paid himself 15,000 *livres*; Le Vau received 6,000 while La Quintinie received 2,000 plus another 2,000 in gratuities. The amount paid to Le Bouteux was more than the combined amount paid to three other gardeners, Collinot, Trumel and Vautier. The accounts can mislead, however, since they conflate an individual's salary with the cost of the services he provided. Le Bouteux had to use his income to purchase plants, which would have been expensive because of their rarity. Le Nôtre incurred no such expenses as *Contrôleur des Bâtiments*, for which job he was paid 5,400 *livres* annually, nor as a designer of parterres, which brought an additional salary of 1,200 *livres*. He would have had to have met some expenses out of the 3,000 *livres* he was paid each year as the contractor responsible for the upkeep of the Grand Parterre at the Tuileries. Le Nôtre's total earnings of 9,640 *livres* per annum as a royal servant might seem substantially less than Le Bouteux's, but it must be remembered that the master-gardener often received substantial gratuities and bonuses, and also earned fees from other design commissions.

By 1674, Athénaïs de Montespan felt secure in the King's affections. In the previous year, though heavily pregnant, she had accompanied him to the front during the siege of Maastricht. Louis loved the company of women when he travelled, but he could be extremely inconsiderate. On such trips he would eat enormous snacks en route which he would insist upon sharing with his queasy companions; yet if anyone needed to heed a call of nature, he would refuse to stop the coach. The journey must have been particularly uncomfortable, because Athénaïs had been obliged to share the carriage not only with Louise de la Vallière but also with the Queen, both of whom were mad with jealousy. Those who saw them pass were astonished to see these 'Three Queens' riding in the same carriage as the King. He was unperturbed, but the women must have had a miserable time. Athénaïs' daughter, Mlle de Nantes, was born at Tournai.

In the same year, the King had found a legal precedent that would allow him to legitimise his children born to Athénaïs. As she was still married to the Marquis de Montespan, this was a tricky business. Her husband was the sort who would cause a fuss. He had already shown his capacity for anger by riding in a coach with a cuckold's horns strapped to the roof and had taken to referring to Athénaïs as his 'late wife'. Louis wanted to keep his legitimised children out of the way, so they were sent initially to a house in a remote suburb of Paris where Mme Scarron, the future Marquise de Maintenon, was engaged to be their governess.

There were fêtes at Versailles throughout the summer of 1674, and though the ostensible motive for holding them was to celebrate the annexation of Franche-

*Illuminations at the fête of 1674, held to celebrate the
reconquest of Franche-Comté. Engraving by Jean Le Pautre.*

*Firework display on the Grand Canal at the fête of 1674,
held to celebate the reconquest of Franche-Comté. Engraving by Jean Le Pautre.*

Comté, overrun by the French for a second time, it is clear from the programme that they were also mounted to please Athénaïs, rather as the fête of 1664 had been designed to impress Louise de la Vallière. It is no coincidence that the first evening of festivities, on 4 July, began with a collation in the Marais, the *bosquet* that bore De Montespan's stamp, nor that the second day of celebrations, a week later, should have centred on the Trianon love-nest. Despite the intensity of the relationship between Louis and Athénaïs, the parties of July and August 1674 were public occasions. The whole court followed the King as he made his way around the gardens, whether by coach or *calèche* or by gondola. Félibien observed that on the fourth day of the celebrations, when their majesties left the château at six o'clock for a tour of the Petit Parc, they were followed by more than thirty carriages, each drawn by six horses. Lesser subjects meanwhile could watch the fireworks from a distance, and peasants climbed the trees within the park to get a better view.

Pity poor Félibien as he strove to do justice to the King's brilliant displays! Not only did he have to note it all down – the architectural derivations of the stage sets, the quantities of fruit in the baskets, the numbers of candles in the chandeliers, the precise movements of the King, the numbers of fireworks in every salvo – but he had to find superlatives to crown his superlatives. Obsequious though the chronicler had to be, there is no doubting, when one reads his descriptions, that these were truly astonishing occasions, although by 1674, as the juggernaut of French power was starting to falter, a certain nostalgia had already crept into the proceedings. There was little that summer that had not been seen before – certainly not the rockets and lanterns and inevitable collations – and the theatrical programme also looked backwards. On 19 July, a year after the playwright's death, there was a performance of Molière's *Le Malade imaginaire*, on a stage constructed outside the Grotto, while on 28 July, Lully's *Les Fetes de l'Amour et de Bacchus* was performed in a temporary theatre at the top of the Allée du Dragon, close to the Tour d'Eau. The only new work presented was Racine's *Iphigénie*, which was staged near the Orangerie. On the fifth day of the festivities, 107 flags taken from the enemy by the victorious Condé were presented to the King. It is almost as if those responsible for planning these celebrations, from the monarch downwards, understood that their like would never be seen again. It was already a time for remembering.

One curious feature of Félibien's reportage is that he scarcely mentions the theatrical performances. He seems far more concerned with architecture, decoration and food. When he is required to describe a buffet, he gets quite carried away. The collation that preceded Lully's opera took place in Le Nôtre's Théâtre d'Eau, which had been decorated for the occasion with apple, pear and apricot trees laden with fruit, between which were vases of flowers and pedestals carrying bowls piled high with colourful pyramids of seasonal fruits. The supper following the performance was even more spectacular. After a promenade in the gardens and a firework show, the court made its way, shortly after midnight, to the Cour de Marbre, where, it seemed to Félibien, all the fires that had appeared in the air above the Canal had now arranged themselves in the courtyard, and a thousand lights, twinkling like stars, formed a Tuscan column of flame. This extraordinary feature, devised by Vigarani and about 18 feet high, was perforated so it seemed that the light of six hundred candles formed a festoon of golden flowers wrapped around it from base to cap. Supported by eight swirling brackets, this central post rose from the middle of an octagonal table, which had been decorated with orange blossom, tuberoses and carnations.

The last two days of this drawn-out fête seem to have been the most breathtaking of all. On Saturday, 18 August, following the performance of *Iphigénie*, the royal party installed themselves in a tent below the Fountain of Apollo, facing the pool at the head of the Canal. A cannon shot announced more fireworks, which were immediately followed by the shock of fifteen hundred *boîtes*, or fire-bombs. At the same time the margins of the water were illuminated by the fiery figures of fleurs-de-lis and royal monograms. A gigantic theatrical dragon, afloat on seven boats, belched fire from its mouth and nostrils. It was swathed in thunder-clouds of red and bluish smoke, crackling with thunderbolts. The beast's mouth was like an abyss out of which poured a thousand flaming imps. These squibs swirled upon the water, often subdividing with a crack, until the whole surface of the Canal appeared to be covered in flame. More rockets were launched. They were so high and so noisy that they seemed to be attacking the stars themselves. The main feature, dreamt up by Le Brun, was an illuminated pyramid-obelisk crowned by a royal sun. For the final act of this pyrotechnic theatre, five thousand rockets took flight, forming a dome of light over the head of the Canal from which a great rain of stars descended, brighter than the real stars in the heavens above. If Félibien's figures can be trusted, the performance turned thirty thousand individual fireworks to soot.

After such magnificence, it must have taxed Le Brun and Vigarani to come up with something appropriate for the final event of the summer, held on the last day of August. An audience sated with fireworks and explosions needed something quieter but equally impressive, so it was decided that this should be a night fête, which would not commence until the early hours of the morning, when the court would take to boats on the Canal.

The scene, as the courtiers left the château, was magical. Pots of fire had been placed in a double row around the margins of the Grand Terrace, and the ramps and steps of the Fer à Cheval, as well as the margins of the Canal, had been treated in similar fashion. The lines of the parterres had been picked out by lights, and every fountain in the Petit Parc had been illuminated. It was, according to Félibien, a particularly black night and very still, which greatly enhanced the air of mystery.

Their majesties stepped aboard beautifully decorated gondolas, followed on to the water by the rest of the court, who boarded a flotilla of other vessels all suitably decked out. The surface of the Canal resembled a looking-glass. Spaced around the banks were 650 illuminated statues and between them an assortment of fishes, lit up by coloured lights, apparently watching open-mouthed as the greatest of kings floated by, the sovereign not just of France but also of their watery realm. When the boats reached the pool at the junction of the main and transverse canals, their passengers were thrilled by the appearance, at the Trianon extremity, of Neptune in his chariot pulled by marine horses and accompanied by Tritons. Then, turning towards the Ménagerie, they saw Apollo, at the reins of his sun chariot, rising into the air accompanied by four female figures representing the hours of the day. Finally, at the farthest end of the Canal, there was a palace, which seemed to have been built on the water out of crystal, with mosaics evidently composed of rubies, emeralds and other precious stones. It was with some reluctance, says Félibien, that the court left this nautical kingdom, paddling slowly back up the length of the Canal to the accompaniment of violins.

View of the Bosquet des Trois Fontaines by Jean Cotelle, commissioned in 1688.

X
Zenith

I N 1677, LOUIS' BUNGLED DUTCH WAR, launched to teach his neighbours a salutary lesson, was at last drawing to a satisfactory conclusion. It might have
ended in 1672, the same year it began, if Louis had taken heed of Condé, that
other warrior-gardener, and dispatched cavalry to take Amsterdam at the criti-
cal moment. Louis hesitated long enough to discover that the Emperor Leopold
and the Elector of Brandenburg had come to the assistance of the Dutch, who
had shown their will to repel the invaders by opening their dykes and flooding
the countryside. Rather than the short, sharp war Louis had envisaged, his troops
had been forced to battle hard for over five years. After prolonged negotiations, a
series of treaties were signed at Nymegen which brought the war to an end. Louis
had to give his more northerly conquests back to the Dutch, but even so 1678
marked the zenith of his power; the Sun King's continental possessions were at
their greatest extent. The Elector of Brandenburg was forced to concede that 'In
the present state of affairs it seems that no prince will henceforth find security and
advantage except in the friendship and alliance of the King of France'.

Considering the country's vulnerable condition when Louis had taken the
throne, this was a remarkable turn-around. Now the whole of Europe feared
France, but for Louis this high point would also be the turning-point. The sixteen
years it took to reach this summit would be followed by thirty-seven of gradual
decline, punctuated by reverses at war and famine at home. But no one could have
known this in 1678. The city of Paris declared that the King should henceforth be

known as Louis *Le Grand*. From this moment he lost interest in playing the role of the Sun King or likening himself to Apollo. Louis was now established in his own right. In the hubristic glow that followed his military successes, it seemed that France might be considered more than the equal of ancient Rome. Had Louis died suddenly at this time, it is conceivable that the soubriquet might have stuck, but in terms of foreign policy the second half of his reign was far less successful. Indeed many of his achievements were undone. In popular memory, Louis remains the Sun King, however, and we recall the spectacle of his court and the magnificence of his palace and gardens rather than any lasting political and military gains.

At the zenith, celebrations seemed in order, and Le Nôtre was given instructions to prepare designs for the replacement of two early *bosquets*, the Pavillon d'Eau and the Berceau d'Eau, which lay on the slope to the north of the château to either side of the Allée d'Eau, otherwise known as the Allée des Marmousets. One of these new creations, the Bosquet de l'Arc de Triomphe, was a direct reference to Louis' military successes. At the northern entrance was Tuby's massive gilded personification of France, armoured and sitting triumphantly in her chariot, lance in hand, quiver full of arrows, while at her feet, amongst abandoned flags and helmets, a young captive and a despondent lion symbolised defeated Spain, and an older prisoner and a dead eagle represented the Austrian Empire. Between them, a writhing three-headed dragon signified the vanquished Triple Alliance of the Netherlands, England and Sweden. The group has recently been restored, and in full sun its fresh gilding blazes against bright white marble and deep green foliage.

This powerful sculpture is all that remains of the once-elaborate scheme of decoration for this outdoor room. At the opposite end of the *bosquet* stood the Arc de Triomphe itself, the work of Pierre Mazeline, a confection of architecture, sculpture and hydraulics. The arch had three apertures, each containing an urn that spouted a jet of water. More water spilled from a series of bowls along the pediment into ladders of seashells at the sides of the structure and, finally, into a large basin at the foot of the façade. Between the Arc de Triomphe and the figure of France triumphant were basins on pedestals, water-buffets made of marble and flanked by tall obelisks which also spouted water, and, just to force the point home, two more meaningful statues, *La Victoire de la France* and *La Gloire de la France*. Walking the length of this *bosquet* up the considerable slope might have seemed arduous, but Le Nôtre made the climb easier by providing curved staircases and gentle ramps.

The landscape architect's skill in handling levels was even more apparent in another *bosquet*, the Trois Fontaines, reputedly sketched out by the King himself. This was a much longer chamber than its neighbour, making use of the full slope. Le Nôtre created three platforms divided one from another by cascades and flights of steps. The highest, which was also the narrowest, had a circular basin with a strong central jet; the slightly larger central terrace had a square pool with vertical jets at its corners and others which created the effect of a crystal vault, while the bottom pool was octagonal with a tiered fountain to match, crowned by a spray of delicate jets. Devoid of sculptural embellishments, the interest of the Trois Fontaines lay in the variety of its water effects. Each level could be appreciated in its own right, but the genius of the design was the way in which the displays related to one another. Not everyone was impressed, however. The English visitor Joseph Shaw wrote that 'crossing the water alley, you come to the three fountains, a pretty melancholy place', but praising the French did not come easily to this observer. In the same account he wrote, 'From Fontainebleau I came to the court, eighteen leagues to Versailles, the French paradise and miracle of the world, but though it is the finest palace I ever saw, yet it is much more inferior to the idea the French had given me of it.'

A letter written to the King by Colbert on 1 March 1678 gives a good impression of the surge in activity at Versailles that accompanied the end of the Dutch War and also demonstrates Colbert's role as project manager. After reassuring the King that his ponds are in good condition and that construction of the reservoir at Satory is nearly complete, he tells the King of a site inspection, or *visite générale*, he has just made. He was accompanied by 'Monsieurs Francines and Denis for all the fountains; Le Nostre and Collinot for all the gardens; Lemaire for all the nozzle taps and other works in copper; Berthier for all the rockwork; carpenter, mason, metalworker, joiner the same, to restore everything to order'. This Collinot would have been Jean Collinot, the expert in trellis-work who had worked on the temporary structures for the *Grand Divertissement* of 1668 and the Labyrinthe in 1673. In the same letter Colbert mentions that Le Nôtre had made a model for a new waterbody; this might be a reference to the Pièce d'Eau des Suisses, which was started in 1678, or to the Pièce des Sapins, later renamed the Pièce de Neptune.

While the *bosquets* were being embellished by fine craftsmanship, immense replanting works were being undertaken in the Grand Parc. Research into the accounts for Versailles has revealed that vast amounts of plant material were carried there. In particular there was huge demand for hornbeam hedging plants to line the *bosquets* and *allées*; 2,870,000 were sent from Lyon in 1685. Between 1668 and 1672, about 130,000 trees were planted, and the pace did not slacken. In the autumn of 1686 alone, 9,000 hazels and maples, 8,400 elms, 255 sycamores and 1.5 million hornbeam hedging plants were delivered from Lyon and Rouen. In 1688 a further 25,000 trees were brought from Artois.

Getting young trees to root is simple enough as long as you plant them in the dormant season and take care to protect the roots from desiccation and frost, but the difficulties increase with older trees. It is clear from the accounts that very large trees were transplanted. A letter from Charles Perrault dated 8 March 1673 mentions the widening of the Allée Royale and, remarking that the height of newly planted trees exceeds that of the surrounding woodlands, adds approvingly that 'the labour of a single day equals the work of Nature during two or three centuries'. Some of the trees brought from the forests of Lyon, Compiègne or Flanders were in excess of 30 feet (10 metres) in height and where possible would be conveyed some of the way by barge. In Claude Desgot's account of Le Nôtre's life, he says that the King depopulated the countryside for 20 leagues around of chestnuts and limes. With regard to the transplantation of such large trees, he observes that 'the expense is great but the pleasure is immediate.'

John James, passing on to the subscribers of his English translation the wisdom of Dezallier d'Argenville, recommended that trees be lifted with a rootball but without being drastically pruned as might be necessary with bare-root stock. It was evident, he wrote,

> that a Gentleman, by planting Trees in their Clod, gains the Time those trees necessarily require to make another Head; besides that they are infinitely more beautiful not discovering their Removal, as those do that have been headed. I have planted Elms in their Clod 30 foot high, and as big as one's Thigh, which have taken again to a wonder; by this Expedient you plant Trees at their full Bigness, which was never done heretofore, and enjoy a Garden ten Years the sooner, by means of this admirable Contrivance.

The transplantation of large trees is still undertaken today and for the same reasons. But small trees establish more surely than big trees and generally catch up with them in height in just a few years, so the mass planting of mature or semi-mature trees is now relatively uncommon, and it is still an uncertain and potentially very costly business. The modern tool for lifting mature specimens is called a hydraulic tree spade. It forces triangular blades into the ground around the trunk of the tree, which can then be lifted whole within a conical plug of earth containing a mass of its roots. Before the tree spade was invented, the process was much slower. The best practice was to begin preparing the tree a couple of seasons before it was to be lifted. In the first dormant season a trench would be dug halfway around the tree, a certain distance from the bole, and the roots would be pruned. The same procedure would be followed on the other side of the tree during the following season. Once the roots had been cut, a root ball could be formed and wrapped in damp hessian to prevent the roots from drying out. The tree was ready for transportation.

It is clear from the records of arboricultural contracts at Versailles that those involved understood the importance of lifting trees without damaging the roots and root-hairs, or the head of the tree. A contract to bring trees from the forest of Compiègne, issued to Pierre Le Clerc on 17 September 1705, stated that the trees should be lifted with good rootballs, with 'all the roots well garnished with earth', but if the soil should be sandy, so that a rootball could not be formed, then the contractor should ensure that there was 'a good collar of hairy roots'. Despite this theoretical understanding, the process of transplantation in Le Nôtre's day seems to have been brutal, involving the infamous machine known as 'the Devil'. Such devices must have done great harm as they wrenched their victims from the earth. Diderot and D'Alembert's *Encyclopaedia* mentions that 'trees are transported with their root balls in baskets, either on small wagons called trolleys or on larger wagons to which the trees are attached with iron chains.'

The most likely explanation for the enormous number of trees shipped to Versailles is the quantity that died during transportation or shortly after planting. It was well understood that trees had a better chance of survival if they were taken from poor conditions and planted into better ones, but Versailles was a reformed bog, not a place that would be hospitable to silvicultural arrivals from the forests of Normandy, Flanders and the Île-de-France. According to Pierre-André Lablaude, seventeenth-century survival rates were deplorable. Louis' constant tinkering with the layout of Versailles did not help, for if there is anything a tree likes less than being transplanted, it is being transplanted twice.

After the indignity of transplantation came the discipline of pruning. With the use of double ladders on rolling carriages, there was little that was out of the reach of pruning shears. It was the young hedging material that was most esteemed because it withstood all manner of rough treatment. *Palissades* were sometimes created using material that was 6 or 7 feet high, but in such cases there was always a risk that the larger stock would not root. John James, in his translation of Dezallier d'Argenville, notes that the hornbeam 'is fit, as the Beech is, to form Walks, Palisades and Woods; but especially Palisades, in which 'tis made Use of more than any other Plant. Then the *French* change its name, and instead of *Charme*, call it *Charmille*, which imports no more than small Plants of Horn-beam about

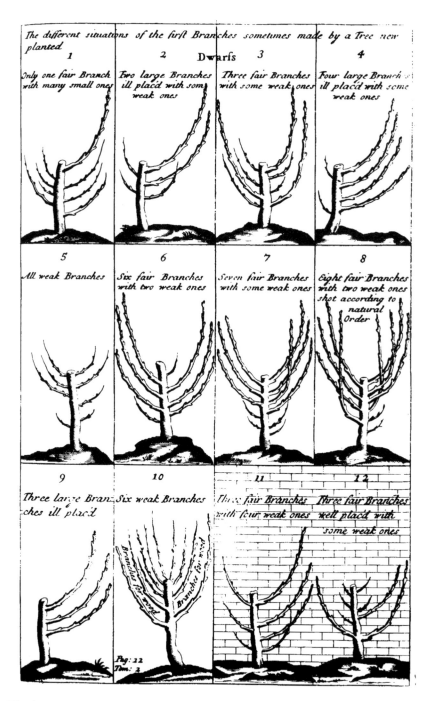

The different situations of the first branches sometimes made by a tree newly planted.
Illustration from John Evelyn's *The Compleat Gard'ner*, 1693.

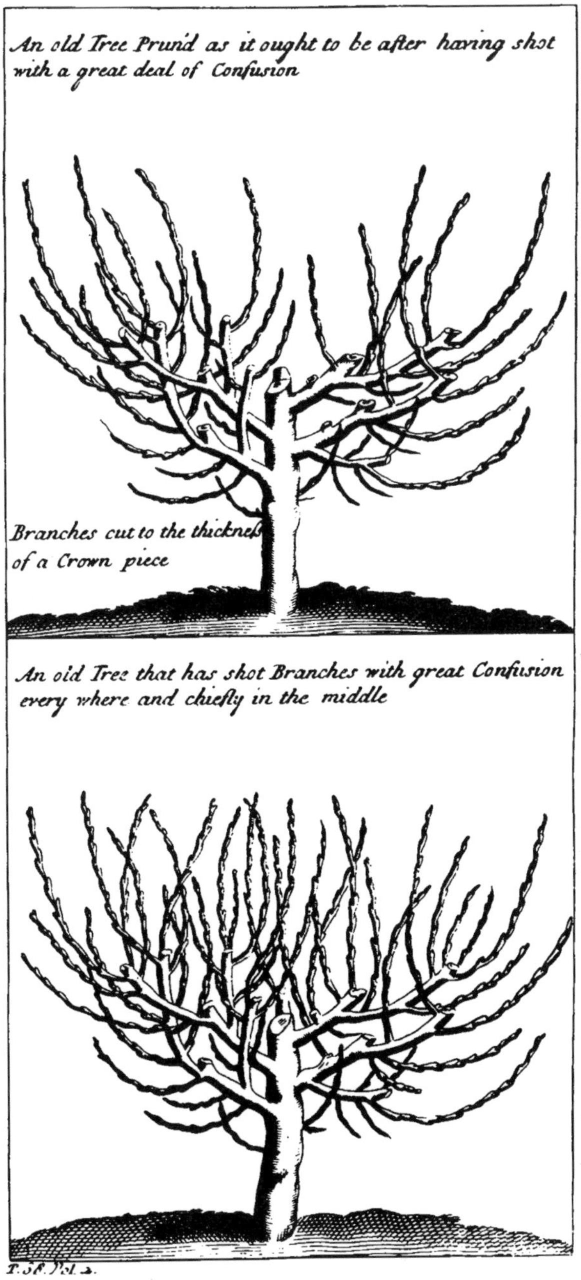
An old Tree Prun'd as it ought to be after having shot with a great deal of Confusion
Branches cut to the thickness of a Crown piece
An old Tree that has shot Branches with great Confusion every where and chiefly in the middle

An old tree pruned as it ought to be after having shot with a great deal of confusion illutration from John Evelyn's The Compleat Gard'ner, 1693.

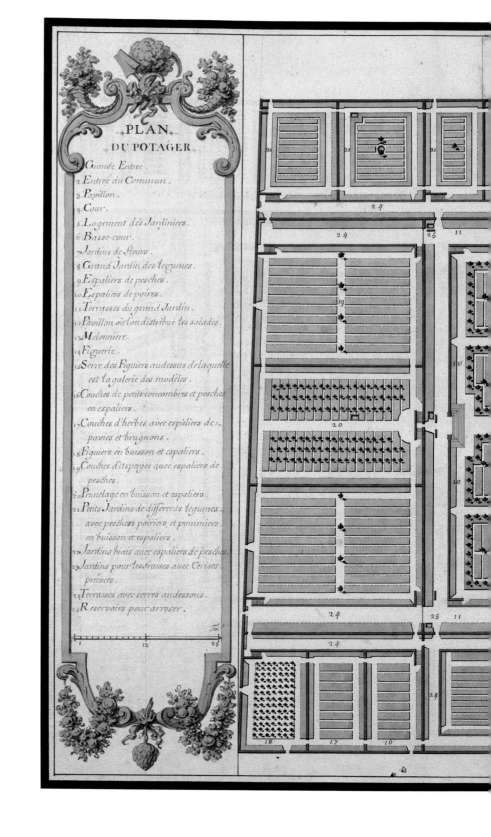

PLAN
DU POTAGER

1. Grande Entrée.
2. Entrée du Commun.
3. Pavillon.
4. Cour.
5. Logement des Jardiniers.
6. Basse-cour.
7. Jardin de Fleurs.
8. Grand Jardin des legumes.
9. Espaliers de pesches.
10. Espaliers de poires.
11. Terrasses du grand Jardin.
12. Pavillon où l'on distribuë les salades.
13. Melonniere.
14. Figuerie.
15. Serre des Figuiers au dessus de laquelle est la galerie des modéles.
16. Couches de petits concombres et pesches en espaliers.
17. Couches d'herbes avec espaliers de pavies et brugnons.
18. Figuiers en buisson et espaliers.
19. Couches d'asperges avec espaliers de pesches.
20. Prunelage en buisson et espaliers.
21. Petits Jardins de differents legumes avec pesches, poiriers, et pommiers en buisson et espaliers.
22. Jardins biais avec espaliers de pesches.
23. Jardins pour les fraises avec Cerises précoces.
24. Terrasses avec serres au dessous.
25. Reservoirs pour arroser.

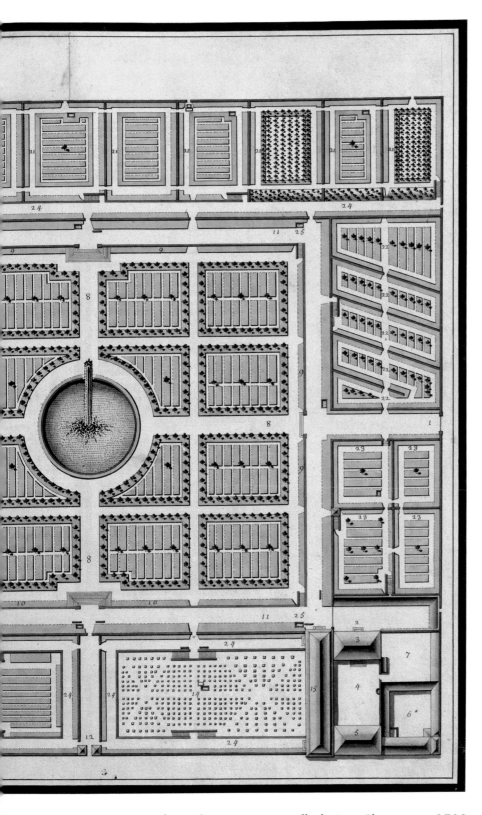

Plan of the Potager at Versailles by Jean Chaufourrier, 1720.

two Foot high, and no bigger than a Wheat Straw.' *Palissades* could be high, to screen views entirely, or waist-height, in which case they were called *banquettes*. For the most part the desired effect was a smooth hedge, like a curtain of greenery, perfectly perpendicular and furnished with leaves from top to bottom, but in the *bosquets* the hornbeam could be forced to behave more like masonry; it could be clipped into arches and piers topped with topiary balls or vases. Even without resorting to trellis-work, niches could be formed for sculpture or natural arbours.

Horticultural technique advanced at Versailles under the guidance of the lawyer-turned-plantsman Jean-Baptiste La Quintinie, an associate of Le Nôtre's from his days at Vaux. La Quintinie was put in charge of the Potager that was established between 1678 and 1683 on a boggy site close to what had been known as the 'Stinking Pond' at the western end of the old village. In the time of Louis XIII there had been a small vegetable plot where the municipal library now stands, but as the château was enlarged this was judged inadequate and a new site had to be found. Conveniently situated for the King's walks, it was hardly an auspicious location for a fruit-and-vegetable garden, although dredgings from the excavations for the Pièce d'Eau des Suisses and good soil from the Satory plateau, mixed with liberal quantities of manure from the stables, improved growing conditions. The Potager was no modest kitchen-garden; it was something between an outdoor laboratory and a early example of agribusiness, and its production was destined for the ever-demanding *Service de la Bouche*. Sometimes the garden produced a surplus, which La Quintinie would distribute to the poor from a small passageway called the 'Public', rather than sell it for profit, as others in the royal service might have done.

La Quintinie built rubble drains and raised planting beds, and the whole garden was enclosed behind walls which kept the precious produce safe from both thieves and biting winds. La Quintinie lined his plants up like soldiers in a layout that was every bit as regimented as Le Nôtre's plan for the Petit Parc, but within this horticultural parade-ground there were specialised sections for the production of figs, melons, plums, strawberries and cherries. A number of techniques were used to optimise growing conditions so that fruit and vegetables could be provided throughout the year. La Quintinie built upon known market-gardening techniques. Olivier de Serres, for example, had already advocated the use of glass cloches, or bell-jars, to grow melons and cucumbers. In the Potager, La Quintinie constructed hotbeds consisting of alternate layers of soil and manure for forcing vegetables and trailing fruit out of season. The King had an infatuation with peas, which had been introduced from Italy around 1660. He had been observed to gobble a whole dish of them and then be sick during the night. One of Mme de Sévigné's letters reports that 'the pea business still goes on. Impatience to eat them, the pleasure of having eaten them and the hope to eat more of them are the three questions constantly discussed by our princes.'

La Quintinie was renowned for his expertise in the cultivation of pears, listing over three hundred varieties but esteeming the *'Bon Chrétian'* above all others. In addition to its virtues of sweetness and succulence, it could be produced for the table when other pears were out of season. The gardener experimented with different methods of pruning and developed the espalier technique to the point where his pear trees resembled candelabra; this flattened form ensured that they did not shade one another. Glass frames were used to cover some of the beds, and glass walls were erected in front of some of the espaliered trees. Glass was a very expensive material, costing about 225 *livres* per square metre, so it was a mark of the King's favour that La Quintinie was afforded the budget for such innovations. Louis also built a house for him in 1682, together with lodgings for his gardeners. Once again, the reason must be sought in the King's relentless appetite for prestige. Having a miraculous garden and a miracle-working gardener not only served the royal table but also piled up *gloire* like so much fruit in a basket.

The King was genuinely interested in the techniques that his gardener had developed and was a regular visitor. Such was his pride in his Potager that he often showed it to his courtiers and guests. The design incorporated a sort of battlement or terrace from which they could watch the gardeners toiling below. In his journal entry from Thursday, 31 July 1684, the Marquis de Dangeau records that 'the King promenaded on foot in his gardens and his potager, where he allowed all those who followed him to pick and eat the fruit.'

The relationship between La Quintinie and Le Nôtre, the King's most favoured gardeners, appears to have been entirely amicable. There seem to have been brotherly bonds between many of the gardeners in the royal service, but these two in particular posed no threat to one another, so complementary were their areas of expertise.

The fortunes of Athénaïs de Montespan began to slide after the fêtes of 1674, but not before Louis had commissioned a house for her and their recently legitimised children at Clagny, not far outside the main gates of the château. The architect was to have been Le Pautre, but Le Nôtre pressed the cause of Jules Hardouin-Mansart, who was then only twenty-eight and still little known. When Louis was sent the plans for his consideration, he replied that he could not give an opinion without first consulting his mistress. Then he wrote to say that Athénaïs was in agreement, adding that 'Madame de Montespan has great desire that the garden should be in a state to be planted this autumn; do everything necessary for her to have this satisfaction and report to me the measures you have taken.' Under Le Nôtre's direction, work on the gardens started in advance of the construction of the château. Characteristically the King monitored progress from afar. 'Continue to do whatever Mme de Montespan wishes,' he wrote from his camp in Franche-Comté in 1675, 'and let me know what sort of orange trees have been brought to Clagny.'

Athénaïs was always the most expensive of mistresses. It took a workforce of twelve hundred men to construct the house and gardens, which cost on the order of 2,862,000 *livres*, about the same amount that Louis spent on pipework in the park at Versailles or a quarter of Colbert's annual budget for the navy. The ambitious Mansart seized his opportunity, creating a château which, with its façade of nineteen windows facing the garden, has been described as 'perhaps the most regularly beautiful house in France'. It formed the basis for his reputation and later career, serving as the model for his completion of the château at Versailles.

For Le Nôtre it was just another exercise in the style he had made so much his own, with the characteristic geometries and parterres. The main axis, passing as usual through the centre of the building, ran west towards the Étang de Clagny, which had an irregular shape that Le Nôtre formalised as best he could. But there were never any elaborate water features at Clagny, possibly because Louis was so preoccupied with Versailles, for which the Clagny pond supplied water, but also because Mme de Montespan was soon to fall from favour.

For the ladies of the court, Clagny was a favourite destination. On 7 August 1675 Mme de Sévigné wrote to Mme de Grignan:

> We were at Clagny. What can I tell you? It is the palace of Armide. The building is up and the gardens are made; you know the style of Le Nôtre. He left a little dark wood standing, which is very fine. There is a grove entirely of orange trees in large boxes; one can walk there in the allées which are shaded. To hide the plant-boxes there are waist-high hedges on both sides, all in flower with tuberoses, roses, jasmine and carnations; it is surely the most beautiful, the most surprising and the most enchanting novelty imaginable.

Within the château, murals depicted Dido on the walls of Carthage. Athénaïs identified with the Phoenician princess, but it was a poignant choice of heroine, since Dido was abandoned by her lover Aeneas. By 1678 Primi Visconti would write that 'the King is tired of Mme de Montespan; she has taken an influence

Françoise d'Aubigné, Marquise de Maintenon
by an unknown French artist in the reign of Louis XIV.

over him which has become a kind of domination.' Louis grew sexually restless, and successive pregnancies took a toll on Athénaïs' figure. Louis had always been promiscuous – he had been known to tumble one of Athénaïs' maids in his mistress's antechamber if his lover kept him waiting – but now he threw himself into a series of public affairs, first with the beautiful but dull Princesse de Soubise; then with Mme de Ludres, one of Madame's maids-of-honour; then, more seriously, with Mlle de Fontanges, another of Madame's ladies-in-waiting, who was regarded as the greatest beauty to have come to court in years.

None of these women had the personality and charm to displace Athénaïs, but Mme de Maintenon had the weapons of intelligence and quiet determination. Devoutly religious, she saw it as her sacred mission to reform the King. She had proven herself to be an excellent governess, and the King doted on his children. She began, slowly and carefully, to insinuate herself into his affections. There was still some embarrassment about the status of her young charges. The Duc du Maine was forbidden from addressing the King as 'Papa', yet one evening, during a family outing in gondolas on the Grand Canal, the boy, who had drunk more red wine than he could handle, asked to be rowed towards the King's boat. Rising unsteadily to his feet, he shouted, 'To the health of the King, my father' before collapsing in giggles into the arms of his governess.

Mme de Maintenon whispered to the King about the state of his soul and gradually became more important to him than Athénaïs. Courtiers could not quite believe that this was happening, but nevertheless a punning joke about her name began to circulate. She became Mme de Mainte*nant*, the woman of the moment.

When Louis resolved to lead a better life, there was no place in it for a racy ex-mistress with extravagant tastes and a sharp tongue. Sensing all of this, Athénaïs did not like to remain at Clagny; Versailles was where the battle for the King's heart and soul would be fought, but it was a battle she would lose despite the love philtres she obtained from Mme Voisin.

Clagny fell into disrepair. When Nicodemus Tessin went there in 1687, he recorded that 'the château is not furnished and the garden not well kept.' The ungrateful Duc du Maine aligned himself with Mme de Maintenon and demanded the house at Clagny as a wedding present. In time it would pass to the Prince de Dombes, all the while remaining a royal residence, but Louis had no use for the place. The Étang was filled in after an outbreak of malarial fever in 1734, and the château itself was demolished in 1769.

Change was in the air at Versailles. Conceived as a pleasure-palace, it had once been only one of a string of châteaux that Louis called home. Throughout the Dutch

Wars the court had followed the practice of earlier monarchs and had been itinerant. Increasingly, however, Louis liked to spend time at Versailles, and in 1677 he announced his intention to make it his permanent residence. Five years later, after Le Brun had finished the State Apartments, he would move the whole court there.

It was a decision that would have a huge impact upon the town, upon the château itself and upon the gardens. There was a need for new offices and much more accommodation. The town expanded quickly around the structure provided by Le Nôtre's avenues. In many ways it was a pioneering piece of urban development. The people who would be coming to Versailles were of such importance that they would not be content with muddy, poorly lit streets, bad water and stinking sewers. In 1674 Colbert had given an instruction to 'plant elms in all the streets and squares of Versailles', but vandalism or theft must have been an issue, because in 1684 the guards who were ordered to look after these plantings were armed with pistols. The marshy waters around Versailles were regarded as unfit to drink, so contractors were employed to bring fresh water to the workers and soldiers who laboured at the château, but this was only a stopgap. Later there would be pipes and aqueducts bringing potable water to eleven drinking fountains in the town. Soon, in fact, there would be little left of the old village. The Grand Commun, built to house the King's officers and where Le Nôtre would have an apartment, was built between 1682 and 1684 on the site of the old church. Versailles had become a modern town.

View of the Bassin de l'Encelade by Jean Cotelle, commissioned in 1668.

XI
Total Control

O NE OF THE MOST MEMORABLE SCULPTURES at Versailles is also the most gruesome. This is the enormous drowning figure of the giant Enceladus, which was placed in the Bosquet de l'Encelade in 1676, just when Louis was thinking of moving his court to Versailles. Astronomers may recognise the name of one of Saturn's moons, but the original Enceladus was one of the mythical giants who rebelled against Zeus. Subdued by a bolt of lightning, his fate was to be buried beneath Mount Etna; and when that mountain rumbles he is said to be adjusting his position on his eternal couch. At Versailles, though, he seems to be mired in something like rocky quicksand, and his efforts to escape are just dragging him deeper. The message could hardly have been clearer. It was a warning to uppity nobility: 'Know your place.' Just as Enceladus, in his folly, had built a mountain in his attempt to reach the heavens, the *Frondeurs* had dared to threaten the authority of the King. This fountain, conceived by Le Brun, made by Marsy, placed amongst rubble by the *rocailleur* Berthier and given a delightful setting of vine-covered trellis-work by Le Nôtre, included a jet as thick as a man's arm, rising to a height of 8 metres and issuing from the giant's throat like a despairing cry. Just as surely, proclaimed the fountain, would the King's enemies be crushed.

Psychoanalytically inclined biographers of Louis XIV have suggested that the whole edifice of Versailles, not just the buildings but also the elaborate rituals and codes of etiquette, stems from the incident in Paris when he had just turned ten and a mob with murderous intent had surged towards the Palais-Royal. Louis was

View of Les Bains d'Apollon by Jacques Rigaud, c. 1730.

awoken in the early hours of the cold January morning and hurried out through a secret door into a carriage made ready for immediate departure for Saint Germain. This incident accounts, say the analysts, for Louis' dislike of Paris, his determination to keep his nobles firmly in place, and even his need to chase away all thoughts of that intimidating winter by blazing forth like the sun.

Whatever Louis' unconscious motivations, he certainly had conscious political ones. His love of control – an aspect of his domestic policy – had a few very simple principles. First, if he could keep all of his high-ranking nobles at court, he could watch them closely and they would not be able to plot against him. Second, if he made life at court diverting enough, they would lose their taste for rebellion. Third, if he made court life very expensive, they would not have the resources to cause him trouble; in fact they would probably have to take administrative posts or army commissions just to pay their costume bills. Finally, if he made all advancement absolutely dependent upon himself, he would have complete power over them all.

To conclude from this, however, that seventeenth-century France was some kind of police state would be a mistake. In most respects Louis was not a tyrant, though historians agree that his domestic record is badly stained by his treatment of the Huguenots, the French Calvinists who lost their right to freedom of worship when he revoked the Edict of Nantes in 1685. Two hundred thousand of them fled the country, and ten thousand would fight for William of Orange in the coming wars, while those who remained in France were cruelly persecuted. Nothing can be said in favour of this policy, which was motivated by a misguided sense of piety, for which some blame the influence of Mme de Maintenon. France lost a wealth of talented artisans, among others, and Louis besmirched his reputation by sending troops to quell Huguenot revolts and quartering unruly dragoons upon families who refused to convert to Catholicism.

The King had no need of dragoons to keep his court under control. Perhaps he realised the power of exclusion when he hosted his hunting-lodge parties for an élite set at the beginning of his reign. By degrees he reduced the most powerful nobles to the role of sycophants. *Les Grands* were effectively excluded from politics and government. Louis took care of that business personally, closeting himself away for at least three hours each morning with his ministers and secretaries. Whilst he insisted that his nobles should attend court – if they stayed away too long they risked the royal rebuke 'I do not know him' – at the same time he kept them at a distance. In *Les Plaisirs* members of the nobility had performed the roles allotted to them by the King, but by the time of the *Divertissement* they were no longer encouraged to be actors, having become mere spectators. As it was in the gardens, thus it was in the state.

Just as sunrise and sunset were the most significant moments of Apollo's day, so were the *lever*, the royal getting-up, and the *coucher*, the royal going-to-bed, the most important occasions in the daily routine at Versailles. It was considered a great honour to see the King rubbed down with rose-water, to watch him shave and have his first bowel movement, and to help him on with his shirt and breeches. Similarly at night time it was considered a privilege to help the King off with his trousers but an even greater honour to hold the candlestick while he got into bed. Far from feeling humiliated by these empty rituals, the grandees were flattered to be so close to their sovereign and even believed that such activities were in their own interests, since it was in these intimate moments that they might petition the monarch for favours, assuming that he was willing to listen.

To advance in the game of courtly snakes-and-ladders, it was necessary to be noticed by the King. 'When the King condescends to glance at someone,' wrote Primi Visconti, 'that person considers his fortune made and says to others "the King looked at me!"', adding that Louis was cunning enough to repay his courtiers with nothing more than a fleeting glance. Louis had mastered the art of keeping people dangling. When they petitioned him for favours, he would turn impassively and reply, 'I will see.'

In contrast to the aloofness the King displayed towards many of high birth, he would talk for hours with his ministers or architects, or walk in the gardens in deep conversation with Le Nôtre. Those with effective influence upon the King, aside from his mistresses and his confessors, were often those who had risen by merit, if not from the middle classes, then certainly from the lower orders of the aristocracy. Yet to say that the entire nobility was reduced to a swarm of useless drones may be an overstatement, since there were still aristocratic bishops, ambassadors and provincial governors, and the majority of military and naval commanders continued to be drawn from the Nobles of the Sword.

Many of the rules of etiquette that monopolised court life strike us as absurd. It is a measure of the King's psychological grip over everyone that he could command a room even if he was not in it. It was customary, for example, to take one's hat off at the King's dining-table, even if His Majesty was not dining, and it was as much of a solecism to turn one's back on a portrait of the King as it would have been to do so to the monarch himself. Apart from the stultifying etiquette, there was often not a lot to do, and much of the time one had to do this nothing while standing completely still. The contemporary writer Jean La Bruyère summed up life at

Versailles elegantly when he wrote that 'the Court does not make one contented; it prevents one from being contented anywhere else.'

The King liked order in his daily life as much as he admired order in his gardens. Saint-Simon remarked that 'with a watch and an almanac, at three hundred leagues from the court, one knows at any given hour what the King is doing.' After the ritual of the *lever*, he would generally spend the hours from ten o'clock until midday in council; then he would pass through the Grande Galerie on his way to take Mass with the Queen and other members of the royal family. This passage gave his courtiers one of their few opportunities to petition the King; they would get another when the service ended. Compelled to wait around while he conversed with his ministers or said his prayers, those concerned must have found these to be edgy occasions. From one until two o'clock he would spend some time with his favourites; then it was time to eat.

According to Saint-Simon, the afternoon meal was always taken *à petit couvert*, which is to say at a small table in the King's own apartment, but it was never a light snack. Louis' sister-in-law, the Princess Palatine, recorded that 'I have often seen the King eat four plates of soup of different kinds, a whole pheasant, a partridge, a large plate of salad, two thick slices of ham, a dish of mutton in a garlic-flavoured sauce, a plateful of pastries and then fruit and hard-boiled eggs. Both the King and Monsieur are exceedingly fond of hard-boiled eggs.' Not that Monsieur ever dined with his brother; the latter's role, on these occasions, was to proffer the royal napkin, though Louis at least allowed him to be seated. Although the meal took place in the King's own room, it was a very public and formal event, witnessed by his principal courtiers and employing the industry of 498 members of the *Service de la Bouche*. Louis was a man of intemperate enthusiasms and appetites who could be more of a glutton than a gourmet. It has been suggested that he might have had a tape worm, for, although he ate prodigiously, he did not get fat. When he died it was found that his intestines were twice as long as those of an average man, though whether this was the cause or an effect of his enthusiasm for food (or whether his innards stretched when they were measured) is not clear.

Some exercise was probably needed after such a substantial dinner. The afternoon was Louis' favoured time to go hunting, take a walk or a ride in his carriage. Once a week he would follow his hounds, in his later years riding in a specially contrived light carriage drawn by four horses, which he would drive at great speed. He had abandoned hawking, the sport of his ancestors, in favour of shooting and was reputedly an excellent shot, who had been known to bring down 250 game in a single day. He would give some of what he had shot to the ladies who had accompanied him; it was a great honour for them to return to the château with such trophies dangling from their belts.

A remark by the Princess Palatine seems to contradict the many reports concerning Louis' enthusiasm for his gardens. 'Although Versailles possesses the loveliest promenades in the world, no one except myself ever walks in them. The King is always telling me: "You are the only one who enjoys the beauties of Versailles."' Surely the King was just making conversation or being playful. Saint-Simon tells us that on those days when the King did not shoot or hunt, he walked in the gardens or inspected his buildings. On these occasions the King would be accompanied by his principal officers, the same select noblemen who had access to the *lever* and *coucher*, while others followed at a distance. The excursion usually reached the Grand Canal, where the King would take to a gondola, accompanied by his favourite ladies. Lully's violinists and vocalists would clamber into another boat, for music was an essential component of the King's leisure. In better weather, the promenade might take place at dusk, replacing the regular indoor concert, and culminating in fireworks. However, these excursions were pallid reiterations of the great fêtes held earlier in the reign, so perhaps there was some truth in the Princess Palatine's remark. Louis' enthusiasm may have flagged since the heady days when Le Nôtre was laying out the main elements of the park.

Even Louis became a prisoner of his own routine. Since talk of serious politics was discouraged, there was only gossip – who was in favour, who had made fools of themselves, who was in fashion, who was not, who was sleeping with whom. Louis was aware of the dangers of boredom and provided a regular programme of concerts and comedies, in the Salon de Diane and the Salon de Vénus, rooms collectively known as *l'appartement*. There were balls on Saturdays and card games on Mondays, Wednesdays and Fridays. The gaming table seems to have been the one place where both men and women could forget etiquette and good behaviour. The Princess Palatine remarked that 'the players behave like madmen, one screaming aloud, another striking the table so hard with his fist that the whole room echoes with the sound, a third uttering blasphemous oaths so terrible as to make one's hair stand on end; they all appear to be completely out of their minds.' For those who lost, the rule was stoical acceptance; those who were truly noble would never complain.

In fact as life ossified at Versailles, it seemed to move out of the gardens and into *l'appartement*. A robust, outdoor type like the Princess Palatine could not stand it: 'The apartment is an absolutely intolerable experience. We all troop into the billiard room and lie on our stomachs or squat, no one uttering a word, until the King has finished his game. Then we all get up and go to the music room where

A lady of the court (la Duchesse de Valentinois) dressed for a masked ball.
French school, seventeenth century.

someone is singing an aria from some old opera which we have heard a hundred times already.' Perhaps it was Madame's intense dislike of such evenings indoors that prompted her complaint that no one seemed to enjoy the garden walks anymore.

Though there were no longer fêtes to match the splendours of 1664, 1668 and 1674, there were still masquerade balls at which the guests were encouraged to appear in the guise of Turks, Moors, Persians or Chinamen. They had to provide their own costumes, another strain on their already pummelled purses. There was nowhere in the world as fashionable as Versailles, and it was a constant struggle to keep up. If the King remarked that he liked a fabric or the cut of someone's dress, everyone had to rush off to update their wardrobes. To be out of fashion was to risk scorn. It was a very difficult balancing act. If one made no effort, one would be ridiculed; if one tried too hard, one could meet the same fate, for, as Molière's comedies served to remind everyone, there was nothing so laughable as pretension. The courtly ideal of the *honnête homme* was a means by which a 'true aristocracy', based upon supposed natural virtue, could be distinguished from a ranking based entirely upon blood-lines. This creed suited those financiers and merchants who sought to rise socially, and also benefited artists, architects and those who were admitted to the Académies, where distinctions between aristocracy and bourgeoisie could be erased. Le Nôtre, a gardener who was ennobled, was a perfect example of this social mechanism in operation. His talent, when considered alongside his open-hearted and straightforward nature, made him a perfect model of *honnêteté*.

Tidiness and control were also the essence of Le Nôtre's gardens, the perfect setting and metaphor for this orderly court. Here nature was clipped and subjugated. The ranked levels of the terraces and the degrees of the cascades spoke of a natural hierarchy in society. If you trace the central axis of the garden at Versailles back towards the château, it will lead you to the room which, from 1701, was the King's bedchamber. The avenues in the town converge towards the same spot. Thus the whole layout – buildings, avenues, lakes, canals, even the town – was focussed upon the royal personage. When he looked out from his rooms, the views seemed to stretch to infinity, and the domination of nature by geometry seemed as absolute as his reign.

Louis' *Mémoires* show that he was fully aware of the symbolic significance of his gardens: 'When foreign visitors in a State see that it is flourishing and well-regulated, see that which is consumed and an expenditure which might seem excessive, it makes a very favourable impression on them of magnificence, power, wealth and grandeur.' Princes were judged by the shows they could mount. This was the reason why ambassadors, envoys and distinguished guests were always given a tour of the gardens. Le Nôtre's style would become so closely identified with such displays of royal power that in eighteenth-century England the Whig oligarchy would reject it completely, turning to the naturalistic style that was so much its antithesis.

Straight lines have been associated with military power ever since the Romans built their unswerving roads for the rapid deployment of their legions. The straight forest rides of the Grand Parc were ideal for hunting on horseback, always a training ground for military leaders. Such thoughts were probably far from Le Nôtre's conscious mind, but the ideas were there in the culture from which he sprang. When Baron Haussmann remodelled Paris for Napoleon III in the nineteenth century, he cut straight avenues through the mediaeval city. Though we might admire them for their aesthetics, they were also designed for rapid troop movements and the deployment of artillery in case of insurgencies.

From its beginnings as a private retreat, Versailles became a very public place once the court had moved there; the King lived his life in the public gaze to an extent that seems remarkable from our security-conscious perspective. With so much precious metalwork on view, there had to be a regular patrol of armed *gardes-bosquets*, and for those who helped themselves to copper or bronze the penalty was death.

Though Versailles could be a frivolous place, and while there was much scope for playfulness in the details of the *salles* and *bosquets*, the overall design is austere. Indeed it seems as though it became simpler and more formalised as Le Nôtre got older, thus playing into the hands of Hardouin-Mansart, whose taste was for setting the gardens in stone. Le Nôtre loved his axes and had visual effects very much in mind, yet he grew to distrust ornamentation for its own sake. We have already noted his indifference towards parterres. He was also no great plantsman, for his woodlands were full of the same species of trees that could be found in the French countryside, and, as we have seen, he relied heavily upon hornbeam to line the *allées* and box hedging to shape the parterres.

For those with money or power, however, collecting plants was becoming an enthusiasm. A garden containing unusual species was an ornament to its owner's prestige in a similar way to a library including rare books or a curiosity cabinet packed with artworks or specimens. Already in the sixteenth century a plant trade had developed to serve this interest, focussed initially on varieties of fruit trees for orchards but expanding later to include ornamental material. The tulipomania that had gripped Holland in the 1630s afflicted France less severely, but the hitherto casual trade in seeds and cuttings brought in by seafarers, botanists and travellers became the basis for organised commercial activity, with nurseries established around Paris, like that of Pierre Morin, who traded in tulips, irises and ranunculi from his well-stocked site at Saint-Germain.

Despite Colbert's mercantile promptings, Louis' dreams of territorial expansion extended no further than the Rhine and the Pyrenees; the great age of botanical exploration and plant-hunting would be linked to colonial expansion and was still a century away. The expedition that would carry the botanist Philibert Commerson to Rio de Janeiro, where he discovered a shrubby climbing plant with vivid purple-red papery bracts and called it *bougainvillea* in honour of his captain, did not set sail from Nantes until December 1766, the same year in which a young Englishman called Joseph Banks, later a founder-member of the Horticultural Society, shipped aboard the HMS *Niger* bound for the coasts of Labrador and Newfoundland. The display of exotic plant material would become a nineteenth-century enthusiasm; the plant palette of seventeenth-century France, like that of the English landscape gardeners of the following century, was relatively limited.

Enormous purchases of plant material were nevertheless authorised by Colbert and his successors, as the account books for Versailles show. If rare flowers carried prestige, then Louis had to have more of them than anyone else. The minister set up supply routes and put in place a network of nurseries, including, in addition to Saint-Germain, those at Aulneau, near Sceaux, Noisy and Rocquencourt, and, most significantly, the Pepinière du Roule, in the Faubourg Saint-Honoré, close to the Tuileries. Of the latter the English traveller Martin Lister wrote, '... this ground, inclosed with high walls, is extremely large, as it ought to be for the supply of the king's gardens; several acres were planted with pines &c. and there were vast beds of bulbous roots and the like.'

As with so much else at Versailles, the planting carried political significance. It was important that France should surpass Italy in horticultural technique as in everything else, and also that France should be regarded as a geographical unity even though it straddled different climatic zones. For these reasons it was necessary that plants from the Mediterranean should be seen flourishing under the cool grey skies of the Île-de-France, so the south-facing Parterre du Midi, above the Orangerie, was created. Aware of the floral richness of Provence, Colbert wrote to Nicolas Arnoul the *Intendant de Marine* at Marseilles asking him to scout for jonquils, jasmines and tuberoses. Writing in April 1674, he was clearly frustrated by the poor quantity that had been supplied: 'It is necessary,' he told M. Arnoul, 'that you strongly advise all those employed in this search to apply themselves more diligently than in previous years.' The *Intendant* was certainly kept busy; in

Flowers including tulips, anemone, bugloss and campanella,
from Les Velins du Roi by Nicolas Robert, seventeenth century.

addition to purchasing plants, he was also under orders to find rocks and shells for the royal grottoes. Colbert had need of 'a very large quantity for the new works which the King is undertaking'.

Louis' early identification with the sun is revealed in the *Comptes des Bâtiments*, where there are several references to expeditions to gather unusual plants and animals from the Levant, which was the name given to the eastern Mediterranean region, including modern-day Lebanon, Syria, Israel and Turkey, and which took its appellation, like Louis' morning ritual, from the verb *lever*, 'to raise'; the Levant was considered to be the land of the rising sun. It was not only tulips that were prized, but also anemones, ranunculi, auriculas, narcissi, irises, carnations, hyacinths, jonquils, lilies and fragrant flowering plants such as jasmines and tuberoses. Plant purchases were recorded in the era of the grand fêtes, but they increased with the construction of the Trianon de Porcelaine in 1670. Spending on flowers stepped up still further in the 1680s when the gardens at Marly were created and those at Trianon extended. Elizabeth Hyde estimates that the King reimbursed his gardeners for more than 165,000 flowers in 1686 alone, with a further 96,500 plants and bulbs purchased in the following year. Almost 30 per cent of these purchases were intended for Trianon, with a further 20 per cent for Marly, but, as Hyde observes, there was no shortage of flowers in the Petit Parc at Versailles, drawing our attention to the 600 hepaticas and 750 primroses planted in the Salle du Conseille in 1690, and the 100 double wallflowers, 300 double carnations and 2,150 double white juliennes that embellished the Salle de Bal in 1691.

Such was the demand for plants that it could not entirely be met from French sources. Loath though he was to buy material from abroad, in 1680 Colbert purchased some land for a garden of acclimatisation at Toulon, which meant that he could at least buy seeds, bulbs and southern plant material as cheaply as possible, bringing it on at Toulon before it was shipped to the various royal gardens. The nursery was under the charge of Nicolas Arnoul.

From time to time there were problems, with royal gardeners in Paris or at Versailles complaining that the Toulon nursery was sending them immature bulbs which would not flower. In 1693, Louvois' successor, the Marquis de Villacerf, put his complaints in writing to De Vauvré, the new *Intendant de Marine*. The bulbs sent were no good, grumbled the Marquis, and the cost of transporting them to Paris was greater than their value. The nurserymen had undertaken to supply sixty-five thousand sound bulbs per annum but were delivering only twenty-four thousand. Toulon nevertheless supplied huge quantities of flowers for the King until 1698, when the ground was sold. Thereafter the royal gardeners had to rely

View of the Orangerie, the staircase of One Hundred Steps and the Palace of Versailles, c. 1695. Attributed to Jean-Baptiste Martin, the Elder.

on the nurseries established in and around Paris, of which Roule remained the most important.

If keeping the King's flower-beds in bloom was a vast undertaking, it was matched by the effort that went into furnishing trees for the woodlands, *bosquets* and avenues of the Parc. If one has time, the cheapest way to create a woodland is to scatter seeds, and Louis' silviculturalists did experiment with acorns and yew seeds, but for the most part the King was in too much of a hurry. From the building accounts we can get a good idea of the species used by Le Nôtre and his colleagues. There are references to the delivery or planting of elms, limes, chestnuts and oaks, with a proportion of evergreen trees such as firs, yews, cypresses, hollies and spruces. The resources of many provinces were utilised. Elms and white poplars were sent from Flanders. Firs and yew trees arrived from Normandy. In 1684 more than four million *charmilles* (young hornbeams) were lifted from the forests of Lyon. The Dauphiné region provided conifers.

When, in later life, Louis' allergies turned him away from flowers, he was still able to enjoy the scent of orange trees, for which he had a particular passion. Citruses were to be found not only in the Parterre du Midi but also around the rest of the Parc and within the château. Most of them were kept in wooden boxes, so that they could be wheeled back to the Orangerie for protection during the winter months. In 1689 an ingenious jack-of-all-trades called Valentin Lopin devised a machine to lift and transport large orange trees.

The Orangerie, vaulted like a cathedral, could accommodate twenty-six hundred boxed trees. On his visit to Versailles, John Locke fell into conversation with a gardener who worked there. The trees 'were all set in square cases & are a great many of them biger than a man's thigh, but most of them with litle heads, having been lately transported i.e. 2,3,4,5 or 6 years since.' Locke tells us that the trees were mostly brought from Italy to Rouen by sea and repeats the explanation of their preparation, as given to him by his guide; they 'cut of the stock where it is entire and not spread into branches & cut of (as the Gardener told me) all the roots'. The sceptical empiricist had his doubts about this account:

> I believe they are most of them cut of, for the boxes seeme not capeable to hold the roots which are necessary for a tree of that bulke as many of them are, & soe, root & branches being cut off, they bring them exposed to the aire like soe many stakes at all times of the yeare without dyeing, but I am afraid in this later part of the story the gardiner made bold with the truth.

The sheer amount of physical labour involved in maintaining the gardens at Versailles is difficult for us to conceive. In 1693 a gardener called Rémy Janson was paid 1451 *livres* 16 *sols* for disbudding 48,000 trees in the avenues at Versailles. Disbudding, which was accompanied by pruning and training, involved the removal of surplus buds from the front and back of a tree to encourage lateral growth, and was undertaken to improve the shape of the tree, and in the case of fruit trees to improve their productivity.

Louis' garden promenades, often undertaken on foot, were in some respects the peacetime equivalents of the military inspections he would undertake while at camp, where he would review the cavalry or make changes to the disposition of the artillery. The Marquis de Dangeau's journal for Sunday, 8 April 1685 notes that 'after the sermon, the King mounted his *calèche* and went to Trianon; then he returned to his *Petit Parc* where he ordered many small adjustments.' For Le Nôtre and his colleagues, the King was an omnipresent client, but as Dominique Garrigues has observed, Louis' involvement could go further than just giving orders and waving his cane. Sometimes it was literally 'hands-on'. On 2 December 1694, for example, Dangeau reports that 'the King entertained himself all day planting in his gardens', which suggests that he might have wielded a spade, and on 11 January 1695 he 'went for a walk at Trianon after dinner, where he amused himself by pruning the Indian Chestnuts.' Just as the Sun King saw himself as the source of all animation, whose royal touch could cure scrofula, so too he was the font of all fecundity. Of course it is easier to enjoy gardening when one can dabble for an evening than when faced with the disbudding of 48,000 trees, but it is still remarkable that the King should have taken such pleasure in this manual (and, to some eyes, menial) occupation.

A story from 1707 illuminates the thrall in which the King kept his courtiers as well as demonstrating the ruthlessness of the age towards growing things. According to Saint-Simon, the King and Mme de Maintenon paid a whirlwind visit to the Marquis d'Antin at his château at Petit-Bourg. D'Antin was the legitimate son of Mme de Maintenon's old rival, Athénaïs de Montespan, and was thus particularly anxious to please his royal visitors in every way, fervently wishing to be accepted into the King's inner circle. Saint-Simon disdainfully lists the lengths to which D'Antin went, including the 'excellent concert, the games, ponies, and numerous decorated carriages for driving in the grounds'. When presented with a plan of the estate, the King found much to admire but drew attention to an avenue of chestnuts which, in Saint-Simon's opinion, 'was vastly becoming to the gardens and landscape but quite obstructed the view from the State bedroom'. Upon waking the following morning, the King looked out of his window to find that the offending avenue had been silently removed while he slept. Not a trace remained, not even the wagon ruts that might have testified to some nocturnal activity. This willingness to please the King served D'Antin well. In the following year he succeeded Mansart as *Surintendant des Bâtiments*.

The King looked favourably upon his gardeners, rewarding them with financial bonuses, building houses for them, and even, in some cases, agreeing to become the godfather of their children yet, like the *palissades* they tended, the royal gardeners were always under strict control. The building accounts give details of the hundreds of contracts that were issued, not just for new works like planting an avenue or building a trellis but for digging drains, delivering manure, spreading river sand on the walks, pruning trees and replanting floral parterres. Le Nôtre's name is not mentioned in relation to this kind of routine work at Versailles, though the accounts show that he was paid an annual wage for the maintenance of the Grand Parterre at the Tuileries, duties which included 'cleaning, packing down, and raking the great terrace facing the said palace', overseeing the 'digging and manuring of the said parterre' and filling it each season with 'flowers of the same variety as those currently found there, which he is to raise, replant, and replenish at his own expense'. He was paid 3,500 *livres* for these services in 1683. It is clear that alongside his duties as a high court official and regardless of his fame as principal designer of the King's gardens, he continued to operate as a garden-maintenance contractor. The names of Collinot, Trumel, Dupuis, Masson and Le Bouteux appear regularly in the details of the contracts for such work at Versailles. The latter all had to submit written reports to the *Contrôleurs Generaux* (one of whom was Le Nôtre himself), who in turn reported to the *Surintendant*, who reported to the King.

It made little difference whether the King was at home or away on campaign. On 19 September 1673, while his forces laid siege to Nancy, he wrote to Colbert:

'I have seen the report that you sent concerning the works at Versailles with which I am very content. I'm readying myself to feel some pleasure on arrival, which won't be so soon. It would be good if Trianon were covered and neat when I arrive, which is why it would be good to start covering the orangeries early so that I find it completed. I expect to find many late or early flowers, because my brother said the garden isn't as full as it usually is and that Le Bouteux has some flowers in reserve, I think this may be the reason. Try to find out.'

Nine days later Colbert was able to reply that everything had been covered up for the winter at Trianon and that Le Bouteux had reassured him that all would be well with regard to the flowers. Everything was always urgent for the King and he knew how to maintain psychological pressure from a distance.

Although Saint-Simon never spoke ill of Le Nôtre, he himself was not impressed with the formal style of gardening: 'Despite oneself, the violence that has been done everywhere to nature repels and disgusts.' Such a sentiment, which seems to conceal a degree of reluctant admiration, anticipated the mood of the eighteenth century. But though England's William Kent would one day be described as the first European to have 'leaped the fence and saw that all Nature was a garden', there is a possibility that Le Nôtre got there first. Those who believe that he always let the ruler and graphometer dictate his designs should consider his two water-mazes, the Bosquet des Sources in the Petit Parc and the later Jardin des Sources at Trianon. The first was situated to the south-west of the Bassin d'Apollon and shared a square block of woodland with the Galerie d'Eau. The wood was diagonal and the Bosquet des Sources occupied the north-eastern portion, where it was laid out to follow the course of an old stream, which trickled through this boggy part of the grounds on its way to the Bassin. Le Nôtre created further meandering streams, followed on each side by winding paths and accompanied by trellis-work. This was a completely novel design for its day, a piece of pure invention, created a couple of months before Le Nôtre set off on his Italian journey in 1679. When he returned from his travels, he embellished the *bosquet* with a culminating fountain, but for some reason this grove was not as popular as he had hoped, and it was soon erased to make way for Mansart's Colonnade. As soon as Le Nôtre was given another opportunity, he revived the concept of an informal water-maze. Tessin has left a description of the Jardin des Sources, the little marsh garden Le Nôtre created at the Trianon, where water flowed 'as the big trees allowed' and ran in grassy channels with occasional waterfalls. Unfortunately this garden was also destroyed, though not until the nineteenth century. It is intriguing to consider that if Le Nôtre had lived in a slightly different period, the style made famous by 'Capability' Brown and so different from that favoured by Louis XIV might have been quite within his reach.

Françoise d'Aubigné, Marquise de Maintenon. Portrait by Pierre Mignard, c. 1694.

XII
Changes

The king's new lover, Mme de Maintenon, was able to appreciate the astonishing beauty of Versailles, but she was less than enamoured with the court. When she wrote that she was 'filled with sadness and horror at the very sight of Versailles', it was a judgement upon the institution, which she condemned as too worldly, rather than its aesthetics, though her attitude is difficult to understand, considering the great efforts she took to acquire her elevated position. It was not an attitude that would make her popular. Beneath her toughness and piety was an underlying melancholy that would change the atmosphere at Versailles. In place of the gaiety and abandon of Athénaïs de Montespan, there would be conformity and gloom. Everyone had to look very serious during Mass, plays were banned for the duration of Lent, and even some of the naked statues in the gardens were fitted with fig-leaves.

Mutual hatred had replaced the friendship between Mme de Montespan and Mme de Maintenon, although they were sometimes seen walking arm in arm and laughing together in the gardens. Lucy Hilton, Mme de Montespan's biographer, suggests that Athénaïs was 'too good tempered to allow a feud to interrupt a good conversation'. Mme de Montespan lost the King's affections after the birth of the Comte de Toulouse, as she put on weight, then consoled herself by overeating, but if the flame of sexual passion between Louis and his mistress was already spluttering, it was Athénaïs's involvement in the biggest scandal to hit the French court that finally extinguished her hopes of winning back her place in the King's heart.

The trouble started in 1676 with the sensational trial of the Marquise de Brin-villiers, a sad and deranged woman who was found guilty of poisoning her father and her two brothers and then attempting to kill her husband. As if these crimes were not ghastly enough, it was discovered that she had tested her poisons on the unfortunate patients of various Parisian hospitals, where she was known as a charitable visitor and friend to the sick. The case inflamed a widespread dread of poisoning, and this fear was not unfounded, since many thwarted lovers and abused spouses turned to the black arts as a way out of their difficulties. The most popular poisons were arsenic and antimony, but all manner of powders and potions were available, including those compounded of hemlock and mandrake root, the remains of bats and moles, viper venom and the slime of toads. These substances were often peddled by women who operated on the shady margins of society, offering services as midwives, abortionists, fortune-tellers and sorcerers. Even though the penalty for witchcraft was to be burnt at the stake, they often did good business, drawing their clients not only from the lower classes but also from the prosperous bourgeoisie and nobility.

The man charged with the task of eliminating these nefarious practices was Gabriel Nicolas de La Reynie, who had in 1667 been appointed to the position of lieutenant of police for Paris by Colbert and who also had responsibilities for the sewers, a clean water supply, public health and street lighting. In 1677 Louvois authorised La Reynie to look into a spate of alleged poisoning cases, and the police chief soon had hundreds of suspects behind bars. In an attempt to quell the mounting hysteria, Louis established the Commission of the Arsenal, which soon became known as the *Chambre Ardente*, the 'burning room', a reference to an old inquisitorial court that had been hung with black curtains and lit by torches. Before the Commission finished its business, thirty-six people would be condemned to death by fire, with others banished or fined and a handful sent to serve on the galleys.

Soon the accused, perhaps in an attempt to prolong proceedings, perhaps out of malice, were spreading allegations which reached the highest echelons of society. Once the name of the fortune-teller Catherine Monvoisin, known as 'La Voisin', had been implicated in this murky business, which became known as the Affair of the Poisons, it was inevitable that suspicion should fall upon Athénaïs de Montespan. There were many who were willing to testify that Athénaïs had consulted La Voisin, but there were also far more serious allegations involving satanic rites, kidnappings, child murder and a plot to assasinate the King.

Was Louis' spirited mistress capable of such crimes? There was certainly enough truth in the accusations for Louis to quickly wind up the business of the

Chambre Ardente. Rather than prolonging the risk that damaging accusations might be proven, he issued *lettres de cachet* ordering that more than 140 prisoners should be locked up at the King's pleasure. To safeguard Mme de Montespan, Louis was willing to perpetrate a miscarriage of justice, for many of the accused were undoubtedly guilty yet escaped the death penalty given to earlier suspects, while any that might have been innocent were incarcerated without trial. It is hard to accept, however, that Louis believed his former mistress guilty of child murder or treason. She remained at court for another eleven years, during which time the King was willing to settle her gambling debts and even accompanied her to a ball in 1681 in honour of their daughter, Louise-Françoise, Mlle de Nantes. Nevertheless, Athénaïs had lost her grip on his soul. It was Mme de Maintenon who was secretly married to the King following the death of the Queen in 1683.

Another pair of rivals, Colbert and Louvois, played opposing roles in the Affair of the Poisons. Many of those implicated in the scandal were friends of Colbert, so the minister did his best to dampen down the rumours, found a good lawyer for Athénaïs and tried to persuade the King of her innocence. Louvois, on the other hand, sided with Mme de Maintenon and was happy to fan the flames of gossip. Colbert's intercession might have saved Athénaïs from those who would have seen her burn, but his own reputation was damaged by the scandal.

The early 1680s thus saw a complete change of regime at Versailles, and with it came a marked change in atmosphere. In 1682 the château became the permanent home of the court. In 1683 Colbert died and, the very same day, was replaced as *Surintendant des Bâtiments* by Louvois. This did not slow down the pace of the works for one moment; indeed Louvois pushed on with military rigour, letting everyone know that things must be 'of higher quality than in the past'. But it did have consequences for those members of the *équipe Colbert* who had enjoyed the late minister's trust. One of the first to be shown the door was his youngest son, the Marquis d'Ormoy. So bad had this boy proved at account-keeping and memo-writing that even his father had been forced to send him on menial missions like counting workmen or checking that the fountains were working. Le Brun, who had been a virtual commissar of culture, became another casualty of the shifting web of power; Louvois became *Protecteur de l'Académie* and never missed an opportunity to undermine the *Premier Peintre*'s authority. Le Brun's rival, the veteran artist Pierre Mignard, was commissioned to design statues for the gardens, while Le Brun's own influence in that sphere evaporated. Mignard had been a bitter critic of the Académie for over twenty years and had never recognised Le Brun's authority. Le Brun also had to face down rumours that he had embezzled over a million *livres* and was destined for the Bastille. When he died in 1690, the Académie, following the orders of the King, appointed Mignard as Associate, Rector, Director and Chancellor, all at a single sitting.

Despite Colbert's initial misgivings, Le Nôtre had proved his worth countless times over, and the two men had established a good working relationship. Le Nôtre would not enjoy the same favoured status under Louvois, and he would lose ground, literally as well as figuratively, to Mansart's architectural initiatives. Though he remained a favourite of the King and even got on well enough with Louvois to design gardens for him at Meudon, he lost an important ally when Le Brun fell so dramatically from favour.

Le Nôtre's last major addition to the gardens, created at the age of sixty-seven, was the Salle de Bal, also known as the Bosquet des Rocailles, situated immediately to the south of the Parterre de Latona, which was built in 1680–1 during the last years of Colbert's life. Le Nôtre had just returned from his trip to Italy, and though he claimed to have found little there to compare with the glories of French gardening, it has been suggested that he drew the inspiration for this new *bosquet* from the ladder-like water features at the Villa Aldobrandini and Villa Ludovisi at Frascati, outside Rome. There is certainly something whimsical and theatrical about this tiered amphitheatre with its turf seats and rusticated cascade, constructed from Fontainebleau sandstone and covered with thousands of shells from Madagascar. One of Le Nôtre's well-hidden surprises, it lies deep within woodland, along a curving path lined with trellis-work, and is only revealed when the visitor stands upon the threshold. One of the best-kept *bosquets* at Versailles, it is still magical today, but the enchantment must have been greater when it was lit by torches and an unseen orchestra played from behind the cascades. This is a very delicate *bosquet*, and the wonder is that it has survived in such good repair. The shells and semi-precious stones of the cascade are wired into place rather than held with mortar, and the whole construction is alarmingly fragile. In 2002 the gilding was restored on the impressive lead candelabra. The original seventeenth-century hydraulics are still in place, including a tank that takes two days to fill. From the Salle de Bal one can gain an impression of how other *bosquets* must have looked in their prime; one can even be transported to the lost and lamented Grotte de Thétis, which, with its shellwork and *rocaillage*, must have been very similar in spirit. They both belonged to the playful era at Versailles, delightful though teetering a little giddily along the brim of bad taste. Soon the place was to shake off these Italianate fripperies and become more seriously French.

When Mme de Montespan fell from favour, Louis had little hesitation in obliterating her memory from the gardens. Mme de Maintenon disliked the Trianon

View of La Salle de Bal by Jean Cotelle, commissioned in 1688.

de Porcelaine, which symbolised her rival's period of ascendancy, and persuaded Louis to have it knocked down. This was not a difficult argument to win, since the building was too small for anything other than its intended use as a love-nest, and it was also costly to maintain. The jaunty blue-and-white tiles had never been suitable for outdoor use and would come clattering down from the roof after every frost. When the Marais, with its tree-like fountain, was removed in 1704, Mme de Maintenon had successfully erased the last trace of Montespan.

Meanwhile a stultifying routine crept upon the court, which was only relieved in 1696 by the arrival of Marie-Adélaïde of Savoy, who was to be the child-bride of the Duc de Bourgogne, the heir to the throne. Louis doted on her and had Mansart extend the Ménagerie as her private residence. There cannot be many children in history who have had their own personal zoo. In the years before Marie-Adélaïde's arrival, life at court was an eternity of waiting and standing, sticking to the rules, and keeping one's face straight.

When the entire court was relocated to Versailles, there was a vastly increased demand for accommodation. The Enveloppe was no longer sufficient. A southern wing was added to the château by Mansart between 1678 and 1682 to accommodate the Princes of the Blood and their households. It was to be matched by a North Wing, with apartments for the nobility, but the Grotto stood in the way of this proposal. The building accounts show that as late as 1681 a sum of money was put aside to find a solution that would wrap the extension to the château around the Grotto, but this plan was abandoned. The King's attachment to the Apollonian theme had waned, as we have seen, and the Grotto was firmly associated with the Age of Montespan, which perhaps sealed its fate.

The North Wing went up between 1685 and 1689 and was soon a bustling place, crammed with courtiers. An apartment at the château, no matter how pokey or ill-lit, was a status symbol, although anyone with the money would also build a town house or château of their own in the vicinity. The North Wing was so overcrowded that there were traffic jams of sedan chairs in the corridors. Another major element in this expansion plan was the construction in 1678 of the Grande Galerie or Galerie des Glaces, a vast, mirrored reception room that replaced the open-air loggia created by Le Vau on the garden front. This is one of the indoor glories of Versailles and must have looked magical when it flickered and shimmered in candle-light, but the external effect of these additions was to create a façade that can seem overpoweringly severe.

In building the Galerie des Glaces, Mansart had to remodel the garden front of the château. Without the first-floor terrace, the old water parterre, with its fancy

Jules Hardouin-Mansart. Print by Gérard Edelinck, seventeenth century.

design and sinuous lines, could no longer be easily viewed. From the ground-floor windows it just did not work. Its many sculptures did not enhance the view; they got in the way.

A rethink was obviously necessary. Whether it was Le Nôtre who had the idea or Mansart, the new design was strong because it was simple. The masterstroke was to do away with any kind of central feature so that the axis could run uninterrupted from the middle of the elevation towards the sculptural groups of Latona and Apollo and then to the Grand Canal beyond. To either side there would be sheets of water with much simpler fountains placed centrally within each. This new parterre, installed in 1683–4, was also to have its sculptural complement, but it would not be allowed to dominate. The principal statues represent gods and goddesses signifying the major rivers of France, the Garonne, the Dordogne, the Seine, the Marne, the Rhône, the Saône, the Loire and the Loiret. Cast in bronze at the royal foundry in Paris, where Jean-Jacques Keller, the commissioner for artillery, usually made cannons, they also represented the work of the greatest sculptors of the era, Antoine Coysevox, Étienne Le Hongre, Jean-Baptiste Tuby and Thomas Regnaudin. Each sculptor produced one male and one female figure. Le Brun created the first sketches. These figures would be reclining so that they would not interfere with the views to and from the palace, while between them, interspersed along the white marble copings surrounding each pool, there would be other groups, children playing innocently with birds or admiring themselves in mirrors, and a series of nymphs with attendant cupids bringing them pearls and flowers or draping them in garlands.

The question of what to do with the twenty-four displaced sculptures from the first water parterre remained. These pieces, which had once been so tightly linked to the Apollonian theme, were now distributed at will around the *allées* and *bosquets*, where they mixed with copies of Roman sculptures done by students from the Académie Française and items which had been bought as a job-lot from Vaux.

Greater resources were available for building during the peaceful period that followed the Treaty of Nymegen. Spending peaked in the middle of the 1680s, at which time the accounts show that at Versailles it amounted to more than eight times the combined expenditure on the Louvre, the Tuileries, Saint-Germain and Marly. The Marquis de Dangeau, in his matter-of-fact chronicle of life at court, noted on Sunday, 27 August 1684, that during the previous week the expenses on the works at Versailles had amounted to 250,000 *livres*, and that there had been twenty-two thousand men and six thousand horses employed there. The Marquis, obviously impressed, returned to this theme on Thursday, 31 May 1685, when he wrote that, 'According to one's calculation of all the people who presently work here or in the surrounding area for the sake of Versailles, one finds that there are currently 36,000 at work.'

Like most engineering and construction works before the era of health-and-safety legislation, lives were lost on the building site almost as easily as they were on the battlefield. In the gardens it was the excavations that were the most dangerous, not just as a result of landslips but because of fevers and poisonings caused by the unhealthy conditions in which the men laboured. Mme de Sévigné mentioned in a letter dated 12 October 1678 to her cousin, the Comte de Bussy-Rabutin, the 'great mortality affecting the workmen'. According to Primi Visconti, the Dauphine had a great aversion to the air at Versailles and blamed the earthworks. During August 1680, Visconti noted, everybody seemed to fall ill, the Dauphin, the Dauphine, the courtiers … just he and the King seemed to be spared. Only the fateful works on the River Eure would be more costly in terms of human life.

Colbert had struggled to keep France's finances in order, but towards the end of his life the scale of Louis' ambition to build would throw him into despair. 'Buildings are such an abyss,' he wrote, 'the more I work with them, the more difficulties I find. Finance gave me no problems at all in comparison.' When Louvois took over, he wasted no time in signalling his intentions. He thought that Colbert had let things slip, and he was going to restore order as quickly as he could. He wrote to Sieur Lefebvre, one of Le Nôtre's fellow *Contrôleurs*, warning him to expect an inspection and demanding a report 'on all the matters that are in hand, of the number of workmen who are employed at each workshop and the point reached in each project'. A military man through and through, Louvois desired obedience above anything and had a tendency to prefer the stick to the carrot. He banned the workers at Versailles from striking and threatened to withhold payments from contractors, or even to lock them up, if they did not meet their obligations. Even artists were not spared this heavy-handed treatment.

There is no doubt that Louvois could be a coarse and abrasive man. Nancy Mitford went so far as to call him 'that horrid man' and 'the King's evil genius'. Like many apologists for the Sun King, she cast Louvois as the villain responsible for the harshness of the *dragonnades* and also for Louis's war crimes, the atrocities committed by French armies in the Palatinate during the Dutch War. However, the responsibility for France's aggressive foreign policy and for internal repression must ultimately rest with the King, in whose name these policies were pursued. As in authoritarian hierarchies everywhere, no doubt Louvois prospered because he was a sycophant, pleasant to those above him but harsh to his subordinates. Even the charming and affable Le Nôtre would have a brush with him. There is equally

213

no doubt that Louvois was an effective minister. Like his predecessor, he was an utter workaholic, capable of writing over seventy letters in a day. However, he had little more success than Colbert in keeping costs down, for even though he tightened everything up, the scale of the building works just went on increasing.

In 1676, in his capacity as minister of war, Louvois had already commissioned Mansart to work on the chapel at Les Invalides. In October 1681 Louvois appointed him *Premier Architecte*, although he had already been involved with the work at Versailles for a number of years. Mansart is sometimes portrayed as Le Nôtre's protégé, sometimes as his rival, or else the relationship is painted as one of friendship which turned to hostility, but these are all oversimplifications.

It is easy to see why Le Nôtre might have felt disposed to help the young Jules when he first appeared at Versailles. There were thirty-three years between them in age, but their backgrounds were similar. Mansart had been born Jules Hardouin in 1646, the son of another Jules, who was a royal painter, and Marie Autier, who was the niece of the architect François Mansart, the first proponent of French Classicism. When Jules Hardouin's father died in 1660, his great uncle took the family in. Six years later, when François died, Jules took possession of his papers and also appropriated his name with a hyphen. Saint-Simon, who disliked the architect, said that he must have done this to make himself better known. If he did, it was surely no crime, and one might also think that Jules acted out of affection and respect, for it was François who first set him on the path to becoming an architect.

In 1671 Hardouin Mansart (called Mansart throughout this volume) was commissioned by various members of the nobility to build town houses for them in Versailles. Just as Le Nôtre had been launched by Fouquet at Vaux, Mansart's career took off in 1673, when he was asked to rebuild a hunting lodge, the Château du Val, situated at the end of Le Nôtre's long terrace at Saint-Germain. It is often suggested that it was Le Nôtre who put Mansart's name forward for this commission. In 1676 the architect was taken up by Mme de Montespan, who asked him to work on the enlargement of her house at Clagny, a site only a few streets away from the gates of the château of Versailles.

In time Mansart became one of those with the closest access to the King, attending him every morning at the *lever*, in itself enough to upset the pecking order at court, but also spending hours closeted tête-à-tête with Louis while they pored over the details of his building plans. Showing a shrewd understanding of the monarch's psychology, Mansart sometimes presented hastily drawn sketches, allowing the King to find faults and play architect himself. By 1685, at the age of thirty-eight, he had been made *Intendant et Ordonnateur Alternatif des Bâtiments*

*View of the Bosquet des Dômes. Illustration from
Pierre De Nolhac's La Création de Versailles.*

and established a drawing office at Versailles where colour-coded plans were prepared. Existing buildings were coloured grey while those to be demolished were washed in yellow, and proposed additions appeared in red. Mansart was made a *Chevalier de Saint-Lazare* in 1682 and ennobled; when that order was reformed in 1693, both he and Le Nôtre were awarded the Ribbon of Saint-Michel. The architect went on to rise still further in the hierarchy, adding the title of *Inspecteur Général des Bâtiments* in 1691 and eventually succeeding the Marquis de Villacerf as *Surintendant des Bâtiments* in 1699. In 1702 he became the Comte de Sagonne. It is no wonder that Saint-Simon detested him. The snobbish duke thought that the architect came from 'the dregs of the people' and that nothing could hide the coarseness of his birth, a verdict which makes it all the more surprising that the writer was comparatively positive about Le Nôtre. Whatever else Mansart might become, in the eyes of Saint-Simon he could never be an *honnête homme*.

By training and inclination Mansart was a mason and his passion was for marble. His first intervention in the gardens was at the Bosquet des Dômes, which shares a block of woodland with the Bosquet de l'Encelade. Originally known as the Bosquet de la Renommée, it had been designed by Le Nôtre in 1675 as a site for Marsy's statute of Fame, a winged female figure carrying two trumpets and poised on one leg atop a globe. A piece of comforting propaganda conceived by Le Brun during the Dutch War, this herald seemed ready to circulate news of Louis' military triumphs. However, as the Princess Palatine observed, 'there was not a single spot in Versailles which was not modified ten times', and this grove was no exception. Mansart put up two white marble pavilions, crowned with trophies and gilded decorations, which are first mentioned in the budgetary allocations of 1676. At this stage the relationship between the architect and his gardening mentor seems to have been amicable and co-operative.

An entry in the journal of the Marquis de Dangeau for July 7 1684 notes that 'The King went to set aside a camp for ten battalions he had brought to Versailles. Afterward he walked about his fountains and directed that the one of Renommée should be removed, wanting to put in that place something even more magnificent.' All change again. The displaced sculptures from the doomed Grotto were soon installed between Mansart's pavilions, Apollo and his nymphs in the centre, flanked by the groups of horses. Thus the *bosquet* became known as the Bains d'Apollon, a name it would keep for twenty years, until the peripatetic marbles were moved again in 1705 and the grove took its present name, not from any sculptural content but from the twin domes of Mansart's early essays in marble.

Le Nôtre must have been irritated by the rash of marble alterations that accompanied Mansart's growing influence in the Parc. The gardener might have tried

*Louis XV as a child, on horseback with his retinue, in view of
the Grand Trianon by Jean-Baptiste Martin, the Elder. c. 1724.*

to ignore the signs, the way in which the stone rims of the fountains in the Allée d'Eau and the lead rims of the Seasons fountains had all been changed to marble, telling himself that these were minor annoyances, but he would not be able to overlook these creeping manifestations for long. He himself had given Mansart the idea of setting off his design for the new Orangerie, which doubled the size of Le Vau's previous building, with the two gigantic stairways known as the Cent Marches, the inspiration for which seems to have been the Villa Ludovisi at Frascati. The extent of Le Nôtre's involvement in the design of the new Orangerie has been an issue for historians of Versailles because of some hearsay evidence from Louis de Bachaumont which gives the gardener more credit than the architect. 'Le Nôtre gave a quick sketch of it to the King,' wrote de Bachaumont in 1751:

> ... this Prince adopted it and placed upon his first architect the responsibility of drawing up its measurement and charged him with the execution. I have this from a respectable old gentleman, a man of parts and taste who recounted it to me in my youth. He was so much the more credible owing to the fact that he had long lived in the greatest intimacy with the famous Le Nostre.

Dominique Garrigues called the tussle between Le Nôtre and Mansart a 'polite struggle'; Jules Guiffrey, the archivist who edited the massive volumes of the *Comptes des Bâtiments*, dismissed talk of a feud as a 'canard'. But as Mansart's ascendancy wore on, there was certainly a tug-of-war over the soul of the garden. For Le Nôtre, the plants, trimmed and ordered, *were* the architecture, while for Mansart the greenery provided a showcase for exquisite buildings. Trellis-work, which had featured so strongly in Le Nôtre's designs, threatened to compete for attention with built structures, so it became less and less favoured. Though Le Nôtre gardened for the most part in a Classical idiom, his materials were close to nature – earth, foliage, lead, water and stone. Marble, though natural, was expensive, hard to come by and highly finished, while bronze, Mansart's favoured material for statuary, was costly to manufacture. Louis *Le Grand*, however, thought that these pricey materials reflected well on his glory, so Mansart had the advantage. Louvois inevitably favoured Mansart, since Le Nôtre was associated with the Colbert era. From 1684, the architect began to push his own agenda at the expense of the gardener.

In 1684 Le Nôtre was already seventy-one years old. Although he clearly did not approve of the outbreak of marble architecture in his gardens, he was sufficiently wise to realise that there was little he could do to oppose it. But if Le Nôtre did not strive to defeat Mansart, he no longer saw any reason to help him. Thomas Hedin has suggested that this antipathy between gardener and architect was not

View of the parterres of the Grand Trianon by John Cotelle, 1693.

mutual. Le Nôtre thought that Mansart was undoing his work, but Mansart saw things differently; he had not lost his admiration for Le Nôtre and would have been happy to work alongside him, but this would have entailed Le Nôtre's acquiescence in the architect's plans, and this the veteran gardener found impossible to give. Yet the two men did co-operate to a degree over the redevelopment of the Trianon from 1687. Whatever the complexities of the relationship, it was certainly not one of contempt.

The Trianon de Porcelaine was to be replaced by a larger building, the Grand Trianon, and since the job was given to Mansart the preferred building material was marble, predominantly the pink Languedoc variety, together with white and touches of the green type from Campan in the Pyrenees. With Louis characteristically pushing the pace, construction was rapid, with the main works undertaken between June 1687 and January 1688. The King gave very precise instructions and at times was almost his own architect. The project also exemplifies his trial-and-error approach to design. By September 1687 the walls of the new building had reached 6 or 7 feet in height; Louis, displeased with the effect on the garden side, ordered them to be pulled down and restarted. He even went so far as to erect a tent from which he could view the works, and in the evenings, after dinner, he would spend the evenings there with Louvois, working on his affairs. Having the royal client camping on the doorstep must have speeded up the works considerably. The King dined in his new pleasure-house for the first time on 22 January 1688, and from that date on there were frequent dinners, suppers and shows, even though the decoration was far from complete.

Collaboration between Mansart and Le Nôtre was required by the King, who insisted that the Grand Trianon should harmonise closely with the existing gardens. Indeed the basic arrangements of the parterres were scarcely affected by the new works, and they remained dedicated to floral display. The two principal pavilions were redressed with marble, and the mansard roofs of the previous building were replaced with flat roofs concealed behind balustrades. The central building of the Trianon de Porcelaine was demolished and replaced with an open portico, an unusual design that allowed views into the gardens upon arrival. 'His Majesty desires that it should be something very light, upheld by columns in the form of a peristyle, and this is what he would like you to design at your earliest convenience, understanding as he does that while you are taking the waters it is difficult for you to apply yourself,' wrote Louvois to Mansart, who was taking a holiday at Vichy.

During construction, an incident occurred that sheds light on Le Nôtre's character and his uneasy relationship with Louvois. On a visit to the building site, the King, who had an extraordinary eye for detail and was a good judge of

View of the Colonnade by Jean Cotelle, commissioned in 1688.

proportion and symmetry, noticed a fault in the casement of one of the ground-floor windows. He quizzed Louvois about it, but the latter became argumentative, maintaining that there was nothing wrong. The next day the King came across Le Nôtre and asked him for a second opinion. Le Nôtre procrastinated. He had no desire to contradict the tyrannical Louvois. After the King had asked the same question on successive days, he got angry and commanded Le Nôtre to meet him at the Trianon the following day during the course of his promenade. Le Nôtre could not avoid this confrontation and duly met the King and his minister. While Louis and Louvois disputed, Le Nôtre remained silent, but eventually the King asked the gardener to check the alignment of the casement. A furious Louvois protested that the window was identical to the others. Le Nôtre began to stammer, but the King commanded him to speak out. Le Nôtre finally admitted that the King was right and that Louvois had made a mistake. Louis declared that he could not stand obstinacy, saying that if he had not intervened the building would have incorporated the defect and would have had to have been condemned as soon as it was completed. Louvois had been soundly reprimanded. In the new political climate that followed the death of Colbert, this incident cannot have helped Le Nôtre's position.

With the construction of the Grand Trianon, the role of this retreat changed significantly. No longer a place for trysts, it was large enough to cater for the whole of the royal family, for hunting companions or those who were temporarily in favour. Nevertheless, its intimate scale and its distance from the château meant that etiquette could be relaxed.

On 11 July 1691 Louis threw a party at the Trianon for the exiled King and Queen of England. The Bourbons felt great sympathy for the displaced Stuarts. The Princess Palatine thought that King James was 'the best prince in the world', whose 'sighs are quite heart rending'. The guests arrived by canal in gondolas and *chaloupes*. An orchestra accompanied them, remaining afloat throughout the evening. Faggots were lit to illuminate the façades of the building from below, while the guests promenaded in the gardens before dining at five sumptuously decorated tables.

For the visual artists of seventeenth-century France, Versailles was the ultimate gallery, and it was natural that Mansart should want to demonstrate his prowess there; the problem was that Le Nôtre, working alongside Le Brun, had more or less finished the place. It left Mansart with no option but to attempt to turn Le Nôtre's *bosquets* into showcases for his own art. The marble basins and rims had been mere preliminaries. The real clash began in the spring of 1684, when it was suggested that the Apollonian sculptures from the Grotto might go into a marble pavilion, designed by Mansart, that would replace the fountain installed less than five years previously in Le Nôtre's cherished Bosquet des Sources. Mansart, it appears, was aware of the gardener's sensibilities and wrote to Louvois in the following terms:

> With regard to the design of which you speak to me, to replace the Sources, I have had several thoughts on this subject, which I send to you, although I would have preferred to express them to you when you were here, in order to work in concert with M. Le Nôtre on the subject of gardening, and myself on architecture, and also to understand better the intentions of the King and yourself.

If this diplomacy was intended to mollify the gardener, it did not work. Le Nôtre ignored the overture, as did Louvois, who told Mansart to get on and make a wax model of the proposal. While the projected building, an open-air interpretation of the Grotto, might have made a fine home for the sculptures, it did not sit easily upon its suggested site. The pavilion would have been open at the front but closed in at the back, which would have created dead ground to the rear. Its proposed orientation with regard to the slope did not help, since Mansart intended to place it facing uphill, which would have only accentuated the blank rear wall. The architect understood the topography less well than the landscape designer.

While these plans were being discussed, the King was away inspecting fortifications along the northern frontier. When he got back on 9 June he seemed unusually preoccupied with his gardens, in which he walked almost daily for the next ten days. We can only imagine the lobbying that went on between Mansart and Le Nôtre. This was one battle that Le Nôtre did win, because the pavilion was dropped, but it was a pyrrhic victory because the *bosquet* would still be lost.

The King's decision had less to do with Le Nôtre's powers of persuasion than with the visit that the monarch had paid to Chantilly on his way back from the border. He stopped there on 8 June and Condé gave him a tour of the gardens. The *Mercure Galant* published details of this stopover:

> The King remained closeted for several hours, after which he amused himself at the waters. The Duc brought him first to the large reservoir, which is of astonishing beauty. His Majesty then went to various places, where the waters make marvellous effects. The Prince waited for him at the first one, and accompanied him for some time, but the Duc guided him everywhere. All the waters of this delightful place are beautiful, and abundant. There is a machine which, while being quite simple, furnishes moving water to all the jets and to the cascades.

The *Mercure Galant* also said that the King praised what he saw and was 'quite satisfied', but subsequent events suggest that he was pricked by the glories he witnessed. Though Condé was beyond censure, the King was taken aback by Chantilly, rather as he had been by Vaux twenty years earlier, and once again it was a garden by Le Nôtre that had set his mind spinning. He had been stunned by the cascades and fountains, and particularly by the feature known as the Bassin Rond des Sources, at the head of the Grand Canal. Le Nôtre had created a circular pool, 70 metres in diameter, at a higher level than the Canal and fed by water from the River Nonette. The pool's shape was emphasised by two concentric rings of trees. From this basin, water tumbled down a three-tiered cascade into a hexagonal pool at the end of the Canal. Most miraculously of all, this water appeared to spring from nowhere, because Le Nôtre had hidden the conduits below ground.

It would be easy to say that the King was simply jealous of Condé's garden, but his envy was mixed with the more noble thought that it was his sovereign duty to have the best of everything. After more than a week of brooding, he announced his decision. Inspired by the Bassin Rond des Sources and its encircling trees, the King commanded Mansart to build a colonnade with fountains on the site of the Bosquet des Sources. Ironically, Le Nôtre had been responsible for his own defeat, since he had created the prototype for Mansart's new building, not knowing that the King's taste would swing so dramatically towards marble. Le Nôtre was completely passed over in the planning of this new feature, which was a blessing for all concerned. It must have been very painful for the gardener to watch trees being felled in his *bosquet* in August 1684 to make room for Mansart's showpiece.

The Colonnade is actually an arcade, made up of thirty-two arched bays, supported on Ionic columns and topped by a cornice, which closes upon itself in a perfect circle. Beneath all but one of the arches there is a pedestal basin spouting a jet. It is, perhaps, another interpretation of the Palace of the Sun described by Ovid, but equally it takes its inspiration from the descriptions and woodcuts in the mysterious erotic novel *Hypnerotomachia Poliphili* by Francesco Colonna, first published in Venice in 1499, in which the hero, Poliphilo, seems to take an almost fetishistic delight in elaborate architecture.

The workforce employed to build the Colonnade included five brigades of the Dauphin's regiment. The King followed progress closely, visiting the site several times in June and December 1685. The choice of building materials was a political statement in itself, since the marble was sourced from within France rather than imported from Italy. Eight columns are of a violet breccia, a dozen are of blue *turquin* marble, and a further dozen are of the pink Languedoc variety, while, for contrast, the bases, capitals and the entire superstructure are in white. The

Mercure Galant boasted that 'this work indicates that the King is the most magnificent prince on earth, and demonstrates that marble is at present more common in France than in Italy.'

It must have galled Le Nôtre to read the panegyric to the Colonnade in the *Mercure Gallant*: 'The woods that enclose it, along with the trellis that adorns the trunks of the trees, create a backdrop advantageous for setting off the architecture, and this work, which is of pure magnificence, is admired as much for the skill of its workmanship as for the richness of its materials.' Le Nôtre's favourite *bosquet* had been reduced to the role of a stage setting for Mansart's exhibit.

Le Nôtre's reaction to the Colonnade must have kept the gossips busy at court; Saint-Simon, who did not arrive at Versailles until 1692, thought that the story was juicy enough to include in his *Mémoires*. He scrambled the dates in the telling, suggesting that the Colonnade was erected while the landscape architect was away in Italy, but in other respects his account has the ring of truth. The King pressed Le Nôtre for an opinion on Mansart's work. 'Well! Sire, what do you want me to say?' replied the old man. 'You have turned a mason into a gardener and he has given you a sample of his craft.' At this the King fell silent and the onlookers smiled, for 'it was true that this piece of architecture, which was anything but a fountain, and yet which was intended to be one, was very much out of place in a garden.'

The remark reveals much about the attitudes of all concerned. Saint-Simon sided readily with the affronted gardener against the King and his despised architect. Le Nôtre, characteristically, dressed his displeasure in courtly wit. Mansart is made to look a little foolish – he was trying to create a fountain but could not do other than build a building. Even the King – assuming that he really did fall silent – is shown in a moment of embarrassment. He still valued Le Nôtre's opinion and wanted the veteran to approve of this new departure. Nevertheless, Le Nôtre's barb was badly aimed, because the gardener had misjudged the King's most recent enthusiasms. Louis liked the Colonnade precisely because it was a shop-front display of all that was excellent in French craftsmanship and materials.

Historians regard Saint-Simon as an unreliable witness, but there is further proof of Le Nôtre's aversion to the Colonnade in the journal of Nicodemus Tessin. When the latter visited Versailles the Colonnade was almost finished, but it was Le Nôtre who acted as tour guide, and his opinions clearly influenced the Swedish architect. Noting that the piece was 'all of marble' and that some of the details produced 'a very ugly effect', Tessin went on to remark that 'the connoisseurs all maintain that the expense must be admired more than the genius; it had already cost more than 400,000 livres.' At least one green-fingered connoisseur was of the same opinion.

Le Nôtre was able to find some consolation by recreating the atmosphere of the Bosquet des Sources in the little Jardin des Sources, which he was able to create at Trianon. This is the garden that the Princess Palatine described to her aunt Sophie, Duchess of Hanover, in a letter written from her apartment at Trianon and dated 21 June 1705:

> I am very well lodged: I have four rooms and the closet where I am writing this looks onto what we call 'Les Sources'. This is a little wood, which is so thick that the sunlight cannot penetrate it even at midday. There are more than fifty springs in it. They make little rivulets, some of them no more than a foot wide and easily crossed. Their grassy banks form little islands, large enough for chairs and a table where one can play card games in the shade.

It was in this garden, according to Tessin, that Le Nôtre made 'a sort of little marsh which he had rendered in the form of different figures, as far as the large trees allowed'. Tessin described small circular pools for water jets and noted that the little watercourses sloped so that the water would gurgle. 'It was beautifully conceived, inexpensive, and an excellent way of conserving the large trees which ruled out any other solution,' concluded the architect. In Le Nôtre's own written description of the gardens, done to accompany a plan presented to his Swedish guest, the designer wrote: 'I do not know how to describe the beauty of this place; it is a cool place where the ladies go to work, to play and to picnic.' Since the Trianon apartments of the highest ladies at court looked out on Les Sources, it is more than likely that he had this particular clientele in mind when he planned his relaxed little garden 'without order'.

When Louis had returned from Chantilly in 1684, the idea of the Colonnade had not been the only vision buzzing in his brain. He had also been stirred by the Grandes Cascades, created by Le Nôtre for Condé in a western corner of the gardens in the 1670s, and he wanted to surpass them at Versailles. He even had a site in mind: a steep slope in the same block of woodland as the Marais, the place now occupied by Hubert Robert's Bains d'Apollon. In the new mood that prevailed at Versailles, he did not simply turn to his trusted landscape designer but initiated a competition between Le Nôtre and Mansart. Drawings showing their entries are held in collections in Stockholm and Paris respectively, and they illustrate the aesthetic gulf that had opened up between the two masters. Le Nôtre's exuberant design is for an entire hillside of water-games, replete with *rocaillage* and shellwork and reminiscent of the Salle de Bal. Mansart's design, as one might have expected, is far more architectonic, with a framing building of columns and pilasters. The impression is of a kind of outdoor theatre where the cascade, topped by a sculptural Parnassus, would take the place of the stage. Considering Louis' new tastes and the drift of events at Versailles, it is not surprising that Mansart's scheme was chosen.

The Marquis de Dangeau recorded that on Thursday, 18 January 1685, the King went 'to see the model of a fountain that will be below the Marais, it will not perhaps be finished for three years, and his majesty told us that it will cost 3,000,000 *livres*'. With the model approved, thirty-six marble columns were ordered, but then work had to stop. In 1688 Louis pitched France into the Nine Years' War. The extent to which it was his own bullying tactics that united the powers of Europe against France is a matter of historical debate, but one undeniable and immediate consequence was that the Sun King's grandest building projects came to a shuddering halt.

Among the casualties were Louis' challenging project to bring water from the Eure, Mansart's cascade, and another ambitious proposal for a vast marble amphitheatre dedicated to the rivers of France, which would have been sited at the eastern end of the Bosquet de l'Île Royale. The outbreak of war spared Le Nôtre the sight of masonry rampaging throughout his rooms of greenery. It is clear that nothing would have been sacrosanct, for in 1687 Mansart planted his mark on the gardener's grand axis when he lifted the Fountain of Latona on to a wedding-cake of tiered marble. The humiliation must have been even greater for the disgraced Le Brun, who had been the author of the original concept back in the 1660s, and who did not die until 1690.

Mansart altered many of Le Nôtre's designs after the gardener's death. The Salle du Conseil of 1671 was renamed in 1705 when it became the Bosquet de l'Obelisque. Le Nôtre's design was replaced by a simplified rectangular pond that included a most impressive tiered fountain, the Cent Tuyaux, or Hundred Pipes. This created an obelisk-like pillar of water, which, by virtue of its location in the lower gardens, had sufficient head to reach 23 metres in height. The Salle d'Antiques, created by Le Nôtre in 1680, was redesigned by Mansart in 1704, becoming the Salle des Marronniers, or Chestnut Hall; chestnuts had been introduced to France during the reign of Louis XIII and were still regarded as arboricultural novelties. All of this, necessarily, was done with the King's approval. Though Louis was not an unfeeling man, he could be ruthlessly unsentimental when it came to changes in his gardens.

View along the Allée d'Eau by Jean-Baptiste Martin, the Elder, 1693. The Bassin de Neptune and the Bassin du Dragon are in the foreground, and the groves of the Arc de Triomphe and the Trois Fontaines are also shown.

XIII
Waterworks

A NDRÉ LE NÔTRE WAS A PRACTICAL TEAM PLAYER who was willing to co-operate with anyone if it helped to achieve the desired results. Like a modern landscape architect, he was a generalist who knew enough about a lot of different subjects – horticulture, arboriculture, hydraulics, mechanics, surveying, geometry, civil and military engineering – to be able to talk intelligently to experts in these fields, but he was also the visionary who saw how to bring all of this expertise together. It is easy to imagine him, on his long walks with the King, becoming rhapsodic about the possibilities.

From time to time his enthusiasm ran away with him. When Tessin visited the château in 1687, Le Nôtre was caught up with an idea for a feature in the vicinity of the Orangerie. Tessin reported that 'Monsieur Le Nôtre showed me his design, which was admirably conceived, but which had cascades of about 100 *aunes* (about 120 metres) in width, leading one to suspect that it would not be executed, since it would take another Seine to provide the requisite water.'

Le Nôtre had also been captivated by the proposal to build a canal system that would connect his Grand Canal with the Loire. As Charles Perrault recorded in his *Mémoires*, Le Nôtre and the King had been strolling along the edge of the Canal when the landscape architect said that it would be a pleasing thing 'to see the vessels descending the river Loire with their masts and sails along the mountain, like a glissade, and to come floating down the Grand Canal'. This plan had been put forward in 1674 by Pierre Paul de Riquet, whose scheme to build a waterway between the Atlantic and the Mediterranean was then under construction. His work on the Canal du Midi gave him considerable standing, but his reasoning in the case of the Loire was erroneous. He thought that because the Loire's bed was steeper than that of the Seine, it must undoubtedly be higher, but he did not allow for the height that Versailles is above the Seine. 'That which I have promised, I shall perform,' boasted Riquet, and Colbert was on the brink of signing a contract with him when Perrault invited the Abbé Picard to check the levels. The 'mountain' mentioned by Le Nôtre was the Satory plateau, south of Versailles. Using his precision instruments, Picard pronounced that there was no conceivable way that it could be crossed. 'It was a pleasure to have helped to divert this irrational and unfortunate enterprise', wrote Perrault. He was right to be pleased, since he had saved the King from the monumental embarrassment of a 100-kilometre-long white elephant costing perhaps 2,400,000 *livres*.

With the King and Le Nôtre both obsessed by the aesthetic possibilities of water, it is easy to see how the number of fountains at Versailles grew to a thousand by 1672 and ultimately reached the staggering total of 2,456. If it is difficult to conceive how a single garden could contain such a number, we must remind ourselves of the vast extent of the Parc and the King's wish that his promenades should be enlivened by the sparkle of splashing water at every juncture. It also helps to look at some of the contemporary engravings that illustrate notable garden features. The Théâtre d'Eau, for example, developed by Le Nôtre in collaboration with Denis Jolly from 1671, had two hundred jets. If the total of 2,456 still seems profligate, it at least starts to make sense.

Louis and Le Nôtre must have egged one another on in their watery excesses, but it is one thing to propose a fountain, another to get it to run. Paradoxically, though Versailles had been infamously swampy, not enough groundwater could be extracted to feed the burgeoning fountains. The King's craving for them went beyond any purely sensory pleasure they might have given him. For most of the population of France, clean water was a precious commodity and potable water was hard to come by. That the King could possess this substance in superabundance and splash it about for the sake of pure pleasure was yet another mark of his glory. Just as the peasants had to subsist on bread and root vegetables while the King regularly munched his way through multiple meat courses and platters of fresh fruit, so the poor were vulnerable to dysentery and other water-borne diseases, as well as periodic famines, while the King diverted streams and built aqueducts to feed his favourite fountains.

In his lavish use of water Louis was following long historical precedent. Running water had been prized in Byzantium and became an essential feature of

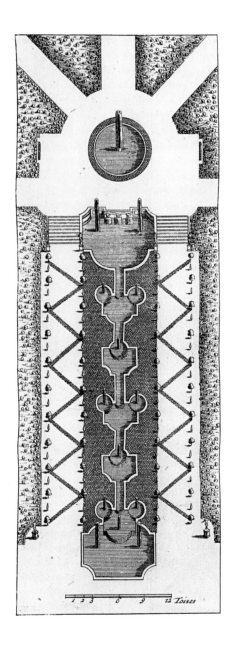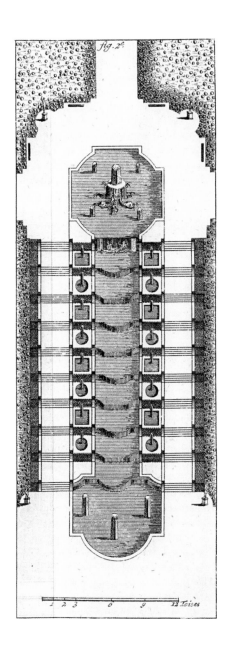

A cascade upon a 'rampe douce' or easy descent (left) and a cascade by
'chutes déscaliers' or falls of steps (right), from La Théorie et la practique
du jardinage by Antoine-Joseph Dezallier d'Argenville, 1709.

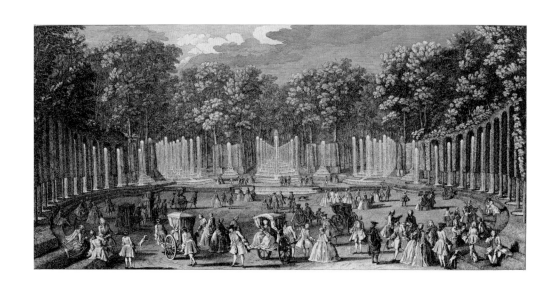

View of the Théâtre d'Eau by Jacques Rigaud, c. 1730.

Islamic paradise-gardens, culminating in the fourteenth-century courtyard pools of the Alhambra. The *Hypnerotomachia* contained sumptuous descriptions of limpid pools frequented by maddeningly beautiful nymphs and sacred fountains attended by naked handmaidens. The château of Gaillon, built by Cardinal Georges d'Amboise, Archbishop of Rouen and one of Louis XII's ministers between 1501 and 1510, included spectacular fountains, with one jet that rose to 22 feet. The main fountain in the courtyard, shipped with great difficulty from Genoa, incorporated lactating graces and micturating youths, while Richelieu's gardens at Rueil had musketeers who squirted surprised visitors with water from their guns.

All of these precedents had established the necessity for water features within the French formal garden, but it was Le Nôtre's work at Vaux which provided the most immediate precedent for Versailles. In addition to the Grandes Cascades and the Grille d'Eau, there were also jets along the Allée d'Eau, described by Madeleine de Scudéry as a 'crystal balustrade' because the jets were kept deliberately low.

For Louis it was necessary that the water features at Versailles should surpass anything that had been seen before in either France or Italy, and, if we accept the opinion of Ellis Veryard, an English traveller who visited Versailles at the close of the century, they succeeded in this ambition. 'The Water-works far exceed those of Frascati and Tivoli, so much boasted in Italy,' wrote Veryard in 1701, 'for as the Italians have been happy in their Inventions, so the French have been prosperous in promoting and perfecting them ... The most expert and famous Artificers ... have been cal'd from all parts, and are daily employed in this stupendous Work.'

The earliest water features were the pools of Saturne, Flore, the Sirène, the Girandole, the Dauphin, the Bois Vert and the Couronnes, as well as those within the Parterre à Fleurs and the Parterre de l'Orangerie. All of these had been constructed by 1663, as was the Bassin du Grand Jet, which would become the Dragon Fountain from 1667. As each new *bosquet* was added to the chequerboard of the Petit Parc, so the demand for water increased. The Labyrinthe alone had thirty-nine fountains, many with multiple jets, and there followed the Pyramide, the Fountain of Latona and the group centred upon Apollo's chariot in the former Bassin des Cygnes. And so it went on. Louis' water-engineers were constantly playing catch-up with the surging imagination of the King and his creative team of artists, garden designers and fountaineers. At first the only water available was that which could be pumped from existing ponds, like the one at Clagny, just north-east of the château, which had been dug in the time of Louis XIII. It soon became evident that these resources were inadequate, and the abandonment of

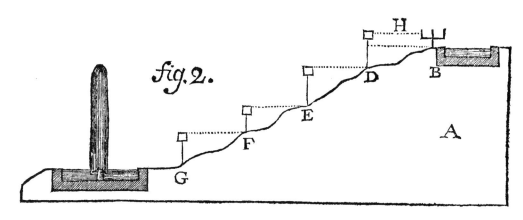

Measuring the head of water for a fountain using the 'level with vials', from La Théorie et la practique du jardinage by Antoine-Joseph Dezallier d'Argenville, 1709.

Amphitheatre at the head of a lake, from La Théorie et la practique du jardinage by Antoine-Joseph Dezallier d'Argenville, 1709.

the Loire project meant that, for a decade or so, no grand solutions were sought. Instead an extensive gravity-fed network of reservoirs and stone-lined channels was developed to bring water from the countryside around Versailles, particularly from sources on the Satory plateau to the south. In the 1680s the grand projects would return, first in the form of a bold plan to raise water from the Seine using technology developed in the coal-mines of Liège, then in the ill-fated Eure scheme. Most of the remnants of this network are to be found within 20 miles of Versailles, although there are vestiges up to 60 miles away, including the gaunt, ivy-covered arches of the Aqueduc de Maintenon.

The significance of fountains in Louis' France was underlined by the size of the payments to those who could create, maintain or nourish them. Denis Jolly, who bore the title of engineer ordinary to the King, earned over 300,000 *livres* for his work at Versailles between 1664 and 1667. He had worked for Fouquet at Vaux and also maintained four pumps at the Pont Neuf in Paris. At Versailles he kept an old pump going, one that had been installed by Francois Robin in 1632 and remade in 1642 by Claude Denis, and he also supplied the pump and pipework for the water features in the Ménagerie. The supply for these came from a nearby well, which would dry up in half a day when they were running, a foretaste of the problems of capacity that were going to dog the fountain-makers of Versailles for decades. In 1664, as the King's vision for his garden began to take shape, Jolly was given the contract for supplying three new pumps at a cost of 2,400 *livres*.

Both the gardeners and the fountaineers came under the 'technical services' branch of the building administration, which must have made life easier for everyone, since it was imperative that these two groups should be able to co-ordinate their operations. On 19 March 1664, Jolly signed a contract, in the presence of 'the noble man André Le Nostre, King's councillor, controller general of the said buildings', for 'a great machine of new construction' that would lift the waters of the Clagny pond into a water-tower designed by Le Vau.

The building consisted of a central tower of brick and stone that supported a lead-lined tank. There were two gins, one to either side, and in each a horse turned an elmwood wheel. These provided the motive force for four piston pumps designed by Jolly. The mechanism was technically advanced, a complex assembly of flanges, cylinders, valves and pistons which incorporated many metal parts at a time when similar devices were mostly made of wood. The pump could lift 600 cubic metres per day into the reservoir in the tower, which provided enough pressure to run the early jets, but the capacity of the tank was less than 100 cubic metres, so the system was still very limited. Nevertheless, the Pompe was a marvel in its day. Mlle de Scudéry mentioned its 'pipes of prodigious size' in her *Promenade de Versailles*, and it even became an object of tourism. Guests at Versailles would be taken to see the machine in action.

According to a contract signed on 1 October 1670, one of Jolly's responsibilities was to break the ice in the reservoirs and pools during the winter months, and also to repair any of the joints in the lead linings that were found to be leaking. His expertise was valued, but he was not reliable. In addition to his own services, he was supposed to supply two further fountaineers and three fountain lads, but to the King's displeasure there came a day when the fountains failed to run. There was worse to come. Jolly had been discovered passing fraudulent accounts for lead and welding materials and had embezzled on the order of 25,000 *livres*. Seeking a pardon, he offered to repay the money, but instead he was excluded from public contracts, including his lucrative appointments in Paris. Surprisingly he continued to be employed at Versailles, presumably because he understood the workings of his pumps better than anyone else. However, Colbert imposed a strict new regime from 1672, insisting, among other things, that the fountaineers had to ask permission for leave of absence. They had to hold themselves in constant readiness in case the King wanted the waterworks to play. Jolly was replaced as overseer by Claude Denis, a poet in his spare time, who, around 1674, wrote an explanation in verse of all the grottoes, rockworks and fountains at Versailles. As a result of the failings of his predecessor, Denis always had Colbert on his back, fining the fountaineers for any dereliction of duty.

Ultimately the Francine brothers, François and Pierre, became more significant figures than either Jolly or Denis. They had worked with Jolly on the pump at Clagny and helped him to install the water effects in the Grotte de Thétis between 1662 and 1668. The Francine brothers made their first important contribution to the water-supply system at Versailles after the excavation of the first branch of the Grand Canal, when they devised an ingenious recycling arrangement whereby water from the Canal could be returned to the pond at Clagny by three windmills that raised it to successive levels.

The problem with windmills is that they are of no use when there is no wind, and it was on still days that the King and court were most likely to wish to view the fountains. In the seventeenth century wind-power had exactly the same virtues that it has today; it was clean, relatively quiet and just about free. Louis' engineers could always fall back on horsepower, but horses were costly to feed, and there was a reluctance to house them close to the château. Increasing the amount of water stored at a sufficient height to run the fountains was an obvious solution but a very difficult one, given that the château had been built on top of a hill.

The lack of capacity in the system was alleviated a little by a tank with a capacity

236

of 580 cubic metres on the roof of the Grotto. By 1666 there was water enough to inaugurate the *Grandes Eaux* and so, for a few hours on 17 April, all the fountains performed for the King and his court. The Grand Jet in the future Bassin du Dragon, and the spouts that issued from the Ovale, where the Fountain of Latona would soon stand, gave the audience a foretaste of the gushing spectaculars they could expect to see one day. In the following year, three clay-lined reservoirs were built close to the Grotto, overlooking what became known as the Rue des Réservoirs, although these original puddled clay pools were later replaced with stone tanks. Holding 5,000 cubic metres, the new reserves allowed impressive displays to be mounted to mark the signing of the Treaty of Aix-la-Chapelle in 1688.

François Francine and Le Nôtre enjoyed an affable professional association, though Primi Visconti left a curious caricature of the two men and their relationship:

> As for the garden with its fountains, it is a marvellous thing … A certain Le Nôtre is the designer, and it all the more astonishing that he traced the whole without schooling, and only from his own characteristic genius, because beforehand he was just a simple gardener. The fountain-maker is a certain Francini, the son of a Florentine, a man heavy in body, but even more so in spirit. He costs the King much, because, when carrying out Le Nôtre's plans, he is very ignorant. For the aqueducts alone he has placed underground lead worth seven millions.

The Italian's dislike for the fountaineer is evident, but there seems to be no support for his poor opinion, and he also does Le Nôtre a disservice by suggesting that he was uneducated. In any event, the two hundred jets of the Théâtre d'Eau, on which the two men collaborated from 1671, placed further strain on the reservoirs. Francine's particular talent was for the fine detail of the waterworks, the nozzles that could shape water into the forms of vases and goblets. His brother Pierre, as indispensable in his way, was the engineer who laid the pipework and made sure that the fountains were supplied.

Despite the additional capacity provided by the new reservoirs, the water supply still had to be rationed. When the King was in residence, some of the fountains played constantly, but some of the most thirsty, such as the Dragon, Ovale and Pyramide, were only turned on as he passed. Thus the *Grandes Eaux* were an elaborate charade. In 1672 Colbert issued an elaborate set of instructions to Claude Denis and his team. 'Whensoever His Majesty comes forth from the château,' it began, 'the master fountaineer shall take care to hold himself in readiness to receive the order, and if His Majesty command that the fountains play, he shall, instantly, by blowing his whistle, signal for the water to be set running at the Couronnes, at the Piramide, at the Dragon, at the Cérès, at the Dosme ...'

These elaborate routines, with whistle blasts and fountain boys skittering through the *allées*, were not in keeping with the King's all-powerful image. He still sought a solution that would allow him to run his fountains constantly. Ways to extend the supply network were sought. Between 1668 and 1674, the River Bièvre was dammed and its waters brought to Versailles. Five windmills were added to this system in 1671, the same year in which the Satory reservoir, with a capacity of 72,000 cubic metres, was created. Although the Loire project was a non-starter, the careful levels taken by the Abbé Picard proved that the area around Trappes was higher than the reservoir on top of the Grotte de Thétis. A partial solution to the fountains' perennial thirst might be found by damming small valleys and then creating channels and aqueducts linked to the reservoirs and tanks close to the gardens. Following the example of the Romans, much of this work was done by soldiers in peacetime. As some of the sources lay behind the Satory plateau, a 1.5-kilometre-long tunnel had to be dug, to allow the water to flow by gravity towards the gardens. Nearly 30 metres deep, it was made by sinking shafts at intervals of 60 metres, then joining them up below ground. Even with such developments it was still not possible to run all of the fountains all of the time, but they could, at least, be turned on for several hours a day.

In 1674 the power of the Clagny pump was augmented. There were now three horses rather than two, driving twelve piston pumps rather than four. The installation became known as the Grande Pompe, and the increase in daily capacity was almost fivefold. The Grande Pompe was a wonder, but its very efficiency underscored another problem – the pond at Clagny was running dry, a situation made worse by the addition of two more windmills in 1676. Denis, his fellow fountaineers and the fountain lads had lodgings at the Pompe from 1686. It was not unusual for workers to be offered accommodation near their place of employment; the Swiss Guards had quarters close to the walls of the Parc, the gamekeepers had lodgings in the woods, and the gardeners lived at the Potager, though Le Nôtre, having risen above their ranks, possessed both a house in town and a fine apartment in the Grand Commun, amongst the high functionaries of the court.

The gravity-fed network of reservoirs was supplemented by a second system of ponds developed by Thomas Gobert, the steward of the King's buildings. Because this second series of ponds, at Saclay, Pré Clos and Orsigny, was some 10 metres lower than the first, it could only feed the fountains that were lower than the Parterre d'Eau. Thirty thousand men were involved in its creation, and once again the engineers had to overcome a serious topographical obstruction, in this case the valley of the Bièvre. Gobert's first solution was to build a ground-hugging siphon consisting of two large-diameter cast-iron pipes, but when it was finished the pressure in the pipes on the valley floor was found to be too much for the seals of lead and leather, and the system leaked copiously. Gobert sought royal authority to build an overhead aqueduct and won support from Louvois, who had become *Surintendant* in the meantime. The nineteen arches of this aqueduct still tower impressively, but it did not greatly augment the water supply for Versailles.

Naturally Louis was particularly concerned about the fountains immediately outside his windows, and the inadequate supply to the Parterre d'Eau, which had to rely upon the tank on the roof of the Grotto, was a constant vexation. It was François Francine who suggested that the solution was to construct three great cisterns, with a total capacity of 3,400 cubic metres, beneath the terrace of the Parterre d'Eau to capture the water for recycling. It fell to the architect François d'Orbay to build them, at a cost of 200,000 *livres*. Two chains of buckets, nick-named 'Rosaries of Return' or 'Jacob's Ladders' and driven by horses, circulated the water back to the roof of the Grotto.

These improvements were conceived in 1672, the same year in which the Dutch flooded their polders and prevented Louis' armies from entering Amsterdam. While the technicians strove to perfect the new pumps, Louis followed their progress from the campaign front. Even in his tent, with pressing military matters to attend to, he could look forward eagerly to his return to Versailles and the pleasure he would take in the increased power of his fountains.

On his visit to Versailles in 1677, John Locke was shown around the gardens by the King himself, in the company of Mme de Montespan, and had this to say about the waterworks: 'The jet d'eaus, basins & cascades in this garden are soe many, variously contrivd & changed in a moment that it would require a great deale of time to describe them.' He added that 'the King seemed to be mightily well pleased with his water works and severall changes were made then to which he himself gave sign with his cane, and he may well be made merry with this water since it has cost him dearer than so much wine, for they say it costs him 3 shillings every pint that run there.' To describe the fountains in detail 'would require a volume', said Locke, who, as a scientist, was more interested in technology than aesthetics:

> The water of all these works is noe thing but the rain water of the winter stopd
> by dams made in the vallys on both sides the Chasteau. From thence it is raisd

by 10 winde mills, 5 on a side, to the reservoire by the Grot de Thetis in the garden. Besides these 10 windemills there are 120 horses kept on purpose to raise water also, where of 40 are always at work night and day. They work 2 hours and rest 4.

When Locke saw something worth emulating, he took detailed notes. He thought one of the windmills the best sort he had seen anywhere and carefully recorded the capacity of the buckets – '16 pints of Paris' – and the number of cogs on the various millwheels. There were taps, he noted, 'a foot French diameter' which cost £2,000. An earlier visitor, Primi Visconti, also commented on this hydraulic system but counted even more horses. 'Windmills have been built,' he noted, 'but just to supply just a small jet of water on the expanse in front of the king's apartment, it takes a hundred and fifty horses to pump the water. This is truly grand for the King, but the fountain maker cuts a really stupid figure.'

At the time of Locke's visit, work on the Canal would have been nearing completion, since the earliest excavations began in 1668, and the second phase, completing the cruciform plan, was dug between 1671 and 1679. Looking out from the King's apartment, the philosopher saw 'almost noe thing but water for a whole league forwards, this being made up of severall basins, supplied by jet d'eaus, & a very large & long canale at the end of a broade walk (which is soe conceald by the hanging of the hill that one scarce sees any of it, but the severall basins seem almost contiguous to one an other & to the canale)'. This, of course, had been exactly the effect that Le Nôtre had desired and Picard's level had delivered.

Even without the flotilla of gondolas and larger craft that came to occupy the water, the very name 'Grand Canal' invited comparison with Venice. During works to lengthen and deepen the feature in 1671, the King took the opportunity to show the Venetian ambassador, Francesco Michiel, around the gardens. 'One of the most remarkable of the creations within the vast enclosure of this domain,' Michiel would later write, 'is a canal of no ordinary breadth.' When the King showed his guest his growing collection of boats, he drew the ambassador's attention to the little *feluccas* of Naples. Michiel saw the opportunity for a diplomatic gesture, perhaps one for which Louis had been angling. 'There would be nothing more appropriate than the gondolas of our city,' said the Venetian, at which the King smiled and nodded his agreement. Two months later, the Senate of Venice agreed to make a gift of two large gondolas to the King of France.

Fittingly the base for the little fleet that was assembled at Versailles was called *Petite Venise* and was built at the eastern end of the Grand Canal by the architect Antoine Bergeron. In addition to a warehouse and lodgings for sailors, there was a boatyard under the authority of the Marquis de Langeron. In 1684 the naval personnel consisted of a captain, a lieutenant, a ship's master and his mate, eleven sailors and six gondoliers, four of whom came from Venice, with two more recruited from Toulon. As the flotilla got larger, so the need for sailors increased; there were generally sixty held in readiness. Alongside the crewmen there was a team of boat-builders, including two Italian specialists, two caulkers and a number of sawmen whose job it was to turn tree-trunks into useable planks.

The gondoliers who conveyed the King upon the water were well paid and handsomely clothed. The accounts for 1685 include an entire section concerned with their costumes. A merchant called Dautecourt was paid for damask and taffeta; another called Laleu was paid for buttons and gold braid; a hosier called Nau supplied four pairs of crimson silk stockings; the Dessart brothers, merchants, provided crimson and gold brocade for the jackets; while another named Brion furnished not only the flags, burgees and pennons that decorated the boats but also shirts and underpants for the crew.

Supplies for the flotilla were truly international. Wood for the construction of the *Grand Vaisseau* came from Amsterdam; two yachts came from England via Le Havre and the Seine, and had to be trundled overland on a machine with enormous wheels, entering the gardens through a breach in the walls of the Grand Parc; sailcloth for the *chaloupes* came from the Levant; fifty-four Moors came as crewmen; even the swans that graced the Canal were imported from Denmark.

In winter the Canal would freeze, preventing excursions by boat but opening up the prospect of sleigh rides and skating. Monseigneur, the Grand Dauphin, seems to have been the greatest enthusiast. Dangeau's journal entires for January 1685 record that the King's son, who was then in his early twenties, went for sleigh rides on the first, second, third, fourth and fifth days of the month. On the 6th he went out again, combining this excursion with a little duck-shooting in the vicinity of the Ménagerie, but a planned excursion for the following day in the company of the ladies was thwarted by a sudden thaw. On the 13th, 14th and 15th he went skating. The Dauphin was as much of an outdoor person as his father, with the same taste for hunting; indeed he is reputed to have killed the last of the wolves in the Île-de-France. The King, however, was losing much of his vigour. He had always enjoyed his water-borne concerts and firework displays, but his doctor, Fagon, counselled him that these excursions might be aggravating his rheumatism, so they became much less frequent.

Primi Visconti thought that the amount of lead piping buried at Versailles made the ground more valuable than any mine. He overestimated the amount, but

View of the Orangerie and the Pièce de d'Eau des Suisses by John Cotelle, 1693.

the actual figures are still startling. Of the total expenditure of 80,000,000 *livres*, 2,800,000 were spent on pipes. Lead pipes were generally only used within the Petit Parc, where there was less chance that they could be stolen. Iron pipes, introduced in 1671, greatly reduced losses. Although this gargantuan system seems self-indulgently extravagant, it has been argued that it provided a model for urban water supplies throughout the world, rather in the way that the formal geometries of the gardens and hunting park would become ubiquitous templates for the rational planning of towns and cities. At the time, of course, public health was not the issue. Indeed the unhealthiness of Versailles is a recurrent theme in contemporary accounts. Fundamental notions of hygiene were unknown. The cause of much of the sickness was almost certainly the practice of throwing dung into the pond at Clagny, from whence it was circulated via the Grande Pompe and the Clagny windmills to the Tour d'Eau, the Grotto and the Parterre d'Eau.

'Miasmas' released during the earthworks were often blamed for deaths among the workforce. According to Primi Visconti, the air at Versailles was still insalubrious in 1681. 'The waters, which are putrid, infest the atmosphere,' he wrote. In a letter to Mme de Sévigné, Bussy-Rabutin took a pessimistic view. 'Kings,' he wrote, 'by means of their wealth, can give to the ground a form different from that which it received from nature, but the quality of the water, and that of the air, is not within their power.' In the context of Louis' court, that was almost a treasonable sentiment. Louis certainly had no thoughts of giving up. These were just the sorts of difficulties that a great monarch ought to be able to surmount.

In 1678 work began to create the large pool now known as the Pièce d'Eau des Suisses after the regiment of Swiss Guards who were forced to dig it. It was excavated on the site of a putrid pond where marsh gases were released during the works. The design superseded plans for a great octagonal basin, conceived in the mid-1660s but shelved after the outbreak of the War of Devolution, which took the military away from such major engineering works. Significantly the Swiss Lake was instigated at the time of the Peace of Nymegen, which brought the Dutch War to a conclusion. At more than 15 hectares, this lake covers an area equivalent to almost forty football pitches.

The aesthetic idea behind this waterbody was that it should balance the northern extension of the cross-axis where Le Nôtre proposed the Bassin des Sapins, named for the encircling conifers, but also referred to as 'below the Dragon', indicating its proximity to the earlier Dragon Fountain. Although some of its jets played for Louis for the first time on 17 May 1685, the central hydraulic group – featuring Neptune and Amphitrite on their thrones, Proteus astride a sea unicorn, Oceanus resting on a conch shell, and assorted walruses and spiny fish – was not inaugurated until 1741, during the reign of Louis XV, at which time the pool was promoted to the Bassin de Neptune.

While some of the pools at Versailles were intended to be full of splashing spouts and jets, the larger sheets of water, like the Parterre d'Eau, the Grand Canal and the Pièce d'Eau des Suisses, were conceived as tantalising mirrors in which evanescent reflections of the sky and the surrounding landscape would shimmer, break up and reform with each passing breeze. As indoor decoration, mirrors were considered extremely luxurious items, and their theatrical appeal, their magical doubling of space, was only enhanced by their expense. Inside the château, in the incomparable Galerie des Glaces, there were seventeen arcades, each clad with mirrors, thus creating a shimmering spectacle when the chandeliers and crystal girandoles were illuminated. Seventeen corresponding windows looked out to the gardens. Le Nôtre's garden mirrors offered an outdoor counterpart, no less costly to create but with the added fascination of natural changeability.

Landscape-architectural works involving significant earthworks are always expensive, for though the work may not be highly skilled, the sheer quantity of soil that must be shifted pushes the price up. It was no different in the case of the Swiss Lake, for which Sieur de Surbeck, major of the Swiss Guards, received 51,900 *livres* 'on account of the movement of earth which the said regiment undertook to complete the large lake and for carrying earth to the potager'. Since the soldiers had to do much of the carrying on their own backs, six hundred baskets with straps were purchased. On 30 July 1679, Swiss carpenters were paid 283 *livres* 10 *sols* to repair the wheelbarrows broken by their countrymen in the course of this strenuous work.

To move the earth from the excavations to the Potager, where it was required to make up the ground, a machine invented by Francine and known as *la lisse* was used. Since no illustrations of this 'smoothing machine' have been found, we are left to speculate about its construction and operation. Dominique Garrigues called it a *tapis roulant*, or 'conveyor belt', but contemporary descriptions mention little carts, so it may have been some sort of waggon-way.

Although the building accounts contain frequent references to compensation payments and surgeon's fees, the true human cost of the waterworks is scarcely to be found in their pages. But we get a glimpse from Mme de Sévigné, who wrote of 'the prodigious mortality of the workmen, of whom every night wagons full of the dead are carried out as though from the Hotel-Dieu; these melancholy processions are kept secret as far as possible in order not to alarm the other workmen'.

244

What is certain is that more men were killed through illnesses contracted on the site than through what we might call 'industrial accidents'. The King must surely have known about the nocturnal convoys of dead bodies. Presumably he regarded garden-making casualties in the same way as he thought of casualties at war. They did not trouble him much at the time, but when his own death was imminent, he confessed to the future Louis XV that he had too often waged war through vanity. Even if it is a mistake to judge Louis by the humanitarian standards of our own times, the King must be thought foolish to have squandered so many élite troops belonging to his personal guard in such a venture.

We do not know if Le Nôtre had any qualms about the death-toll. He might not have known about the fatalities, but this seems improbable, for although his main residence was at the Tuileries he would have often been on site to check the progress of particular works. But Le Nôtre would never have questioned the will of his King, and as a devout Catholic he may well have considered that such deaths, since most of them were not directly caused by accidents, were but the will of God.

View of the Machine and Aqueduct at Marly (detail) by Pierre-Denis Martin, 1724.

XIV

The Machine and the Aqueduct

I F ONLY THE WATERS OF THE SEINE could be brought to Versailles, thought Louis, there would be no need for piecemeal responses to the problem of supply. The river lay just 7 kilometres to the north, but some 100 metres below the level of the château, with the intervening hill of Louveciennes adding a further obstacle. The King is reputed to have suggested an ideas competition to Colbert and Mansart: 'Ask the wise men of France when there will be a machine that can raise the waters of the Seine.' 'I will ask the scholars tomorrow and the water will ascend to the skies, if it please your Majesty,' replied Mansart, ever eager to satisfy.

Town-criers throughout the kingdom announced the competition, which came to the ears of a certain Arnold de Ville, an alderman of Liège. Although he was a lawyer rather than an engineer, he had some awareness of hydraulics, since pumps were used to keep coal-mines dry in the region. He knew of a craftsman-carpenter called Rennequin Sualem, a native of Jemeppe-sur-Meuse, who, about 1668, had installed a hydraulic machine at the château of Modave that raised water 50 metres from the River Hoyoux to a water-tower in the park. The men joined forces and in 1678 submitted a proposal for a similar machine to serve the needs of Versailles.

A lift of roughly 50 metres was about the maximum that the plumbing of the era could accommodate. Pipes were simply not strong enough to withstand the pressures that would be needed to raise water 150 metres in a single stage. The

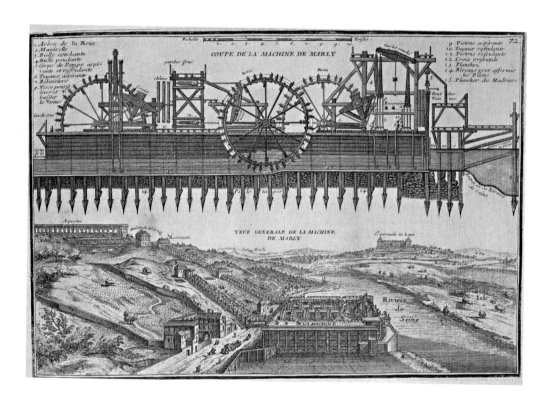

Elevation and Perspective of the Machine de Marly by Nicolas de Fer, c. 1715.

idea was to use the flow of the Seine, harnessed by giant waterwheels, to send water up the hill in three stages via two intermediate reservoirs, each with its own bank of pumps. Power for the pumps would be supplied via a complicated system of connecting-rods and camshafts.

Fresh from the embarrassment of the Loire scheme, Louis and his advisors commissioned a pilot project at Saint-Germain, the Pompe de Palfour, built between 1679 and 1680, which lifted water as far as the terrace at Saint-Germain. This machine was tested in the presence of the King. According to an old story retold by Pascal Lobegeois, De Ville intended to exclude Sualem from this demonstration, until the carpenter removed a vital piece of the machinery, compelling the lawyer to send for him. De Ville was a smooth talker, skilful in presenting proposals and negotiating contracts, but it seems to have been the illiterate Sualem who provided the technical expertise. In truth the two men could not do without one another. De Ville was no inventor or craftsman, even though he liked his name to appear on the drawings, while Sualem would never have obtained the commission without his well-placed collaborator.

Reassured by the success of the Palfour pump, the King sanctioned the construction of the full-scale engine, and in 1681 a site was chosen between Bezons and Bougival where a chain of small islands almost divided the river. By constructing dykes, it would be possible to complete this division, reserving the northern channel for shipping while the fourteen great waterwheels, (each almost 12 metres in diameter), aligned in two parallel rows, could be partially submerged on the southern side. In total there would be 221 pumps. The practically minded Sualem knew that it would be better to increase capacity by multiplying the number of pumps rather than by attempting to build bigger pumps that would be liable to fail. An initial bank of sixty-four sucked water out of the river and discharged it into the first reservoir at 48 metres above the Seine, where another tier of pumps, this time numbering seventy-nine, sent it on its way to the second reservoir, 56 metres further up the slope. A final assemblage of seventy-eight pumps lifted the water to the top of the slope, where it was received by the Louveciennes aqueduct, built to convey it towards Marly and Versailles. The connecting-rods often broke, while the wooden components would sometimes catch fire due to friction.

The surgeons of Bougival were kept busy while the so-called 'Machine de Marly' was being built. One called Godefroy was paid for the treatment of ten injured workers in June 1684, and his services were needed again in June 1687, once the contraption was working, to treat a carpenter called Sauvage. The workings of the Machine had none of the guards and safety devices that we would demand today, and it earned an unenviable reputation for crushing and maiming those who served it.

During construction, De Ville and Sualem were provided with a house on site, where there was also a forge, a stables and accommodation for a model of the engine. This house became the lodging of the controller, while De Ville, who became *Guverneur à vie de la Machine*, occupied a beautiful lodge at the top of the hill. (In 1769 this lodge was given to Mme du Barry by Louis XV when she became his principal mistress.) De Ville was handsomely rewarded for his part in the Machine's creation. In addition to his salary of 6,000 *livres* per annum, he was awarded an exceptional bonus of 100,000 *livres*, plus a generous annual pension. Sualem was rewarded too, though not in proportion to his contribution. He became first engineer to the King and received an annual payment of 1,800 *livres*. It was enough for him to set up in a mansion in Paris, and his subsequent career was prosperous. However, the elevation of De Ville must have rankled, because after his death his descendants had the words 'sole inventor of the Machine de Marly' inscribed on his tombstone in the church at Bougival.

The Machine was a qualified success. It came into full operation in 1685, but because of leakages and breakdowns it only delivered 3,200 cubic metres of water per day, which was about half of its theoretical capacity. Over fifty craftsmen were employed just to keep it running. In addition to the inherent dangers of the machinery, it caused navigation problems on the Seine, where sandbanks formed in the supposedly navigable channel, leading to wrecks and even drownings. The Machine was also horrendously noisy. The neighbours were still complaining about it in the second half of the following century, when Mme du Barry protested that it kept her guests awake.

On the other hand, it was undoubtedly spectacular, and even its noise was a source of fascination. It remained operational until 1817, when it made way for a short-lived steam engine, but while it worked it was firmly on the itinerary for foreign dignitaries and received visits from the Siamese ambassadors, Peter the Great and the King of Denmark. In 1786 Thomas Jefferson described the beauties of the Seine in a letter to Maria Cosway, mentioning not only the châteaux and gardens but also the 'rainbows of the machine of Marly'.

The aqueduct of Louveciennes was an unnecessary expenditure, since there was no valley to cross, but the King favoured such structures as they conjured up visions of ancient Rome. Another aqueduct, known as the Wall of Montreuil, was built between Marly and the new reservoir at Montbauron, located on high ground between the avenues of Paris and Saint-Cloud in the town of Versailles. The King and his entourage rode up to inspect the new reservoir, and the painter

Jean-Baptiste Martin captured the scene, the King resplendent in his blue coat and red stockings, leaning on his cane, with his advisors clustering round making promises of increased flow and unlimited supply.

The Machine was a very costly undertaking. In 1685 alone, 2,532 *livres* were spent on earthworks, 285, 348 *livres* on masonry, 98,069 *livres* on carpentry, 144,872 *livres* on metalwork, and 81,335 *livres* on copperwork. It has been estimated that the works employed around eighteen hundred men and cost in excess of 3,500,000 *livres*. These were just the capital costs and take no account of the ongoing expense involved in keeping this timber-splitting and bone-crunching behemoth in operation. Ironically most of the water was used not for the fountains at Versailles but to develop new gardens on a fresh site at Marly.

The Machine routinely delivered 3,200 cubic metres of water per day. Even if most of this had not been diverted for use at Marly, it would not have been enough, since the fountains at Versailles, running *à l'ordinaire*, which is to say at half-pressure, used four times the amount. More than three times the quantity lifted daily from the Seine was needed to mount the *Grandes Eaux* just for the course of an afternoon, and consequently this display was reserved for only the most important of visitors. Even though more water was supplied to Versailles than to the whole of Paris, fountain-rationing was still a necessity, a situation that could not please the King for long.

Following the death of the Abbé Picard in 1682, Louis had come to rely on the opinions of the mathematician and cartographer Philippe La Hire. The latter had established that the River Eure at Pontgouin, beyond Chartres, was some 26 metres above the level of the Grotto reservoir. The Loire debacle had not been forgotten, so La Hire, aware of the implications, reported his findings with some trepidation. If the King showed the will to tap the waters of the Eure, at a point more than 160 kilometres away from Versailles, the engineering works would outstrip anything undertaken thus far to feed the fountains.

It was Louvois who had to determine the feasibility of the idea. As a military man he had come to have enormous respect for Vauban, and it was to Vauban that he now turned. In the company of a little band of experts, which included De Ville, whose reputation now rode high upon the success of the Machine, the great military engineer crossed and recrossed the terrain during February 1685. In the middle of the month, Louvois went to see the ground for himself, returning to the King on the 23rd to say that it could be done. On the 25th, showing his characteristic impatience, Louis ordered troops from the regiments of La Ferté and Languedoc, who had been working on the Montbauron reservoirs, to go to the Eure.

Essentially the idea was to construct a canal, 5 metres wide, 2.5 metres deep and 83 kilometres long, that would connect with the pond of La Tour at the furthest extremity of the upper-gravity network, deep in the forest of Rambouillet. In addition to the daunting distances involved, there were two great natural obstacles that would have to be crossed. The first of these was the Larris valley at Berchères, while the other was the valley of the Eure itself, which describes a great curve through Chartres, so that water extracted at Pontgouin, cutting across this loop in a canal, would have to be carried across its own valley at a point below the cathedral city. The most suitable crossing point, the surveyors determined, was just a few hundred metres away from the windows of the former widow Scarron's house at Maintenon.

Louvois was able to call upon the finest engineering talents and the best minds of the Académie. In addition to Vauban, La Hire and De Ville, the team included Thomas Gobert, who had proved his worth in the creation of the pond network around Saclay; an engineer called Mesgriny, who acted as Vauban's assistant; another called Parisot, who was given responsibility for construction of the locks; and an inspector of works called Isaac Robelin, who was paid a handsome salary of 6,000 *livres* per year.

Despite Louvois' faith in Vauban, when the latter proposed that the valley of the Eure might be crossed not by an aqueduct carried proudly on an arcade but in the form of an enclosed masonry conduit or ground-hugging siphon, Louvois opposed him, since he shared the King's taste for monuments. He consulted the scientists of the Académie to find arguments he could use against the engineer, but since Vauban was hard to persuade, Louvois finally resorted to his authority. On 7 February 1685 he sent a stern memorandum: 'It is pointless you thinking about a creeping aqueduct, the King does not wish to hear any more of it.'

After five months of concentrated effort, Louvois produced an estimate for the necessary 'works of masonry' together with plans, elevations and sections. The aqueduct would be open to the sky, more than 5 kilometres long and, at over 70 metres high, taller than the towers of Notre Dame. It would consist of three storeys of arches, stacked upon one another, each smaller than the last.

With Vauban in charge, the works got off to an impressive start. The Eure was rendered navigable as far as Maintenon, and a port was created between Coulombs and Nogent-le-Roi to receive materials from Normandy. To facilitate the transport of sandstone from the quarries at Gallardon and Epernon, soldiers under Parisot canalised the rivers Voise and Drouette, building four locks on the former and nine on the latter. The stone was carried by a fleet of a hundred barges.

The initial deployment of troops was soon reinforced by men from the regiments of Enghien, Champagne and Maine. The scale of the works kept pace with Louis' mounting impatience. There were between nine and ten thousand troops employed on the works in 1685, but more than twenty-two thousand in 1686. In the following year the number of infantry battalions employed there rose from twenty-two to thirty-seven while the squadrons of dragoons increased from three to six. Frédérick Tiberghien estimated that the French army consisted of twenty-two thousand infantrymen and sixty thousand cavalrymen and dragoons in 1678, and that a tenth of these forces were put to work at the Eure.

There were some eight thousand civilian workers employed by various contractors, particularly in the more skilled trades like carpentry or masonry, but soldiers were less costly, and as they were subject to military discipline they could be given the most gruelling tasks to do, like earth-moving or the transport of heavy materials. The regiment of Languedoc, which contained many Protestants, often paid the price for this allegiance when they were assigned the heaviest work. Soldiers even had to take the place of horses for hauling the barges. It is hardly surprising that they frequently deserted, but Louvois had an uncompromising attitude towards discipline. Deserters would be tracked down and either executed or condemned to the living death that was life on the galleys of the Mediterranean fleet. Those selected for the latter fate would have their noses or ears cut off. One officer who showed too much zeal, slicing off a man's entire nose, was rebuked by Louvois. It was the King's intention, said the minister, that just the fleshy tip should be cut.

While Vauban and the chief engineer, Robelin, were in charge of the technical aspects of the project, military discipline was in the hands of the Marquis d'Huxelles, who, if we are to accept Saint-Simon's opinion, 'looked like a fat brutal butcher, sluggish, voluptuous from the excess of all sorts of comforts'. The camp commander might have been a sybarite, but the urgency with which the works were pursued meant that no one else had any time for pleasure. In 1685, when the canalisations of the Eure, Voise and Drouette were under way, Louvois asked permission from the Bishop of Chartres for the men to work on Sundays. The relentless regime applied to officers as well as the lower ranks. According to Saint-Simon, even officers of the rank of colonel and brigadier needed permission to leave the works for more than a quarter of an hour. When certain high-born officers protested their right to go hunting, Louvois would have none of it. 'The King will be pleased if you prevent them,' he told Huxelles, and even offered the flimsy pretext that to hunt in that season would damage the crops. So it might have done, but that was not usually much of a consideration.

Although the civilian workers were fewer in number, without them there could have been little progress. Amongst the contractors, the most important was the veteran mason Pierre Le Maistre, who was paid over 1,421,412 *livres* between 1685 and 1687 for work on the aqueduct. Such large disbursements were not unusual.

Although Louis had shown, during the War of Devolution, that he was prepared to wage war in winter, dispatching a force under Condé to take Franche-Comté during February 1668, most of the Sun King's campaigns took place in more open weather. When nature was put under siege at the Eure, the seasons still had the upper hand. Frost and snow made it difficult and dangerous to move materials by land or water, so it was necessary to demobilise the troops in October and bring them out from their barracks the following spring.

Progress reports reached Versailles, where they mixed with rumour. Mme de Sévigné was certainly excited. Her daughter told her of 'this great beauty that is to appear at Versailles, so totally fresh, so totally pure, so totally natural that it must eclipse all other beauties.' In the precious style of the seventeenth century, she affected astonishment to learn that this new belle, expected at court, was actually 'a river, diverted from her course, precious though that is, by an army of forty thousand men'. Gloomier prognostications abounded. The River Eure was too far away; perhaps the surveyors had got their levels wrong. The King had embarked upon his greatest folly.

On 3–5 September 1685, Louis himself toured the works on horseback, sleeping at Gallardon and dining at Berchères. Despite heavy rain, he was reassured by the progress he saw. He returned twice in 1686, an indication of the importance he attached to the project. In June of that year he reviewed his troops on the plain of Maintenon. The works appeared to be well up to schedule, and success seemed to be assured.

There is no record that Le Nôtre ever visited the Eure works, which is perhaps surprising in light of his presence at sieges during the Dutch War. Considering his interest in military engineering, one might have expected him to have been eager to witness the growth of the aqueduct that would deliver an inexhaustible supply of water to his fountains. But he was already in his seventies by the time the works commenced, and though not officially retired, he had been effectively displaced by Mansart, whose Colonnade was also begun in 1685. With his great works behind him, perhaps he had lost the curiosity he had shown as a younger man, or maybe he was just sparing his old bones the jolts of a journey to yet another building site.

By this time Louis was firmly under the influence of Mme de Maintenon, who from 1684 had a beautiful four-roomed apartment at Versailles, where the King would come to work each evening in her company. During the works on the Eure, Louis would often stay at the house at Maintenon, which had been extended to accommodate his suite. Mme de Maintenon does not seem to have objected to the construction of a gigantic aqueduct across her gardens, but she reveals an opportunistic streak in her correspondence with her son. 'Don't distress yourself about Maintenon,' she wrote; '… the compensation will amount to more than the damage.'

In August 1686 an outbreak of fever hospitalised almost sixteen hundred of Louis' soldiers. Conducting his second troop review of the year at Maintenon that September, he found his soldiers diminished and weary and immediately sent them to their winter quarters. Although he had proudly shown the Siamese ambassadors around the works at the start of the month, he now felt the first fluttering of anxiety.

The illness to which Louis' workforce was succumbing was almost certainly a form of malaria. We are used to thinking of malaria as a disease exclusive to the tropics, but until the middle of the twentieth century it was endemic in temperate climates. The 'ague' mentioned by Chaucer and Shakespeare was a form of malaria, as was the 'Essex ague' described by Daniel Defoe on his tour through Britain, which he began in April 1722. This 'damp part of the world' was associated with high rates of mortality, particularly amongst incomers, such as the unfortunate brides brought to the marshes by local farmers. One man was said to have married twenty-five times. As it was in England, so too in the Marquis d'Huxelles's camp on the Eure.

Isaac Robelin requisitioned the Benedictine monastery at Coulombs as a military hospital. It had two thousand beds, and by 1687 all of them were needed. Sick officers were sent to another hospital, in Chartres. Care was rudimentary. Patients were given clean shirts, sheets and bonnets and subjected to the seventeenth century's universal remedy, which was to be bled. The only effective treatment was the so-called 'Jesuits' Powder', made from cinchona bark imported from South America. This contained quinine and may have helped some of the sick, though the death rate was very high. No one has been able to determine exact figures, since the deaths were not entered into the local parish registers, but some accounts have placed the total at ten thousand. Just as the bodies of the Guards who had died during the excavation of the Pièce d'Eau des Suisses were smuggled out of the palace grounds at dead of night, so too were the fever victims of the Eure interred at five o'clock in the morning, when the only people stirring were the hospital attendants bringing the first broth of the day to their patients. When the regiments that had toiled on the Eure were called to the front in the Nine Years'

War, some were down to almost half their effective strength and needed to be substantially reinforced before being sent into battle.

In seventeenth-century France human life was literally held cheap. The widow of Size Renault 'killed while working' received only 30 *livres* in compensation, while Noël Poulain, injured while hauling sand from Dangers, was awarded 20 *livres*. A worker who broke an arm might receive 30 or 40 *livres*, and one who lost an eye might get 50 *livres*, but there was no recognition of the loss of earning potential that a serious injury might entail. Indeed it seems that the value of a horse was higher than that of a man. On 8 December 1686 the *terrassier* Orry was paid 367 *livres*, which represented half the value of two horses that had died and two that had been crippled while turning the draw pumps associated with the piling works for the aqueduct. Ninety-two *livres* for a dead horse but only a third of that amount to the widow of a dead workman.

Louis' anxieties increased during 1687. It seemed to rain constantly, and it was rumoured at Versailles that two-thirds of the workforce was ill. From time to time an ailing colonel or brigadier would appear at court with grim tales of sickness. Even Louvois was afflicted in 1688. Despite the threat of severe punishment, absenteeism remained very high. Nevertheless the situation did not seem hopeless. By the start of 1688, the canal had been finished and only the crossing at Begères and the aqueduct at Maintenon remained to be completed. When Louis inspected his troops at Maintenon in May, they appeared much improved, so it seemed that all that was needed was one final push.

The fate of the aqueduct was about to be overtaken by events on a larger political stage, however. In 1686 Louis' aggressive foreign policy had provoked the Austrian Emperor, several German princes and the rulers of Sweden and Spain to form a defensive alliance against him, known as the League of Augsburg. Louis, always fearful about weaknesses on France's eastern border, had also become entangled in a dispute with the Pope about who should become the new Archbishop of Cologne, a strategically important city. When France's preferred candidate failed to be elected by the cathedral chapter, Louis decided to act to consolidate his frontier.

The outbreak of hostilities coincided with the end of the construction season on the Eure. When Louis stood his troops down at Maintenon on 16 August 1688, he did not think he was abandoning the project, but by late September Vauban, Huxelles and most of the French army were laying siege to Philippsburg. Initial French successes were overshadowed by reversals in a wider theatre, not least by

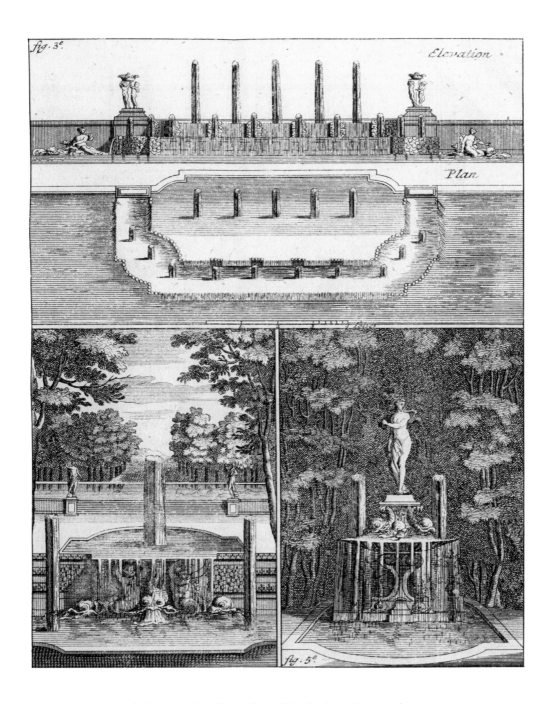

A cascade 'en Bufeta' at the head of a lake (top), with a cascade on a terrace (below left) and a cascade in a niche (below right), from La Théorie et la practique du jardinage by Antoine-Joseph Dezallier d'Argenville, 1709.

William of Orange's successful invasion of England and the ensuing Glorious Revolution, which displaced Louis's ally, James II. Magnanimously Louis offered the palace of Saint-Germain to the deposed monarch, but he showed poor judgement in backing James's attempts to regain his kingdom. The course of what Louis had hoped would be a short war turned long and bloody.

Louis thought that he might be able to complete the aqueduct using only civilian contractors. Vauban believed that it could be done in two years. The planned aqueduct at Berchères would be replaced by a siphon, and the completed first stage of the Maintenon aqueduct could be adapted to carry pipes rather than an open canal. Payments for work on the canal, which had been averaging 2,000,000 *livres* per annum between 1685 and 1688, plummeted to 40,000 *livres* by 1690 and dwindled still further in subsequent years. Louis might not have believed that he was abandoning the project, but from the moment the troops were sent to the front, the dream was over. By 1697, when France was again at peace, he lacked the funds to resume the works. The aqueduct became a useless, if picturesque, ruin, one that had cost 9,000,000 *livres* and thousands of lives. Rather than being one of the crowning glories of the Sun King's reign, it was a bitter humiliation.

Saint-Simon called the works on the Eure 'the ruin of the infantry', expressing the view that they were a monumental mistake. Napoleon took a different view; it was not the idea that was wrong but the execution. If he had been in charge, he would have kept a closer eye on progress, and the project would have been finished. Considered in purely practical terms, the problems presented by the scheme were not insurmountable. In terms of scale, Riquet's Canal du Midi, successfully completed at the start of the 1680s, had been an even more adventurous undertaking. Whatever we might think of the human cost of the enterprise, it was not the delusion of a madman, and, had the aqueduct been completed, an estimated 50,000 cubic metres of water would have been delivered to Versailles daily, solving Louis' supply problem permanently.

On the other hand, there was certainly something obsessive about the Sun King's love of fountains. The scale of this fixation becomes clear when we consider that the cost of the water-supply system at Versailles amounted to a third of the entire building costs, including everything that was spent on the château. The failure of the Eure project has kept the fountains short of water, and those who maintain the system today must ration the displays in the same way that Claude Denis and his fountain boys had to. The current fountaineers have the advantage of a large pump that recycles water from the Grand Canal back to the reservoirs of the North Wing and Montbauron, but leakages and evaporation mean that resources must be carefully husbanded. The gravity-supply network created in the seventeenth century is much attenuated, and the fountaineers must rely upon rainwater gathered for the most part within the boundaries of the Parc. Gauges in the Grand Canal tell them whether they have enough water to run the fountains, but it is still a point of honour to use only their own resources without having to tap into the local drinking-water supply. Impressive though the *Grandes Eaux* remain, with only three hundred jets and these limited in height, visitors never see the full glory of Versailles as it must have appeared to the Sun King and his guests.

Supervised by military engineers, undertaken by soldiers and organised like siege warfare, the campaign to bring water from the Eure ended in a defeat that must have injured Louis' martial pride as much as any battlefield reversal. The expansion of the water supply at Versailles was undertaken at a time when France's borders were also expanding. That the end of Louis' hydraulic dreams should coincide with the opening of the Nine Years' War is symbolic, since the terms of the Treaty of Ryswick of 1697, which brought this bloody and inconclusive conflict to a close, were not particularly advantageous to France. As the century drew to a close, Louis still believed in his own myth of invincibility, but the stream of victories that sustained that illusion would soon dry up altogether, and France would be fighting for her survival.

View of the Château and Pavilions of Marly by Pierre-Denis Martin, 1724.

XV

Escape to Marly

THE MOTIVATION FOR BUILDING ANOTHER OFFSHOOT from Versailles was much the same as that which had originally attracted Louis to his father's hunting lodge. The Sun King liked to throw house-parties, and when Versailles became the hub of the court it lost the sense of intimacy which Louis had previously enjoyed. It was around 1676, while following his hounds through his recently extended hunting forests, that he came upon the site for his new house. 'Weary of splendour and crowds, the King became persuaded that he desired simplicity and solitude,' wrote Saint Simon, although these terms must be understood in a relative sense. Marly was never a hermitage, and Louis was incapable of becoming a hermit. Even with the vast scale of Versailles available for comparison, Marly still seems sufficiently grand, while the gardens, now sadly mere ghosts of their former splendour, are revealed in contemporary engravings to have possessed a similar level of elaboration.

In his petulant way, Saint-Simon could exaggerate the supposed deficiencies of the site. It was steep, hemmed in by hills, a 'sewer' of a valley where the inhabitants of a nasty village threw their rubbish. In reality, compared to the main site at Versailles, this new plot had considerable advantages. It was a site that offered seclusion and a beneficial aspect. Perhaps Louis could not face the thought of another struggle against nature; this site had 'capabilities' without too many constraints. Martin Lister was certainly impressed. 'I must needs say it is one of the pleasantest Places I ever saw, or, I believe, is in *Europe*,' he wrote in his journal. 'It is seated

261

in the bosom or upper end of a high Valley, in the midst of and surrounded with Woody Hills. The valley is closed at the upper end, and gently descends forwards by degrees, and opens wider and wider, and gives you a prospect of a vast plain Countrey, and the River Seine running through it.'

The extent of Le Nôtre's involvement in the gardens at Marly is academically mooted, for there is no documentary evidence to link him with the elaborations that took place in the late 1690s and continued until 1714. When the plans were being conceived, around 1679, he was away in Italy, and he was already in his late sixties when the foundations for the new house were laid two years later. A letter from Crönstrom, the Swedish ambassador, to Nicodemus Tessin says that 'it is no longer Le Nôtre who is in charge of the gardens nor of Trianon: it is Monsieur Mansart.' Nevertheless, considering his closeness to the King, it is almost inconceivable that Le Nôtre should not have acted at least as an advisor, and there is evidence to suggest that the principal water feature, the Rivière, was one of the fruits of his Italian study tour.

The topography at Marly provided natural seclusion which the designer could easily augment. Diderot wrote that 'He who planted this garden realised that it was necessary to keep it out of sight until the moment one could see it in its entirety.' The constellation of buildings which Mansart created might remind us of the most exclusive of resort hotels, for in addition to the royal apartments in the main house, Palladian in character and square in plan, there were twelve pavilions for guests, arranged with characteristic symmetry on either side of the lake known as La Grande Pièce.

There are parterres and *allées*, goosefoots and groves, axes and cross-axes at Marly, indeed all the elements of the design vocabulary brought to perfection by Le Nôtre, yet the domination of the garden by its buildings and the rigidity of its symmetry seem to confirm that it was Mansart who had the King's ear. On such a sloping site the opportunities for mirror-like expanses of water was reduced, so there could be no Grand Canal; instead there was a return to Italian precedents with a series of water features arranged along the principal north–south axis, which was carried by the Rivière to the south of the Royal Pavilion and by La Grand Pièce, Les Napes and then the basin of the Abreuvoir, or Watering Place. The latter lay outside the confines of the gardens but could be viewed from the balustrade of the terrace above. As its name suggests, it was intended as a place for horses to drink, although it became a popular, if unauthorised, swimming pool for the children of Marly village during the reign of Louis XVI. The axis was closed by a circular pool some 150 *toises*, which is to say about 300 metres, further north, where a magnificent fountain called the Grosse Gerbe would play.

The linearity of the garden was most evident in the area around La Grand Pièce, itself a sort of modified rectangle which sat in the floor of a shallow, straight-lined amphitheatre, with parallel walks carried on a series of terraces to either side. The unswerving regularity of these *allées* was emphasised by rows of elms pruned into balls, by fanciful topiary yews and by the *portiques*, or colonnades, of clipped hornbeam on the intermediate levels below the guest-houses, which were themselves linked by trellis-work arbours. This lake still exists, surrounded by conical conifers, but these are in thin lines, not multiple ranks, and the effect is forlorn.

The first works at Marly were begun in 1679, in advance of the court's move to Versailles, and the main buildings were substantially complete by 1683, although Louis did not spent a night there until 1686. The new complex was less than 4 miles from Versailles and even closer to Saint-Germain. Louis would regularly visit on foot, taking the most direct route and entering the upper gardens at the goosefoot to the south of the Rivière, but when the court came in their carriages, the approach was from the east, down a treacherous slope. In March 1688 the carriage that contained the King's musicians overturned, and 'four of the best were hurt,' while in May 1697 an equerry who jumped from his careering carriage was carried off, apparently dead.

The solar theme made a reappearance at Marly, for each of the guest pavilions took a sign of the zodiac, while the King's pavilion represented the sun. The painted pediment of the western façade picked up the theme, showing Apollo at the reins of his chariot, the same imagery found in the Apollo Fountain at Versailles. Since all the guests at Marly were either members of the family or favoured at court, there was no need for the stern iconography of slain dragons and chastened giants to frighten would-be rebels, and since the house was not an official residence where ambassadors would be received, the rhetoric of power and glory could also be toned down. Instead the groves would be animated by nymphs and deities: Diana, Mercury, Bacchus, Amphitrite, Arethusa and Narcissus.

South of the Royal Pavilion were parterres stocked with narcissi, tulips and hyacinths, which gave way to summer flowers: pinks, crown imperials, wallflowers, ranunculi and rocket. To the east and west were the four Cabinets de Verdure whose contents and design were frequently changed in response to the royal inclination. To the south-east and south-west respectively were the Salon du Midy and the Salon du Couchant, while to the north-east and north-west lay the Salle du Levant and the Salle du Nord. Each of these spaces began as a shady retreat, with little in the way of decoration except for busts on pedestals. The Salon du Midy was used for a game called *passe de fer*, which involved bowling a ball through the gaps in a row of metal rods set into the ground like an upturned comb, while the

Salon du Couchant was equipped for the more elaborate game known as *l'anneau tournant*, the 'turning ring'. In time these amusements would be relocated to allow Louis to indulge his new passion for pools of decorative carp.

The sense of seclusion and peaceful relaxation within these garden rooms extended to the remainder of the park. At Marly the *bosquets* did not take the form of chequerboard blocks of woodland as at Versailles. Instead, to either side of the central concourse there were woodlands within which walks and clearings had been made to echo the linearity of the principal spaces. To the east, on sloping ground, lay the Bosquet de Louveciennes or Levant, within which were various rooms containing fountains and statuary, including an elaborate Cascade built at about the same time as the Rivière. Still further east was the Bois de la Princesse, yet another tribute to the Dauphine, Marie-Adélaïde. Planted with sweet chestnuts and horse-chestnuts during the winters of 1697–8 and 1698–9, it was threaded with meandering paths reminiscent of Le Nôtre's designs for the Bosquet des Sources and another indication of an incipient change of taste.

To the west, on flatter land close to the village, lay the Bosquet de Marly, which before 1702 incorporated a large, irregularly shaped reservoir. It was to this that the Princess Palatine was referring in July 1702 when she wrote: 'This morning I went for a walk with the king. One would think that fairies were busily at work here, for where I had left a great lake, I found a wood or grove.' Such rapid transformations, so typical of the King's trial-and-error approach to design, were commonplace at Marly.

Perhaps the most surprising feature of the Bosquet de Marly was the Escarpolette, a giant swing-boat of the sort that used to be seen in British playgrounds until the authorities recognised how dangerous they could be. The version at Marly was more sumptuous, of course, as the gondola seats were covered with red velvet. The entertainment was a hit with Marie-Adélaïde and the younger members of the court, although even the Grand Dauphin, who was getting on for middle age, liked to play on it. The same clientele were regular passengers on the Roulette or Ramasse, a kind of roller-coaster constructed amidst the wooded slopes to the south-east of the Rivière and consisting of a gilded bob-sleigh that ran on copper wheels for speed and had shock-absorbing cushions in blue, silver and gold. Sometimes the Duke and Duchess of Bourgogne and their friends would play until nightfall. These strenuous pastimes were not all that was on offer at Marly, however. The more sedate could retreat to a shady corner like the Vestibule de la Table for a game of chess or backgammon, or to the Vestibule du Portique, which took its name from a game something like a cross between roulette and bagatelle.

Another popular pursuit was *mail*, or pall-mall, the forerunner of croquet, which was played on level ground at the summit of the Rivière.

In 1702 Louis removed the Escarpolette and replaced it with a fish-pond. Again the Princess Palatine expressed her surprise: '… there where I had left a clearing and a swing, I found a reservoir full of water, into which will be placed this evening over one hundred fish of various species and thirty admirably fine carp.' The glittering carp, which bore names like 'Golden Sun' or 'Silver Mirror', were such a source of pleasure for the King that he soon created carp ponds in the four green rooms close to the Pavilion, as well as a Canal des Carpes at the western side of the southern parterre. Unfortunately the King's enthusiasm for these ornamental creatures was out of step with their natural preference for muddy pools and stagnant water. Louis wanted to be able to see his prize fish, and for this purpose the sparklingly clean water delivered by the Machine de Marly seemed ideal to everyone except the carp, which died in prodigious numbers. Louis was forced to raid other royal pools to keep those at Marly stocked, and in October 1703, in scenes reminiscent of the days following Fouquet's downfall, carp were seized from the pools of Vaux. The Princess Palatine thought that Louis' fish looked sad. 'They are like me,' she said, 'they are regretting their native mud.'

Trees also played an important part in creating the secluded ambience of Marly. In a letter to her Aunt Sophie, written on 3 February 1700, the Princess Palatine remarked: 'Now that a way has been found to take trees as tall as houses from the woods, gardens will soon be made. Today we met more that thirty wagons with trees this size. We hear that when they are transplanted they do well and don't die'. In the light of what we know about the rates of successful transplanting at Versailles, this seems like an overly optimistic or ill-informed view, and Saint-Simon was probably closer to the truth when he wrote that 'great trees were unceasingly brought from Compiègne or farther, three-fourths of which died and were immediately after replaced.'

Once again it was the humble hornbeam that proved the most versatile, serving, according to Martin Lister, for '*Arcades, Berceaus*; and also *Standards* with Globular Heads'. They were often planted in low hedges, which could be almost 4 metres wide. Lister suggests that such 'hedges' were even used as a sort of ground cover or at least as an alternative to grass. There was an on-site nursery for which sacks of oak, yew and spruce seeds were purchased. The accounts also mention acquisitions of Scots pines and silver firs, maples, sycamores, sweet chestnuts, limes, ash trees, alders and silver birches. Lister, who found it commendable that the King, 'who pleases himself in Planting and Pruning the Trees with his own

Hand, to make use of no other Trees, but what the neighbouring woods afford', also seems to have been badly advised, for it is clear that both trees and other plant material were brought from considerable distances. Sieur de Lelès was paid 466 *livres* 10 *sols*, for example, for six hundred elms from Flanders and Artois destined for the gardens of Versailles and Marly in June 1687.

Even in his retirement Le Nôtre continued to visit the King at his residences, and his nephew, Claude Desgots, reported that on one occasion in spring he was surprised at Marly to find groves and dense woods where the previous autumn there had been only meadow and arable land. Though Le Nôtre had never shied away from taking a firm hand with nature, even he was taken aback by the transplanting of mature trees, some thirty years old, on such a colossal scale. It was Louis' answer to a problem that faces all gardeners, amateur or professional, when they arrive at late middle age. In the normal course of events they are unlikely to live long enough to witness their plantings in the mature condition they manifest in their mind's eye. Desgots noted, with a hint of professional scorn, that 'for twenty leagues about', Louis had 'denuded the countryside of chestnut and linden trees'.

Rare flowers were as valued at Marly as they were at Trianon. Elizabeth Hyde has tabulated the flower purchases for Marly in 1690. By far the most in demand were narcissi, of which 148,850 were purchased, but the list also includes 1,604 double orange hyacinths, 1,300 single orange hyacinths, 1,075 irises, 3,650 *Oculus christi*, 1,100 Spanish carnations, 1,100 valerians, 300 double violet juliennes and 144 cases of tulips. Lister found little difficulty in believing the head gardener of the Pépinière du Roule when he asserted that 'in the space of four years he had sent to Marli, eighteen millions of tulips and other bulbous flowers'. In one of her letters, the Princess Palatine mentioned 'the King's admirable tulipans, which all the *curieux* come to see'. According to the Princess, a Scottish milord, with a reputation as a connoisseur and grower, placed a value of 2,000 francs on a particularly fine specimen.

Flowering shrubs were also used in great numbers. Roses were imported from Holland and bought from Provence. Lilacs, guelder-roses and roses of Sharon appear among the purchases, as do climbers like jasmine and honeysuckle. The gardens were also renowned for their topiary, though the species used were not restricted to box and yew; juniper, phillyrea, myrtle, holly, bay, spurge laurel and cherry laurel were also employed. Hawthorn and hazel were probably used in the woodlands and less formal areas; as Dezallier put it, the hawthorn is 'one of the finest shrubs for garnishing groves'.

* * *

If Marly gave Louis the opportunity to indulge old passions, such as his love of flowering plants, and to develop new ones, such as his fascination with showy fish, there was one great enthusiasm which had always been shackled at Versailles and which now seemed free from constraints – his love of fountains. Although the Machine de Marly did not perform up to its specification, it did provide hitherto unimaginable quantities of clear water, and there would soon be fountains throughout the gardens. Louis combined a child-like acquisitiveness with an obsessive demand for perfection. It was not just that he wanted more of everything; he also demanded the best. Saint-Simon, for one, found it all quite wearying. 'I speak of what I have seen in six weeks,' he wrote; '… basins were changed a hundred times; cascades the same; carp ponds adorned with gilding and the most exquisite painting, scarcely finished, were changed and differently arranged by the same hands, and this an infinite number of times.' The biggest of the fountains could be seen playing in the tree-tops from outside the park, but inevitably Louis' ambitions for his gardens outstripped even the formidable power of the Machine, and after 1700 some of the fountains were suppressed in order that the power of the others should not be diminished.

The Rivière, which poured down the central axis from the Reservoir du Trou d'Enfer towards the Royal Pavilion, was the most impressive water feature at Marly. Like the previous decade's abandoned project for a cascade at Versailles, it was motivated by the King's envious regard for similar features at Chantilly and at his brother's garden at Saint-Cloud. Claude Desgots was studying at the Academy of Rome when his great-uncle made his trip to Italy. When he returned to France, Desgots produced a drawing showing a cascade proposal that could have been the inspiration for the Rivière. The evidence for Le Nôtre's influence, if not for his direct involvement, is persuasive though not conclusive.

Like most of the features at Marly, the Rivière went through various iterations. The earliest version combined straight steps with curved ones, and rockwork gave the whole structure a rustic appearance. The cascade was bordered by grass and lined with rows of globe-headed elm trees. By 1703–4 Mansart had imposed his taste for marble and the rockwork was removed. The curved steps also vanished. Later the elms, whose roots were threatening the fabric of the cascade, were also removed, thus opening up the view. From a distance, the sixty steps of the cascade merged so that it really did resemble a river flowing freely down a hillside. Louis was delighted with the effect, which easily outclassed his brother's celebrated water feature, but the cascade did not survive much beyond the end of his reign. By 1728 Louis XV had been persuaded that it was too expensive to maintain, and that – rather than spending the necessary sums required for its restoration – it should be filled in and grassed over. Only a ghostly trace remains today, though the cascade at Chatsworth House in Derbyshire gives us a good idea of how it must have looked. The latter was designed in 1694 by a Frenchman called Grillet, who is thought to have been one of Le Nôtre's disciples.

Those fortunate enough to be included on the invitation list drawn up by Bontemps, the royal butler, could feel that little bit closer to the King at Marly. The Princess Palatine was not entirely sure that she approved. 'When the King walks in the gardens here,' she wrote to her Aunt Sophie, 'the lady [Mme de Maintenon] sits in a chair mounted on four wheels, pulled by four men. His Majesty walks alongside like her lackey, and the others follow on … It seems an upside-down world to me, and I don't like anything but the place.' Louis, however, must have enjoyed the opportunity to let his royal mask slip a little.

Etiquette was only relaxed, of course, not abandoned. Gentlemen were allowed the privilege of keeping their hats on when walking with the King in the gardens, but only after Louis had given them permission with a shout of '*Chapeaux, Messieurs*'. The habits of sycophancy did not disappear either. One day the soft-spoken Abbé de Polignac was in the company walking in the gardens, when it started to rain. The King expressed his concern that the Abbé was not dressed for this change in the weather. To the great amusement of the court, De Polignac replied, 'It is no matter, Sire. The rain of Marly does not wet.'

'No one could deny that Marly is … much lovelier than Versailles,' wrote the Princess Palatine, expressing a widely held opinion. The King's preference for the place grew steadily until, at the end of his reign, he was spending about a third of his time there. Marly, like Trianon, played a part in his great game of inclusion and exclusion, since invitations to both places were highly prized. Courtiers would petition the King with calls of 'Marly, Sire?', but there was a subtle distinction between invitations to the two places. If a lady was offered the opportunity to visit Marly, her husband would be able to accompany her without a separate invitation, but the same did not hold for Trianon, presence at which was considered the greater honour. Saint-Simon shows us how such niceties of etiquette could be used by the King to express his displeasure. Louis consistently gave invitations to Trianon to the Duchesse de Saint-Simon but just as regularly refused her petitions for Marly, leaving the Duke in no doubt about where he stood.

It is impossible to separate Saint-Simon's opinions concerning Marly from his resentment of the King. Louis had chosen the site, so the Duke was ready to dismiss it as an 'abode of serpents, and of carrion, of toads and frogs, solely chosen to avoid expense'. He grumbled about the expenditure involved in transforming the place, about the incessant alterations, and generally 'about the bad taste of the King in all things, and his proud haughty pleasure in forcing nature; which neither the most mighty war, nor devotion could subdue'. Yet when the Regency Council was considering the destruction of Marly as a cost-cutting exercise following Louis' death, it was, by Saint-Simon's own account, the Duke himself who spoke up against the proposal. The expenses involved in maintaining Marly were 'but drops in the ocean', he told the Regent. It had cost millions of *livres* to create this 'fairy palace', but the receipts from selling off salvaged materials, including the vast quantities of lead pipework, would not compensate for the injury that the demolition would do to the reputation of the deceased King. All of France would be indignant if this ornament were to be swept away, and France's international reputation would also suffer.

Saint-Simon's arguments won the day, but the fate of Marly was only postponed. In 1793, the same year that Louis XVI went to the guillotine, the estate was put up for sale and bought by a manufacturer who wished to turn it into a cotton-mill. When this enterprise failed, the owner tried unsuccessfully to sell the buildings to Napoleon. The manufacturer sold off what he could, so that when Mme Vigée-Lebrun, who had known 'noble, smiling Marly' in the reign of Louis XVI, was at last able to return in 1802, she was devastated to find that 'the palace, the trees, the cascades, the basins, all had vanished.' Louis' enchanted realm had been effectively dismantled.

View of the Galerie des Antiques by Jean Joubert, c. 1688.

XVI
Honourable Old Age

IN 1679, AT THE AGE OF SIXTY-SIX and with his greatest work behind him,
André Le Nôtre finally made the journey to Italy of which he had dreamt
for the whole of his adult life. At last he had the chance to see the gardens
that had so influenced the development of French design theory. Although this
trip was a mark of the King's favour, Le Nôtre was also given some assignments
to carry out. As we have seen, the King was always anxious that France should
surpass Italy in aesthetic matters, so Le Nôtre was to act as sort of scout, seeking
out anything new, meritorious or beautiful in gardening or the visual arts that
might serve as inspiration for improvements in the royal houses and gardens. To
this end, Colbert wrote to the Duc d'Estrées, the French ambassador in Rome,
asking him to help Le Nôtre gain access to all the palaces and fine residences in
the region.

Le Nôtre travelled in the lively company of the Duchesse de Sforza and the
Duc and Duchesse de Nevers. The Duke, a nephew of Mazarin, had been a way-
ward youth – he once got in trouble for baptising a pig and is thought to have
introduced the King's brother to sodomy – while his wife was a niece of Mme de
Montespan and shared her aunt's vibrant personality. The trip began in late January and lasted until the late autumn, but in one respect it was a disappointment.
Although there are reasons to believe that Le Nôtre was impressed by some of the
water features he saw at the Villa Aldobrandini and elsewhere, and that – as we
have seen – these might have had some influence on his proposals for Versailles

and Marly, in the main he was unmoved by the Italian gardens. He had pictured them so well in his imagination that the reality had nothing to add. He even came to the conclusion that 'the Italians have no taste in gardens which can approach ours. They do not know how to make them.'

Le Nôtre's visit to the sculptor Bernini to enquire after the promised equestrian statue of the Sun King went very well. Le Nôtre was after all the sort of person who could readily appreciate the work of others. At the time of Bernini's trip to Versailles, Le Nôtre had been working there for three years, and he had been happy to show the distinguished visitor around the site and to discuss his designs frankly and openly, producing his drawings and explaining the details of his proposals. It seems that the two men talked for a long time and in depth, for when they reached the Orangerie they measured its width. Bernini thought Versailles was the most beautiful place he had visited that week, and wondered why the itinerary arranged for him only allowed for a single visit. Perhaps he and Le Nôtre were able to get along because they were not rivals. The Italian was interested in gardening but was not a gardener, while Le Nôtre had a keen interest in both sculpture and architecture but was not hoping for a commission to rebuild the Louvre.

Bernini made Le Nôtre very welcome; in fact he disarmed him. It is said that when the gardener walked into the sculptor's studio, lying on the desk was a pile of sketches and engravings showing French garden designs. 'Who are they by?' asked the great Bernini, adding that he admired them enormously. Le Nôtre flushed, because, of course, they were his own work. In return Le Nôtre must have given his approval of the equestrian sculpture, because in time it made its way, via Toulon, Le Havre and the Seine, to Versailles – where, as we have seen, Louis took an instant dislike to it.

Another task given to Le Nôtre was to report on the activities of the Academy de France in Rome (directed by Charles Errard), where the gardener's great-nephew, Claude Desgots, was enrolled as a student. Preparing the way for the King's artistic emissary, Colbert wrote to Errard, '… you know his ability and you must try to follow the advice he will be able to give you concerning the studies of the students and everything regarding the Academy.' Once again we can see that Le Nôtre was esteemed for far more than just his knowledge of garden design.

When Pope Innocent XI heard from the Duc d'Estées that Le Nôtre was in Rome, he wished to see him. This placed Le Nôtre in an almost ambassadorial position, since the relationship between the Church and Louis' absolute monarchy was developing into a power struggle that would escalate alarmingly during the following decade. Thankfully, on this occasion, the Pope seemed interested only in gardens. Knowing of his enthusiasm, the gardener took a roll of drawings with him, and once the genuflections were over he began to explain his designs for Versailles. His Holiness was particularly impressed by the number of canals, jets, fountains and cascades to be found there and wanted to know where the river was from which all this water must come. Le Nôtre proudly told him that there was no river and explained the elaborate system of ponds, pipes, pumps and conduits. The Pope was duly amazed by this French ingenuity and even more so by the cost of it all. Such was the warmth of the conversation that Le Nôtre got quite carried away: 'Now I have no regret in dying. I have seen the two greatest men in the world, Your Holiness and the King, my master.'

'There is a difference,' replied the Pope. 'The King is a great and victorious prince while I am a poor priest and the servant of the servants of God. He is young and I am old.' This was too much for the elderly gardener, who slapped the Pope on the shoulder, saying, 'Reverend Father, you are in good health and you will bury the whole Sacred College.' Innocent XI laughed at this prediction. More and more charmed by the Pope's kindness, and by the special esteem he seemed to profess for the King, Le Nôtre forgot himself completely. He was so used to embracing those who praised his master that he threw his arms around the Pope and kissed him.

Le Nôtre sent an account of this encounter to his friend Alexandre Bontemps, the King's valet, who read it out at the *lever*. The French court could not quite believe the story. The Duc de Créqui even wagered 1,000 *louis d'or* that Le Nôtre had not gone so far as to embrace the Pope, but Louis had no doubts. The cultivated and even fearful distance he maintained with most of his courtiers had not prevented Le Nôtre from displaying similar outbursts of affection towards him. 'When I return from campaign,' he told his courtiers, 'Le Nôtre always kisses me.'

Having been lauded by a polymath and a pope, Le Nôtre can be forgiven a little pride. While in Rome and sitting for a portrait by Maratta, one of the city's leading painters, he chose to be depicted in the robes of *Contrôleur des Bâtiments* with the red ribbon and medal of the Order of Saint-Michel, awarded by the King in 1693, flashing beneath the white lace of his cravat. Le Nôtre had been made a chevalier of the Order of Saint-Lazare back in 1675, but when that order had been rescinded in 1692 he graduated to the Saint-Michel, a distinction he shared with a mere hundred Catholic men of rank.

It used to be thought that Le Nôtre also visited England. In 1662 Charles II, not long restored to the throne, had plans for improvements in the royal houses and

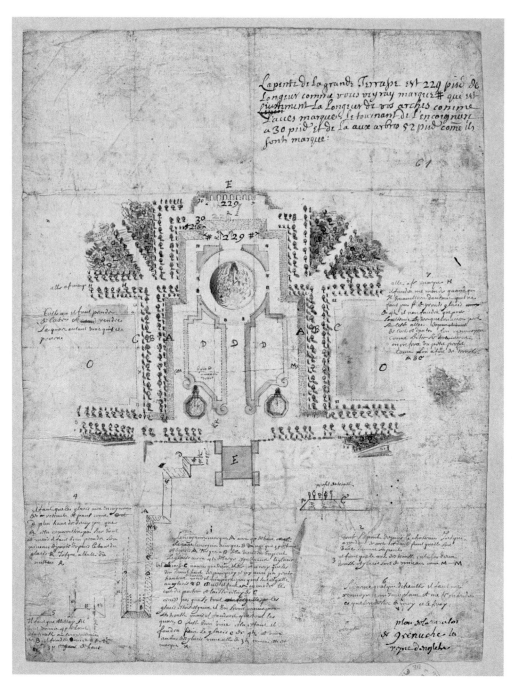

Plan of the gardens of the Queen's House, Greenwich. Attributed to Le Nôtre by
Ernest de Ganay (most of the annotations are in the landscape architect's hand).

asked, through the French ambassador in London, whether Louis could spare Le Nôtre for work at Greenwich. The King replied that 'although I have need of Le Nostre every day while he is busy working for me at Fontainebleau, I shall willingly allow him to make a tour of England since the King desires it ...' Despite the polite wording, Louis was very reluctant to release Le Nôtre, and the settled opinion is that he never made the trip. Had he done so, he would surely have been received with some fanfare, and diarists of the day like John Evelyn and Samuel Pepys could not have failed to notice. Evelyn, in particular, had a passionate interest in gardening, as well as close links to France. Though Le Nôtre never saw the Greenwich site, he did supply a plan for a grass parterre to be implemented within the deerpark to the south of the Queen's House. Towards the end of his life, he also supplied plans for Windsor, but as he was too old and infirm to travel he entrusted the supervision of the work to Desgots.

Le Nôtre returned from his Italian journey with his international reputation confirmed despite the fact that he was losing influence at Versailles to Mansart. If the King asked him for advice less often, his guidance was still sought from abroad. In 1698 Tessin, who was designing a palace in Copenhagen for the Danish King, sent his drawings to Le Nôtre for a frank evaluation. The main door was too small, the gardener replied, and the pavilions too rich and ornamented to correspond to the centre.

In 1693 Le Nôtre, weary perhaps from his concealed struggle against Mansart, asked the King whether he might retire from his official duties. Louis agreed but only on condition that the gardener would honour him with his presence from time to time. If Le Nôtre was forced out, it was done in the gentlest of ways. Having been awarded a pension of 6,000 *livres*, the following year he asked Louis to convert this annuity into a capital sum of 42,000 *livres*. He transferred his positions and responsibilities to Jean-Michel Le Bouteux (the son of Michel II Le Bouteux) and to Claude Desgots, the latter becoming *Contrôleur Général des Bâtiments*.

Remarkably for someone so energetic and influential, Le Nôtre enjoys one of the least sullied of historical reputations. When we consider the character of the court at Versailles, where courtiers competed vigorously for the merest glance of approval from the King, Le Nôtre's social achievement starts to seem as extraordinary as his influence on garden design. He was certainly more sophisticated than the *bonhomme* he liked to play. Saint-Simon wrote a generous eulogy in which Le Nôtre is described as 'honest, honourable and plainspoken'. We are told that 'everyone loved and respected him, for he never stepped out of his place nor forgot it and was always perfectly disinterested'. Perhaps there is a hint of condescension in Saint-Simon's pen-portrait. When he says that there was artlessness about Le Nôtre, 'a simple-hearted candour that was perfectly delightful', perhaps we can detect the superciliousness of a sophisticated man towards one whom he deemed to be his social and intellectual inferior. After all, one of Saint-Simon's principal reasons for liking Le Nôtre was that the gardener seemed to know his place.

But this picture of Le Nôtre as a guileless rustic does not withstand close examination. Not just a gardener but also a high-ranking court official, André seems never to have lost his common touch, for there are no records of any animosity or resentment towards him on the part of the gardeners from whose ranks he had risen and with whom he necessarily had regular contact. Surely a real innocent would have tripped up in such a social mine-field? It seems that Le Nôtre's art lay in his artlessness. In fact he was the antithesis of the bumbling rustic; he was a man in possession of enormous and unforced social skills.

Being both perverse and inconsistent, Saint-Simon could praise Le Nôtre in one paragraph but pour contempt on his life's work in another:

> The gardens [of Versailles] astonish by their magnificence, but cause regret by their bad taste. You are introduced to the freshness of the shade only by a vast torrid zone, at the end of which there is nothing for you but to mount or descend; and with the hill, which is very short, terminate the gardens. The violence everywhere done to nature repels and wearies us despite ourselves. The abundance of water, forced up and gathered together from all parts, is rendered green, thick, muddy; it spreads humidity, unhealthy and evident; and an odour still more so ... I might never finish upon the monstrous defects of a palace so immense and so immensely dear, with its accompaniments, which are still more so.

Of course it is not the gardener's 'bad taste' that is the object of Saint-Simon's scorn here but that of the King, the real target of his invective. In the eyes of the disaffected Duke, nothing that sprang from the King's inclinations could be any good.

Such sentiments were often expressed in the eighteenth century on the opposite side of the English Channel. Horace Walpole called Versailles 'a garden for a great child' and thought that it showed Louis 'in his proper colours, where he commanded in person, unassisted by his armies and his generals, left to the pursuit of his own puerile ideas of glory'. But such opinions might be anticipated from the youngest son of a Whig prime minister, whereas Saint-Simon was a highly placed French nobleman and a contemporary of Le Nôtre. The mainstream of French opinion is better represented by a remark made by the Duc de Croÿ during the reign of Louis XVI. In his opinion, Versailles was 'much nobler than the English fashion'. In any event, when La Quintinie came to write his *Instruction*, he did not neglect to pay his respects to his friend. 'Our century,' he wrote, 'which has excelled in everything that human industry was able to think up, has given, particularly, through the skill of the famous M. Le Nôtre, the ultimate perfection to that part of gardening which is apparent in so many canals, lakes, cascades, gushing fountains, labyrinths, bowling greens, terraces, etc. ornaments in effect numerous, but which in truth bring out marvellously the natural beauty of gardening.'

Le Nôtre lived long enough to see Mignard usurp his old friend Le Brun and for his own rival, Mansart, to become *Surintendant des Bâtiments*. Molière had died in 1673 after a performance of the *Imaginary Invalid*, while Lully had died in 1687 in tragicomic circumstances. Accustomed to conduct his musicians by banging a staff upon the ground, he accidentally stabbed himself in the foot and succumbed to the ensuing infection. Depleted of its greatest talents, the *Grand Siècle* drew to a cheerless close.

Despite the reverses that came at the end of his career, Le Nôtre's legacy and his achievement are still remarkable, considering the social conditions that existed in seventeenth-century France. Although society was strictly hierarchical, the cult of the *honnête homme* allowed for a degree of social mobility on the basis of merit. Colbert was the son of a draper, hired initially to help Mazarin with his finances. Vauban emerged from a family of notaries and merchants. La Quintinie was destined to become a lawyer before he discovered the allure of vegetable gardening. Le Nôtre's father maintained the parterres at the Tuileries. Talent was one of the keys to advancement, but it was not enough to know one's business; one also had to know one's place. Whatever class the *honnête homme* might have emerged from, he had an almost instinctive understanding of how to behave in social situations and could always summon up an appropriate phrase.

Le Nôtre played the courtly game far better than many of his social superiors. By apparently eschewing ambition to concentrate on his gardens, he ensured that honours and financial rewards came his way regardless. He was never boastful and cleverly allowed Louis to take personal credit for the gardens at Versailles. Since he lived mostly in Paris, he preferred to guide visitors around the gardens at the Tuileries, where he could show more personal pride, free of the proprietorial aura of the King. Nor do we find Le Nôtre voicing the social concerns that troubled Vauban, for example, who had seen great poverty and suffering on his travels around France's borders. Le Nôtre was a dutiful but apolitical man, focussed on his work, his family and his friends, to whom he was unfailingly loyal. We might label him a conservative, but a wish to preserve order is forgivable in someone who, as a young man, would have witnessed the turmoil brought to the streets of Paris by the *Frondes*.

The translator of Jules Guiffrey's short biography of Le Nôtre, George Booth, tucks away a provocative suggestion among his endnotes and personal observations. Though Le Nôtre was a brilliant designer and a 'bit of a light-hearted wag', Booth concludes that he was also 'a most consummate toady ... who flattered and sucked up to anyone who could help or hinder him'. This would seem to be a harsh and anachronistic judgement which mistakes the conventional courtesies of seventeenth-century French society for sycophancy. It is certainly true that Le Nôtre tried to avoid direct confrontation; his reluctance to become involved in the dispute between Louis and Louvois over the window at the Trianon is proof enough. But he was forthright about Mansart's Colonnade and criticised Louis for his excesses at Marly.

Claude Desgots certainly did not leave us with the portrait of a sycophant. 'Though Louis XIV did not cease to admire the rare genius of Le Nôtre for gardens,' wrote the gardener's protégé, 'this great Prince wanted to see some created which owed their charms only to himself. Le Nôtre was then eighty years old; his long service at the Court had not been able to diminish his love of the truth. He did not find that the greatest King in the world understood the art of the gardens as perfectly as he did, and said so without restraint.'

That Le Nôtre had the ability to soften an unpleasant message with humour is shown in two letters he wrote, late in life, to Louis Phélypeaux, *Contrôleur Général des Finances*, concerning overdue payments for design work he had undertaken at the château of Pontchartrain. In the first, written in 1696, he refers to all the 'strokes of the pen' he had made in producing the designs for the garden, before asking the finance minister to make a single mark, with his 'beautiful white hand', which will release the payment of 3,000 *livres* due to him. Payment had still not been made by the following year, and the amount of the debt had increased. 'Friends are friends,' wrote Le Nôtre. 'I have many who frequently shower me with flattery – crowned heads, princes, cardinals, bishops, chancellors, first presidents, ministers of finance, and royal treasurers. But, alas! Monseigneur, there is only you, true and good friend, who is able to authorise payment to me of five thousand two hundred and eighty *livres*.'

Le Nôtre kept his health and his good humour until the end of his life. Martin Lister was delighted with the reception he received from the veteran gardener. 'This Gentleman is 89 years old, and quick and lively,' he wrote. 'He entertained me very Civilly.' Louis Petit de Bachaumont, who was brought up at Versailles, also remembered a visit to the elderly Le Nôtre with warmth, though he was only six or seven years old at the time, with a grandfather who had an apartment in the

Grand Commun close to that belonging to the retired gardener: 'He was the most pleasant old gentleman that there could be, always jolly, correct and well-disposed, with a very cheerful face, and always laughing.' De Bachaumont was fascinated by the drawings strewn around the old man's floor, so Le Nôtre supplied him with drawing materials and encouraged him to make some of his own. When the gardener noticed that the boy liked drawing figures better than anything else, he entertained him by making caricatures in the style of the engraver Jacques Callot. The young boy and the octogenarian were both reduced to giggles.

After a life of cheerfulness, temperate habits and innumerable long walks around vast gardens, Le Nôtre remained a robust and energetic pensioner. A painting of Pontchartrain attributed to Jean-Baptiste Martin shows the château and the gardens. In the foreground is Phélypeaux with a group of riders, one of whom, according to Hamilton Hazlehurst, is Le Nôtre on a tour of inspection, although he would have been in his eighties when the canvas was painted.

Le Nôtre was also a good husband and a dutiful son who looked after his mother until her death at the age of eighty-eight in 1675. He also showed great kindness to his wife's sister, Marie-Anne Langlois, who came to live with his family. When she married in 1677, he contributed a generous dowry of 23,990 *livres*. Although home was a house built in a corner of the Tuileries gardens, Le Nôtre also had his residence in Versailles, which he sold in 1686, and an apartment in the Grand Commun, which he kept until his death. The master-gardener had the good sense not to aspire to an aristocratic way of life, so there was never any large country house, but the Le Nôtres enjoyed an affluent bourgeois existence, with a household staff that included a cook, a chambermaid, a lackey and a coachman. We know from an inventory of furnishings made at the time of André's death that their house was well appointed, with expensive tapestries in the living rooms and many copper cooking vessels in the kitchens, while Madame's white satin dressing table, jewels and fine dresses are also recorded, along with several bags of gold and silver.

Le Nôtre's will and the inventory of his possessions made at his death show him to have been an avid collector of artworks and beautiful objects. Lister mentions three apartments, the 'uppermost of which is an Octagon Room with a Dome'. It was here that Le Nôtre displayed

a great Collection of choice Pictures, Porcellans, some of which were jars of a most extraordinary size, some old *Roman* Heads and Busto's, and intire Statues; a great Collection of *Stamps* very richly bound up in Books; but he had lately made a Draught of his best Pictures, to the value of 5,000 Crowns and had presented them to the King at Versailles.

Accumulating a private art collection was a shrewd way for Le Nôtre to invest his money without appearing to be too ostentatious, while at the same time marking himself out as a man of taste and learning. He had a taste for Italian painters such as Francesco Alberti, Filippo Napoletano, Domenico Fetti and Domenichino, but he also had seven canvases by Poussin, including *The Woman Taken in Adultery*, which he had commissioned, landscapes and seascapes by Claude Lorrain, and works by Flemish artists such as Brueghel de Velours, Paul Bril and Cornelis van Poelembourg.

It was considered a great honour to be allowed to make a gift to the King, so in 1693, when Le Nôtre invited the monarch to select any items he desired from the collection, he was enhancing his own reputation. The King selected twenty paintings, which were initially displayed in a small gallery within his apartment. Several of these are now in the Louvre, including Albani's *Acteon Changing into a Stag, Apollo and Daphne* and *Salmacis and Hermaphrodite*, Lorrain's *Seaport at Sunset* and *Village Fête*, and Poussin's *Woman Taken in Adultery, Moses Saved from the Waters* and *Saint John Baptising the People*. This was a significant gift, but, seen in the context of the remaining collection, which included 250 paintings, it made a mere dent and was far outweighed by the prestige and honour it brought Le Nôtre. Knowing that he must be nearing the end of his life, he possibly thought it was better to give his best pieces to the King rather than to allow them to be sold off at his death. The timing is significant, since it coincided with his official retirement and was a way of marking the transition. Le Nôtre was thanking the King for his patronage. In return he would soon receive his generous annuity.

On one of his visits to the gardener's house, Martin Lister was shown an upper closet where Le Nôtre kept a 'great Collection of medals in 4 Cabinets'. Commemorative medals, which were expensive when compared with other forms of reproduction such as woodcuts, etchings and engravings, were correspondingly collectable. They might be struck in their hundreds to memorialise great events or military conquests. Louis' image-making machine cranked them out throughout his reign, and, knowing his garden designer's predilection, the King would often give sets to him. It is rather more surprising to read in Lister's account that this ever-so-loyal subject had three drawers containing some three hundred medals created for King William and a fourth devoted to 'King William's Ancestors and Family'. Le Nôtre would swap medals with Nicodemus Tessin, another enthusiast, while his collection of prints ran to twenty-four bound volumes and included items given to him by Louis, among them images of the *Carrousel* of 1662 and a set of the fountains of Versailles.

When the King came to visit Le Nôtre, the old man would often show him his medal collection. According to Lister's account, it seems as though Le Nôtre took a mischievous delight in showing the monarch King William's medals, for he would say, ' *"Sire, voyla une, qu'est bien contra nous!"* as though the Matter pleased him, and he was glad to find it to show the King.' Louis might have regarded himself as God's anointed, but he still enjoyed a bit of fatherly teasing. 'Monsieur le Nostre spoke much of the good Humour of his Master,' wrote Lister; '… he affirmed to me that he had never seen him in Passion, and gave me many Instances of Occasions that would have caused most Men to have raged, which yet he put by with all the Temper imaginable.'

Le Nôtre's collection of medallions indicates a fascination with the country across *La Manche* which he was never able to visit. This interest is also revealed by the catalogue of his personal library, which contained more books about the history of England than any other subject. More surprisingly, the library did not contain a single treatise on gardening. This does not necessarily mean that Le Nôtre had never read or possessed one, but it does suggest that he regarded his library as a hobby or another form of collection rather than as a reference source. As a young man he had learnt his craft first-hand from the master-gardeners of the previous generation. Perhaps he had never had much time for books, or perhaps in his maturity he had given his textbooks away, to Desgots or some other young gardener who still had to make his way. Such a gesture would have been entirely in character. Le Nôtre was not possessive or over-protective about his collections, and would leave the key to his cabinet in a place known to his servants so that visitors might be admitted in his absence. Remarkably, even though he owned some very portable pieces, nothing was ever lost.

As his family showed little interest in his collections, Le Nôtre made provision for their sale in his will, which was drawn up in February 1700, while he was still active but felt himself to be weakening. Even in his testament he could not resist a little self-deprecating humour and the opportunity to gently tease his wife. He thanked his spouse, who 'by her good management and economy took in hand the preservation of their wealth, whereas he, the testator, has always had the inclination to spend money on his studio and his collection with no thought to conserving wealth but only thinking of glory and honour'.

The health of the old gardener only became a matter of concern to his friends in 1698. The Swedish ambassador Cronström wrote to Le Nôtre's friend Tessin in January of that year, mentioning that André had suffered various infirmities over the winter, but wrote again in March saying that he had revived with the return of the sunshine. His strength was failing, but his mind was as alert as ever and his interest in gardens had not diminished. He had prepared plans for Windsor and was still corresponding with the Earl of Portland regarding this commission in July 1698. Ever the prudent planner, on 13 March 1700, he obtained the promise of a life pension of 6,000 *livres* for his wife in the event of his death. He died that autumn.

To the end there can be no doubt that Le Nôtre loved his King, but could someone as remote and dazzling as a Sun King form an ordinary friendship? It seems that he got as close to it as he could with Le Nôtre. When the old gardener visited him at Marly, he invited him to take a drive around the new forests. Desgots tells us that the King climbed into a covered chaise, carried by his Swiss Guards, then invited André to be seated in a similar conveyance. This was a stupendous honour for the elderly gardener, but what made it all the sweeter was that his old rival, Mansart, was left to follow on foot. 'You can imagine,' wrote Desgots, 'how touched a loyal subject, sincerely devoted to his master, must have been by such a distinguishing act of kindness.' Le Nôtre, with tears in his eyes, turned to Louis and said, 'In very truth, sire, the *bonhomme* who was my father would stare to see me in a carriage alongside the greatest King on earth,' adding with a twinkle of his old wit that 'it must be said that Your Majesty treats his mason and his gardener well.'

Le Nôtre is thought to have written his own epitaph, inscribed on a pillar in the Saint-André Chapel at Saint-Roch, beneath a bust of the gardener commissioned by his family from Antoine Coysevox. For someone known all his life as a modest man, the words seem, if not downright boastful, at least to reflect a very healthy plateau of self-esteem, but as ever he expresses his gratitude to the Sun King:

> To the glory of God. Here lies the body of André Le Nôtre, Chevalier of the Order of Saint-Michel, Councillor of the King, Controller General of His Majesty's buildings, crafts and manufactories of France, and appointed to embellish the gardens of Versailles and other royal houses. The strength and scope of his genius made him so outstanding in the art of gardening that he may be considered as having invented the chief beauties of that art and brought all the others to their ultimate perfection. The excellence of his works accorded with the greatness and magnificence of the Monarch whom he served and who showered him with honours. France was not the sole beneficiary of his talents. All the princes of Europe sought his apprentices. He had no rival that could be compared to him. He was born in the year 1613 and died in the month of September 1700.

Reputations rise and fall. A steady tide of recent scholarship has tended to show how much Le Nôtre was a man of his times, and how great his debt was to earlier French gardeners such as the Mollet family, but there is really no way that his achievement can be taken away from him. When he asserted that there was no one who could be compared with him, he was speaking the straightforward truth, and it is equally true that his apprentices carried his ideas into all of the courts of Europe.

Le Nôtre met his end with an untroubled soul. In his own eyes and in the opinion of his contemporaries, he had lived a blameless life. Historically his reputation has been tarnished by the closeness of his association with absolutism, and we must wonder about his complacency regarding the hardships suffered by some of those who laboured to create his designs. But it is worth maintaining a sense of historical proportion. The gardens at Versailles were begun in the same decade in which London was visited by the Plague and the Great Fire. Most of the deaths on the works at Versailles and Maintenon were caused by malarial fevers, the causes of which were as unknown to the science of that time as the rat fleas that carried the Black Death. Construction work, particularly heavy engineering, has always put lives in peril.

Even if Le Nôtre could have foreseen the scale of the casualties, there would have been little he could have done to prevent them. The infantry regiments who suffered and died in the attempt to build the aqueduct at Maintenon were there not because of the landscape architect's liking for fountains but because of the inexorable will of his master. Such politics as Le Nôtre displayed were of the courtly kind, and it must be remembered that during Louis' reign even *Les Grands* had little effect on policy.

Unlike his King, the gardener also knew how to keep clear of scandal. Literature contains some famous examples of the sexual magnetism that sons of the soil can exert, *Lady Chatterley's Lover* being the prime case, and it is difficult to believe that Le Nôtre did not have his admirers and opportunities, since infidelity was almost a way of life at Versailles. Yet there are no records of any amours. It is probably another indication of André's common sense and intuitive understanding of his place at court, for love affairs would have been certain to attract negative attention and jealousy. Instead he stayed faithful to Mme Le Nôtre, who in turn supported him and ran his household.

Le Nôtre's form of gardening has gone in and out of vogue. In the eighteenth century, the Marquis de Girardin, an enthusiast for the more natural style pioneered in England, echoed Saint-Simon's criticisms and slated the formal manner. The famous

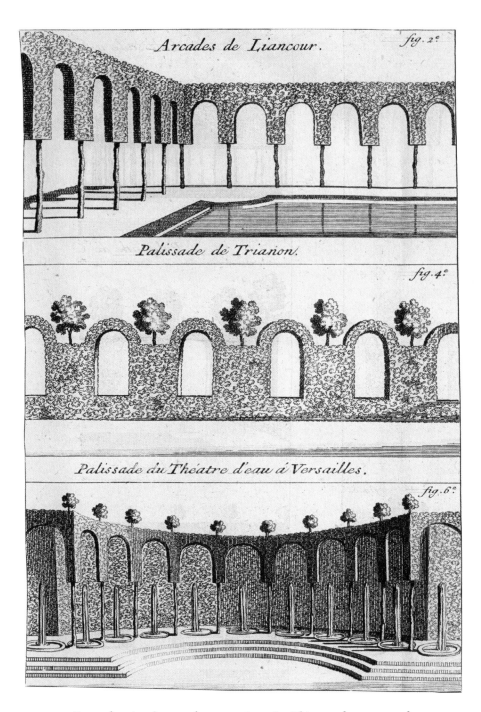

Examples of architectural topiary, from La Théorie et la practique du jardinage *by Antoine-Joseph Dezallier d'Argenville, 1709.*

Le Nôtre had 'massacred nature and subjected everything to the compass of Architecture'. He had encircled the palace of Versailles with 'surroundings of boredom'. As an opponent of absolutism, the Marquis shared the sentiments of the English Whigs.

At the distance of three centuries, we need not be royalists to see that everything Le Nôtre achieved at Versailles was a perfect expression of the wealth and taste of a nation. It was packed with messages about the military might of France, about technological progress, the superiority of French art over Italian, the commanding reach of the Most Christian King and the futility of insurrection. Even the little fleet that bobbed around the Grand Canal was an effective piece of propaganda about France's status as a maritime power. And even if we are unsympathetic to this content or dislike the style, it is still necessary to admire the scale of the achievement. We might even agree with the anonymous author of Le Nôtre's obituary in the *Mercure de France*:

> The King has lost a rare and zealous man from his service, a man of unique art, to whom he gave honour. Monsieur Le Nostre, Controller-General of His Majesty's Buildings and Gardens. No man knew better than he everything which contributes to the beauty of gardens, and even Italy acknowledges this. For proof of this it is only necessary to cast one's eyes upon the gardens of Versailles and the Tuileries and it is impossible to withhold the admiration which the work inspires. He left less cover in his gardens than some might have wished; but he could not abide restricted views, and felt that fine gardens should not be like forests. He was admired by all European Royalty, all of whom sought his designs for gardens.

Louis XIV, at the age of sixty-three, in full regalia. Portrait by Hyacinthe Rigaud, 1702.

XVII
Hard Times and Sunset

ATE WAS KIND TO LE NÔTRE throughout his life and even spared him at the end. He was excused the last fifteen turbulent years of Louis' reign, the long War of the Spanish Succession, the defeats at Blenheim, Ramillies and Oudenarde, and the series of royal deaths that sent the court reeling in 1712 and 1713.

Saint-Simon arrived at the Sun King's court in 1691, in time to record its ossification and decline. In the same year Louvois suddenly died, and there were inevitable rumours about poisoning. Harsh and unpleasant though he might have been, he had been an efficient war minister whose skills would soon be missed. Louis himself had retired from active military campaigning during the Nine Years' War at the age of fifty-five, leaving the armed forces under the less than inspired leadership of Marshall Villeroy. In 1701 Monsieur died of a stroke, possibly brought on by a quarrel with Louis, and the King also lost another great supporter when Alexandre Bontemps, the manservant who had been with him all his life, died at the age of nearly eighty.

Louis' last great conflict, the War of the Spanish Succession, was essentially defensive, although his history of opportunism and territorial aggrandisement prepared the way for it. His brother-in-law was such a chronic invalid that he was known as Carlos the Sufferer, and his death was expected for decades. The French King and the Austrian Emperor supported rival candidates for the succession, threatening to plunge Europe into a wasteful conflict. Much diplomatic manoeuvring was employed to avoid this outcome.

*View of the Bassin d'Apollon and the Grand Canal
(detail) by Pierre-Denis Martin, 1713.*

When Hans Willem Bentinck, the Earl of Portland, visited Versailles, it was not primarily to swap horticultural tips with Le Nôtre, although he did have responsibilities for the upkeep of William of Orange's gardens and had a genuine interest in the subject. His real mission was far more delicate and important. He was supposed to discover Louis' intentions regarding the Spanish throne and to persuade him to stop sheltering James II at Saint-Germain. Under the terms of the Treaty of Ryswick, Louis had been forced to recognise William III's right to the English throne, though he had apologised profusely to King James for having done so. At the same time, William was not only the King of England but also the Stadholder of Holland, and thus the most powerful Protestant prince in Europe. Louis could not just ignore him; indeed elaborate arrangements had to be put in place to ensure that King James, who had been given rights of precedence over just about everyone at Versailles, never met the Earl in the course of his embassy.

Bentinck had been William of Orange's first gentleman-in-waiting before the Stadholder had been offered the English throne. He spoke French better than he spoke English, which was a distinct advantage, considering the nature of his assignment. He impressed everyone he met with his good taste and manners, and he was even invited to visit Marly, a break with the usual protocol that indicates how much effort was being put into this diplomacy. Unfortunately the mission took place in winter, during abominable weather, when the gardens there and at Versailles were covered in frost and the fountains were frozen. During his stay Bentinck probably had conversations with Le Nôtre and certainly visited his most famous gardens, because the designer would later write to him urging him to 'remember everything you have seen of the gardens of France; Versailles, Fontainebleau, Vaux le Vicomte and the Tuileries, and above all Chantilly'. Le Nôtre also expressed the hope that he would be able to converse with Bentinck again, if it would not be too inconvenient.

Though Bentinck returned to England loaded with favours and goodwill, his mission must be accounted a failure. Louis politely refused to send King James anywhere that he did not want to go, while all diplomatic attempts to avert a crisis over the Spanish succession seemed fated to fail. While these efforts were ongoing, Carlos II destabilised the situation by making a will. Then, in November 1700, the Sufferer finally died. His hatred of France is said to have run so deep that he once poisoned his wife's parrots because they spoke French, yet he astonished the whole of Europe by naming the French candidate, Philip d'Anjou, Louis' grandson, as his heir. He seems to have reasoned that only France had the might to preserve the Spanish Empire intact. Louis was now faced with a dilemma: Should he accept the will and provoke a war, or should he contest it, at the risk of handing everything to the Hapsburgs on a plate?

Louis was always likely to decide in favour of family, and had he taken steps to mollify the rest of Europe, he might have avoided a war, since both England and Holland promptly recognised Philip V. Then Louis, showing the same rashness and lack of judgement that had tripped him up at other points in his reign, made three big mistakes. First he put it on record that Philip V had not renounced his claim to the French throne, raising the spectre of complete union between France and Spain. Then he ordered Dutch troops to vacate their defensive fortresses in the Spanish Netherlands. His third blunder reflects the depth of sympathy he felt towards James II. As the exiled King lay dying, Louis told him that he would recognise his son, James Edward Francis Stuart, the 'Old Pretender', as King of England, Scotland and Ireland. It is hard to imagine anything that could have provoked the English more. By May 1702, France was at war with the combined forces of England, Holland, Austria and most of the German states.

The war went badly for the French, but the court was not used to hearing of misfortunes. According to Saint-Simon, it was not until 21 August 1704 that a courier arrived from Villeroy to tell the King about the French defeat by forces under the command of the Duke of Marlborough at Blenheim, a battle fought on the 13th of that month. Those who wrote letters from the front were afraid to tell the truth, since the defeat had been the result of bad generalship, so the scale of the catastrophe only emerged slowly. But there was not a noble family that had not suffered a personal loss. More defeats were to follow. The lowest point was reached at the Battle of Oudenarde on 11 July 1708, when Marlborough was able to exploit the disharmony that existed between two French commanders, the Duc de Vendôme, a battle-hardened veteran, and the Duc de Bourgogne, the King's grandson. Soon after the battle, Lille was taken and the allies invaded France.

There was also gloomy news at home. On 27 May 1707 a repentant Athénaïs de Montespan died at the spa of Bourbon. Although she had borne him many children and presided over the most glorious years at Versailles, the King did not shed a tear when he was told. In the following year Jules Hardouin-Mansart was struck by colic while working at Marly. Twelve hours later he was dead. The King's doctor, Guy Fagon, pronounced that he had been killed by an overindulgence in peas and other novelties from the kitchen-gardens, although there were the usual suspicions of poison. The Marquis d'Antin, who had once moved an avenue of trees by night to please the King, became the new *Surintendant*.

The sufferings of 1709 were made immeasurably harder by the worst winter that anyone could remember. The frost was so severe that the Seine froze. Then there was a thaw for seven or eight days before everything froze again. The

Princess Palatine sat in front of a roaring fire with her neck wrapped in sable and her feet in a bearskin sack, trying to describe it all to her Aunt Sophie, but she was almost too cold to hold her pen. Wine froze solid in bottles, but the Sun King, now seventy, seemed warmed by his own internal fires. Saint-Simon recorded the damage to the gardens: '… the second frost ruined everything. There were no walnut-trees, no olive-trees, no apple-trees, no vines left, none worth speaking of, at least. The other trees died in great numbers; the gardens perished, and all the grain in the earth. It is impossible to imagine the desolation of this general ruin.'

Beyond the walls of the Grand Parc, the situation of the poor was even more desperate. Thousands died and the ground was often too hard to give them a decent burial. Two hundred bonfires had to be lit in the streets of Paris just to try to keep the population warm. There were lurid tales of small children who had turned to cannibalism. A hungry mob of Parisian women marched on Versailles but was turned back by troops at Sèvres.

The situation had not improved much by the spring. 'If the famine gets any worse, perhaps they will send all the extra mouths away, including me,' wrote the Princess Palatine to Sophie. In June the King sent all his tableware to be melted down at the mint, and many loyal members of the aristocracy followed his example. A satirical parody of the Lord's Prayer was in circulation:

> Our Father who art in Versailles,
> Unhallowed is thy name,
> Thy Kingdom is no longer great,
> Thy will is no more done by land or sea,
> Give us our bread which we lack on all sides,
> Forgive our enemies who have beaten us,
> But not your generals who let them do so,
> Do not succumb to all the temptations of La Maintenon
> but deliver us from Chamillart.

The string of misfortunes gave ammunition to the King's critics both at home and abroad. Forty years of image-weaving was gradually unravelled. Louis was being repaid for his insatiable ambition, his lack of scruples, his revocation of the Edict of Nantes and the devastation of the Palatinate. A German pamphlet entitled 'Self-praise Stinks' drew attention to the Sun King's vanity, as exemplified by the extravagance of Versailles. His foes scoffed that he had always been better at making love than making war.

*   *   *

At the height of the famine, when there was a real threat of domestic insurgency, the Princess Palatine wrote to Sophie describing a bread-riot in the streets of Paris in August 1709, during which troops fired on a mob that had broken into a baker's shop. Louis was surrounded by enemies and did not have the money to pay his troops. There was no way out but to sue for peace, but the King needed a final victory in order to escape without loss of lands or honour.

In September 1709 Louis was granted not a victory but a gloriously stubborn defeat at Malplaquet. The allies ranged against France lost twenty thousand men, killed or wounded, while the French losses were barely two-thirds of that number, and the defeated army was able to retreat in good order. Although the war rumbled on for another three years, the threat of invasion had receded.

Louis sued for peace and would have accepted harsh terms, giving up Alsace and a string of border fortifications, recognising the Archduke Charles as the Spanish King and Queen Anne as the legitimate successor to William III, but then the allies went too far, demand that he should supply troops to help them chase Philip V off the Spanish throne. Louis refused, saying that if he had to fight, he would rather fight his enemies than a member of his own family. There was a patriotic revival, Vauban's defences prevented an allied breakthrough, and then came a French success against the Dutch and Austrians at the Battle of Denain (1712). At the Treaty of Utrecht, Louis obtained better terms than had ever seemed likely, and Philip V remained King of Spain, though he promised to renounce any claim to the French throne. France had survived but at great cost.

A sad incident that occurred in the middle of the war was a foretaste of greater tragedies to follow. The King was often so gloomy that he needed the Dauphine, Marie-Adélaïde (Duchesse de Bourgogne), with him at all times, even though she was heavily pregnant and her doctors had advised her not to travel. When he decided to visit Marly shortly after Easter 1708, he insisted that she join him there. He was at one of the ponds, feeding his carp, when the Duchesse de Lude rushed up, impatient to speak to the King privately. When she had gone, Louis returned to his fish. Something was wrong, but no one dared say a word. Finally the King turned round and announced, 'The Duchesse de Bourgogne has miscarried.' There were exclamations and expressions of pity, but the King, who was wrestling with feelings of guilt, snapped, 'Thank God, she has miscarried, since it was bound to happen. Now I shall no longer be annoyed in my journeys and in everything I wish to do, by the representations of doctors, and the reasonings of matrons. I shall go and come at my pleasure, and shall be left in peace.' This outburst was followed by a silence so profound that 'an ant might be heard to

Marie-Adélaïde de Savoie. Portrait by Pierre Gobert, 1704.

walk.' According to Saint-Simon's account, it was fifteen minutes before the King broke the silence, leaning on a balustrade to speak of a carp with his estate workers. Saint-Simon thought the episode revealed that the King 'loved and cared for himself alone', but more subtle psychologists might say that it revealed just how much he cared for Marie-Adélaïde.

In the last few years of Louis' life, the court of Versailles was a sorry place. The region was hit by smallpox in 1711, and the Grand Dauphin, Louis' heir, caught it at Meudon. It appears to have been the doctors, rather than the illness, that killed him, because it was his heart, strained by a regime of purges and bloodletting, which gave out. Smallpox also reached Versailles, followed swiftly by an outbreak of measles. Marie-Adélaïde succumbed and did not recover. She was only twenty-six. The King and Mme de Maintenon were so overcome with grief that they hardly noticed that her husband, the new Dauphin, was also grievously ill. He went with the King to Marly, retired to bed and never got up again. Their sons, both infants, now yielded to the same infection. The oldest boy died, but the youngest survived, hidden away from the doctors and their so often fatal purges by his nanny. While Versailles was reeling from these multiple shocks, the Duc de Berry, who was next in line for the succession after the young sons of the Duc and Duchesse de Bourgogne, had an accident while out hunting and died within two days. The Bourbon succession, which had looked so secure, now depended upon the fragile health of the two-year-old Duc d'Anjou.

The château, which had long since ceased to be a fashionable place, was now under a permanent shadow of mourning. The Sun King lost his cheerful and sanguine disposition; for the first time in his life he was clouded by depression. Gloomy and pious, Mme de Maintenon lacked the ability to lift the darkness. The gardens no longer echoed to the sound of fireworks, and the frivolities of the grand fêtes were remote memories.

The King became crotchety in his old age. He often had gout and toothache, and his fabulously robust digestive system never recovered from an operation for an anal fistula which he underwent in November 1686. He had prepared himself for this ordeal by walking in his gardens, and though the surgeon had cut him eight times with scissors and sliced him twice with a lancet, he insisted upon receiving ambassadors the following day. Troubled physically as well as in his spirit, the King could be difficult. The cabinet-style government of the early years of his reign was replaced by a stubborn wilfulness.

Louis' own death was not long in coming. On 9 August 1715 he went hunting from Marly for what would be the last time. Returning to Versailles he complained of pains in his leg, which were thought at first to be sciatica but turned out to be gangrene. Not surprisingly, bathing the leg in burgundy and ass's milk did no good. It was too late for amputation, and Louis, suspecting that he was dying, would not let the doctors bleed him. It took him a week to die, but throughout he maintained that same self-control which had characterised his life.

Historians, when considering the life of a figure of such significance, feel obliged by their calling to draw up balance sheets of achievements and failures. Our usual standards of morality seem to fall apart in such assessments, for how can any piece of territory gained be balanced against the hundreds of thousands of lives lost or blighted in Louis' wars? His apologists will say that he fought only necessary wars, and that attack was really his best form of defence, but his detractors will argue that many of his campaigns were fought out of personal vanity. And if the gardens and château of Versailles are the most lasting monument to his reign, are they really worth the hundreds, if not thousands, of lives that were lost during the excavations and the building of the aqueduct at Maintenon?

Having lost a son-and-heir and also a grandson-and-heir in such devastating succession, it was for his great-grandson, the future Louis XV, then only a boy of five, that Louis called as he lay on his death-bed. As he prepared to meet his God, he had been reviewing his life and preparing his own balance sheet, and he was inclined to be harsh in his self-assessment. 'Mignon,' he advised the future King, 'do not copy me in my love of building or in my love of warfare.' The Sun King did not, however, caution the boy against gardening. The new King would turn out to have green fingers, just like his great-grandfather.

The Great Palace and the Great Cascade, Peterhof, by I. K. Aivazovsky, 1837.

XVIII

Influence

ALL GARDENING INVOLVES RESISTANCE to natural processes. The lawn cannot be allowed to turn into scrubland, then into forest. The lake must not be allowed to silt up and become a swamp. Le Nôtre would be astonished to find that his garden is essentially intact, three hundred years after his death. Its survival is remarkable but not as astonishing as its influence, for Versailles has been one of the most copied gardens in history.

Perhaps the least surprising imitations were those made by other Bourbon monarchs. Louis' gloomy grandson, Philip V, whose right to rule had been confirmed by the War of the Spanish Succession, pined for the carefree days of his youth at the French court, so this northerner, who could not bear the heat of his sweltering capital, selected a site in the cool hills near Segovia, at an altitude of 1,200 metres, and commissioned two French garden architects, René Carlier and Étienne Boutelou, to create a Spanish Versailles. Known as La Granja (The Farm), the palace was built of a rose-coloured marble that evoked Trianon. The gardens were laid out on a sloping site that required terracing on a scale that rivalled anything attempted by Le Nôtre. When it came to the creation of water effects, Philip V faced none of his grandfather's difficulties, for in this mountain setting water was abundant and readily tapped to fill the canal, the basins and the cascade, which, with its steps of pink marble and jasper, was a pleasing reminder of the Rivière at Marly. Philip even commissioned a Fountain of the Frogs, an almost direct copy of the Fountain of Latona.

In Italy the Savoy monarchy, a family entwined with the Bourbon line, developed a crown of residences around their capital, Turin, which bears comparison with the circlet of royal houses surrounding Paris But if there is a candidate for the 'Italian Versailles', it must be the palace created at Caserta by the son of Philip V and Isabella Farnese, who reigned as Charles III, King of the Two Sicilies.

To inaugurate these building works in 1752, Charles had two regiments of infantry and two squadrons of cavalry form up to make the footprint of the palace. Following the French model, the house and gardens were arranged about an axis; there would also have been a town, except that it was never built. The scale of Caserta is quite disproportionate to the power possessed by such a tiny kingdom. Its designer, Luigi Vantivelli, had never been to Versailles, but he was familiar with the design through engravings and descriptions, and he understood that if he was to emulate the French style, he would have to design on a far more extensive scale than had been customary in Italy. It might even be thought that he overdid it, for the colossal cascade that is the glory of Caserta starts some 2 miles away from the palazzo, where it tumbles down 78 metres of wooded hillside. This cascade is the longest of its kind in the world, and to keep it charged with water Vantivelli had to emulate Louis' engineering projects for Versailles. He located mountain springs which had been known to the Romans in the Monte Taburno region to the east and constructed the 25-mile-long Acquedotto Carolino to deliver their waters to Caserta.

Imitation of Versailles was not confined to Louis' family and friends. William of Orange, the Sun King's greatest foe, nevertheless admired French gardens. He regretted that he had to send the Earl of Portland to France as his ambassador, for although Bentinck sent him reports of all he had seen at Saint-Cloud, Meudon, Fontainebleau and Vaux, William would have liked to have seen these places with his own eyes.

The homesickness that Queen Mary had first felt when she had married William and gone to live in Holland had been eased somewhat by her love for the palace which the couple built at Het Loo, near Apeldoom. Mary laid the foundation stone herself in 1685, and the building work was finished by 1702. The design of the garden is attributed to Daniel Marot, a French Huguenot who emigrated to Holland in 1685, the year in which Louis revoked the Edict of Nantes, and to Jacob Roman, a Dutch sculptor and architect. The design of Het Loo, with its sunken parterre, shows that William shared French tastes. To call Het Loo a 'Dutch Versailles' would be to raise completely false expectations about the size of the mansion and its garden. In a small country where land was at a premium, the extravagant scale of Versailles would have been out of keeping, so both house and garden are neat and contained. As one might expect in Holland, there are flower-beds, and the arabesques of boxwood that fill the compartments of the lower garden, close to the residence, are so neatly clipped that they could almost have been carved. The elaborate patterns appear to best effect from the flanking terraces, which introduce a degree of elevation into the flat Dutch landscape.

Perhaps the most surprising thing about Het Loo today is that the gardens have been completely reconstructed. When Louis Napoleon, one of the brothers of Napoleon Bonaparte, became King of Holland, he took Het Loo for his summer residence, but he covered the overtly French features of the formal garden with a layer of sand so that he could have a fashionable English-style garden instead. Shortly after Het Loo became a national museum in 1970, the decision was taken to remove all the nineteenth- and twentieth-century additions and return the gardens to the condition in which William and Mary would have known them. This meticulous work of restoration was completed in 1984.

As Het Loo demonstrates, it was not always possible to transpose the Versailles model without adapting it to the local context, climate and topography. This was true in Sweden, where Le Nôtre's great friend Nicodemus Tessin guided royal tastes. Tessin has been described as Le Nôtre's best foreign student, but he was astute enough to realise that the French style would have to be modified to suit his native country. The climate also imposed constraints; box, for example, does not flourish in Sweden, so Tessin often used a variety of cranberry in its place. His most important work was at Drottningholm Castle, built for the dowager Queen Hedvig Eleonora, on an island in Lake Malar on the outskirts of Stockholm.

For the seven years of the Regency, the thousands of shutters on the windows of Versailles remained closed, though the public were still allowed to roam in the empty grounds. But while the place appeared to be sleeping, its influence upon the palaces and gardens of Europe continued to grow. Peter the Great had hoped to visit Paris on his first tour of Europe in 1697, but the Sun King had politely refused him an invitation. On his second tour, his curiosity would not be denied, although the Duc d'Orléans was less than enthusiastic. Entertaining the Russian party would be expensive, the Tsar had a reputation for wilfulness, and the manners of his courtiers were considered barbarous.

When the Russian visitors arrived at Versailles, Peter was given a suite in the château. His courtiers scandalised their French hosts, including Saint-Simon, who relished such gossip, by taking women into the apartments formerly occupied by Mme de Maintenon. The governor of the château was shocked to see this temple of prudery profaned. The Tsar explored the whole of the gardens, including the Trianon and the Ménagerie. He sought out the fountaineers and got them to recreate the display he would have seen had he been the guest of the Sun King. It is sometimes said that this visit inspired Peter to create the Peterhof Palace on the Gulf of Finland, 18 miles outside St Petersburg, but this project was well under way before the Tsar went to Paris. Peter had first discovered his site while travelling by boat from Krondstadt to St Petersburg in 1705. Within five years he had built the first house out of timber on a natural terrace overlooking the sea. By the spring of 1714 he had started to construct the pleasure-house called Monplaisir – a name that reveals French preoccupations, although its garden owes more to the Dutch – as well as a more substantial and permanent mansion on the terrace.

Nor is it true that Jean-Baptiste-Alexander Le Blond, Le Nôtre's pupil, returned with Peter in 1717 to help him with the Peterhof and with the planning of St Petersburg. In fact Le Blond had arrived in Russia in September of the previous year, when he had come to the assistance of a capable German architect, Johann-Friedrich Braunstein, who had already started to create the Peterhof gardens, bringing in fertile topsoil, improving the drainage and building a dyke to protect the lower parts of the site from flooding. Trees were brought from around Moscow and Novgorod, but Peter was forced to look abroad for his materials, just as Louis had been compelled to do at Versailles. Thousands of limes, elms, ashes, beeches, hornbeams and maples were brought from Holland, Germany and Estonia to furnish the walks, avenues and groves.

Like Louis at Versailles, Peter was so involved in the creation of the Peterhof that he could be described as his own architect. He sketched out his personal ideas for his professional designers while covering their drawings with his notes and amendments. The central canal was one of the first garden features to be constructed, and it seems to have been the Tsar's own concept. Nevertheless, it was the arrival of Le Blond that enabled him to create an ensemble that really did match the grandeur of the French original. Although the Frenchman was to die suddenly in St Petersburg in 1719, in the course of three energetic years he completely reviewed the designs produced by Braunstein, correcting errors in composition and adjusting faulty proportions.

It could be argued that the water features at Peterhof, although fewer in number, trump the horticultural aspects of the garden even more decisively than do the fountains at Versailles. There are over 170 jets, and they are entirely gravity fed. The discovery of a water source some 12 miles away prompted the construction of a linking canal and enabled the designers who succeeded Le Blond, principally the Italian Niccolo Michetti, to embellish the Great Cascade with jets

The Imperial Summer Residence at Schönbrunn,
Court Façade by Canaletto (Bernardo Bellotto).

and to create new fountains in the Lower Park. The most famous one depicts a gilded Samson, bearing a strong resemblance to Peter, prising apart the jaws of a lion, and was created to commemorate the twenty-fifth anniversary of the Tsar's victory over the Swedes at the Battle of Poltava. Among the pleasures of Peterhof are a number of water-jokes, like a bench that one cannot sit on without being sprayed from hidden nozzles, just the sort of games that amused the Sun King in his grottoes. The venerable hydraulic system still keeps the fountains of Peterhof working for ten hours every day.

Techniques of construction had not advanced much since Le Nôtre's time. The work was still strenous and labour-intensive. In the early years, three to five hundred men were employed in the gardens, but the workforce fluctuated with the country's political and military fortunes just as had been the case in France. After the Peace of Nystadt, which brought the Great Northern War to an end in 1721, Peter was able to employ up to five thousand men on works in the Lower Park. Like Louis, he constantly changed his mind about the details of the design, and construction work often had to be started over.

As at Het Loo, much of what the visitor sees at Peterhof has been reconstructed. A popular summer residence for the Romanov family, the palace was preserved by the Communist government after the Revolution as a cultural symbol, but during the Second World War the Germans overran Peterhof and the gardens suffered extreme degradation. Trees were ripped up, fountains destroyed and many bronzes plundered, although the Russian curators tried to hide the greatest treasures underground before the invading troops arrived. After the war understandable anti-German feeling led to the renaming of the palace as Petrodvorets, while restoration work began almost immediately.

The spread of the Versailles model was astonishingly wide. There would also be a 'Polish Versailles' – the Branicki Palace at Bialystok – and a 'Hungarian Versailles' at Esterháza, as well as an 'Austrian Versailles' at the Schönbrunn Palace in Vienna, but the country in which the dream of glory and absolutism proved most intoxicating was Germany. Germany had emerged from the Thirty Years' War as a mosaic of duchies, electorates and bishoprics whose rulers were anxious to inscribe their authority and underline their autonomy with gardens which followed the absolutist template laid down by the Sun King. As Europe's dominant cultural power, France was still the arbiter of taste. The *Kavalierstour* – the German equivalent of the Grand Tour undertaken by young English nobles – always included a visit to Versailles. Frederick the Great thought that any young man who had not been there would 'pass for an imbecile'. French architects such as

Robert de Cotte, who was the brother-in-law and protégé of Mansart and who designed the Rohan Palace in Strasbourg, were in great demand.

The garden with the strongest claim to be the 'German Versailles' is Herrenhausen, near Hanover, which was begun as early as 1666 under Duke Johann Friedrich but was substantially developed during the last two decades of the century under the guidance of the Electress Sophie, a favourite correspondent of the Princess Palatine. However, the rigorous compartmentalisation and strictly orthogonal layout are more Dutch than French. Born in the Hague, Sophie spent much of her childhood in Holland and was an enthusiast for Dutch gardens, although she employed a French gardener called Martin Charbonnier, who belonged to the school of Le Nôtre. In 1696 she sent him to study the gardens at Het Loo, Niewburg and Honslaerdyck. When he returned, ambitious plans to double the size of the Herrenhausen garden were implemented. The new extension, known as the Grosser Garten, shows Dutch influence in its strict division into triangular orchard plots by the main axes, cross-axes and diagonals, and by the rigorous enclosure of these behind clipped hedges. When Sophie's son became George I of England in 1714, the entire court moved to London, an event that paradoxically saved the gardens at Herrenhausen from the fate of so many formal gardens in the eighteenth century: a fashionable makeover in the English style.

Augustus the Strong, King of Poland and Elector of Saxony, had visited Louis at Versailles. He copied the Sun King not only in his enthusiasm for gardens but also in his taste for costly festivities, including equestrian ballets, firework displays and operas that could last for days. The grounds of the Zwinger Castle in Dresden were laid out in Baroque fashion to provide spaces large enough for public pageants and courtly entertainments. This formed part of a system of parks in that city which included the Grosse Garten, Gross-Sedlitz, Pillnitz and Moritzburg.

In Bavaria the Elector Max Emanuel, who had been governor of the Low Countries between 1692 and 1701 and had spent some time in exile in France during the War of the Spanish Succession, built the palaces of Schleissheim and Nymphenburg near Munich. Schleissheim, which included parterres designed by a Frenchman called Dominique Girard, was soon being hailed as the 'Bavarian Versailles'. It features a central canal that stretches between the new castle and the little lodge of Lustheim. The grounds at Nymphenburg were more extensive and even more consciously French, although Dutch influence might be detected in the generous use of canals. There are two main channels, both occupying the central axis, one running towards the palace from the town, another slicing through the park. Max Emanuel even aped the Sun King in his choice of Venetian gondoliers to ferry his guests around the gardens.

The Sun King was certainly not a role-model for Frederick II of Prussia, who saw himself as an enlightened monarch; nevertheless he spoke French and held French culture in high regard. He began a garden at Potsdam in 1744 which went by the name of Sans Souci, meaning 'without a care' – thus indicating that it was intended as a place of recreation rather than a site for ostentation. The spirit would be more of Marly than of Versailles, but Sans Souci would deliberately be more modest. The King had definite ideas about what he wanted, and provided his master-builder, Georg Wenzeslaus von Knobelsdorff, with sketches. Frederick desired a terraced vineyard that would pay ironic respect to the French Grand Style but that would be altogether lighter and more playful. The plan was innovatory in that the terraces would be gently curved to make the best use of the available sunlight. The retaining walls were supplied with niches that could be covered with glazed panels to protect figs and vines, an idea that owed much to the experiments of La Quintinie.

Though the Grand Style may often be out of favour, it is a slumbering archetype that is periodically reanimated. No discussion of the influence of Le Nôtre in Germany can be concluded without mention of the Herrenchiemsee, the most extraordinary and anachronistic tribute of them all. Ludwig II of Bavaria, often called Mad Ludwig on account of his well-documented eccentricities, is usually associated with the toweringly romantic Schloss Neuschwanstein, the fairy-tale castle that was imitated by the imagineers of Disneyland, but he also built a replica of Versailles, placing it on an island in the Chiemsee, Bavaria's biggest lake.

This particular fixation was born of a visit that Ludwig made to Paris in 1867, during which he saw Versailles and developed an obsession with the grandeur and style of the Bourbon kings. Ludwig's Neues Palais was built between and 1878 and 1885, and although it was never completed, in some respects it exceeded the French original. Its Hall of Mirrors, for example, was bigger than the one created by Mansart. The palace also benefited from technological improvements. There were better lavatories, a heated pool for bathing, and an extraordinary lift that could lower the dining-room table into the nether regions of the building, where it could be reset, a device that enabled Ludwig to avoid distasteful contact with his servants.

The marshlands of the Île-de-France have very little in common with an island in the middle of a Bavarian lake. At Versailles, proper avenues of trees and forest rides serve to make the countryside for miles around subservient to the palace, but at Herrenchiemsee there was no park to be dominated, so the whole apparatus of axes, *allées*, goosefoots and *rondpoints* became superfluous. There was insuf-

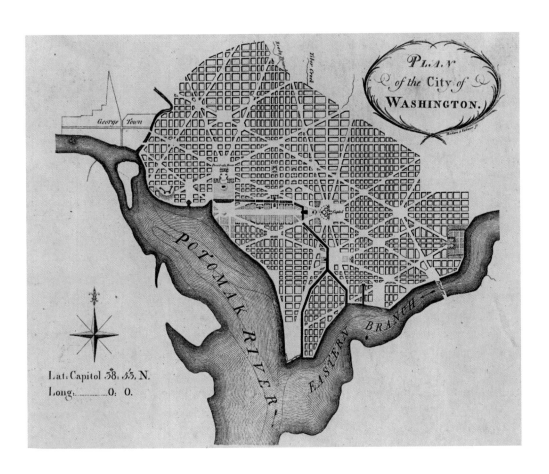

Plan of Washington D.C. by Thackara & Vallance after L'Enfant.

ficient space to develop *bosquets*, so Ludwig put most of his energy into the main water features. He commissioned a presentable copy of the Latona fountain for the main axis, but when it came to the two fountains in front of the palace, the Bavarian King did not have the benefit of a Le Nôtre or a Mansart to guide him. Louis had refrained from erecting any large monuments within the two basins of the water parterre so that the views from his château would be kept open, but without such sage counsel, Ludwig's tastes were left to run free. They had always veered towards the Romantic rather than the Classical – he was, after all, a friend of Richard Wagner – so where Louis limited himself to a scattering of putti and recumbent river goddesses, the pools in front of the Neues Palais are embellished with towering pyramids of rock, winged warriors and vanquished serpents. It is certainly true that Louis commissioned his share of grotesque statuary but never in such bad taste as this.

Versailles also had a marked effect on urban planning. Le Nôtre had a direct influence upon the street map of Paris, for in 1664, when he finally got his chance to redesign the Tuileries gardens, he took the far-reaching step of demolishing the wall and laying out a goosefoot on what is now the Place de la Concorde, thus opening up a vista along what would one day become the Champs-Élysées. This axis would later be extended to La Défence. The system of axes, grids, diagonals and *rondpoints* developed by Le Nôtre at Versailles appealed strongly to city planners in subsequent centuries, along with avenues of trees, monumental statuary, celebratory fountains and all the other paraphernalia of the Grand Style. These things speak of Empire, which is why they were used by the British in colonial capitals like Lusaka, Nairobi and New Delhi, and why they also appealed to Hitler, Stalin and Mussolini. The town-planner Peter Hall is perhaps right to be wary of all plans that set out to turn cities into monuments. Behind the elegant façades of Haussmann's Paris, or the wedding-cake architecture of Stalin's Moscow, lay desperate slums.

For the most direct example of Versailles's influence on a city plan, however, we must cross the Atlantic. Ninety years after the death of Le Nôtre and only two years after the fall of the Bastille, George Washington needed someone to prepare a master plan. He had chosen the site for America's capital city; the diamond-shaped tract of land that would become the District of Columbia had been marked out with forty boundary stones, laid at 1-mile intervals, but who would design the city? During the Revolutionary War he had met a French artist and engineer called Pierre-Charles L'Enfant, whose father had worked as a court painter at Versailles. Major L'Enfant had written to Washington requesting the honour of working on the project. Washington's secretary of state, Thomas Jefferson, who would later become the third President and would also earn a reputation as an amateur landscape architect, had spent time in France and was enthusiastic about working with the Frenchman. When L'Enfant produced the first plan in 1791, he wanted to call the new city 'Washingtonople' to reflect its significance in the emerging world order, but his suggestion was not taken up. This plan was inspired by Le Nôtre's for Versailles, using axial geometries and long avenues connecting important buildings and monuments that were to become the New World equivalents of Le Nôtre's *allées* and *pattes-d'oie*. The plan appealed to both Washington and Jefferson. Why should America's capital not have a plan that had all the Classical dignity of Rome? It would remain the basis of Washington's urban planning for a hundred years.

L'Enfant understood the manner in which geometry could represent power radiating out from a central source. The irony is that his plan for the capital of a fledgling democracy and the leading nation of the Free World should have been based on the garden designed for the Sun King, the monarch who, above all others, has come to epitomise absolutism.

The Bosquet des Bains d'Apollon during felling operations
in the winter of 1774-75 by Hubert Robert, 1775-77.

Epilogue

THE LAST DECADE OF LOUIS XIV'S REIGN had ruined French finances. Whenever budgets have to be trimmed, of course, it is usually those for maintenance which are the first to be slashed. The royal accounts show that the amount spent on Marly's terraces, for example, fell from 100,000 *livres* in 1698 to only 5,000 *livres* in *1712*. For a while this sort of benign neglect can produce a pleasing effect. Trees planted during the era of the Sun King now reached maturity, filling the *bosquets* with their billowing canopies, while the crispness of Le Nôtre's austere geometry was softened and blurred in a pleasingly Romantic way. Nevertheless the clockwork set in motion by the Sun King had not wound down. Gardeners still raked the sand on the *allées*, climbed ladders from time to time to clip *palissades*, and replaced the flowers in the parterres, while the fountaineers still hurried through the groves with their lyre-shaped handles, opening the valves for a water display that had lost its audience.

This new look was popular, particularly with visual artists like Antoine Watteau, who could make an overgrown park resemble the Arcadian scenes depicted by Claude Lorrain. A later painter, Hubert Robert, would develop an even more profound taste for scenes of decline and decay, earning himself the nickname 'Robert des Ruines'. One of his fantasies depicted the Grand Galerie of the Louvre, roofless and crumbling like some relic of Antiquity. Where the Sun King's propagandists had produced images which associated the French monarchy with the imperial glory of Rome, the message that Robert conveyed, during the reign of Louis' great-grandson, was that all glory is transient.

When the court returned to Versailles in 1722, the whole population of the town came out to greet the procession of royal carriages as they rattled into the Place d'Armes. People were expecting a firework display to announce the return of the great days of fêtes and spectacles, but the Regent, Philippe, Duc d'Orléans and nephew of the Sun King, cancelled it because he thought it inconvenient. There would be no return to the *Grand Siècle*, but at least the gardens would be maintained.

Louis XV became known as the *bien-aimé*, the 'well-beloved'. He was most at ease in domestic situations, becoming tense whenever he had to play the public role of monarch. In Louis XIV a sense of duty and a love of theatre had happily coincided, and the Sun King had lived most of his life in public, but this was an act his great-grandson was psychologically unable to follow. Nevertheless he was caught up in the machinery. Every morning, highly placed nobles came to help him on with his shirt, while others came dutifully at eleven o'clock to bring him his silk nightshirt, slippers and cap. He tried to keep up the old forms, but he was just too shy to take all his meals in front of an audience. Easily bored, he shunned his great-grandfather's hands-on approach to government, although he was capable of enthusiasm, particularly when it came to his three main hobbies: hunting, architecture and botany. His mistress, Mme de Pompadour, was said to be the only person who knew how to amuse him, but even she admitted that the King was only truly happy when he had a roll of architectural drawings unfurled on his table.

Despite the penury of the monarchy, Louis XV was still able to get contractors to work for him, though they might wait a long time for payment. Mercifully, though he was passionate about interior decoration, the 'well-beloved' did not inherit his great-grandfather's mania for new buildings. He disliked the public aspect of the vast château of Versailles, and found the place uncomfortable. There was better plumbing, and a lot more of it, in the gardens than in the apartments. The edifice was also judged by eighteenth-century critics to be in poor taste. The King's architect, Ange-Jacques Gabriel, harboured a project for adjusting the whole place to the preferences of the day, but Louis showed slight interest. Little was done in the gardens. Some sea monsters were added to the Bassin de Neptune between 1738 and 1741, and the pond at Clagny was filled in – a matter of public health rather than aesthetics – but no one came forward with any bold new proposals. Formal gardens were out of fashion.

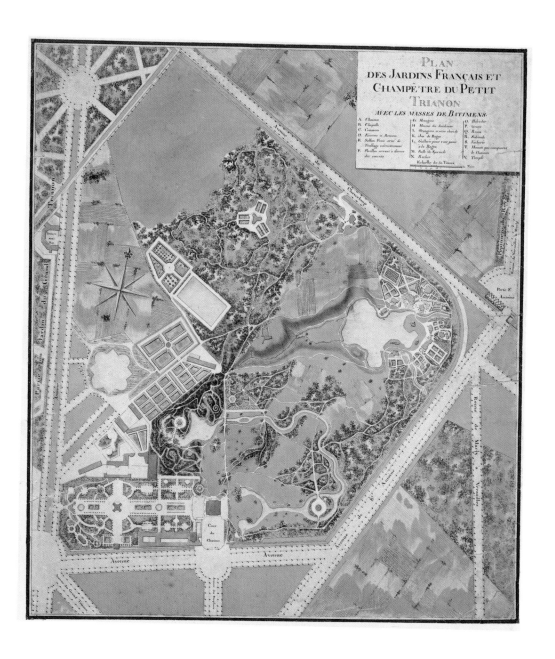

*Plan of the Petit Trianon Showing the Relationship between the Formal Gardens,
the Jardin Anglais and the Hameau. Attributed by Richard Mique, 1786.*

The King much preferred the domestic scale of the Trianon, which afforded him the privacy he craved, to the echoing rooms of Versailles. Mme de Pompadour prevailed upon him to build a new menagerie there, but this would be one where there were no fierce beasts from distant lands, just a collection of domestic animals, poultry and pigeons. The Sun King's Ménagerie had also possessed elements of the farm, but this initiative was spiritually connected to a new mood in which the rustic life was culturally exalted. Rousseau censured the artificiality of social customs and the corruption of institutions, for which his suggested remedy was a return to nature. This was a theme that Robert would develop in his paintings, where happy peasants grazed their cows among the remnants of an overblown and degenerate empire. At the same time, François Quesnay – Mme de Pompadour's physician, who interested himself in economics – promoted the 'Physiocratic' view that a country's wealth depended not upon its stocks of gold or silver but upon the extent of its agricultural surplus. Unlike Colbert, who had promoted industry and commerce, Quesnay thought that all wealth ultimately came from the land. Marie-Antoinette, the wife of Louis XVI, was thus not the first to play the farmer's wife at Versailles, and her make-believe seems more forgivable in the context of a well-established fashion that was underpinned by philosophers, artists and economists.

The Nouvelle Ménagerie was designed by Gabriel for a site to the north-east of the Jardin du Roi at Trianon. It included a farmyard with hen-coops, cow-barns, sheep-pens and pigeon-houses, and was integrated with a garden on a cruciform plan centred around Gabriel's French Pavilion, which was large enough for supper parties, card games and music, while the smaller Salon Frais was used for light refreshments.

Louis XV's passion was for botany rather than garden design. His friend the Duc d'Ayen took him to the botanical garden at Saint-Germain (run by Claude Richard), which became one of his favourite destinations. In 1750 Richard was rewarded with the title *Jardinier-Fleurist* and went to work at the botanical garden newly established at Trianon, taking his orders directly from the King. Strawberries were as much Richard's speciality as pears had been La Quintinie's.

Louis was also patron of the Jussieu brothers, Bernard and Antoine, who had travelled together, plant-collecting in Spain, Portugal and southern France. In 1758 Bernard Jussieu was made superintendent of the botanical garden at Trianon, where he worked with Richard to develop a system of plant classification. He corresponded with the great Swedish botanist Carolus Linnaeus, who paid him the tribute of naming the genus *Jussieua* after him. Under Jussieu, the Trianon garden contained some four thousand varieties, all neatly catalogued. The garden also had a large greenhouse, modelled on Dutch designs, which had a large, sloping glass roof, thick masonry walls to retain the heat of the sun, and a stove to keep frosts at bay.

Louis spent so much time at Trianon that in 1761 he decided that another building was required, but as he had not inherited his great-grandfather's taste for the grandiose, it was to be a house on an intimate, domestic scale. Louis did however share the Sun King's wish to be involved in all of the details and often insisted that Gabriel should work in his company, an echo of Louis XIV's decision to camp on the site of the Grand Trianon. The result was a delightfully proportioned mansion, the Petit Trianon, which possessed a great purity of line and simplicity of ornament. The interior decoration reflected the King's botanical interests, with lilies in circular wreaths on the panels in the Grand Salon, festoons of fruit on the panelling of the dining room (with the strawberry taking pride of place), and yet more flowers carved into the wainscoting of the King's study, which overlooked the garden tended by Richard and Jussieu. The dining table was served by an ingenious dumb-waiter system, which might well have inspired Mad Ludwig's table-elevator at Herrenchiemsee. Those for whom the building had been intended had little opportunity to enjoy it, unfortunately. Mme de Pompadour died in 1764, at the age of forty-six, while the Petit Trianon was still just a shell. It would be several years before the decoration was complete, and Louis did not spend a night there until August 1770. He died of smallpox four years later.

Under Louis XV, Versailles saw few spectacles to rival the great fêtes of the Sun King's reign, but there was one notable exception. On 16 May 1770, six thousand guests from all ranks of society attended the wedding of the Dauphin, the future Louis XVI, to the Archduchess Marie-Antoinette, the daughter of the Austrian Emperor. To mark this momentous union between two great royal families, Versailles mounted the full panoply of pomp and pyrotechnics. The court, in full regalia, watched the fireworks and illuminations from the Grand Galerie; it was all too much for the Duc de Croÿ, who climbed on to the roof of the château to get a better view. No one alive could remember a better show.

The same Duc de Croÿ, who was first gentleman of the bedchamber, took a tour of the gardens on the day before the wedding, to check the preparations for the fireworks. 'It was the best day of Spring,' he noted in his journal; he 'could not cease to marvel at the height of the trees'. Here were oaks as tall and straight as pines, sheltering innumerable birds. The Duke was a staunch defender of the

The entrance to the Tapis Vert during Felling Operations
in the Winter of 1774-75 by Hubert Robert, 1775-77.

French style of gardens against the advances of the English fashion, but his glowing praise for the trees at Versailles overlooked an uncomfortable fact. They were getting too old and would soon have to be cut down unless they were to fall. Louis XV had been aware of this difficulty but had procrastinated, leaving the bulk of the problem to his successor.

Le Nôtre's garden faced its most perilous moment when Louis XVI took the throne. It was one of those periods when nothing old seemed worth preserving. Molière was considered in bad taste, Lully was passé, and the château created by Le Vau and Mansart was an anachronism. Le Nôtre's clipped gardens were equally outdated, and they were also costly to maintain. Was this not the right time to sweep them away and replace them with something informal and naturalistic? There was a political difficulty here, since the English style was so closely associated with the Whig oligarchy, which had been so hostile to the rights of the monarchy. How could Louis XVI adopt this style without undermining his own divine authority? If this were not problem enough, there was also the cost. Landscape-style gardens might ultimately be cheaper to maintain, but the expenditure involved in erasing all of Le Nôtre's straight lines and Mansart's marble embellishments in order to replace them with Brownesque clumps and a serpentine lake was too much to contemplate.

The replanting took place over the winters of 1774 and 1775 under the direction of the Comte d'Angivillier, who sold off the timber at auction. It was a fitting subject for 'Robert des Ruines', who recorded the sad event on two canvases now kept in the museum at Versailles. In Robert's paintings there are logs everywhere and workmen labouring with two-handed bandsaws to cut them up into manageable pieces. One canvas shows men heaving on a rope to topple the last of the trees in the Bosquet des Bains d'Apollon, while the other shows a view towards the Tapis Vert, with children in the foreground playing on a hastily improvised see-saw. It looks as though some unforgiving storm has ravaged Le Nôtre's masterpiece. The Duc de Croÿ was understandably heartbroken, but there was one consolation, in that statues which had been hidden for years behind overgrown foliage emerged suddenly, looking rather startled to be seen again.

The replanting went ahead using mostly native trees as in the original design, more for reasons of economy than of aesthetics. To cut down on maintenance, single rows of limes or chestnuts replaced many of the hornbeam *palissades*, a change in keeping with the Romantic style that people had come to appreciate. To cut costs still further, some of the old *bosquets*, like the Arc de Triomphe and the Théâtre d'Eau, were finally abandoned. The Dauphin and the Girandole, the two longest-serving groves on the site, were converted to simple quincunxes, while the

The Illumination of the Belvédere by Claude-Louis Châtelet, 1781.

Labyrinthe, long out of vogue, became the Bosquet de la Reine, much simpler in design although graced by rare trees including a Corsican pine, a cedar of Lebanon and tulip trees from Virginia.

Hubert Robert was not restricted to recording the replanting of the Petit Parc; he was also commissioned to create a new setting for the statues of Apollo and his horses, which had begun their wanderings when they had been transferred from the Grotte de Thétis to the Bosquet des Dômes in 1684. Their original home had been a building with an interior designed to look like a shell-encrusted cave. Their final domicile was a more literal cave, though one assembled from rocks in accordance with Robert's picturesque vision, and thus every bit as artificial as anything designed by Le Nôtre.

Robert became one of the most significant landscape designers working in the new style, designing gardens for the Marquis de Laborde at Méréville and for the Marquis de Girardin at Ermenonville, where he created the island setting for the tomb of the philosopher Rousseau, who had spent his last years as a guest of Girardin and died on the estate. Despite his sympathies, Robert was arrested during the Terror but escaped the guillotine when someone else was mistakenly executed in his place. He survived to become, in 1795, one of the first curators of the Louvre, the building he had once painted in ruins.

When Marie-Antoinette arrived at Versailles in 1770, she would have found a good deal that was familiar, since she had spent much of her childhood at the Schönbrunn Palace outside Vienna, where the glorious gardens owed much to the style of Le Nôtre, and where there was an orangery full of tropical plants and a menagerie that boasted a camel, a rhino and a puma, as well as parrots and squirrels. When she turned her attention to gardening, she was following family tradition, as well as the example set by Mme de Montespan and Mme de Pompadour. But when Louis XVI made her a present of the Petit Trianon soon after becoming King, he could hardly have predicted the consequences.

No one could have been higher-born than Marie-Antoinette, yet she quickly displayed her dislike of the excessive formality of the French court. The Trianon offered her respite, just as it had done for Louis XV and the Sun King. Versailles already had a 'Little Venice'; now tongues wagged about the 'Little Vienna' nearby. The Queen had no interest in botany and soon swept away the hothouses and experimental beds of Richard's research garden. The fashion now being for the sweeping curves and asymmetry of the English garden, Marie-Antoinette, nothing if not fashionable, was determined to have one of the best. It would be difficult to overstate the revolutionary nature of this change in taste. Le Nôtre's geometries seemed tired, rigid and dull, while the fluid lines of the Jardin Anglais were exotic and carefree, and spoke of freedom. The lives of people in such a garden could be as unconstrained as the vegetation, which was liberated to follow its own inclinations, not clipped and tied into unnatural shapes. Ironically the paintings that inspired this new taste were those by the very artists whom Le Nôtre had liked to collect – Bril, Lorrain, Poussin – but the veteran gardener had only been able to make tentative steps towards the emerging style.

Marie-Antoinette first turned to Richard to provide her with a design. He had the chance to protect his life's work by suggesting a layout that avoided obliteration of the experimental garden, but he simply was not up to the task. Although he had visited Stowe and Kew in England, the plan he served up in 1774 was like a bowl of spaghetti, with far too many winding paths. Rejecting this fussy approach, the Queen turned to the Comte de Caraman, whose own garden in Paris was considered one of the best in the new style. He was appointed *Directeur des Jardins de la Reine* and produced a satisfactory master plan with the assistance of the architect Richard Mique and the painter-*cum*-landscape architect Hubert Robert. The Queen took great interest in the progress of the design. Since plans can be hard to read and often fail to convey a sense of three dimensions, the sculptor Deschamps was asked to model the proposals, using wood, wax, moss and horn shavings dyed green. Only after fourteen iterations was the Queen satisfied with the design.

Caraman was gradually eased out in favour of Mique, while Richard became responsible for sourcing plants. He must have been dismayed to watch his glasshouses being unceremoniously demolished to make way for a range of hillocks, although the botanical collection was transferred to the Jardin des Plantes in Paris. Soon there was a cascade pouring from a grotto to feed an irregular lake and a wandering stream that divided to form the island site for Mique's Temple d'l'Amour, an elegant rotunda sheltering a statue of Cupid by Bouchardon. Around the lake the setting was wild and rocky. The spiralling paths of the Montagne de l'Escargot joined terraces which seemed untamed but were systematically planted with pines, larches, firs and junipers brought back by Antoine Richard from his expeditions to the Alps. The octagonal Belvédère, begun in 1778, was set on a promontory above the lake, but the most outlandish element of the gardens was the Jeu de Bagues, a mad little merry-go-round, more Chinese than English, which really belonged in a fun-fair. Guests would sit in seats shaped like peacocks or kneeling Chinamen on a revolving platform turned by two servants concealed in a subterranean chamber, and would try to throw hoops over pegs as they were whirled around.

The Queen's mother, the Empress Maria Theresa, had been the first to have

The Hameau de la Reine at the Petit Trianon by Pierre-Joseph Wallaert, 1803.

doubtful premonitions about the King's 'charming first present' to her daughter, hoping that it would not 'provide occasions for too large expenditure, let alone for dissipation'. No one seemed to mind much initially, only the Comte d'Angivillier, who, as *Directeur des Bâtiments*, had been rather ignored, and Turgot, the finance minister, who was the next to worry about the cost. Gradually others began to notice the expense, and people started muttering about excess. The Duc de Croÿ confessed that he thought he was dreaming: '… never had two acres of land changed so completely, or cost so much money.'

If Marie-Antoinette had been more willing to share her garden with a wider public, she might have avoided much criticism, but she kept a very close circle. Following the fashion for amateur dramatics that took hold in the 1780s, she asked Mique to design a miniature theatre in the grounds of the Trianon, where she started a company and liked to take the part of laundry girls or village maidens in the escapist rural fantasies that were then in vogue. The audience, however, consisted entirely of members of the royal family and her own retinue. Most of those excluded already associated the theatre with licentiousness and dissipation, and were happy to stoke rumours about the Queen's private life.

'I have no Court at Trianon,' Marie-Antoinette once wrote; 'I live as a private individual.' It was her custom to lunch there every day, and the King would often join her later in the afternoon. The problem was that she spent so much time there that it seemed like she kept no court at all. Louis XIV had set impossible standards to live up to, yet even he had been constantly in search of privacy, first at Versailles, then at Trianon, finally at Marly. Louis XV had not strutted the regal part so well, but at least his retiring habits had not antagonised anyone. Marie-Antoinette's attitude, however, was symptomatic of the age. She wanted to enjoy all of the benefits that came with being a queen just as long as she could step out of the role as often as she felt like it. Though she played at being a private person, she could mount the most regal of performances at Trianon whenever royalty came visiting. Trenches would be dug around the Belvédère and the Temple d'l'Amour and filled with faggots, which, when lit, would illuminate the buildings flickeringly. Chinese lanterns would be hung from branches and little pots of fire would be concealed like footlights shining up into the canopies of the trees. It was not only Marie-Antoinette who liked to avoid ceremony during this era; many monarchs chose to travel incognito. So in 1780 these magical illuminations were lit not for the Grand-Duke Paul of Russia but for the 'Comte du Nord', while in 1784 the festivities were in honour not of King Gustav III of Sweden but of the 'Comte de Haga'.

Driven still further by her taste for informal living, Marie-Antoinette next asked Mique to design her a whole village, complete with thatched cottages, a mill and a dairy, all carefully disposed beside a lake overhung with poplars and weeping willows. Cattle would graze in the meadows and picturesquely attired peasants would bring their corn to the mill to grind. Popular history has exaggerated the extent to which Marie-Antoinette liked to play the dairy-maid, but she did like to dress in white muslin and wear straw sun bonnets, and her husband was sympathetic towards this more relaxed fashion. Her hands did not become calloused with hard work, but she was fond of the Dairy, rather better appointed than most, where there were fifteen marble tables and porcelain utensils for the making of butter, cream and cheese.

From the outside, the buildings of the Hameau were artfully dilapidated. They were an architectural amalgam of vernacular styles, borrowing stepped gables from Flanders, half-timbering and thatch from Normandy, and tiled roofs from the local traditions of the Île-de-France. The village was decorated with a thousand white faience flowerpots bearing the Queen's monogram in blue. Even today, restored to something close to its original condition, there is something of the theme-park or film set about this contrived place. No real hamlet would have anything remotely as whimsical as the Tour de Marlborough, with its balconies and spiral staircases decorated with pots of gillyflowers and geraniums, which stands beside the pond like a lighthouse built for ducks. If it seems strange that this oddity was named after one of France's greatest foes, the victor of Blenheim, the explanation lies in the sentiments of brotherhood that followed the signing of treaties in 1783 to bring the American Revolutionary War to a close. English tourists and diplomats had flooded back into France, and polite society was in the grip of a rampant Anglomania.

The King and Queen played the roles of country squire and lady rather than peasant or milkmaid, and within the apparently run-down buildings the rooms were as sumptuously decorated in gold, silk and marble as those within the château at Versailles. One of the houses was set apart for the Queen's own use, and here etiquette was greatly relaxed. A farm was built near by, and there was a herdsman and his family as well as a garden boy. The Hameau is often invoked as evidence that the King and Queen were living in a make-believe world, detached from all social realities. It is true that the idealised version of the countryside at Trianon bore little relation to the realities of French rural life, where families were starving to death, but the paradox of the Hameau is that it also represented a loosening of the old order, an experiment in a different way of living, which recognised value in the land, in country ways and the rural economy. If there was a yearning for progress wrapped up in this fantasy, it was sadly too little and too late.

When the Queen chose to be painted in her muslin dress and bonnet by Mme Vigée Le Brun in 1783, the painting was received with hostility. This was not the way the Queen of France was supposed to look. Although Marie-Antoinette was nowhere near as frivolous as history has made her seem, she did make all the wrong choices. By seeking a private, secluded life, she angered all those at court who were not part of her coterie, while by refusing to play the part of a grand queen, she disappointed the peasantry, whose day-to-day struggles might have been assuaged by the sort of public pageantry mounted by Louis XIV. At the same time, she promoted costly projects like the theatre, the Jardin Anglais and the Hameau, which were judged to be self-indulgent at a time when France was impoverished.

As a foreigner, Marie-Antoinette was always likely to be a target for anti-monarchical feeling, but she did not deserve some of the slanders heaped upon her. She had been given the Petit Trianon, not built it, and its rooms were not encrusted in gold and diamonds as the rumours suggested. She certainly liked to associate with a young set, which included the King's lively young brother, the Comte d'Artois, and the Swedish soldier and diplomat Count Axel Fersen. Her marriage went unconsummated for seven years before the King was persuaded to have an operation to cure his erectile problems, and there were countless rumours of liaisons. Even the Swedish ambassador noticed that there was a frisson of attraction between Marie-Antoinette and Count Fersen, but solid evidence of an affair has never been found, and her behaviour may have amounted to no more than courtly coquetry.

All of the Queen's amusements, though mostly innocent and certainly not so very different from those of earlier generations, provided coal for the engine of rumour. Did she not cavort with actors, and were actresses not the closest things to harlots? Was there not a grotto in her garden designed for sexual assignations? The Queen was derided in pornographic songs and political pamphlets. She was portrayed as a woman of insatiable appetites, an Austrian spy and a schemer who planned to poison the King in order to place the Comte d'Artois, her alleged lover, on the throne. No slander was too outrageous to be widely believed.

As the Queen matured, she made some attempts to improve her public image which were undone by a scandal in which she was entirely blameless, the so-called Affair of the Diamond Necklace. The Parisian jewellers Boeher and Bassenge had created a fabulous necklace incorporating 647 diamonds for Mme du Barry, Louis XV's last mistress. Louis had died before the necklace could be delivered, so Charles Boehmer offered it to Louis XVI as a suitable present for the Queen, at the bargain-basement price of 1,600,000 *livres*. It was not the sort of object that could be worn comfortably with a muslin frock and straw bonnet, so Marie-Antoinette demurred, observing that the King could equip a man o'war for the same price.

That would have been the end of the matter, except that Cardinal de Rohan, who had been frozen out of the Queen's circle and was anxious to regain her good-will, had been persuaded that she desperately wanted to own the necklace. He had come under the influence of an adventuress who called herself the Comtesse de Lamotte Valois and had shown him forged letters suggesting that she was a close confidante of the Queen. The sting involved a series of bogus notes, purportedly from Marie-Antoinette, which urged the Cardinal to purchase the necklace on her behalf, suggesting arrangements by which he might be gradually repaid. But the master-stroke that closed the trap involved a prostitute called Nicole d'Oliva, recruited by the Comtesse and her co-conspirators because of her close resemblance to the Queen.

Nicole was to meet Cardinal de Rohan in the gardens of Versailles by night, wrapped in a muslin headdress of the sort sometimes worn by Marie-Antoinette. The meeting is said to have taken place in the Bosquet de la Reine, which had small green rooms linked by a winding path within a belt of woodland, similar in some ways to the Labyrinthe, which it replaced. Close to the palace, it was suitably secluded, an ideal place for a secret meeting, and in the half-light the Cardinal was completely taken in. The faux Marie-Antoinette gave him a rose and whispered that her former displeasure was at an end, but this scene, with its element of farce, would soon lead to tragedy.

Convinced that he had recovered the Queen's good favour, Cardinal de Rohan immediately purchased the necklace, passing it to the Comtesse de Lamotte for delivery to the Queen. Instead the Comtesse gave it to her husband, who swiftly took it to London to be broken up and sold. For a while Jeanne de Lamotte kept up modest payments to Boehmer and everyone remained in the dark, though the Cardinal no doubt wondered why the Queen still treated him coldly and why she never wore her new necklace. When the scandal broke, there was a sensational trial, at which the Cardinal was acquitted and the royal impersonator got off with a reprimand, but the Countess was sentenced to be whipped, branded with a 'V' for *voleuse* and thrown into prison.

The real victim of the Diamond Necklace Affair was Marie-Antoinette. Her conduct had been blameless, yet her whole way of life was put on trial. People were prepared to believe that she had wanted the necklace and had been willing to use devious means to obtain it. They thought that she had used the Comtesse de Lamotte to settle a score with the Cardinal, who was seen not as a fool but as someone wronged. Surely, they said to themselves, if half the stories we hear about

Marie-Antoinette are true, then the Cardinal made an excusable mistake. Marie-Antoinette was just the sort of person to make nocturnal trysts in the groves of Versailles.

Marie-Antoinette had tried to live down her reputation for extravagance, but she could not shake off the hurtful nickname she had been given – 'Madame Déficit'. In reality the country's problem was not that it had an Austrian queen with a penchant for the theatre and gardening but that it had a vast population, an unreformed agricultural system and an economic crisis caused by decades of overspending. When Louis XVI took the radical step of summoning the States-General, which first met in May 1789, it was with a view to enacting fiscal reforms, and for a moment it seemed as though a transition to a new social order might be possible. But throughout the political wrangles of that summer, bread prices in Paris remained at the highest levels of the century, while in the countryside peasants had begun to tear down the walls of their lords' manor houses. In the midst of these tribulations, the royal family was dealt another blow with the death, on 4 June at Meudon, of the Dauphin, who was not yet eight years old but had long been suffering from tuberculosis of the spine.

Although the nobility, gripped by fear, had started to flee France's borders, the King and Queen chose escapism rather than escape. On 5 October 1789, a cold, overcast day, the King was out hunting at Meudon while the Queen sought comfort walking in her garden. Her stroll took her to the grotto behind the Belvédère, where she lay down on a moss-carpeted bed to contemplate the unfairness of life. A mob of market-women from Paris, fired up with Revolutionary fervour, was on its way to Versailles. Angry at the price of bread and stirred up by militants, their purpose was to bring the King back to Paris to ensure that the Revolution would continue. Eighty years earlier, the Sun King had successfully turned such a mob back, but the situation in France had changed, and Louis XVI was powerless to prevent their arrival. During the night the mob attacked Versailles, and on the following day the royal family was transported to Paris in a cortège that took seven hours to reach its destination. The events that would lead to Marie-Antoinette's execution were already in train. When the Queen departed, the contractors and suppliers working on her unfinished garden presented bills totalling almost half a million *livres*. This was a gift to the Revolutionary propagandists. Surely it was this woman, with her earthworks and her rockeries, who had brought France to its knees?

It is a wonder that Versailles survived the Revolution. It was such a symbol of the monarchy that one might have expected it to be put to the torch. Yet it is a curious fact that even the most bloodthirsty of revolutionaries prefer to convert buildings rather than to destroy them. While the guillotine did its work in Paris, the people of Versailles left the château alone, not just out of loyalty but from some sense that their lives were still bound up with that of the estate. In 1792 the citizens petitioned against the removal of artistic treasures to the Museum of Paris. It was decided that the building should be preserved at the expense of the Republic for the benefit of the people, and that there would be a small art gallery exhibiting about 350 paintings of the French School.

The Potager was divided into eight plots and let to tenants, but in 1798 Antoine Richard, who had converted to republicanism at an opportune moment, was given the task of setting up an experimental garden, and the leaseholders were evicted. Various subsequent regimes brought differences in emphasis. Sometimes the Potager was valued for educational purposes, sometimes it reverted to its original function of providing fresh produce, but it always survived because it was so evidently useful. In 1849 it became the National Agronomic Institute, under the direction of August Hardy; then in 1874 it became the National Horticulture School, where, in time, the teaching of design became important. Since 1976 the National School of Landscape has been based at Versailles, and since the departure of the horticulturists to a new site in Angers, the historic vegetable garden has been left in the care of the landscape designers, who take this responsibility very seriously. The fruit trees are still pruned by hand, and the old shapes – the spirals, triangles, cordons and candelabra – can still be seen. But among La Quintinie's ordered layout, today's visitor might also find some surprises, since the design students are allocated plots for aesthetic experimentation.

Beyond the fortress-like walls of the Potager, there was a danger that the rest of the gardens, more ornamental than useful, would be ploughed up and distributed to the local peasantry. Indeed, under the National Convention of 1792, many trees were felled and some land in the Grand Parc was dispersed, but Richard's timely change of political persuasion enabled him to lobby on behalf of the gardens that had been his life's work. He got himself appointed *Directeur des Jardins Botaniques de Trianon* and convinced his new masters that Versailles could be of benefit to the people by turning parterres into vegetable plots and planting orchards around the Fountain of Latona, the Tapis Vert and the head of the Grand Canal. These wily tactics saved the gardens from dismemberment and destruction, but – in keeping with the egalitarian spirit of the times – the gardens were left open to the public, and there are accounts of soldiers' wives washing their laundry in the Buffet d'Eau and hanging it out to dry on the hornbeam *palissades*.

The Sun King's princely Menagerie, forerunner of the modern zoological garden, was one of the casualties of the Revolution. Such an aristocratic frivolity irritated the Jacobins. The *Encyclopédie* declared that it was shameful to feed beasts kept for pleasure when human beings were dying of hunger, and saw parallels between social injustices and the apparent oppression of nature involved in keeping animals in captivity. So in 1793 the animals at Versailles were sent to the skinners.

Whatever virtues Napoleon might have possessed, they did not include an interest in gardening. When he went to live in the Grand Trianon, he was more concerned with security, removing planting to improve surveillance, something which park managers today are often under pressure to do, though Napoleon was more afraid of assassins with bombs than muggers with flick-knives. He presided over a further erosion of features when the *bosquets* of the Arc de Triomphe and the Trois Fontaines were cut down. Little changed at Versailles after the Restoration, though when the elderly Louis XVIII (the youngest brother of Louis XVI) became King, he created the English-style Jardin du Roi on the site of the former Île Royale.

In 1820 the landscape designer Gabriel Thouin produced a plan for Versailles that would have left the gardens and the area around the Canal untouched but converted the rest of the park into a romantic landscape in the Anglo-Chinese style. The Swiss Lake would have acquired a naturalistically dithered edge and a picturesque island, while there would have been much larger serpentine lakes beyond the western limit of the Grand Canal. The shading suggests an undulating landscape, cut through by sweeping paths and dotted with Brownian clumps. The scale is such that the cost would likely have exceeded everything the Sun King had done in his gardens, so it is not surprising that it was never constructed.

The gardens continued to be neglected throughout the nineteenth century. King Louis-Philippe turned the château into a museum to 'all the glories of France'. At the opening ceremony on 10 June 1837, Mme de Boigne, the daughter of a lady-in-waiting in Louis XVI's court, later an accomplished hostess and the author of memoirs, looked out from the windows of the Galerie des Glaces as the sun sank slowly at the far end of the Grand Canal. 'I appreciated in that moment and for the first time,' she wrote, 'the merit of the talent of Le Nôtre,' adding that under present circumstances only the whole nation was grand enough to replace Louis XIV in his palace. Louis-Philippe showed little interest in his gardens, however, which was probably a good thing, since most architectural historians agree that he made a mess of the buildings. He shamelessly filled in the colonnade of the Grand Trianon with windows which a later conservator had no hesitation in removing.

When Mad Ludwig built his copy of Versailles in the middle of a Bavarian lake towards the end of the nineteenth century, the original could hardly have been less popular. After defeat in the Franco-Prussian War, political sentiment in France became predominantly republican. Monarchists had supported the claims of the Comte de Chambord, but he had destroyed his own cause by refusing any sort of constitutional monarchy. The white flag of the Bourbons was not destined to flutter over the palace of Versailles again, and what place was there in a progressive country for this gargantuan stone relic of the *Ancien Régime*?

When a young curator, Pierre de Nolhac, was appointed to Versailles in 1887, it was regarded as a sinecure and a dead-end, since the place was of no interest to anyone. Nolhac, however, was an energetic scholar with an enquiring mind who threw open rooms that had been locked for decades, and pored over documents and plans in the archives to reconstruct the life of the château. His books were widely read, and gradually a narrow republican distaste for the style of absolutism gave way to recognition that Versailles was a treasure in which the whole nation could take pride.

Efforts at restoration were hampered, however, by lack of funds, until the American multimillionaire John D. Rockefeller, Jr, who had been stationed in France during World War I and had seen for himself the ruinous decline that had set in at Versailles, pledged what today would amount to $2 billion for essential repairs, including the reroofing of the château. The gift also made possible the restoration of Marie-Antoinette's theatre and the Hameau. The recent restoration of the Bosquet des Trois Fontaines continues this tradition of American philanthropy. The works were partially funded by the American Friends of Versailles, a group led by an upper-crust Chicagoan called Catherine Hamilton. At a glittering party on 12 June 2004, Mrs Hamilton inaugurated the reinstated display with a blast on a golden fountaineer's whistle, and, after a few moments of suspenseful delay, water shot out of the nozzles to recreate the lances and plumes of Le Nôtre's water show, lit up by the slanting rays of the slowly setting sun.

Pierre-André Lablaude, the landscape architect in charge of the restoration of the Trois Fontaines and indeed of all the recent replanting at Versailles, has studied the history of earlier renovations. The replanting cycle operates over periods of about a hundred years, so that trees planted under Louis XVI matured during the Second Empire and had to be felled and replaced in the 1860s. Following a hurricane in 1870, there was a general replanting in 1883. No one likes to chop down mature trees, but by the end of the twentieth century, the felling and restocking process needed to be carried through again. Nature, in her unsentimental way, intervened where the custodians had become reluctant. A storm on 3 February 1990 brought down more than thirteen hundred trees, shocking the authorities out of their inertia. Preparations were being made to celebrate Le Nôtre's tercentenary, which corresponded with the advent of the new millennium. Then another calamitous storm hit the park in 1999. In the long term, these hurricanes may come to be seen as a blessing, since they greatly accelerated the pace of renewal at Versailles.

The garden restoration work, which is progressing at the time of writing, has been carefully phased, *bosquet* by *bosquet*, not just to spread the cost but also because it is less drastic visually than wholesale felling, although there have been corners of the gardens that have resembled modern-day equivalents of the scenes painted by 'Robert des Ruines'. The team currently working at Versailles has determined that it would be most appropriate to restore the gardens to their condition at the end of the reign of the Sun King, fifteen years after the death of their principal designer. It could not be otherwise, since too much of Le Nôtre's earlier work had already been altered or destroyed, while Mansart's additions and alterations – whether we side with Le Nôtre in his distaste for what the mason had served up, or with Louis in his appetite for coloured marble – have become characteristic features of the place. New plantings of lime, field maple and hornbeam will soon re-establish the towering walls of architectural greenery favoured by the greatest gardener of the seventeenth century, however. Meanwhile, at Trianon, Marie-Antoinette's landscape garden, perhaps more neglected than any other part of the estate, has also been restored – another response to the storm of 1999, which struck particularly hard in this sector. Here the aim has been to re-establish the eighteenth-century character of the garden, with its meandering streams and winding paths, and to reintroduce trees and shrubs of botanical interest.

Should anyone think that the French formal garden is a spent force, or that tinpot dictators are now the only ones ever tempted to emulate the gardens of Versailles, the new gardens at Alnwick Castle might be reason enough to reconsider. Here, adjacent to parkland laid out by 'Capability' Brown, the present-day Duchess of Northumberland has created a garden that manages to be both floridly Baroque in plan and modern in much of its detailing. The garden, which covers 26 acres and which has cost an estimated £15 million, has been created in a former walled garden, given to the Duchess in 1995 when her husband inherited the estate. Designed by a father-and-son team from Belgium, Jacques and Peter Wirtz, the new garden includes box hedging and trained hornbeam, but its central feature is a curvaceous Grand Cascade, beneath which are chambers containing the banks of pumps and computers which ensure that forty jets will dance and play upon each half-hour, and that water spouts will leap across the path above the lower basin, drenching anyone foolish enough to get in their way – you can imagine the Sun King laughing. This garden has divided opinion in the professional world of landscape and garden design, there being many who are ready to condemn it as an anachronism or a pastiche in poor taste, but the visitor numbers are impressive, and it has caused a surge in tourism that has delighted the local community.

Throughout its history, of course, Versailles has remained a controversial landscape. For Louis XIV's courtiers, who could not understand why their King threw money away on a piece of swampland, it was the 'undeserving favourite'. Even in his own lifetime, Le Nôtre's works could divide opinion. While Mlle de Scudéry, in her gushing way, could say of the gardens and *bosquets* that 'here was everything that could make a place agreeable,' and the Princess Palatine could write that Versailles 'possesses the loveliest promenades in the world', Saint-Simon could complain that 'the violence everywhere done to nature repels and wearies us.' It was not a controversy that would go away, for even as rulers throughout Europe were fervently copying Le Nôtre's gardens, Horace Walpole could dismiss their 'impotent displays of false taste'.

Weather and season have a huge effect upon Versailles. Seen on a cold, overcast day, when there is no one about, it can seem as mournful as it must have looked in the boarded-up days of Louis XV's Regency. On a moist and misty autumnal morning, this mournfulness becomes a romantic melancholy, but on an Easter day, when the crowds are flooding through the entrance gates, horse-drawn carriages are trotting along the freshly raked *allées*, rowing boats are out upon the Canal, and the fountains are playing against bright blue skies, the place is as animated and as happy as it must have been when the King and his entourage set off to inspect the latest addition to a *bosquet*.

What difference does knowing the history of this place make to its enjoyment? Do we admire it less when we realise that it was a piece of propaganda and an expression of power? Are we troubled when we read that thousands of troops gave their lives in a futile attempt to get the fountains to run all day? Knowing that an immense amount of toil and suffering went into the creation of Le Nôtre's masterpiece can only increase the grip that this serene and stately place exerts upon the imagination. There is not a single tree alive at Versailles that was planted in the time of Le Nôtre, and even some of the statues are copies or restorations – the lay viewer has no way of knowing – yet the sense of continuity is palpable. The straight paths that bustle with parties of camera-clicking schoolchildren were laid out by Le Nôtre and his men, with curious brass instruments and bundles of ranging sticks. The grassy banks where lovers lie were made by men with picks and shovels who carried earth on their backs in baskets. The grove where a family has stopped to eat sandwiches once witnessed a rendezvous between a cardinal and a prostitute dressed as a queen.

Versailles is far more than a good destination for a day out. It is a place that asks an almost endless series of questions. Some of these are technical – Where does all the water come from? How do they cut those tall hedges? Others bring us closer to another age – What was it like to be a under-gardener, or a courtesan, or a Swiss Guard? But there are also deeper questions about meaning and purpose. Why was this garden so important to Louis, and why does it continue to be significant today? Was the Sun King justified in making such a colossal park? Is glory an end worth pursuing for its own sake? Are rulers ever right to lavish such sums on pure ostentation? Do straight lines produce beauty or boredom? Is it appropriate to treat nature this way? What is the appeal of geometry? Versailles is impressive, but is it a place to admire? Or is it somehow shocking, even repellent?

In the gardens, even more than in the château, we might also feel that gentle melancholy that comes with the contemplation of time passing. With an acute sense of history, Louis set out to create a monument to himself that would endure long after his death. In this he was spectacularly successful, but is Versailles, like the statue of Ozymandias described by the poet Shelley, a monument to the transitory nature of temporal power? Perhaps it is, after all, more than that, since Louis saw himself not as an individual but as the embodiment of France, and, as a symbol of French prestige, Versailles is as potent now as it was three hundred years ago.

GLOSSARY

Allée: Derived from the verb *aller* (to go), this is essentially the term for a place to walk. *Allées* were straight paths, usually surfaced with sand. We get the English term *alley* from this root (a 'bowling alley' is a long, straight, narrow area).

Avenue: An *allée* lined with regularly spaced trees.

Bassin: A geometrically shaped pool, often with a fountain.

Bosquet: From the Italian *boschetto*, this means a little wood or grove. The English word *bosky* comes from the same root. At Versailles these were usually planted in the square plots formed by intersecting *allées*. They were often cut through with walks, and geometrically shaped openings could be created within them: *see cabinet* and *salle*.

Boulingrin: A corruption of the English 'bowling-green', this referred to a level grass area, usually bounded by grassy banks. Generally not used for playing bowls.

Buffet: The literal translation would be 'sideboard', but in gardening it is a fountaineer's term for an arrangement of cascades, like a stepped table. Playful fountain designers could make a *buffet d'eau* resemble a collation.

Cabinet: A small, intimate chamber, which could be a building but which usually referred to a small space formed by clipped vegetation.

Caisse: A planting box (rather than a tub). The characteristic 'Versailles box' is a square-sided wooden case raised on four small feet.

Canal: A large, regular expanse of water within a garden. Often rectangular, although the Grand Canal at Versailles is cruciform in plan.

Collation: An outdoor banquet laid out on tables within a cabinet or *salle*.

Fleuriste: A cultivator, amateur enthusiast or merchant of flowers.

Fontaineer: One responsible for the design, installation and running of fountains.

Lac: An ornamental expanse of water, generally larger than a *bassin*, but smaller than a canal.

Orangerie: A building for keeping orange trees warm during the winter months. In the summer months the trees would be placed outside in *caisses*.

Palissade: In gardening terms, a tall, curtain-like hedge created by growing trees closely together. Constantly pruned to maintain an architectural effect.

Parc: Originally this meant an enclosed area, usually large in extent, reserved for hunting. Usually wooded, it would be cut through with rides. Gradually the aesthetic appearance of such areas assumed significance, particularly if they could be seen from the house. As in England, the distinction between *parc* and *jardin* began to blur, and the meaning of the word *parc* is no longer automatically associated with hunting.

Parterre: A largely horizontal design laid out on a flat area of earth (*terre*), although topiary and statuary could provide vertical interest. The decorative patterns were generally made from low hedging in box (*buis* or *buxus* L.), infilled with coloured sands and earths. They were designed to be seen from above.

Parterre à l'anglaise: Of the many parterre variations, this was the simplest. It was essentially a turfed lawn into which a pattern of flower-beds was cut.

Parterre de broderie: The most complicated variety of parterre, which featured elaborate patterns based on foliage and scrollwork and similar to those used in embroidery.

Patte-d'oie: A goosefoot. This feature was formed at the point where a radial pattern of *allées* or avenues converged.

Pépinière / Pépinièrist: A plant nursery / specialist in the raising of plants in the nursery.

Pièce d'eau: A formal lake.

Plante-bande: A decorative flower-bed or border, generally long and thin (no more than 3 metres wide).

Potager: Vegetable garden.

Quinconce (quincunx): A pattern of tree-planting resembling, in plan, the five spots on a die. This could be replicated throughout a grove.

Rocaille / Rocailleur: Ornamental rockwork / one who assembles such features.

Salle: In garden terms, an outdoor room, often created within a *bosquet* and enclosed by *palissades*. Some of these were large enough to hold balls, theatrical performances or banquets.

Terrasse / Terrassier: A levelled area created by earth-moving and retained by banks or walls / one who carries out earthworks.

Topiare (Topiary): The art of shaping and clipping trees or shrubs, usually box or yew, into particular shapes, which could be abstract or geometrical, such as spheres or pyramids, or could resemble birds or animals.

Trelliage / Treilliageur: Elaborate trelliswork, often of an architectural quality, with columns, alcoves, pergolas and tunnels / one who constructs such features.

KEY TO THE PLAN OF VERSAILLES

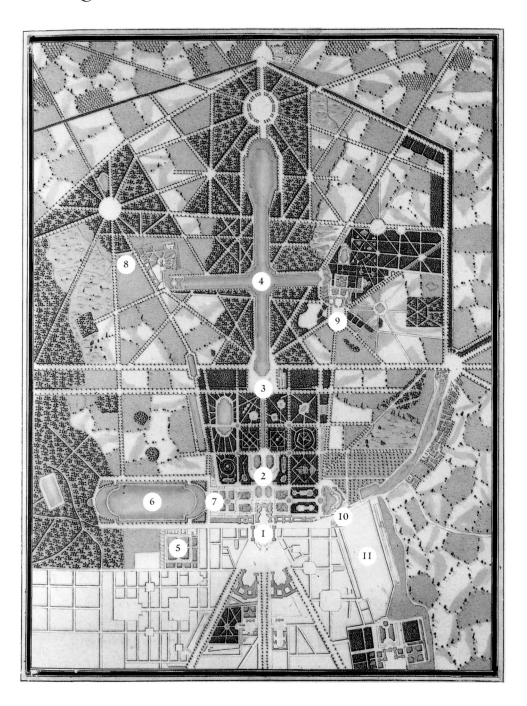

1   Le Château (The Château)

2   Le Bassin de Latone (The Fountain of Latona)

3   Le Bassin d'Apollon (The Fountain of Apollo)

4   Le Grand Canal (The Grand Canal)

5   Le Potager (The Kitchen Garden)

6   La Pièce d'Eau des Suisses (The Swiss Lake)

7   L'Orangerie (The Orangery)

8   La Ménagerie (The Menagerie)

9   Le Grand Trianon (The Grand Trianon)

10 Le Bassin de Neptune (The Fountain of Neptune)

11 L'Étang de Clagny (The site of Clagny Pond)

KEY TO THE MAIN FEATURES OF THE GARDEN

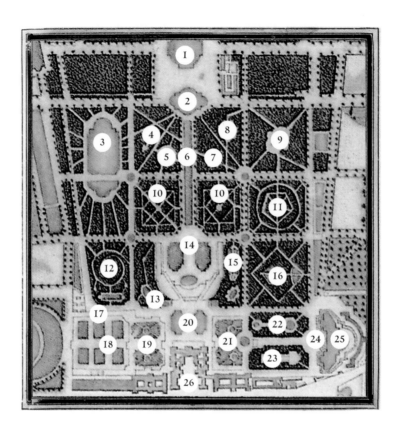

1	Le Grand Canal (The Grand Canal)	14	Le Parterre de Latone (The Parterre of Latona)
2	Le Bassin d'Apollon (The Fountain of Apollo)	15	Les Bains d'Apollon (The Baths of Apollo)
3	Le Jardin du Roi (The King's Garden)	16	Le Bosquet du Rond-Vert (The Grove of the Green Circle)
4	La Salle des Marroniers (The Chestnut Hall)	17	Les Cents Marches (The Hundred Steps)
5	La Colonnade (The Colonnade)	18	L'Orangerie (The Orangery)
6	L'Allée Royale (The Royal Avenue)	19	Le Parterre du Midi (The South Parterre)
7	Le Bosquet de Dômes (The Grove of the Domes)	20	Le Parterre d'Eau (The Water Parterre)
8	Le Bosquet de L'Encelade (The Enceladus Fountain)	21	Le Parterre du Nord (The North Parterre)
9	Le Bosquet de l'Obélisque (The Grove of the Obelisk)	22	Les Trois Fontaines (The Three Fountains)
10	Les Quinconces (The Quincunxes)	23	L'Arc de Triomphe (The Arc de Triomphe)
11	Le Bosquet de l'Étoile (The Grove of the Star)	24	La Fontaine du Dragon (The Dragon Fountain)
12	Le Bosquet de la Reine (The Queen's Grove)	25	Le Bassin de Neptune (The Fountain of Neptune)
13	La Salle de Bal (The Ballroom)	26	Le Château (The Château)

NOTES

Introduction

p.1 **'Although reduced in ...'** This figure is given in M. Baridon, *Jardins de Versailles* (Paris, 2001), p. 153. Central Park has an area of 843 acres. However P.-A. Lablaude, *The Gardens of Versailles* (London, 1995), p. 34, gives a figure of 700 ha, or 1,729 acres.

'In 1689 the Grand Parc ...' See F. Tiberghien, *Versailles, Le Chantier de Louis XIV 1662–1715* (Paris, 2003), p. 23. P.-A. Lablaude, *The Gardens of Versailles* (London, 1995), p. 34, gives an area of 6,500 ha, enclosed within a 43-kilometre-long wall punctuated by twenty-two guarded entrances.

'But Louis, whose ...' Various authorities quote different figures, presumably because they have reached different conclusions about what to include. The figures used here are taken from Baridon, *Jardins de Versailles*, p. 153. Using figures from Tiberghien, *Versailles, Le Chantier*, the total area would be 32,816 acres. Tiberghien estimates Marly at 2,280 ha (5,634 acres) while on p. 25 he says that the *domaine* of Versailles was 11,000 ha (27,182 acres) by 1715.

3 **'This elaborate ensemble ...'** The figure of 93 ha (230 acres) is given in Lablaude, *Gardens of Versailles*, p. 34. Hyde Park covers 140 ha (350 acres) (http://www.royalparks. gov.uk/parks/hyde_park/).

'The roads were clogged ...' Quoted in Tiberghien, *Versailles, Le Chantier*, p. 209.

'The King became ...' See *Manière de montrer les jardins de Versailles*. An edition with a preface by Jean-Pierre Babelon and commentaries by Simone Hoog was published by the Réunion des Musées Nationaux, Paris, in 2001.

4 **'Responding to reports ...'** L. de Rouvroy, Duc de Saint-Simon, *Mémoires*, ed. Yves Coirault (Paris, 1985), vol. V, p. 534.

5 **'One commentator has ...'** Michel Baridon compares Le Nôtre to Shakespeare in the introduction to *Le Nôtre, Un Inconnu illustré?*, a collection of papers presented at a conference in 2000 to mark the tercentenary of the gardener's death and published in Paris in 2003. See p. 24.

'Recent scholarship has ...' See, for example, T. Mariage, *The World of André Le Nôtre*, trans. Graham Larkin (Philadelphia, 1999).

6   'In fact he often provided ...' See C. Mukerji, *Territorial Ambitions and the Gardens of Versailles* (Cambridge, 1997), p. 142.
     'The Italian sculptor ...' A quotation from the *Mémoires* of Charles Perrault, reproduced in P. Burke, *The Fabrication of Louis XIV* (New Haven and London, 1992), p. 54.

10   'The competitiveness and ...' Quoted in R. Wilkinson, *Louis XI: France and Europe 1661–1715* (London, 2002), p. 28.

11   'Le Nôtre replied ...' D. Garrigues, *Jardins et jardiniers de Versailles au Grand Siècle* (Seyssel, 2001), p. 69.
     'They were very different . . .' Saint-Simon, *Mémoires*, ed. Yves Coirault (Paris, 1985), vol. I, p. 738.

I   *The Fateful Party*

15   'It was decided ...' A. France, *Vaux-le-Vicomte* (Étrépilly, 1987 [1933]), p. 171.

16   'According to Anatole France...' Ibid., p. 122. Vatel has entered legend as a chef – there is even a Club Vatel for top chefs – but the evidence suggests that he was more of a head-butler than a cook. He was also someone else who changed his name; of Swiss parents, he had been christened Fritz Karl Vatel.
     'The King would like . . .' quoted in I. Dunlop, *Louis XIV* (London, 2001), p. 88.

19   'At Vaux, as at Versailles ...' In *Gardens of Illusion* (Nashville, TN, 1980), F. Hamilton Hazlehurst has provided a wonderful analysis of these spatial effects, including diagrams, line drawings and sets of sequential photographs. See pp. 17–45 for the chapter on Vaux-le-Vicomte. Several other Le Nôtre gardens are analysed in this thorough way, including Versailles; see chap. 4, pp. 59–151.
     'The poet La Fontaine . . .' quoted in I. Dunlop, *Louis XIV* (London, 2001), p. 88.
     'Thoughtfully Fouquet had ...' This tradition is kept alive by the golf buggies that visitors can hire close to the entrance.
     'According to Helen Fox ...' H. M. Fox, *André Le Nôtre, Garden Architect to Kings* (London, 1962). Fox's biography was the first written for the English-speaking world. She approached her subject as a landscape architect and writer on gardening rather than as an historian, and her book, though engagingly written, has no system of referencing. I have not been able to find primary source material to support some of her anecdotes. This is a case in point.

20   'The anonymous author ...' Anon., *Relation des magnificences faites par Monsieur Fouquet à Vaux-Le-Vicomte lorsque le Roi y alla, le 17 Aout 1661, et de la somptuosité de ce lieu.*

21   'When the King reached ...' Scaling from a plan drawn by Israel Silvestre, this distance appears to be about 500 *toises*. Since a *toise* is about 1.95 metres, the distance is some 1,170 metres, or 1,279 yards.
     'I'm surprised you're ...' Fox, *André Le Nôtre*, p. 68. The story is also mentioned in P. Morand, *Fouquet ou Le Soleil offusqué* (Paris, 1985).
     'The food was served ...' In *Vaux-le-Vicomte* Anatole France refers to 'thirty-six dozen plates of solid gold' (p. 101), but the essay by Jean Cordey included in the 1987 edition suggests that the dinner service was actually vermeil.
     'Some accounts say ...' The lottery is mentioned in France, *Vaux-le-Vicomte* (p. 101), but Cordey thinks he may have been mistaken, suggesting a confusion with a lottery during a fete given by Mazarin (p. 178).
     'An artificial rock ...' See Jean La Fontaine's letter 'À monsieur de Maucroix, relation d'une fête donnée à Vaux', in *Oeuvres diverses* (Paris, 1958), pp. 523–5.

22   **'Between the acts …'** *Paulme* was the French version of real tennis; *mail* or *paille-maille* was a croquet-style game involving hoops and mallets. The English version was 'pall-mall'; the origin is Italian from *palla* 'ball' and *maglio* 'mallet'; *boules* was and remains the popular bowling game.

        The full list of performers is *'joueurs de paulme, de mall, de boules, de frondeurs, de savetiers, de suisses et de bergers'*. The games are easily understood, but it is difficult to see what links the shepherds, *frondeurs* and the Swiss. Possibly the Swiss were Swiss Guards.

    'Thankfully the indefatigable …' The Abbé de Choisy suggested that the fête ended with a ball, but Cordey doubted the truth of this, since nothing is mentioned in the accounts given by La Fontaine and the anonymous author of the *Relation*. See Cordey's essay in France, *Vaux-le-Vicomte*, p. 178.

    'There is a story …' A. S. Weiss, *Mirrors of Infinity: The French Formal Garden and 17th-Century Metaphysics* (New York, 1995), p. 46.

23   **'Don't you wonder …'** Mme de Sévigné, *Correspondance* (Paris, 1972), p. 59, Letter to Pomponne, Paris, 20 November 1664.

    'All the orange …' F. Tiberghien, *Versailles, Le Chantier de Louis XIV 1662–1715* (Paris, 2003), p. 194. For example, on 26 December 1665, M. Léonard was paid 3,816 *livres* to carry 1,250 shrubs from Vaux to the Tuileries and to Versailles.

24   **'Érik Orsenna suggests …'** É. Orsenna, *André Le Notre: Gardener to the Sun King*, trans. Moishe Black (New York, 2000), p. 42.

    'In the face of …' Fox, *André Le Nôtre*, p. 68. The quotation is not referenced, and I have not been able to find it mentioned in any other source. The interpretation seems strained. In the light of what we know about Louis' character, it seems unlikely that he would have revealed any such signs of inferiority or insecurity.

    'On the other hand …' T. Mariage, *The World of André Le Nôtre*, trans. Graham Larkin (Philadelphia, 1999), p. 91. Also see Cordey's essay in France, *Vaux-le-Vicomte*, pp. 156–7.

II *Born to Garden*

30   **'It was fairly common …'** T. Mariage, *The World of André Le Nôtre* (Philadelphia, 1999), p. 30.

    'Here he remarks …' J. Boyceau de la Barauderie, *Traité du jardinage selon les raisons de la nature et de l'art*, facsimile edn (Nördlingen, 1997 [1638]), p. 30.

    'Physically he should …' Ibid., p. 30.

31   **'Though he thought …'** Ibid., p. 31.

    'If he wished to …' Mariage, *World of André Le Nôtre*, pp. 31–2.

33   **'One of the explanations …'** Mariage also dismissed the suggestion that Le Nôtre might have received some of his education from François Mansard or Louis Le Vau. Ernest de Ganay suggested that Le Nôtre might have studied under Jacques Lemercier, Pierre Le Muet or François Mansard. See E. de Ganay, *André le Nostre, 1613–1700* (Paris, 1962).

    'Horace Walpole went …' H. Walpole, *The History of Modern Taste in Gardening* (1771–80).

35   **'In 1637, when …'** The King had granted use of the Tuileries to his brother, so it seems that at this time Le Nôtre would have had two masters, Louis XIII and the Duc d'Orléans.

    'André must have …' Louis XIII, Archives Nationales, 01 1046 21.

37   **'The *contrôleurs* were …'** Marriage, *World of André Le Nôtre*, p. 94.

    'It also gave him …' At various times there were other *contrôleurs* working alongside Le Nôtre, including Charles Perrault, Michel Hardouin and Jacques V Gabriel. The administration also included *Intendants et Ordonnateurs Généraux des Bâtiments* and *Trésoriers Généraux des Bâtiments*. For a full list, see F. Tiberghien, *Versailles, Le Chantier de Louis XIV 1662–1715* (Paris, 2003), app. 2, pp. 333–4.

38   **'It has been estimated ...'** These figures originated with Ernest de Ganay and Antoine Schapper respectively. They are included in S. Castelluccio, 'La Personalité d'André Le Nôtre (1613–1700)', in *Le Nôtre, Un Inconnu illustre?* (Paris, 2003).

'The French King ...' M. Lister, *A Journey to Paris in the Year 1698* (London, 1698), pp. 36–8.

'His involvement in ...' E. A. Riedinger, 'Le Notre, André 1613–1700', entry in C. A. Shoemaker, ed., *Chicago Botanic Garden Encyclopedia of Gardens, History and Design*, vol. 2 (Chicago, 2001), p. 790. See also M. Baridon, *Jardins de Versailles* (Paris, 2001), p. 175, where it is suggested that Mansard and Le Nôtre worked together at Evry-Petit-Bourg.

39   **'The tone of Louis XIV's reply ...'** See Garrigues, *Jardins et Jardiniers*, p. 67, and J. Guiffrey, *André Le Nôtre*, trans. George Booth (Lewis, 1986 [1913]), p. 45.

40   **'Remember the gardens ...'.** E. Cecil, *A History of Gardening in England* (London, 1911), p. 192.

41   **'There is a phrase ...'** L. de Rouvroy, Duc de Saint-Simon, *Mémoires*, ed. Yves Coirault (Paris, 1985), vol. I, p. 739.

III   *The Sun Rises*

44   **'Despite her title ...'** I. Dunlop, *Louis XIV* (London, 2001), p. 12.
46   **'I have lost all my friends ...'** Quoted in I. Dunlop, *Louis XIV*, p.27.
48   **'It was a career ...'** R. Astier, 'Louis XIV, "Premier Danseur"', in D. L. Rubin, *Sun King: The Ascendancy of French Culture during the reign of Louis XIV* (Cranbury, NJ, 1992), pp. 73–102.

'In 1653, with ...' This performance was part of the *Ballet Royal de la Nuict* given on 23 February 1653.

'In another *ballet* ...' *Le Ballet des Nopces de Pelée et de Thétis*, 1654.

'Quote from R. W. Berger, *In the Garden of the Sun King*, Dumbarton Oaks, 1985, p. 11.
51   **'The King proved himself ...'** Quoted in Dunlop, *Louis XIV*, p. 110.
56   **'In it he wrote ...'** Olivier de Serres, *Théâtre d'agriculture et mesnage des champs* (Paris, 2001 [1600]), p. 782.

'The warrior-king ...' N. Tessin, *Relation de la visite à Marly, Versailles, Clagny, Rueil et Saint-Cloud, en 1687*, published by Pierre Francastle in *Revue de l'histoire de Versailles et de Seine-et-Oise* (1926), p. 165.

IV   *The Unpromising Site*

59   **'Saint-Simon, admittedly ...'** L. de Rouvroy, Duc de Saint-Simon, *Mémoires*, ed. Yves Coirault (Paris, 1986), vol. V, p. 532.

'The very landscape ...' Jean-Baptiste Primi Visconti, *Mémoires sur la cour de Louis XIV, 1673–1681*, ed. Jean-François Solon (Paris, 1988), p. 152.

60   **'The water-table ...'** J. F. Mondot, 'La Construction d'un site artificiel', in *Les Cahiers de science & vie*, no. 74 (April 2003), p. 34.

'The Maréchal de Bassompierre ...' Quoted in W. H. Adams, *The French Garden 1500–1800* (London, 1979), p. 79.

62   'The first building ...' Saint-Simon, *Mémoires*, vol. V, p. 522.

64   'Only members of ...' C. Mukerji, *Territorial Ambitions and the Gardens of Versailles* (Cambridge, 1997), p. 233.

       'We know that ...' W. Blunt, *Sebastiano: The Adventures of an Italian Priest, Sebastiano Locatelli, during His Journey from Bologna to Paris and Back, 1664–1665* (London, 1956), p. 162.

       'I saw her once ...' Ibid., p. 163.

67   'He told his ministers ...' C. Perrault, *Mémoires de Charles Perrault ... contenant beaucoup de particularités & anecdotes intéressants du ministère de M. Colbert* (Paris, 1759).

69   'Le Brun determined ...' P.-A. Lablaude, *The Gardens of Versailles* (London, 1995), p. 23.

       'Colbert thought that ...' J.-B. Colbert, *Lettres, instructions et mémoires*, ed. Pierre Clément (Paris, 1868), vol. V, pp. 269–70.

71   'Make a count of ...' The Collinot family were another of the important royal gardening dynasties. Both Jean and his brother Pierre were royal gardeners at Versailles. See the genealogical tables in D. Garrigues, *Jardins et jardiniers de Versailles au Grand Siècle* (Seyssel, 2001), p. 312.

       'At the Tuileries ...' Quoted in T. Mariage, *The World of André Le Nôtre*, p. 97.

73   'When it became clear ...' Mme de Sévigné, *Correspondance*, ed. Roger Duchêne (Paris, 1974), p. 632.

       'His assessment of ...' Colbert, *Lettres, instructions et mémoires*, vol. V, p. 267.

       'Only the items for ...' The figures from the building accounts are quoted in M. Baridon, *Jardins de Versailles* (Paris, 2001), p. 126.

       'Thousands would be killed ...' Tibergien estimates that thirty-two hundred workers were compensated for work-related injuries at Versailles between 1660 and 1700. However, it was the construction of the aqueduct over the River Eure that claimed most lives. See F. Tiberghien, *Versailles, Le Chantier de Louis XIV 1662–1715* (Paris, 2003), pp. 164–7.

V   *Geometry and Earthworks*

75   'By the time that Le Nôtre ...' For a fuller account of the Masson/de Noiron affair, see D. Garrigues, *Jardins et jardiniers de Versailles au Grand Siècle* (Seyssel, 2001), pp. 49–55.

       'His daughter Geneviève ...' Genealogical tables are provided in Ibid., annex III.

76   'As one might have ...' This information was taken from a website maintained by the present gardener at Anet: http://www.patrick-pochon.com/anet1.htm (accessed 22.10.03).

79   'Linked by stairs ...' The parterres at Saint-Germain were first designed by Claude Mollet and illustrated in Olivier de Serres' *Le Théâtre d'agriculture et mesnage des champs*. These were later modified by Jacques Boyceau and then altered again in the time of Louis XIII. See F. Hamilton Hazlehurst, *Gardens of Illusion* (Nashville, TN, 1980), p. 204.

       'On the third landing ...' Some of these details were gathered from 'The Role of Automata in the History of Technology', an article by Silvio Bedini posted at http://xroads.virginia.edu/~DRBR/b_edini.html (accessed 23.10.03).

       'They had been laid out ...' F. H. Hazlehurst, *Jacques Boyceau and the French Formal Garden* (Athens, GA, 1966), p. 49. The attribution of the parterres to Boyceau is secure, but his role as author of the overall plan is an intelligent supposition.

       'Those who have studied ...' Ibid., pp. 51–2.

80 **'The English diarist ...'** Quoted in Ibid., p. 60.

'Evelyn says that ...' Quoted in W. H. Adams, *The French Garden 1500–1800* (London, 1979), p. 57.

'In his *Traité*...' J. Boyceau de la Barauderie, *Traité du jardinage selon les raisons de la nature et de l'art*, facsimile edn (Nördlingen, 1997 [1638]), p. 75.

81 **'He also refers ...'** Ibid., p. 66.

'There were just three fountains ...' Adams, *French Garden*, p. 79.

85 **'It has been suggested ...'** Mukerji, *Territorial Ambitions*, p. 297.

'It is in the second part ...' A.-J. Dezallier d'Argenville, *La Théorie et la practique du jardinage* (Paris, 2002 [1709]), p. 103

87 **'The terms of staking out ...'** J. James, *The Theory and Practice of Gardening* (London, 1969 [1712]), pp. 108–9.

'Dezallier d'Argenville noted ...' Ibid., p. 131.

88 **'Here he laid out ...'** Hazlehurst, *Gardens of Illusion*, p. 77.

'When the earth ...' Dezallier d' Argenville, *La Théorie et la practique*, p. 131.

'In France, he notes ...' James, *Theory and Practice*, pp. 108–9.

89 **'When all went well ...'** Dezallier d'Argenville, *La Théorie et la practique*, pp. 131–2.

'Those injured during ...' F. Tiberghien, *Versailles, Le Chantier de Louis XIV 1662–1715* (Paris, 2003), pp. 160–1.

91 **'Here are none ...'** Dezallier d'Argenville, *La Théorie et la practique*, pp. 136–42.

'The author cautions ...' Ibid., p. 145.

'It is much better ...' Ibid., p. 146.

'A little further on ...' Ibid., p. 151.

95 **'Your Majesty knows ...'** J.-B. Colbert, *Lettres, instructions et mémoires*, ed. P. Clément (Paris, 1868), vol. V, p. 269.

VI *First Plans*

97 **'Louis Gourlier the Eldest ...'** J.-C. Le Gillou, 'Le Domaine de Versailles se l'Aube à l'Aurore du Roi Soleil', in *Versalia: Revue de la Société des Amis de Versailles*, no. 5 (2002), p. 52.

'In a similar fashion ...' Ibid., p. 53.

99 **'Louis Petit, a member ...'** Letter dated 17 February 1663, quoted by Pierre de Nolhac in *La Création de Versailles* (Paris, 1925), p. 37.

102 **'The cruel pitting ...'** For more on the fascinating history of animal collections, see E. Baratay and E. Hardouin-Fugier, *Zoo: A History of Zoological Gardens in the West* (London, 2002).

'The collection at Versailles ...' Ibid., esp. pp. 42, 48–9.

'The word ménagerie ...' Ibid., p. 41.

'In 1665 the Italian ...' Quoted in Ibid., p. 34.

103 **'Like Le Nôtre's ...'** See, for example, A. S. Weiss, *Mirrors of Infinity* (New York, 1995), p. 25.

104 **'In his journal ...'** J. Locke, *Locke's Travels in France, 1675–1679*, ed. John Lough (Cambridge, 1953), p. 168.

106 **'One of the stories ...'** H. M. Fox, *André Le Nôtre, Garden Architect to Kings* (London, 1962), p. 80. Fox presents this story as fact. In Jules Guiffrey's *Andre Le Nostre*, first published 1913 (p. 21), it is described as 'an old legend'.

'Gilles Loistron, Sieur de Ballon ...' D. Garrigues, *Jardins et jardiniers de Versailles au Grand Siècle* (Seyssel, 2001), vol. I, p. 364.

107   'As numerous entries ...' Ian Dunlop says that in 1665 Le Nôtre planted 5.5 million trees, but he does not give the source of this figure. See *Royal Palaces of France* (London, 1985), p. 93.

'But there is evidence ...' J. Guiffrey, ed., *Comptes de bâtiments du roi sous le règne du Louis XIV* (Paris, 1881–1901), vol. I, pp. 255–7.

'In February 1669 ...' Ibid, vol. II, p. 336, Entry for 17 May 1669.

'In order to transplant ...' Dunlop, *Royal Palaces of France*, p. 142.

'The gardening writer Dezallier d'Argenville ...' A.-J. Dezallier d'Argenville, *La Théorie et la practique du jardinage* (Paris, 2002 [1709]), p. 248.

'Mme de Sévigné . . .' Quoted in H. Fox, *André Le Nôtre, Garden Architect to Kings* (London, 1962), p. 106.

'To safeguard the trees ...' Dezallier d'Argenville, *La Théorie et la practique*, p. 208.

108   'Despite this knowledge ...' Fox, *André Le Nôtre*, p. 108. Fox suggests that three-quarters of the trees transplanted from the forests died.

'The preferred species ...' Dezallier d'Argenville, *La Théorie et la practique*, pp. 205–6.

'Monsieur le Nôtre ...' Quoted in Dunlop, *Royal Palaces of France*, p. 93.

'According to Saint-Simon ...' L. de Rouvroy, Duc de Saint-Simon, *Mémoires*, ed. Yves Coirault (Paris, 1986), vol. I, p. 739: 'Il disait des parterres, qu'il n'étaient que pour les nourrices qui, ne pouvant quitter leurs enfants s'y promenaient des yeux et les admiraient du second étage.'

'The Swedish architect ...' N. Tessin, *'Relation de la visite de Nicol Tessin à Marly, Versailles, Clagny, Rueil et Saint-Cloud, en 1687'*, *Revue de l'histoire de Versailles et de Seine-et-Oise*, no. 28 (1926).

'As we have seen ...' J.-M. Apostolidès, *Le Roi-machine* (Paris, 1981), p. 86.

'The precise nature ...' Fox, *André Le Nôtre*, p. 96. When Le Nôtre went to Italy in 1679, as well as being asked to check on the progress of Bernini's equestrian statue, he was tasked with visiting two Italian painters concerning a minor issue regarding their pensions from Louis. Le Brun thought that Le Nôtre had ignored this second request and wrote a sharp letter about it to Charles Errard at the French Academy in Rome, but it seems that Le Nôtre had done what was asked of him, only he had reported directly to Colbert. Coming late in both the gardener's and the architect's careers, this incident seems to have been more of a misunderstanding than an acrimonious row.

VII   *The New Rome*

111   'Nancy Mitford estimated ...' N. Mitford, *The Sun King*, London, 1966, p. 35.

112   'Nor do there seem ...' G. Treasure, *Louis XIV*, Harlow, 2001, p. 143.

'It seems that his ...' Ibid., pp. 147–8.

'He certainly enjoyed ...' Ibid., p. 142.

'Sometimes an orchestra ...' Treasure, *Louis XIV*, p. 144.

114   'Louis himself wrote ...' Quoted in M. Baridon, *Jardins de Versailles* (Paris, 2001), p. 128.

'It has also been suggested ...' T. Mariage, *The World of André Le Nôtre*, trans. Graham Larkin (Philadelphia, 1990), p. 31.

115   'The heights, angles ...' C. Mukerji, *Territorial Ambitions and the Gardens of Versailles* (Cambridge, 1997).

'It also seems that ...' D. Garrigues, *Jardins de jardiniers de Versailles au Grand Siècle* (Seyssel, 2001), p. 227.

116   'Although he was unable ...' Mariage, *World of André Le Nôtre*, p. 138.

'Implementing Louis' policy ...' Mme de Sévigné, *Correspondance*, ed. Roger Duchêne (Paris, 1978), vol. III, p. 496.

117 **'Although Britain would not ...'** George II commissioned a military survey of the Scottish Highlands in 1746, the job going to a far-sighted young engineer called William Roy, but Roy's vision of a national military survey was not implemented until after his death in 1790, prompted by fears that the French Revolution might cross the Channel.

'Some of the most beautiful ...' Marquis de Dangeau, *Journal du marquis de Dangeau, Volume I, 1684–85* (Clermond-Ferrand, 2002), p. 193, Entry for 27 August 1685.

'The Grande Galère ...' Ibid., p. 234, Entry for 20 November 1685.

'Other vessels were brought in ...' Definitive details of the fleet on the Canal are difficult to establish, and the secondary sources do not always agree. The details included here are mostly taken from Garrigues, *Jardins et jardinieres*, pp. 202–4, but Pierre Verlet, in *Le Château de Versailles* (Paris, 1985), p. 193, mentions a gilded *galliote* that came from Rouen in 1679 and another from Dunkirk which arrived in 1682; a new 'yack', perhaps from 1682; a vessel built by the Marquis de Langeron using wood from Amsterdam and boat-builders from Le Havre, launched in August 1685; a galley built at Versailles; a *heu hollandais*; a gondola and a *piotte*.

'This pocket-sized fleet ...' Baridon, *Jardins de Versailles*, p. 73; Garrigues, *Jardins et jardinieres*, pp. 202–4.

118 **'In 1660 the ...'** R. Wilkinson, *Louis XI: France and Europe 1661–1715* (London, 2002), p. 191.

'Figures supplied by ...' http://www.navynews.co.uk/articles/2000/0005/0000052601.asp (accessed 03.12.03).

'Each of Colbert's ...' Quoted in Mariage, *World of André Le Nôtre*, p. 109.

120 **'In the bleak winters ...'** Ibid., p. 177.

'These huge, meticulous ...' Originally housed in the Louvre, they were transferred in 1776 to the Hôtel National des Invalides, where some are still on display in a darkened gallery in the Musée de l'Armée. A number of the original models were taken to Berlin by the Prussians in 1814 as war booty and were later lost in air raids during World War II. Some of the collection is housed the Museum of Fine Arts, Lille.

'Discussing Le Nôtre's ...' Quoted in T. Hedin, 'Le Nostre to Mansart: Transition in the Gardens of Versailles', *Gazette des Beaux-Arts* (December 1997), p. 231.

121 **'The inscription on ...'** The examples in this paragraph are taken from Peter Burke's *The Fabrication of Louis XIV* (New Haven and London, 1992), an excellent account of the efforts of Louis' publicists that proves that the dark arts of presentation were flourishing in the seventeenth century. For the Roman connection, see esp. pp. 35, 93, 192–7.

122 **'Colbert must have ...'** J.-B. Colbert, *Lettres, instructions et mémoires*, ed. P. Clément (Paris, 1868), vol. V, p. 422.

'The King "walked ..." Dangeau, *Journal du marquis de Dangeau*, vol. 1, p. 231.

125 **'He saves his greatest praise ...'** A.-J. Dezallier d'Argenville, *La Théorie et la practique du jardinage* (Paris, 2002 [1709]), p. 44–7.

127 **'Nobles who walked ...'** Mukerji, *Territorial Ambitions*, pp. 91–3.

VIII   *Divertissements*

135 **'One of the more ...'** J. Guiffrey, ed., *Comptes des bâtiments du roi sous le règne du Louis XIV* (Paris, 1881–1901), vol. I, p. 429, Entry for 20 September 1670. The payment of

140 *livres* was to a *frippier* called Fortier. It appears in a section of 'extraordinary payments' and probably relates to the fête of 1668.

'**On the fourth day ...**' Details of the fête are given in Molière's *La Princesse d'Elide: Comédie du Sieur Molière [sic] : les plaisirs de l'isle enchantée, course de bague, collation ornée de machines, mêlée de dances & de musique, ballet du palais d'Alcine, feu d'artifice, et autres fêtes galantes de Versailles*, which can be accessed online at the Bibliotheque Nationale (http://www.bnf.fr/).

137   '**The Labyrinthe can ...**' F. H. Hazlehurst suggested in *Gardens of Illusion* (p. 71) that some form of labyrinth might already have existed in 1663, but this is disputed by Robert Berger in *In the Garden of the Sun King* (p. 30), who believes it was started in 1666 and finished in 1673/4.

139   '**Perrault also wrote ...**' Charles Perrault, 'Le Labyrinthe de Versailles', in *Recueil de divers ouvrages en prose et en vers* (Paris, 1675).

        '**In Perrault's words ...**' Ibid.

141   '**The moral is ...**' See R. W. Berger, *In the Garden of the Sun King*, Studies on the Park of Versailles under Louis XIV (Washington DC, 1985), pp. 32–5, for Perrault's original verses.

143   '**It appeared as ...**' C. Perrault, *Mémoires de Charles Perrault ... contenant beaucoup de particularités & anecdotes intéressants du ministère de M. Colbert* (Paris, 1759), pp. 109–10.

        '**Inside there were three ...**' I. Dunlop, *Royal Palaces of France* (London, 1985), p. 118.

        '**A sculpture by Girardon ...**' The horses were sculpted by Marsy and Guérin.

        '**Mlle de Scudery ...**' M. de Scudéry, *La Promenade de Versailles, dédiée au Roi*, ed. Marie-Gabrielle Lallemand (Paris, 2002), p. 90.

        '**It took Denis Jolly ...**' Dunlop, *Royal Palaces of France*, p. 118.

147   '**As described by Félibien ...**' A. Félibien, *Relation de la fête de Versailles* (Maisonneuve and Larose, 1994), p. 34.

        '**Félibien paid a rare tribute ...**' Does not name the individual, but Dominique Garrigues in Jardins et Jardiniers de Versailles suggests that it was Michael II Le Bouteux.

148   '**This display continued ...**' A. Félibien, *Relation de la fête de Versailles* (Maisonneuve and Larose, 1994), p. 89.

IX   *Pleasure Works*

152   '**Whoever was responsible ...**' T. Hedin, 'Le Nostre to Mansart: Transition in the Gardens of Versailles', *Gazette des Beaux-Arts* (December 1997), p. 218. Hedin argues that this design should be attributed to Mansart rather than Le Nôtre, although there exists a period drawing of the finished work that credits the gardener with the design. Hedin's argument, backed up by a drawing in the hand of Mansart's assistant, Robert de Cotte, is that, in form and material, the twin basins seem to have much in common with Mansart's other changes in the Petit Parc at about this time.

        '**Colbert sent him ...**' J.-B. Colbert, *Lettres, instructions et mémoires* (Paris, 1861), vol. V, pp. 355–6.

153   '**There were to be ...**' See F. Hamilton Hazlehurst, *Gardens of Illusion* (Nashville, TN, 1980), pp. 78–82, and J. Lablaude, *Les Jardins de Versailles* (Paris, 1998), pp. 51–2.

154   '**It has been said ...**' A. Zega and B. H. Dams, *Palaces of the Sun King* (London, 2002), p. 70.

'**Work on site …**' Some did not work so hard. Vigarini explained his ideas in a mere six lines; Le Pautre and Gobert missed the deadline. See F. Tiberghien, *Versailles, Le Chantier de Louis XIV 1662–1715* (Paris, 2003), pp. 83–4.

155   '**It came down to …**' Colbert, *Lettres, instructions et mémoires*, vol. V, p. 287.

'**For example, Solomon de Caus …**' S. de Caus, *Les Raisons des forces mouvements, avec diverses machines tant utiles que plaisantes, Livre II Fontaines* (Amsterdam, 1973 [1615]).

156   '**If he wanted …**' From a distance the Carré d'Eau at Vaux appears to be a rectangle, but from closer to it one is ready to accept that it is a square. The great Belgian landscape architect René Pechère measured it and found it to be 62.7 by 60 metres, a rectangle after all. See R. Pechère, *Grammaire des Jardins* (Brussels, 1995).

'**With due regard …**' Quoted in I. Dunlop, *Louis XIV* (London, 2001), p. 160.

158   '**Perhaps it is …**' See J. Lablaude, *Les Jardins de Versailles* (Paris, 1998), p. 177. In the English translation of the first edition of this book by Fiona Biddulph (London, 1995), *Char embourbé* becomes 'mud-wagon'.

'**The stem of the tree …**' Colbert, *Lettres, instructions et mémoires*, vol. V, p. 330.

160   '**Each canal seemed …**' A. Félibien, *Description du château de Versailles, de ses peintures et d'autres ouvrages faites pour le Roy* (Paris, 1696), pp. 64–5.

161   '**This palace was seen …**' A. Félibien, *Description sommaire du château de Versailles* (Paris, 1674), p. 329.

162   '**There were so many …**' L. de Rouvroy, Duc de Saint-Simon, *Mémoires*, ed. Yves Coirault (Paris, 1986), vol. II, p. 269.

'**Félibien called this …**' Quoted in Dunlop, *Louis XIV*, p. 214.

'**Elizabeth Hyde describes …**' E. Hyde, 'The Cultivation of a King, or the Flower Gardens of Louis XIV', in J. D. Hunt and M. Conan, eds, *Tradition and Innovation in French Garden Art: Chapters of a New History* (Philadelphia, 2002), pp. 1–21.

163   '**In his diplomatic way …**' D. Garrigues, *Jardins et Jardiniers de Versailles*, p. 31.

'**Like the Le Nôtres …**' This was Michel I Le Bouteux (1600–50) who was gardener to the Duc de Vendôme. He was the son of Jean Le Bouteux, a master-gardener of Paris, who died in 1636.

'**Le Bouteux's name …**' See Hyde, 'Cultivation of a King', p. 15, for more details of Le Bouteux's contribution.

'**In the minister's …**' Colbert, *Lettres, instructions et mémoires*, vol. V, p. 368.

164   '**To facilitate the …**' N. Tessin, '*Relation de la visite de Nicodème Tessin à Marly, Versailles, Clagny, Rueil et Saint-Cloud, en 1687*', quoted in D. Garrigues, *Jardins et jardiniers de Versailles au Grand Siècle* (Seyssel, 2001), p. 234.

'**The building accounts …**' Garrigues, *Jardins et jardinieres*, p. 233.

'**Large quantities of …**' 1 *muid de Paris* = 268.2 litres.

'**The head gardener …**' M. Lister, *A Journey to Paris in the Year 1698* (London, 1698), p. 215.

165   '**Le Bouteux was …**' J. Guiffrey, ed., *Comptes de bâtiments du roi sous le règne du Louis XIV* (Paris, 1881–1901), vol. II, p. 1175, Payment for 1679 (there are many other references).

'**Le Nôtre's total …**' T. Mariage, *The World of André Le Nôtre*, trans. Graham Larkin (Philadelphia, 1990), pp. 96–7.

167   '**One curious feature …**' A. Félibien, *Les Fêtes de Versailles: Chroniques de 1668 & 1674* (Maisonneuve and Larose, 1994 [1674]), pp. 127–38.

168   '**A cannon shot …**' *Boîtes* were a kind of mortar. 'Fire-bomb' seems to be the closest modern English translation.

'**If Félibien's figures …**' Félibien, *Les Fêtes de Versailles*, pp. 139–53.

X *Zenith*

171   'The Elector of Brandenburg ...' Quoted in R. Wilkinson, *Louis XI: France and Europe 1661–1715* (London, 2002), p. 107.

172   'At the northern entrance ...' The full title for this piece is *France Triumphing over Spain and the Empire* (1682–3).

'Between the Arc de Triomphe ...' Both created by the team of Mazeline, d'Houzeau and Blanchard.

'The landscape architect's ...' P. Lobegeois and J. de Givry, *Versailles, les Grandes Eaux*, Paris, 2000, p. 105.

173   'The English visitor ...' J. Shaw, *Letters to a nobleman travelling thro' Holland, Flanders and France* (1709), British Library 303.d.21, p. 123.

'In the same account ...' Ibid., p. 121.

'He was accompanied ...' J.-B. Colbert, *Lettres, instructions et mémoires* (Paris, 1861), vol. V, pp. 381–2.

'This Collinot would ...' See the Collinot family tree in D. Garrigues, *Jardins et jardiniers de Versailles au Grand Siècle* (Seyssel, 2001), p. 312.

'In particular there ...' I. Dunlop, *Royal Palaces of France* (London, 1985), p. 136.

'In the autumn of 1686 ...' M. Baridon, *Jardins de Versailles* (Paris, 2001), p. 156.

174   'A letter from Charles Perrault ...' Quoted in Dunlop, *Royal Palaces of France*, p. 142.

'Some of the trees ...' Garrigues, *Jardins et jardiniers*, p. 138.

'In Claude Desgot's ...' C. Desgots, *Abrégé de la vie d'André le Nostre*, included in Père Pierre Nicolas Desmoulets' *Continuation des mémoires de littérature et d'histoire de Monsieur de Salengre*, vol. X, chap. IX, (Paris, 1726), p. 469.

'It was evident ...' J. James, *The Theory and Practice of Gardening* (London, 1969 [1712]), p. 158.

175   'A contract to bring ...' Garrigues, *Jardins et jardiniers*, p. 148. Garrigues quotes a contract between the King and Pierre Le Clerc dated 17 September 1705.

'Despite this theoretical understanding ...' Dunlop, *Royal Palaces of France*, p. 142. Dunlop does not provide a source for the name of this machine. It seems to have been a different machine from the one invented by Valentin Lopin for moving orange trees in their tubs. There is an anonymous drawing showing a *Machine pour transporter des arbres*. It seems likely that this is Lopin's contraption, not the 'Devil' mentioned by Dunlop. See Garrigues, *Jardins et jardiniers*, pp. 152–3. 'Capability' Brown certainly used such a fiendish apparatus in England during the following century.

'Diderot and D'Alembert's ...' T. M. Russell and A.-M. Thornton, *Gardens and Landscapes in the Enyclopédie of Diderot and D'Alembert*, vol. II (Aldershot, 1999), p. 535.

'According to Pierre-André Lablaude ...' J. Lablaude, *Les Jardins de Versailles* (Paris, 1998), p. 56.

'John James, in ...' A.-J. Dezallier d'Argenville, *La Théorie et la practique du jardinage* (Paris, 2002), p. 199.

180   'Horticultural technique advanced ...' The Potager replaced a kitchen-garden established in the time of Louis XIII (the municipal library now stands on the site). La Quintinie became 'director of the fruit and vegetable gardens of the royal houses' in 1670.

'One of Mme de Sévigné's ...' Quoted in J. Levron, *Daily Life at Versailles in the Seventeenth and Eighteenth Centuries*, trans. Claire Eliane Engel (London, 1968), p. 112.

181   'La Quintinie was ...' S. de Courtois, *Le Potager du Roi*, trans. Carol Brick-Stock (Versailles, 2003), p. 21.

'Louis also built ...' Verlet, *Le Château de Versailles* (Paris, 1985 [1961]), p. 205.

'In his journal ...' Marquis de Dangeau, *Journal du Marquis de Dangeau, Volume I, 1684–85* (Clermond-Ferrand, 2002), p. 45.

182   'Continue to do whatever ...' I. Dunlop, *Louis XIV* (London, 2001), p. 217.

'It took a work-force ...' This is the figure given in Ibid., p. 217. Lisa Hilton gives the figure of 2,074,592 *livres*, which she equates to about £7 million at today's prices. See L. Hilton, *Athénaïs, The Real Queen of France* (London, 2002), p. 121.

'The ambitious Mansart ...' Dunlop, *Louis XIV*, p. 217.

'For the ladies ...' Mme de Sévigné, *Correspondance*, ed. Roger Duchêne (Paris, 1978), vol. II, p. 38.

'By 1678 Primi Visconti ...' Jean-Baptiste Primi Visconti, *Mémoires sur la cour de Louis XIV, 1673–1681*, ed. Jean-François Solon (Paris, 1988), p. 117.

184   'The Duc du Maine ...' Sévigné, *Correspondance*, vol. II, p. 363.

'Clagny fell into ...' F. Hamilton Hazlehurst, *Gardens of Illusion* (Nashville, TN, 1980), p. 334, n. 1.

185   'In 1674 Colbert ...' F. Tiberghien, *Versailles, Le Chantier de Louis XIV 1662–1715* (Paris, 2003), pp. 29–30.

'Later there would be ...' Ibid., p. 174.

XI   *Total Control*

187   'This fountain, conceived ...' The *bosquet* was altered by Hardouin-Mansart in 1706 but was restored to Le Nôtre's designs between 1992 and 1998.

189   'Two hundred thousand ...' R. Wilkinson, *Louis XI: France and Europe 1661–1715* (London, 2002), p. 41.

190   'When the King ...' Jean-Baptiste Primi Visconti, *Mémoires sur la cour de Louis XIV, 1673–1681*, ed. Jean-François Solon (Paris, 1988), p. 100.

'The contemporary writer ...' Quoted in I. Dunlop, *Royal Palaces of France* (London, 1985), p. 128.

191   'Saint-Simon remarked ...' Quoted in J.-M. Apostolidès, *Le Roi-Machine, Spectacle et politique au temps de Louis XIV* (Paris, 1981), p. 156.

'Louis's sister-in-law ...' Quoted in G. Ziegler, *The Court of Versailles in the Reign of Louis XIV*, trans. S. W. Taylor (London, 1966), p. 149.

'He would give ...' J. Levron, *Daily Life at Versailles in the Seventeenth and Eighteenth Centuries*, trans. C. E. Engel (London, 1968), pp. 53–5.

192   'Although Versailles possesses ...' Quoted in Ziegler, *Court of Versailles*, p. 151.

'The Princess Palatine ...' Ibid., p. 152.

194   'If you trace ...' In Le Vau's scheme of 1688, this room was known as the Grand Salon. It lay between the King's *appartement* and the rooms belonging to the Queen, and it played the role later filled by the Hall of Mirrors. When it became the King's bedroom, it revived the tradition that the monarch should sleep at the very centre of the palace. See G. van der Kemp, *Versailles* (London, 1978), p. 82.

195   'The tulipomania that ...' C. Mukerji, *Territorial Ambitions and the Gardens of Versailles* (Cambridge, 1997), pp. 171–81.

196   'The minister set up ...' Many of these nurseries are referred to in J. Guiffrey, ed., *Comptes de bâtiments du roi sous le règne du Louis XIV* (Paris, 1881–1901). See, for example, the entries for 1681 in vol. II, p. 29.

'Of the latter ...' M. Lister, *An Account of Paris at the Close of the Seventeenth (sic) Century,* (London, 1823), p. 180.

'Writing in April 1674 ...' J.-B. Colbert, *Lettres, instructions et mémoires* (Paris, 1861), p. 363.

198 '**Colbert had need ...**' Ibid., p. 334.

'**Louis' early identification with ...**' E. Hyde, 'The Cultivation of a King, or the Flower Gardens of Louis XIV', in J. D. Hunt and M. Conan, eds, *Tradition and Innovation in French Garden Art: Chapters of a New History* (Philadelphia, 2002), p. 5.

'**Almost 30 per cent ...**' Ibid., p. 2. Hyde tabulated flower purchases in 1686 and 1687, as well as specific flower purchases for Marly in 1690.

'**The nurseryman had ...**' Ibid., p. 7.

200 '**In 1684 more than ...**' J. Guiffrey, ed., *Comptes de bâtiments du roi sous le règne du Louis XIV* (Paris, 1881–1901), vol. II, p. 508, Entries for 29 October–19 November 1684 and 16 November–10 December 1684.

'**The Dauphiné region ...**' See F. Tiberghien, *Versailles, Le Chantier de Louis XIV 1662–1715* (Paris, 2003), pp. 167–8.

'**On his visit ...**' J. Locke, *Locke's Travels in France 1675–1679*, ed. John Lough (Cambridge, 1953), p. 155. Locke is also the source for the figure of twenty-six hundred boxed trees within the Orangerie.

'**In 1693 a gardener ...**' Guiffrey, *Comptes de bâtiments du roi*, vol. III, p. 873.

201 '**Sometimes it was literally ...**' Entries from the journal of the Marquis de Dangeau for 2 December 1694 and 11 January 1695, quoted in D. Garrigues, *Jardins et jardiniers de Versailles au Grand Siècle* (Seyssel, 2001), p. 12.

'**According to Saint-Simon ...**' Duc de Saint-Simon, *Mémoirs*, ed. and trans. Lucy Norton (London, 2001), vol. I, p. 339.

202 '**The names of ...**' D. Garrigues' excellent *Jardins et jardiniers de Versailles au Grand Siècle* (Seyssel, 2001), already much cited, dispels the idea that Le Nôtre somehow created the gardens at Versailles all by himself, by highlighting the contributions of all the relatively unsung gardeners who were employed there. The book includes genealogical tables of the main gardening families – Le Nôtre, Mollet, Trumel, Dupuis, Collinot, Masson, Le Bouteux, Desgots and La Quintinie – along with annexes detailing contracts and payments to various gardeners.

'**On 19 September 1673 ...**' Colbert, *Letters, instructions et mémoires*, vol. V, p. 354.

'**Although Saint-Simon never ...**' Quoted in Verlet, *Le Château de Versailles*, p. 167: 'La violence qui y a été faite partout à la nature repousse et dégoûte malgré soi.'

203 '**But though England's ...**' From Horace Walpole's 'The History of the Modern Taste in Gardening' (1780), quoted in J. D. Hunt and P. Willis, *The Genius of the Place* (London, 1975), p. 31.

'**Tessin has left ...**' *Relation de la visite de Nicodème Tessin à Marly, Versailles, Clagny, Rueil et Saint-Cloud, en 1687*. The full text is given in app. IV-22 of Garrigues, *Jardins et jardiniers*.

XII *Changes*

205 '**When she wrote ...**' Quoted in N. Mitford, *The Sun King*, London, 1966, p. 122.

'**Mutual hatred had ...**' L. Hilton, *Athénaïs, The Real Queen of France* (London, 2002), p. 221.

207 '**This did not slow ...**' I. Dunlop, *Royal Palaces of France* (London, 1985), p. 140.

208 '**Though he remained ...**' T. Hedin, 'Le Nostre to Mansart: Transition in the Gardens of Versailles', *Gazette des Beaux-Arts* (December 1997), pp. 200–3.

211 '**The building accounts ...**' Ibid., p. 280.

212 '**Spending peaked in ...**' See the graph in P. Verlet, *Le Château de Versailles* (Paris, 1985 [1961]), p. 141.

'The Marquis de Dangeau …' Marquis de Dangeau, *Journal du Marquis de Dangeau, Volume I, 1684–85* (Clermond-Ferrand, 2002), p. 45.

'The Marquis, obviously …' Ibid., p. 163.

213   'Madame de Sévigné …' Mme de Sévigné, *Correspondance*, ed. Roger Duchêne (Paris, 1974), vol. II, p. 632.

'According to Primi Visconti …' Jean-Baptiste Primi Visconti, *Mémoires sur la cour de Louis XIV, 1673–1681*, ed. Jean-François Solon (Paris, 1988), p. 152.

'Buildings are such …' This is Perrault in his *Mémoires,* quoting Colbert. It is quoted in Hedin, 'Le Nostre to Mansart', p. 196.

'He wrote to sieur …' Quoted in I. Dunlop, *Louis XIV* (London, 2001), p. 140.

'Nancy Mitford went …' N. Mitford, *The Sun King*, London, 1966, p. 37.

214   'In October 1681 …' Frédéric Tiberghien thinks that Hardouin-Mansart might have been acting as de-facto premier architect as early as 1673. He was certainly functioning as such from 1676.

'If he did …' Jules Hardouin-Mansart was to become far more famous and successful than François Mansart, so the appropriation of the latter's name is now almost complete. When one sees 'Mansart' in this book, as elsewhere, it is usually a reference to Hardouin-Mansart, not to his great uncle.

216   'Whatever else Mansart …' For a more detailed account of Mansart's life, see F. Tiberghien, *Versailles, Le Chantier de Louis XIV 1662–1715* (Paris, 2003), pp. 44–50.

'However, as the Princess …' M. Kroll, ed., *Letters from Liselotte* (London, 1970), p. 90.

'An entry in . . .' Marquis de Dangeau, *Journal du Marquis de Dangeau, Volume I, 1684–85*.

'The displaced sculptures …' Hedin, 'Le Nostre to Mansart', p. 281. Hedin argues that the marbles from the Grotto only found their way to the Bosquet de la Renommée by default, and that the King might have been thinking of a completely new centrepiece when he made the remark reported by Dangeau.

218   'He himself had …' Le Nôtre had seen a similar arrangement with three flights of steps combined to make a monumental balustraded stair.

'Le Notre gave …' Louis de Bachaumont, *Essai sur la peinture, la sculpture, et l'architecture* (Paris, 1751), pp. 56, 62, quoted in F. Hamilton Hazlehurst, *Gardens of Illusion* (Nashville, TN, 1980), p. 122.

'Dominique Garrigues calls …' D. Garrigues, *Jardins et jardiniers de Versailles au Grand Siècle* (Seyssel, 2001), p. 180.

'Jules Guiffrey, the …' J. Guiffrey, *André Le Nôtre*, trans. George Booth (Lewes, 1986 [1913]), p. 25.

220   'The Trianon de Porcelaine …' Tiberghien, *Versailles, Le Chantier*, p. 198.

'By September 1687 …' Ibid., p. 34. See also Dunlop, *Royal Palaces of France*, p. 151.

'His Majesty desires …' Quoted in I. Dunlop, *Royal Palaces of France*, p. 151.

222   'In the new political …' H. Fox, *André Le Notre, Garden Architect to Kings* (London, 1962), pp.158–9. See also Guiffrey, *André Le Nôtre*, pp. 54–5.

'The Princess Palatine thought that …' Kroll, ed., *Letters from Liselotte*, p. 57, Letter dated 20 October 1690.

223   'With regard to …' Letter from Mansart to Louvois, quoted in Hedin, 'Le Nostre to Mansart', p. 234.

'The King remained …' Account of the King's visit to Chantilly on 8 June 1684, *Mercure Gallant* (June 1684), quoted in Hedin, 'Le Nostre to Mansart', p. 240.

224   'The King followed …' Verlet, *Le Château de Versailles*, p. 176.

225   'The *Mercure Gallant* …' Description of the Colonnade in *Mercure Galant* (Novem-

ber 1686), quoted in R. W. Berger, *In the Garden of the Sun King, Studies on the Park of Versailles under Louis XIV* (Washington DC, 1985), p. 47.

'It must have galled ...' Quoted in Hedin, 'Le Nostre to Mansart', p. 243.

'Well! Sire, what ...' L. de Rouvroy, Duc de Saint-Simon, *Mémoires*, ed. Yves Coirault (Paris, 1986), vol. I, pp. 738–9: 'D'un maçon vous avez fait un jardinier (c'etait Mansart); il vous a donné un plat de son métier.'

'Louis liked the Colonnade ...' Berger, *In the Garden of the Sun King*, p. 44.

'Noting that the piece ...' Berger, *In the Garden of the Sun King*, p. 43. The full text in French is also quoted in the endnotes.

226   'This is the garden ...' Kroll, ed., *Letters from Liselotte*, p. 120. Also in Hedin, 'Le Nostre to Mansart', p. 232.

'It was beautifully ...' N. Tessin, *Relation de la visite de Nicodème Tessin à Marly, Versailles, Clagny, Rueil et Saint-Cloud, en 1687*.

'In Le Nôtre's ...' The French text is reproduced in Garrigues, *Jardins et jardinieres*, annex 23, pp. 355–6.

'Since the Trianon ...' Hedin, 'Le Nôtre to Mansart', p. 233.

227   'The Marquis de Dangeau ...' Dangeau, *Journal du marquis de Dangeau*, p. 92.

'It is clear that nothing ...' Hedin, 'Le Nostre to Mansart', p. 298.

XIII *Waterworks*

229   'Tessin reported that ...' N. Tessin, 'Voyage de Versailles en 1687', *Revue de l'histoire de Versailles et de Seine-et-Oise* (1926), p. 160.

'As Charles Perrault ...' C. Perrault, *Mémoires de ma vie*, ed. Paul Bonnefon (Paris, 1909), p. 105.

230   'It was a pleasure ...' Ibid., p. 107.

'With the King ...' This is the figure supplied by Pascal Lobegeois, following P. Lardellier, 'Splendeurs et misères du Versailles bleu', *Monuments historiques*, no. 188 (1993), p. 132. The figure of fourteen hundred fountains is often mentioned in earlier estimates. According to Lardellier there are now 617 functioning jets at Versailles.

233   'The main fountain ...' W. H. Adams, *The French Garden 1500–1800* (London, 1979), pp. 19, 57.

'In addition to ...' See F. Hamilton Hazlehurst, *Gardens of Illusion* (Nashville, TN, 1980), p. 32, where the author quotes from Mlle de Scudéry's ode to Vaux.

'The Water-works far ...' E. Veryard, *An Account of Divers Choice Remarks as well as Geographical, Historical, Political, Mathematical and Moral; Taken in a Journey through the Low Countries, France, Italy, and Part of Spain with the Isles of Sicili and Malta* (London, 1701), p. 68.

'All of these had ...' See chronological table in Lobgeois and de Givry, *Versailles, Les Grandes Eaux* (Paris, 2000), p. 180.

235   'On 19 March 1664 ...' Quoted in Hazlehurst, *Gardens of Illusion*, p. 146, n. 46.

'Mlle de Scudéry mentioned ...' Quoted in F. Tiberghien, *Versailles, Le Chantier de Louis XIV 1662–1715* (Paris, 2003), p. 232.

236   'Jolly had been ...' Ibid., p. 315. Tiberghien estimates the true extent of the swindle at between 24,000 and 25,000 *livres*, noting that when he was denounced Jolly was accused of having stolen 50,000 *livres*.

'However, Colbert imposed ...' J.-B. Colbert, *Lettres, instructions et mémoires* (Paris, 1861), vol. V, p. 340.

237   **'As for the garden …'** Jean-Baptiste Primi Visconti, *Mémoires sur la cour de Louis XIV, 1673–1681*, ed. Jean-François Solon (Paris, 1988), p. 45.
'Whensoever His Majesty …' See D. Garrigues, *Jardins et jardiniers de Versailles au Grand Siècle* (Seyssel, 2001), p. 176, where a longer extract from Colbert's instructions is given in French as a footnote.

238   **'Even with such developments …'** Lobgeois and de Givry, *Versailles, Les Grandes Eaux* (Paris, 2000), pp. 45–6.

239   **'It was François Francine …'** Pascal Lobgeois questions this figure on the grounds that a recent technological monograph states that the capacity of the two remaining underground reservoirs is the higher figure of 4,140 cubic metres.
'Even in his tent …' Lobgeois and de Givry, *Versailles, Les Grandes Eaux* (Paris, 2000), pp. 33–4.
'On his visit to Versailles …' J. Locke, *Locke's Travels in France 1675–1679*, ed. John Lough (Cambridge, 1953), p. 152.
'The water of all …' Ibid., p. 166.

240   **'There were taps …'** Ibid., p. 167.
'An earlier visitor …' Primi Visconti, *Mémoires*, p. 45.
'Looking out from …' Locke, *Locke's Travels in France*, p. 152.
'One of the most remarkable …' Quoted in I. Dunlop, *Louis XIV* (London, 2001), p. 210.

241   **'A merchant called …'** J. Guiffrey, ed., *Comptes de bâtiments du roi sous le règne du Louis XIV* (Paris, 1881–1901), vol. II, pp. 717–18 (chapter on 'Habits des Gondoliers Vénitiens, Servans sur le Canal' [1685]).
'Wood for the construction …' Tiberghien, *Versailles, Le Chantier*, pp. 186–7.
'Of the total expenditure …' These figures, quoted in Lobgeois and de Givry, *Versailles, Les Grandes Eaux* (Paris, 2000), p. 32, come originally from Joseph-Adrien Le Roi, *Travaux hydrauliques sous Louis XIV* (Versailles, 1865). See also Primi Visconti, *Mémoires*, p. 46.
'Iron pipes, introduced …' Lobgeois and de Givry, *Versailles, Les Grandes Eaux* (Paris, 2000), p. 180.

243   **'Although this gargantuan …'** See T. Mariage, *The World of André Le Nôtre*, trans. Graham Larkin (Philadelphia, 1990), p. 102.
'According to Primi Visconti …' Primi Visconti, *Mémoires*, p. 152.
'In a letter to Mme de Sévigné …' Sévigné, *Correspondance*, vol. II, p. 634.
'At more than 15 hectares …' Different dimensions have been offered. Frédéric Tiberghien, in *Versailles, Le Chantier de Louis XIV* (p. 128), says that the lake measures 618 by 213 metres and covers an area of 13 ha, whereas Dominique Garrigues, in *Jardins et Jardiniers de Versailles* (p 193), says that it measures 682 by 234 metres and covers 16 ha. The author has not had the opportunity to make his own measurements.

244   **'It was no different …'** Guiffrey, *Comptes des bâtiments du roi*, vol. I, p. 1173.
'Since the soldiers …' Ibid., vol. I, pp. 1185–6, Entry for 4 June 1679–14 January 1680.
'Since no illustrations …' Garrigues, *Jardins et jardinieres*, p. 194.
'But we get a glimpse …' Sévigné, *Correspondance*, vol. II, p. 632.

XIV   *The Machine and the Aqueduct*

247   **'The King is reputed …'** This story is related in F. Tiberghien, *Versailles, Le Chantier de Louis XIV 1662–1715* (Paris, 2003), p. 233.

249   'According to an old story ...' Lobgeois and de Givry, *Versailles, Les Grandes Eaux*, (Paris, 2000), p. 54.

'One called Godefroy ...' J. Guiffrey, ed., *Comptes de bâtiments du roi sous le règne du Louis XIV* (Paris, 1881–1901), vol. II, pp. 554, Entry for 25 June 1684; 1254, Entry for 15 June 1687.

250   'During construction De Ville ...' Ibid., vol. II, p. 848, Entry for 7 January–18 November 1685.

'In 1786 Thomas Jefferson ...' http://world.std.com/~hmfh/louvec.htm (accessed 10.5. 04).

251   'In 1685 alone ...' Guiffrey, *Comptes des bâtiments du roi*, vol. II, pp. 835–46.

'It has been estimated ...' This figure is taken from Lobgeois and de Givry, *Versailles, Les Grandes Eaux* (Paris, 2000), p. 60, which in turn cites J.-A. Le Roi, *Traveaux hydrauliques sous Louis XIV, 1664–1688* (Versailles, 1865), p. 8.

'More than three ...' I. Dunlop, *Royal Palaces of France* (London, 1985), p. 138. There have been numerous studies of the water consumption at Versailles, and estimates vary. Following Blondel, Dunlop gives a figure of 12,960 cubic metres for the fountains to run at half strength between 8.00 a.m. and 8.00 p.m., and a figure of 9,458 cubic metres for two and a half hours of *Les Grandes Eaux*. Pascal Lobgeois suggests a slightly higher figure of 13,250 cubic metres for running *à l'ordinaire*. He also suggests that if *all* the fountains were to have played at full strength throughout the day, a quantity of 75,600 cubic metres would have been required daily. See Lobgeois and de Givry, *Versailles, Les Grandes Eaux* (Paris, 2000), p. 86.

'Even though more ...' W. H. Adams, *The French Garden 1500–1800* (London, 1979), p. 88. According to Adams, the supply to Versailles had already exceeded that to Paris by the time of the fête in 1668, i.e. before the construction of the Machine.

252   'Essentially the idea ...' Verlet, *Le Château de Versailles* (Paris, 1985), p. 187.

'On 7 February 1685 ...' Tiberghien, *Versailles, Le Chantier*, p. 246.

'After five months ...' Most writers agree that the aqueduct would have been over five kilometres long. In *Territorial Ambitions and the Gardens of Versailles* (p. 190) Chandra Mukerji says it was 5,047 metres and 72 or 73 metres high. Tiberghien, however, in *Versailles, Le Chantier* (p. 119), gives a figure of only 2,750 metres.

253   'Frédérick Tiberghien estimated ...' Tiberghien, *Versailles, Le Chantier*, p. 129.

'It was the King's intention ...' Ibid., p. 156.

'While Vauban and ...' Quoted in Ibid., p. 120.

'In 1685, when ...' Ibid., pp. 149–50.

'According to Saint-Simon ...' L. de Rouvroy, Duc de Saint-Simon, *Mémoires*, ed. Yves Coirault (Paris, 1986), vol. V, p. 534.

'The King will be pleased ...' Tiberghien, *Versailles, Le Chantier*, p. 155.

254   'In the precious style ...' Mme de Sévigné, *Correspondance*, ed. Roger Duchêne (Paris, 1974), vol. III, p. 165. Mme de Sévigné overestimates the number of men involved, which was closer to thirty thousand.

255   'Don't distress yourself ...' Quoted in Tiberghien, *Versailles, Le Chantier*, p. 81.

'The "ague" mentioned ...' P. Reiter, 'From Shakespeare to Defoe: Malaria in England in the Little Ice Age', *Emerging Infectious Diseases*, 6/1 (2000). Accessed online at www.cdc.gov/ncidod/EID/vol6no1/contents.htm (26.5.04).

'When the regiments ...' Tiberghien, *Versailles, Le Chantier*, pp. 164–5.

256   'The widow of Size Renault ...' Guiffrey, *Comptes des bâtiments du roi*, vol. II, p. 690, Entry for 10 June 1685.

'On 8 December 1686 ...' Ibid., vol. II, p. 1068, Entry for 8 December 1686.

'Louis' anxieties increased ...' Verlet, *Le Château de Versailles*, p. 189.

258   'Saint-Simon called ...' L. de Rouvroy, Duc Saint-Simon, *Mémoires* (Paris, 1986), vol. V, p. 534.

'Napoleon took a ...' I. Dunlop, *Louis XIV* (London, 2001), p. 300.

'Whatever we might ...' Lobgeois and de Givry, *Versailles, Les Grandes Eaux* (Paris, 2000), p. 81.

'The scale of this fixation ...' Tiberghien, *Versailles, Le Chantier*, p. 85.

259   'Impressive though Les Grandes Eaux ...' See Lobgeois and de Givry, *Versailles, Les Grandes Eaux* (Paris, 2000), pp. 89–94 for a fuller account of the present condition of the fountains and their supply system.

XV   *Escape to Marly*

261   'Weary of splendour ...' L. de Rouvroy, Duc de Saint-Simon, *Mémoires*, ed. Yves Coirault (Paris, 1986), vol. V, pp. 534–5.

'In his petulant way ...' Ibid., vol. V, pp. 534–5.

'Martin Lister was ...' M. Lister, *A Journey to Paris in the Year 1698* (London, 1698), p. 205.

262   'A letter from Crönstrom ...' Quoted in I. Dunlop, *Royal Palaces of France* (London, 1985), p. 158.

'Diderot wrote that ...' From a letter to Mlle Volland, quoted in Ibid., p. 155.

'The axis was ...' The *toise* was a pre-metric measure of length, approximately equivalent to 1,949 millimetres. The *toise* was divided into 6 *Paris feet*, each of which was divided into 12 *pouces*.

263   'In March 1688 ...' S. Castelluccio, 'Views of Old and New Marly', in *Views of the Gardens at Marly: Louis XIV, Royal Gardener* (Paris, 1998), text accompanying pl. 2. These incidents are recorded in the journals of the Marquis de Dangeau.

264   'To the west ...' Ibid., text accompanying pl 73. Also quoted in Dunlop, *Royal Palaces of France*, p. 160.

265   'In 1702 Louis ...' Castelluccio, *Views of the Gardens at Marly*, text accompanying pl. 75.

'The Princess Palatine thought that ...' Quoted in Dunlop, *Royal Palaces of France*, p. 161.

'In a letter to her aunt Sophie ...' M. Kroll, ed., *Letters from Liselotte* (London, 1970), p. 91, Letter dated 3 February 1700.

'In the light of ...' Saint Simon, *Mémoires*, vol. V, p. 535.

'Once again it was ...' Lister, *A Journey to Paris in the Year 1698*, p. 209.

'The accounts also mention ...' L. Benech, 'Louis XIV: Royal Plantsman', in *Views of the Gardens at Marly: Louis XIV, Royal Gardener*, p. 28.

'Lister, who found ...' Ibid., p. 209.

266   'Sieur de Lelès ...' J. Guiffrey, ed., *Comptes de bâtiments du roi sous le règne du Louis XIV* (Paris, 1881–1901), vol. II, p. 1216, Entry for 15 June 1687.

'Desgots noted, with a hint ...' C. Desgots, *Abrégé de la vie d'André le Nostre*, included in Père Pierre Nicolas Desmoulets' *Continuation des mémoires de littérature et d'histoire de Monsieur de Salengre*, vol. IV, chap. IX, (Paris, 1726), p. 469.

'Rare flowers were ...' E. Hyde, 'The Cultivation of a King, or the Flower Gardens of Louis XIV', in J. D. Hunt and M. Conan, eds, *Tradition and Innovation in French Garden Art: Chapters of a New History* (Philadelphia, 2002), p. 3, table 3.

'Lister found little ...' Lister, *A Journey to Paris in the Year 1698*, pp. 187–9.

'According to the Princess ...' Kroll, ed., *Letters from Liselotte*, p. 108, Letter dated 7 May 1702.

'The gardens were also ...' Benech, 'Louis XIV: Royal Plantsman', p. 29.

'Hawthorn and hazel ...' A.-J. Dezallier d'Argenville, *La Théorie et la practique du jardinage* (Paris, 2002 [1709]), p. 203.

267 'Saint-Simon, for one ...' Saint Simon, *Mémoires*, vol. V, ed. Yves Coirault (Paris, 1985), pp. 534–5.

'The evidence for ...' F. Hamilton Hazlehurst, *Gardens of Illusion* (Nashville, TN, 1980), pp. 354–9.

268 'When the King ...' Kroll, ed., *Letters from Liselotte*, p. 87, Letter dated 2 July 1699.

'To the great amusement ...' Saint-Simon, *Mémoires*, vol. II, p. 664.

'No one could deny ...' Kroll, ed., *Letters from Liselotte*, p. 87, Letter dated 2 July 1699.

'He grumbled about ...' Saint-Simon, *Mémoires*, vol. V, ed. Yves Coirault (Paris, 1985), pp. 535–6.

269 'All of France ...' Duc de Saint-Simon, *Mémoirs*, ed. and trans. Lucy Norton (London, 2001), vol. III, p. 105.

'The manufacturer sold off ...' E. Vigée-Lebrun, *Souvenirs* (Paris, 1962), vol. I, pp. 47–8.

XVI   *Honourable Old Age*

272 'He had pictured ...' H. Fox, *André Le Notre, Garden Architect to Kings* (London, 1962), p. 125.

'It seems that ...' Le Sieur de Chantelou, *Journal du voyage en France du cavalier Bernin par Chantelou* (Paris, 1930), pp. 156–7.

'Bernini thought Versailles ...' F. Hamilton Hazlehurst, *Gardens of Illusion* (Nashville, TN, 1980), pp. 4,12 (nn. 35–7). Also D. Garrigues, *Jardins et jardiniers de Versailles au Grand Siècle* (Seyssel, 2001), p. 68.

'Preparing the way ...' Letter from Colbert to the Duc d'Estrées, 20 January 1679, quoted in Ibid., p. 70.

'There is a difference ...' Desgots' account of this meeting is included in his '*Abrégé de la vie d' Andre le Nostre*', in P. N. Desmolets, *Continuation des mémoires de littérature et d'histoire de Monsieur Salengre* (Paris, 1726–31), vol. IV. There is no indication that the Pope was displeased by Le Nôtre's outburst. Saint-Simon tells us that the Pope asked Louis to lend him Le Nôtre for a few months, though it is not clear when this request was made. See Saint-Simon, *Mémoires*, vol. I, ed. Yves Coirault (Paris, 1985), p. 738. Saint-Simon got the Pope's name wrong; it must have been Innocent XI, not Clement X, who died in 1676.

'The Duc de Créqui ...' A *louis d'or* was a gold coin worth 24 *livres*.

'When I return ...' É. Orsenna, *André Le Notre: Gardener to the Sun King*, trans. Moishe Black (New York, 2000), p. 110.

'Le Nôtre had been ...' There is some question about which medal is depicted. Hazlehurst, in *Gardens of Illusion* (p. 7), thinks it the Order of Saint-Michel; De Ganay, in *André Le Nôtre, 1613–1700* (Paris, 1962), identified it as the Order of Saint-Lazare.

275 'The King replied ...' Letter from Louis XIV to M. Batailler. See Garrigues, *Jardins et jardinieres*, p. 67, and J. Guiffrey, *André Le Nôtre*, trans. George Booth (Lewes, 1986 [1913]), p. 45.

'The main door ...' Hazlehurst, *Gardens of Illusion*, p. 4; also p. 12, n. 30.

'Saint-Simon wrote ...' Saint-Simon, *Mémoires*, vol. I, ed. Yves Coirault (Paris, 1985), pp. 738–9.

276   'Being both perverse ...' Ibid., vol. V, p. 533.
       'Horace Walpole called ...' H. Walpole to Richard West Esq. from Paris, 1739.
       'The mainstream of ...' Quoted in Verlet, *Le Château de Versailles* (Paris, 1984), p. 167.
       'In any event, when La Quintinie ...' J.-B. de la Quintinie, *Instruction pour les jardins frutiers et potagers* (Arles, 1999), pp. 27–8.
277   'Since he lived ...' C. Mukerji, *Territorial Ambitions and the Gardens of Versailles* (Cambridge, 1997), pp. 222, 272.
278   'Though Le Nôtre ...' Guiffrey, *André Le Nostre*, translator's note 1.
       'Claude Desgots, certainly ...' C. Desgots, *Abrégé de la vie d'André le Nostre*, included in Père Pierre Nicolas Desmoulets' *Continuation des mémoires de littérature et d'histoire de Monsieur de Salengre*, vol. IV, chap. IX, (Paris, 1726), pp. 465–7.
       'In the first, written in 1696 ...' Quoted in Hazlehurst, *Gardens of Illusion*, p. 8. Original documents in Archives Nationales, Paris (AE^{II} 900, CXII 91 and 139).
       'Martin Lister was ...' M. Lister, *A Journey to Paris in the Year 1698* (London, 1698), p. 36.
       'Louis Petit de Bachaumont ...' The account of this visit appears in *Magasin littéraire* (Paris, 1890) and is reproduced in Hazlehurst, *Gardens of Illusion*, p. 398, n. 2.
279   'In the foreground ...' Hazlehurst, *Gardens of Illusion*, pp. 365–6.
       'Lister mentions three ...' Lister, *A Journey to Paris in the Year 1698*, pp. 36–7.
280   'It is rather more ...' Ibid.
281   'According to Lister's ...' Ibid.
       'Monsieur le Nostre ...' Ibid., p. 39.
       'Remarkably, even though ...' Hazlehurst, *Gardens of Illusion*, p. 6.
       'He thanked his spouse ...' Quoted in S. Castelluccio, 'La Personalité d'André Le Nôtre (1613–1700)', in *Le Nôtre, Un Inconnu illustre?* (Paris, 2003), p. 36.
282   'Ever the prudent planner ...' Ibid., p. 30.
       'Le Nôtre, with tears ...' Ibid., p. 31.
285   'He had encircled the palace ...' R.-L. de Girardin, *De la composition des paysages* (Seyssel, 1999 [1777]).
       'The King has lost ...' Obituary in *Mercure de France* (September 1700).

XVII *Hard Times and Sunset*

289   'During his stay ...' Le Nôtre to the Earl of Portland, 2 June 1698. Erik de Jong claims that it not certain that Bentinck and Le Nôtre ever met. See 'Le Nôtre dans le Nord ou le grand "eventeur de jardinages", in *Le Nôtre, Un Inconnu illustre?* (Paris, 2003), p. 206.
290/1 'The Princess Palatine ...' M. Kroll, ed., *Letters from Liselotte* (London, 1970), p. 133, Letter dated 10 January 1709.
291   'Saint-Simon recorded ...' Duc de Saint-Simon, *Mémoires*, ed. and trans. Lucy Norton (London, 2001), vol. I, p. 416.
       'If the famine ...' Kroll, ed., *Letters from Liselotte*, p. 135, Letter dated 23 May 1709.
       'A satricial parody ...' Chamillart was one of Louis' ministers, made minister of war from 1701. The public blamed him not just for the string of military defeats but for the increases in taxation that seemed to go with them.
       'His foes scoffed ...' P. Burke, *The Fabrication of Louis XIV* (New Haven and London, 1992), pp. 136–8.

292   'At the height …' Kroll, ed., *Letters from Liselotte*, p. 137, Letter dated 22 August 1709.
'There were exclamations …' Saint-Simon, *Mémoires*, vol. III.

XVIII *Influence*

298   'To inaugurate these …' E. Kluckert, *European Garden Design* (Cologne, 2000), p. 182.

299   'Tessin has been described … E. de Jong, 'Le Nôtre dans le Nord ou le grand "eventeur" des jardinages', in *Le Nôtre, Un Inconnu illustre?* (Paris, 2003), pp. 209–11.
'His courtiers scandalised …' Mme de Maintenon was, by this time, in retirement at Saint Cyr.

300   'He sought out …' I. Dunlop, *Versailles* (London, 1970), p. 112.

302   'Like Louis, he …' For a more detailed history of the Peterhof gardens, see http://www.peterhof.org/history/ (accessed 30.7.04).

303   'The garden with …' Sophie married Ernest Augustus, Duke of Hanover from 1779 and Elector from 1692.

306   'Behind the elegant …' P. Hall, *Cities of Tomorrow* (Oxford, 1988). The chapter entitled 'The City of Monuments' offers a fascinating critique of the City Beautiful Movement, which Hall traces back to Baron Haussmann's reconstruction of Paris under Napoleon III. See pp. 175–202.

Epilogue

309   'The royal accounts …' Figures from the *Comptes des bâtiments*, quoted in W. H. Adams, *The French Garden 1500–1800* (London, 1979), p. 104.

312   'Unlike Colbert, who …' P.-A. Lablaude, *Les Jardins de Versailles* (Paris, 1998), p. 121.
'In 1750 Richard …' I. Dunlop, *Versailles*, pp. 143–4.
'He corresponded with …' This belongs to the family of the *Onograceæ*, which contains some thirty-six tropical species, chiefly South American.

315   'To cut costs …' Lablaude, *Les Jardins de Versailles*, pp. 132–4.

318   'Only after fourteen …' A. Fraser, *Marie Antoinette: The Journey* (London, 2001), p. 211.
'The spiralling paths …' S. de Courtois, 'Claude Richard 1705–1784, Antoine Richard 1735–1807', in Michel Racine, ed., *Créateurs de jardins et de paysages en France de la Renaissance au XXIe siècle* (Paris, 2001), p. 108.

320   'The Duc de Croÿ …' Ibid., p. 108.
'I have no Court …' Quoted in Dunlop, *Versailles*, p. 190.

324   'When the Queen departed …' Lablaude, *Les Jardins de Versailles*, p. 160.

325   'In 1792 the …' Dunlop, *Versailles*, p. 200. The Museum of Paris later became the Musée du Louvre.
'It was decided …' These paintings were later sent to the Louvre.
'The fruit trees …' S. de Courtois, *Le Potager du roi* (Paris, 2003), pp. 49–67.
'These wily tactics …' T. Mariage and N. Bruant, *Trianon, l'autre rivage* (Paris, 2000), p. 47.
'there are accounts of Soldiers' wives …' Lablaude, *Les Jardins de Versailles*, p. 164.

326   'I appreciated in …' Quoted in I. Dunlop, *Royal Palaces of France* (London, 1985), p. 271.

329' **'While Mlle de Scudéry ...'** M. de Scudéry, *La Promenade de Versailles, dédiée au Roi*, ed. Marie-Gabrielle Lallemand (Paris, 2002), p. 89.
'Saint-Simon could complain ...' Saint-Simon, *Mémoires*, vol. V, p. 532.
'It was not a controversy ...' H. Walpole 'The History of the Modern Taste in Gardening' (1780), quoted in J. D. Hunt and P. Willis, *The Genius of the Place* (London, 1975).

ACKNOWLEDGEMENTS

There are two groups of people I want to thank. One is made up of people known to me who have helped in some way. The second consists of those authors whose books have been so helpful in the writing of this one.

Pride of place must go to Julia Darling. I was tempted to write 'the late Julia Darling' because she died before I completed the manuscript, but although Julia was always very matter-of-fact about the cancer that was going to take her away from us so cruelly, I don't think she would have liked the word 'late', and, anyway, it feels as if she is still amongst us, exhorting us to write and to pursue dreams. Julia ran the lunchtime writing group in the School of English at Newcastle University which gave me the confidence to send work to publishers and agents. She was always so warm, encouraging and upbeat that for a long time none of us could believe that she was ill. Julia, if you are reading this, I'm sure you won't mind if I extend the thanks to the rest of the writing group. As you once said in your weblog, those sessions drew the nicest people from all corners of the university. Julia also introduced me to my agent, John Saddler, whom I must thank for his invaluable coaching and his ability to spot where a good story truly lies.

As it was impossible to go and live in France while researching this book, I employed an agency called CPEDERF to assist with archival research and translations. Julia McLaren from CPEDERF provided prompt, accurate and enthusiastic support throughout. I would also like to thank Monique Hanley for her help in France, and particularly for introducing me to the wonderful gardening bookshop tucked away inside the gates of the Tuileries. Closer to home, I must thank Michael Downing, for introducing me to landscape history about twenty-five years ago, for lending me books and for reading the manuscript before submission. It is customary at this point to acknowledge that any mistakes in the text are entirely my own.

At Bloomsbury I would like to thank Bill Swainson and Sarah Marcus for leading me gently through an unfamiliar process, and Victoria Millar for ironing out the wrinkles in my unruly manuscript.

Thanks also to all of those patient people, my friends, colleagues and family (and most of all my supportive wife Mine) who have understood just how much time it takes to complete a book.

A NOTE ON SOURCES

Anyone with an academic interest in the gardens of Versailles can find detailed references to the sources used in the Notes, but there certain books which were so useful that I feel they deserve special mention here. The most comprehensive book about André Le Nôtre's life and achievements is F. Hamilton Hazlehurst's *Gardens of Illusion* (1980) to which I found myself often turning for detailed descriptions of garden features and chronology. Thierry Mariage's *The World of André Le Nôtre* (1999) provided an up to date perspective on the landscape designer's life, setting his achievements into the context of the most recent scholarship. For the association between gardening and military engineering in seventeenth-century France, I am indebted to Chandra Mukerji's *Territorial Ambitions and the Gardens of Versailles* (1997). Peter Burke's *The Fabrication of Louis XIV* (1992) explained the role played by the gardens and their associated iconography in the Sun King's propaganda machine. Among the many biographies of the Sun King, I found Ian Dunlop's *Louis XIV* (2001) to be the most useful and readable. The same author's *Versailles* (1970) and *The Royal Palaces of France* (1985) provided much valuable information about the stages of the building of the château and the development of the grounds. Two books which, to my knowledge, are not available in English translations, provided very useful detailed information. Frédéric Tiberghien's *Versailles, Le Chantier de Louis XIV* (2002) is a fascinating account of the château of Versailles as a building site, which is particularly strong on the hazardous lives of those involved in construction. Dominique Garrigues' *Jardins et Jardiniers de Versailles* (2001) is a terrific resource for anyone interested in the lives of the ordinary gardeners and under-gardeners at Versailles in the time of Le Nôtre. Chapters 13 and 14 would have been much more difficult to write without reference to Pascal Lobegeois and Jaques de Givry's *Versailles, Les Grandes Eaux* (2000). I found Pierre-André Lablaude's *The Gardens of Versailles* (1995) particularly helpful for understanding the more recent history of the gardens and their restoration.

I am also grateful to writers long dead, like the Duc de Saint-Simon for his waspish descriptions of life in the Sun King's court, Dezallier d'Argenville for recording the essentials of baroque gardening technique, André Félibien for his chronicles of fêtes and fireworks and Jules Guiffrey for his painstaking transcriptions of the royal building accounts (also thanks to the anonymous librarian at Leeds University library who made the latter available through inter-library loans).

SELECT BIBLIOGRAPHY

Adams, W.H., *The French Garden 1500-1800* (London: Scolar Press, 1979)

Baridon, M., *Jardins de Versailles* (Paris: Actes Sud, 2001)

Baratay, E. and Hardouin-Fugier, E., *Zoo, a History of Zoological Gardens in the West* (London: Reaktion Books, 2002)

Berger, R.W., *In the Garden of the Sun King* (Washington: Dumbarton Oaks, 1985)

Boyceau de la Barauderie, J., *Traité du Jardinage Selon Les Raisons de la Nature et de L'Art*, (Nôrdlingen: Verlag Dr. Alfons Uhl, 1997 [1638])

Burke, P., *The Fabrication of Louis XIV* (New Haven and London: Yale University Press, 1992)

Colbert, J.-B, *Lettres, instructions et mémoires*, (Paris: Imprimerie Impériale, 1861)

Courtois, S. de, *Le Potager du Roi* (Paris: Actes Sud, 2003)

Dangeau, Marquis de, *Journal du Marquis de Dangeau*, Volume I, 1684-85 (Clermond-Ferrand: Éditions Paleo, 2002)

De Ganay, E., *André le Nostre*, 1613-1700 (Paris: Vincent Fréal, 1962)

De Nolhac, P., *La Création de Versailles* (Paris: Louis Conard, 1925)

Dezallier d'Argenville, A-J., *La Théorie et la Practique du Jardinage*, (Paris: Connaissance et Memoires, 2002 [1709])

Duchamp, E. (ed) *Views of the Gardens at Marly; Louis XIV Royal Gardener* (Paris: Alain de Gourcuff, 1998)

Dunlop, I., *Louis XIV* (London: Pimlico, 2001)

Dunlop, I., *Royal Palaces of France* (New York: Norton, 1985)

Félibien, A., *Les Fêtes de Versailles, Chroniques de 1668 & 1674* (Maisonneuve et Larose: Éditions Dédale, 1994 [1674])

Fox, H.M. *André Le Nôtre, Garden Architect to Kings*. (London: B.T. Batsford, 1962)

France, A., *Vaux-le-Vicomte* (Étrépilly: Les Presses du Village, 1987 [1933])

Fraser, A., *Marie Antoinette* (London: Phoenix, 2001)

Garrigues, D., *Jardins et Jardiniers de Versailles au Grand Siècle* (Seyssel: Champ Vallon, 2001)

Guiffrey, J. (ed.) *Comptes du bâtiments du roi sous le règne de Louis XIV* (Paris: Imprimerie Royale, 1881-1901)

Hazlehurst, F. H., *Gardens of Illusion*, (Nashville, Tennessee: Vanderbilt University Press, 1980)

Hilton, L., *Athénaïs, the Real Queen of France* (London: Little Brown, 2002)

Hedin, T., 'Le Nostre to Mansart. Transition in the Gardens of Versailles' in *Gazette des Beaux-Arts* (December 1997)

Hyde, E., 'The Cultivation of a King, or the Flower Gardens of Louis XIV' in Hunt, J.D. and Conan, M. (eds.) Tradition and Innovation in French Garden Art; Chapters of a New History (Philadelphia, University of Pennsylvania Press, 2002)

James, J., *The Theory and Practice of Gardening* (London: Gregg International Publishers Ltd., 1969 [1712])

Kroll, M., (ed.) *Letters from Liselotte* (London: Victor Gollancz, 1970)

La Quintinie, J.-B. de, *Instruction pour les Jardins Frutiers et Potagers*, (Arles, Actes Sud / ENSP, 1999

Lister, M., *A Journey to Paris in the Year 1698* (London: 1698)

Lablaude, P-A., *Les Jardins de Versailles* (Paris: Editions Scala, 1998)

Lobegeois P. and de Givry, J., *Versailles, Les Grandes Eaux* (Les Loges-en-Josas, JDG, 2000)

Locke, J., *Locke's Travels in France, 1675-1679* (edited by John Lough) (Cambridge, Cambridge University Press, 1953)

Mariage, T., *The World of André Le Nôtre*, translated by Graham Larkin, (Philadelphia, University of Pennsylvania Press, 1999)

Mitford, N., *The Sun King* (London: Penguin, 1994 [1966])

Mondot, J.-F., 'La construction d'un site artificiel' in *Les Cahiers de Science & Vie*, No. 74 (Avril, 2003)

Monum, Le Nôtre, *Un Inconnu Illustre?* (Paris: Éditions du Patrimoine, 2000)

Mukerji, C., *Territorial Ambitions and the Gardens of Versailles* (Cambridge: Cambridge University Press, 1997)

Orsenna, É., *André Le Notre; Gardener to the Sun King*, (trans. Moishe Black) (New York: George Braziller, 2000)

Primi Visconti, *J.-B., Mémoires sur la Cour de Louis XIV, 1673-1681*. (edited by Jean-François Solon) (Paris: Perrin, 1988)

Saint-Simon, L. de Rouvroy, *Duc de, Mémoires*, ed. Yves Coirault (Paris: Gallimard, 1985)

Serres, Olivier de, *Théâtre d'Agriculture et Mesnage des Champs*, (Paris: Actes Sud, 2001 [1600])

Madame de Sévigné, *Correspondance* (Paris: Gallimard, 1972)

Tiberghien, F., Versailles, *Le Chantier de Louis XIV 1662-1715* (Paris: Perrin, 2003)

Tessin, N., *Relation de la visite à Marly, Versailles, Clagny, Rueil et Saint-Cloud, en 1687* in *Revue de l'histoire de Versailles et de Seine-et-Oise*, 1926.

Treasure, G., *Louis XIV* (London: Longman, 2001)

Verlet, P., *Le Château de Versailles* (Paris: Fayard, 2002 [1961])

Wilkinson, R., *Louis XIV, France and Europe 1661-1715* (London: Hodder & Stoughton, 2002)

PICTURE SOURCES AND CREDITS

The publishers and the author are particularly grateful to the Réunion des Musées Nationaux, Paris, and especially to Anne Lesage, Noëlle Pourret, Laurent Bergeot and Leila Audouy in the Agence de Photo, for their help with finding a great many of the images reproduced in this book, a task that would have been much less swift and enjoyable without their great patience, diligence and courtesy. Thanks also to Agnès Noël and Lénaïck Le Moigno in the Département de la reproduction of the Bibliothèque Nationale de France.

INDEX

Page numbers in italics refer to illustrations